The Creative Cognition Approach

The Creative Cognition Approach

edited by Steven M. Smith, Thomas B. Ward, and Ronald A. Finke

A Bradford Book
The MIT Press
Cambridge, Massachusetts
London, England

This book was set in Palatino by DEKR Corporation and was printed and bound in the United States of America.

Library of Congress Cataloging-in-Publication Data

The creative cognition approach / edited by Steven M. Smith, Thomas B. Ward, and Ronald A. Finke.
    p.   cm.
"A Bradford book."
Includes bibliographical references and index.
ISBN 0-262-19354-X
1. Creative ability. 2. Creative thinking. 3. Cognition.
I. Smith, Steven M. II. Ward, Thomas B. III. Finke, Ronald A.
BF408.C745   1995
153.3'5—dc20
                                                    94-21947
                                                    CIP

Contents

Preface

When we originally set out to compile this volume on creative cognition, we were worried that many cognitive scientists might find the subject matter frivolous or unscientific. Like other topics that were once considered unrealistic or unresearchable, such as consciousness or mental imagery, written work on creativity has often lacked scientific rigor. Our worries were quickly dispelled, however, as soon as we contacted the contributors to this book. We discovered that the authors had already done a good deal of thinking on the subject of creative cognition, and that they were eager for the opportunity to discuss their research in this area. The resulting chapters provide a vision of how cognitive science can explore creativity in the coming years.

The first part deals with one of the most controversial issues in creative cognition, namely, the use of existing knowledge in creative thinking. Some note the importance of utilizing expert knowledge to avoid reinventing the wheel. Others, however, note that there are times when expertise must be suspended if one is to discover truly novel ideals and insights. The chapters in part I lay out the issues in this controversy and in some cases attempt to resolve these seemingly paradoxical points of view.

The second part of the book concerns visual and computational processes in creative cognition. These chapters help in demystifying creativity. Without minimizing the extraordinary nature of creative thinking, they show how the systematic implementation of ordinary cognitive processes can give rise to creative discoveries.

The last part of the volume deals with general issues in creative cognition, such as interactions of cognitive and motivational factors, and practical considerations in creative imagination. Creativity is a vast and varied domain and cannot be completely understood from underlying cognitive structures and processes. The general issues considered in part III are important for placing the cognitive approach to creativity into a broader perspective.

Although this volume is broad in scope and brings together disparate elements in cognitive science, it is by no means a complete and final treatment of creative cognition. On the contrary, it is our intention to encourage cognitive scientists to consider their work in the context of creative processes and to stimulate new research in all areas of creative cognition.

Introduction

Cognitive Processes in Creative Contexts

Steven M. Smith, Thomas B. Ward, and Ronald A. Finke

Creativity depends on how people think. Obviously, it depends on many other factors as well, such as the environment, one's culture, and individual abilities (e.g., Sternberg 1988). Nonetheless, mental processes are, in our view, the essence and the engine of creative endeavors. Although there are many useful and productive approaches to understanding creativity, the creative cognition approach (Finke, Ward, and Smith 1992) focuses on the cognitive processes and structures that underlie creative thinking. This book unites the theoretical ideas and research findings of cognitive scientists who have studied various aspects of creative cognition.

One basic goal of the creative cognition approach is to improve understanding of creative processes by using the methods and concepts of cognitive science. Most of the contributors to this book would agree, however, that there is no single process that we can identify as *the* creative process. Instead, creative thinking encompasses special combinations and patterns of the same cognitive processes seen in other noncreative endeavors.

A second goal of the creative cognition approach is to learn more and raise new questions about cognition by examining it in creative contexts. For example, research on how creative thinking is inhibited or blocked may stimulate new ideas about how noncreative thinking is inhibited. The creative use of categories may yield insights about the way categories in general are represented. Theoretical models for inducing new ideas may have implications for models of text comprehension. Just as ecological approaches have uncovered important properties of cognition by examining it in naturalistic contexts (Neisser 1982), so, too, does a creative cognition approach suggest new ideas about cognition by placing it in a creative context.

The creative cognition approach has roots in associationism (Thorndike 1911; Watson 1958), Gestalt psychology (Duncker 1945; Maier 1940; Wertheimer 1959), and computational modeling (Newell, Shaw, and Simon 1962). The associationist approach reflected a work ethic:

more work should be rewarded with more products and greater success. Because creative behavior was conceived as generalizations of learned behaviors, it was thought that learning more associations should improve creativity. This work ethic can be seen in the more contemporary context of this book in chapters 2 and 3, by authors who maintain that creative ideas are produced incrementally.

The Gestalt point of view, in contrast, posited special processes in creative thinking, particularly insight, which is a major topic of concern in chapters 3 through 7. These authors deal with such traditional issues as whether insight involves incremental processes or rapid restructuring and whether it plays any role in creative discovery.

Computational approaches to creativity have emphasized precisely defined operations that can yield the same sorts of ideas that are produced by creative humans. Although they consider different types of symbolic operations, chapters 9 through 11 deal with current computational approaches to creative cognition.

The claim that the same underlying structures and processes involved in noncreative cognition can explain creative thinking may be thought of as an approach for demystifying creativity. The hidden and fascinating ways in which new ideas are created may seem less mysterious when expressed in terms that are used to explain everyday cognition. The idea of demystification, however, presupposes that creative thinking is not an everyday activity and that noncreative cognition is perfectly well understood. Neither assumption is valid. On the contrary, creative thinking evidently involves many aspects of everyday cognition, and noncreative thinking remains somewhat mysterious. Creative cognition should therefore help our understanding of both creativity and cognition.

Finally, the creative cognition approach should lead to a better understanding of how to improve or optimize creativity. Whereas a personality approach is better suited to identifying creative people or assessing their creative talents, the creative cognition approach focuses on the cognitive processes themselves that lead to creativity. The better we understand these processes, the more we will be able to improve them. Furthermore, theories about creative cognitive processes should be empirically testable, as clearly demonstrated by many of the contributing authors.

The chapters in this book represent a diversity of interests in cognitive psychology and creativity. We begin with a contemporary treatment of the ancient issue of dreams. George Mandler ("Origins and Consequences of Novelty") considers the dream as a natural mechanism and model for the type of unstructured thinking that can produce novelty. Cognitive processes that occur during dreaming encourage new organizations, classifications, and concepts. Mandler also considers affect as an important consequence of novel thought rather than an irrelevant by-product of it.

Kenneth Bowers, Peter Farvolden, and Lambros Mermigis ("Intuitive Antecedents of Insight") tackle intuition and insight from a contemporary cognitive perspective. Blending theory and empirical research, they extend the idea that intuition can implicitly guide one to coherent ideas and correct solutions using incremental mechanisms, such as spreading activation. Also, using indirect measures of performance, they show that subjects make progress toward problem solutions without being aware they are doing so.

Robert Weisberg ("Case Studies of Creative Thinking: Reproduction versus Restructuring in the Real World") proposes that real-world creativity often involves incremental progress toward solutions rather than restructuring. Citing examples from artists and scientists, he traces the development of highly successful, creative ideas. Weisberg emphasizes the importance of using prior knowledge in creative thought, whether or not restructuring is involved.

In contrast to the incremental view of creative problem solving advocated by Bowers, Farvolden, and Mermigis and by Weisberg, Roger Dominowski ("Productive Problem Solving") asserts the importance of special insight processes in problem solving. Tracing ideas from early Gestalt work to contemporary research, Dominowski cites evidence of various forms of fixation and sudden insight and makes some general proposals about how insight problem solving can be improved.

Like Dominowski, Jonathan Schooler and Joseph Melcher ("The Ineffability of Insight") regard insight as a special process. Using protocols from subjects' verbalizations during insight and analytic problem solving, they find detrimental effects of verbalization only on insight problems. Their studies provide new methods for distinguishing insight problem solving from analytic problem solving.

Steven Smith ("Fixation, Incubation, and Insight in Memory and Creative Thinking") integrates a number of theoretical ideas from memory and problem solving, including interference and recovery, contextual fluctuation, plans as long-term knowledge structures, and memory probes, to provide a general description of recall, problem solving, and creative thinking. The patterns of cognition are used to explain fixation, incubation, and insight experiences. Smith provides relevant experimental evidence from tasks that involve memory and creative idea generation.

Thomas Ward ("What's Old About New Ideas") also addresses creative idea generation but from the point of view of concept formation and representation. He proposes that imagination is not random but is structured by underlying conceptual constraints. He also argues that creative ideas are often a mixture of old and new information, and he uses principles of noncreative categorization to predict the established frameworks within which new variations will be embedded. Numerous laboratory studies of creative idea generation are described that reveal the conceptual structures that give rise to imaginative thinking.

Jennifer Freyd and Teresa Pantzer ("Static Patterns Moving in the Mind") relate dynamic perceptual properties of mental representations to dynamic aspects of creative thinking. These dynamic qualities are considered in the context of memory distortions and generating and interpreting "preinventive forms," rudimentary structures that can be used to develop creative ideas.

Peter Cheng and Herbert Simon ("Scientific Discovery and Creative Reasoning with Diagrams") also focus on visual representations as they discuss the use of diagrams in scientific discovery. Special qualities of these diagrams are embodied in a computational model that is capable of discovering scientific principles.

Roger Schank and Chip Cleary ("Making Machines Creative") use a different computational approach to creative thinking, modeling operations for comprehension and creative explanation. The models they discuss help to clarify the relation between comprehension and creativity.

Colin Martindale ("Creativity and Connectionism") provides a novel integration of ideas from diverse areas, such as primary and secondary process thinking, conditioning, genetic algorithms, chaos theory, and the thermodynamics of crystallography. Martindale characterizes remote association in terms of arousal in a connectionist framework, providing yet another computational approach to creative cognition.

Todd Lubart and Robert Sternberg ("An Investment Approach to Creativity: Theory and Data") present a multivariate investment approach to creative performance. Their theory states that creative individuals "buy low" by investing their efforts in new ideas that are not yet popular and "sell high" by moving on to new ideas once an idea has become popular. Their studies show that those who are identified as more creative are more likely to risk judgment of their work for a high reward.

Ronald Finke ("Creative Realism") proposes that creativity must be more than fun and wild imagination; realistic impact is also essential. Distinguishing creative realism from creative idealism and conservative thinking, Finke details criteria for assessing and enhancing creative realism and discusses the concept in terms of "preinventive forms" generated in his creative visualization research.

In the final chapter ("Conclusion: Principles, Paradoxes, and Prospects for the Future of Creative Cognition") we summarize the major themes of the book, highlighting, and in some cases resolving some of the paradoxes of creativity research. We conclude by discussing the potential value of the creative cognition approach.

Each of the chapters deals with central issues in cognition and creativity. Many of them consider new ways in which creativity can be studied under controlled conditions. We hope that the creative cognition approach will help reveal the basic cognitive processes underlying creativity and will offer exciting new directions for contemporary work in human cognition.

Acknowledgments

This chapter was supported by grant R01MH-44730 awarded to Steven M. Smith.

References

Duncker, K. (1945). On problem solving. *Psychological Monographs*, 58 (5, Whole No. 270).

Finke, R. A., Ward, T. B., and Smith, S. M. (1992). *Creative cognition: Theory, research, and applications.* Cambridge, MA: MIT Press.

Maier, N. R. F. (1940). The behavior mechanisms concerned with problem solving. *Psychological Review*, 47, 43–58.

Neisser, U. (ed.) (1982). *Memory observed.* San Francisco: Freeman.

Newell, A., Shaw, J. C., and Simon, H. A. (1962). The process of creative thinking. In Gruber, H. E., Terrell, G , and Wertheimer, M. (eds.), *Contemporary approaches to creative thinking.* New York: Atherton Press.

Sternberg, R. J. (ed.) (1988). *The nature of creativity: Contemporary psychological perspectives.* New York: Cambridge University Press.

Thorndike, E. L. (1911). *Animal intelligence.* New York: Macmillan.

Watson, J. B. (1958). *Behaviorism.* Chicago: University of Chicago Press.

Wertheimer, M. (1959). *Productive thinking.* New York: Harper & Row.

Part I

Knowledge and Insight in Creative Cognition

Chapter 1

Origins and Consequences of Novelty

George Mandler

Nil posse creari de nilo
Lucretius, *De Rerum Natura*

I take as my motto Lucretius's observation that nothing can be created from nothing. The mental products that we call novel, and the creative acts that produce novel thoughts and actions, need a prepared mind, just as much as well-practiced and habitual actions do. I shall argue that the mechanisms that produce novel acts and thoughts are part of our general mental armamentarium. A psychology of creation needs to postulate those mental processes and states that make possible the production of something novel. Therefore, one of the ways of approaching creativity is the exploration of how creative or novel acts or thoughts can be generated by the everyday processes of the human mind and body. Before discussing that problem directly, I examine various dimensions that characterize creation and novelty in significant ways, discuss the nature of dreams, and then use some apparent dream mechanisms to deal with the occurrence of novelty when it comes about in a nondeliberate way, when novel thoughts suddenly come to mind. Specifically, I deal with cases when one is not deliberately trying to solve a problem or task because such unbidden novel constructions have much in common with the construction of dreams.[1] I then turn to the consequences of producing or encountering novel events, arguing that such encounters have emotional consequences, which may affect their production.

Varieties of Creation

The topic of creativity, and the related topic of novelty, occupies a chapter heading or umbrella concept rather than a single characteristic of human (or other animals') minds. Few, if any, psychologists will consider a single mechanism for all creative acts, and different psy-

chologists consider different mechanisms, as a perusal of recent com-
pendia of approaches and theories will confirm (Findlay and Lumsden
1988; Finke, Ward, and Smith 1992; Goleman, Kaufman, and Ray 1992;
Roskos-Ewoldsen, Intons-Peterson, and Anderson 1993). I start with
several distinctions that segregate different kinds of creativity and
novelty, in part to limit my discussion and in part to define topics that
I consider in some detail later.

Individual versus Social Definitions of Creativity
A creative act, the production of something novel, exists in a social
context that defines a degree of novelty. A particular act may be novel
for all of humanity, for a specific social-cultural unit, or for an individual. Along that continuum, anything new for all of humanity is also
novel for all levels below it, whereas a novel act for an individual may
not be novel for each of the higher levels. At the higher levels, a
creation that is new only at a lower level may or can be essentially
uninteresting; "reinventing the wheel" has become a cliché to describe
that disinterest. From a psychological point of view, the focus of
interest is, of course, a creative or novel act by an individual, whether
or not the same novelty has been produced by any or many other
individuals before. The psychological question will always be: How
did he or she come to think of that?

Deliberate versus Nonintentional Creations
Is a particular novel construction deliberate at the time of production?
We may have the goal to produce something novel, but the novel
thought or act may come to mind deliberately, or it may pop into mind
unintentionally. Consider the constructive nature of language. All of
us, probably every day, generate a sentence or phrase that we have
never uttered before and that may possibly never have been uttered
by any other human being. More dramatically, the newly verbal young
child generates novel sentences and phrases at an astounding rate.
But neither the adult nor the child *intends* his or her speech to be novel,
nor is either generally aware of the novelty of these linguistic productions. When we do produce novel language constructions deliberately,
then our productions are not mere daily social intercourse but rather
special constructions in novels, stories, lectures, poems, and other
productions. It is when we are conscious of wanting to "say it just
right" that deliberate novel constructions come into play.

Goal-Defined Creativity
The deliberate creation of novelty introduces another dimension of
creativity—the kind of goal or end state required.[2] Most so-called

problem-solving situations require some degree of creativity. There is a search for a solution that is novel to the individual; it is not available at the beginning of the search. The search requires some prior notion as to the *kind or type* of solution that is required, followed by a search for a *token* that fits the problem encountered. If a particular goal exists, then the act of creation is deliberate in the long term, though it may be nondeliberate at the moment of production. The solution may come to mind unexpectedly.

Subjective Sense of Novelty

The subjective sense of novelty is another dimension that cuts novelty in important ways. When producing a novel thought or act, are we aware of its novelty? The example of language is also relevant. We are rarely aware of the novelty of our language productions; in fact, we tend to become aware of their novelty primarily when we deliberately seek to generate novel constructions. Thus, subjective awareness of novelty goes hand in hand with deliberate attempts at novelty. We are frequently aware of the novel constructions produced by others, though not usually in the course of social interaction.

Degrees of Novelty

We need to consider the continuum from the truly old and habitual to the strikingly novel or creative. In the extremes, there is no difficulty in distinguishing the old from the new, but no repetition is every truly entirely that; there is always something novel in whatever we do or say. Creativity, however, is usually thought to include only the truly novel; there is no argument as to the novelty.

Continuous versus Discontinuous Problem Solving

Problem solving that requires creative solutions may be continuous (ongoing until such time as the solution is reached) or discontinuous (the active deliberate search is stopped or abandoned for some time before being taken up again). The latter case is usually subsumed under the topic of incubation; the solution occurs after a pause or interval following attempts at solution.

With these parameters established, I will be particularly concerned with *individual, subjective* acts of creation of some significant *degree* of novelty that are *goal directed* and come to mind *nondeliberately* and *discontinuously*. I introduce the topic by drawing attention to a daily nondeliberate set of creative acts in which all of us participate every day (or rather night), the production of dreams. Dreams, in contrast to much of daily thought, are usually novel and creative (though not goal-directed) productions. Can we derive some principles or clues from this creative activity that can be applied to other acts of creation in the awake state?

Dreams: Novelty and Consciousness

Some characteristics of dreams provide important clues to the occurrence of nonintentional and usually novel thought.

Dreams come to consciousness without any intent on the part of the dreamer. The manifest content of dreams (its actors and objects) has long been known to be in part a reflection of our recent experiences, of material of which we have been conscious before. These residues tend to include actions that have not been brought to a conclusion, unsolved problems, rejected or suppressed thoughts, and often mundane occurrences that have not been further attended to in the pressure of everyday life (Freud, 1900). At the same time, manifest dream content may include subsidiary and unnoticed memories, as well as material that seems long forgotten. Thus, dreams contain to a large extent recent activations but not always the most activated events of one's recent life. The manifest content of dreams—in contrast to their deeper or dynamic meaning—does not necessarily, or even usually, reflect the dominant preoccupation of the dreamer, perceiver, or rememberer; it may be initially a depiction of rather peripheral events or objects. At the manifest level, at least, there seem to be no exclusive privileged sets of prior experiences.

Dreams are a creative activity that nearly all of us engage in nearly every night. With few exceptions, dreams are novel constructions—concatenations of previously registered and encoded knowledge and experience. In dreams, existing mental contents are configured to produce new views of the world and its objects and actors. This novel reconstruction of what we have known or experienced before characterizes some aspects of what we call creative thought. A reasonable answer to the question of how that is achieved in dreams with high frequency and apparent ease might provide some leads to the origins of creativity in general.

To understand some of the more interesting aspects of dreams, we need a framework within which we can talk about consciousness in general, so that we can consider dream consciousness and its novelty in particular. My own account of consciousness views current conscious content as responsive to the immediate history of the individual as well as to current needs and demands (Mandler 1985a, 1992, in press). These current contents are constructed from activated representations in a way that best assimilates the available evidence. Activated representations are equivalent to preconscious representations; underlying representations can be in one of three states: resting state activation (unconscious), recently activated (preconscious), and recently activated and used in conscious constructions (conscious). The evidence for conscious constructions comes from both extra- (real world) and intrapsychic sources and activates the relevant schemas. Both specific (concrete) and more abstract (generic) schemas will be activated and combined with memories. Most of the time, however, more than one schema or generic hypothesis will be activated by any set of sensory evidence. The selection (conscious representation) of a schema will depend on current as well as prior activation. I will experience (be conscious of) whatever is consistent with my immediate preceding history, as well as with currently impinging events. The most important schemas that determine current conscious contents are those that represent the demands and requirements of the current situation. Thus, sitting in a lecture room activates possible schemas (hypotheses) of university actions, scenes, and occurrences. Absent surviving personal preoccupations I will not be conscious of the roof at home that needs fixing but rather of the themes developed by the lecturer. In that way, current consciousness makes sense of as much evidence as possible that is available and relevant to current expectations and requirements (Marcel 1983b). In most, if not all, instances of consciousness in the waking state, what we are conscious of is constrained by the evidence from the external world that activates specific "world-related" schemas.

What is different in dreams? In dreams there is very little constraint by the reality and lawfulness of the external world on the possible constructions. There is no or little privileged activation of the schemas that represent the structured world. But dreams are highly structured; events in dreams are not random but occur in (often peculiar) connected sequences. Dreams present a structured mixture of real-world events, current events (sensory events in the environment of the dreamer), contemporary preoccupations, and ancient themes. They may be weird and novel, but they are meaningful. What they are not is dependent on the imperatives and continuity of the real world— inhabited by physically and socially possible problems and situations. In the waking world, our conscious experience is historically bound, dependent on context and what is possible in the real world. In contrast, dreams do not depend to a great extent on current sensory activations; they are constructed out of the activation of the previous hours and days. These constructions are meaningful in some way but not in terms of the usual meaning of the world around us. Similar arguments have been made by other investigators of dreams: Thus, "in REM [rapid eye movement] sleep the brain is isolated from its normal input and output channels" (Crick and Mitchison 1983, p. 112). And Hobson and associates (1987) note that the brain-mind is focused in the waking state on the linear unfolding of plot and time, whereas in REM dreaming the brain-mind cannot maintain its orientational focus.

The leftovers of our daily lives that are the building blocks of dreams are both abstract themes—our preoccupations and our generic view of the world—and concrete and specific activated schemas of events and objects encountered. These active schemas are not organized with respect to each other initially; they are, in that sense, random leftovers of our daily experiences and thoughts. Without the structure of the real world, they are free floating—free to find accommodating higher-order structures. The major part of these leftovers represent experiences during the preceding one to eight days of the dreamer's life.[3] The higher-order structures may combine quite separate, unrelated thoughts about events—happy or unhappy occurrences—but since there are no real-world constraints, they may be combined into sequences and categories by activating higher-order schemas to which they are relevant. It is in this fashion that abstract (and unconscious) preoccupations and complexes may find their expression in the consciousness of dreams. I leave open the question why and how these higher-order schemas use the leftovers and detritus—either because schemas tend to fill in the values of their features whenever possible or because of a general tendency to classify and order mental contents.

The residue of daily life produces some of the actors and events, whereas the *scenario* is free to be constructed by otherwise quiescent higher-order schemas. The higher-order schemas—the themes of dreams—may be activated by events of the preceding days, or they may be activated simply because a reasonable number of their features have been left over as residues from the days before. Cartwright (1990) has suggested that memory networks (much like themes) are activated in response to persistent (usually emotional) issues and that dreams are creative constructions that are a function of these networks throughout a night of dreaming. Hobson's activation-synthesis hypothesis of dreaming supposes that, apart from aminergic neurons, "the rest of the system is buzzing phrenetically, especially during REM sleep" (Hobson 1988, p. 291). Such additional activations provide ample material to construct dreams and, as Hobson suggests, to be creative and generate solutions to old and new problems.[4]

In short, dreams are unintentional and novel; they are constructed out of a large variety of activated mental contents, or of mental contents activated by a rather wide-ranging process of spreading activation, and they are organized by existing mental structures. Thus, except for the unusualness of their constructions, dreams are not much different from everyday experience. Dreams may even be confused with reality, when we sometimes are not sure whether we have lived or dreamed something. There is anecdotal as well as experimental evidence that we are sometimes confused between events that actually happened and those that we merely imagined—events that were present in consciousness but not in the surrounds. Clearly imagined and dreamed events seem to be stored in a manner similar to the way actual events are stored (Anderson 1984; Johnson and Raye 1981).

Activation, (Un)consciousness, and Creativity

We can take dreams, in part and only in part, as a model of some kinds of creative activity. There are two main reasons for using dreams as a model. First, they exhibit a great ease of producing novelty; second, there is extensive anecdotal evidence that creative solutions to problems may occur in dreams. Most of that evidence comes from studies of scientific creativity.[5] Apart from citing solutions that occur in dreams (Poincaré 1905; Hadamard 1945; Loewi 1953), scientists and their biographers frequently refer to the creative process as having the appearance of being irrational and undirected. This description of creativity once again ties it to the very similar character of dreams.

The processes that I have invoked are not unusual or peculiar. What is unusual in the construction of dreams is the absence of the constraints of reality, the structure and requirements of the world in which we live and to which we have learned to adjust by conformity and compromise. "Be realistic" is a reasonable commandment for social peace and satisfaction; it is deleterious for creative activity—and absent in dreams. The "voice of judgment" inhibits creativity (Goleman, Kaufman, and Ray 1992).

Given these suggestions on the creation and the appearance of novelty in dreams, I move on to use this framework in order to understand some aspects of creative constructions in the waking state. I will be primarily concerned with thoughts and solutions' coming to mind nondeliberately. This phenomenon, which I call mind popping, occurs when there is no immediate conscious intention to retrieve or generate some creative production. In the wider sense, it applies when solutions to problems suddenly come to mind—whether or not there has been a previous attempt to find that particular solution or to consider that particular problem at length. The evidence comes from cases from a variety of different areas of investigation when the individual is instructed to perceive, recall, or judge some event *different from the actual target* or to try to be nonintentional—that is, not to try to perceive or remember anything in particular, instead reporting "whatever comes to mind." The purpose of this collection is not to claim that the same mechanisms are necessarily operating in all these cases but rather to demonstrate that the mind-popping effect exists. The evidence comes from anecdotal as well as experimental sources and covers *perception* (Nelson 1974; see also Dixon 1981, pp. 93–94), *memory* (Pine 1964; Koriat and Feuerstein 1976), *priming and identification* (Marcel 1983a, experiment 1; Graf and Mandler 1984, experiment 3), *neuropsychology* (Coslett and Saffran 1989; Weiskrantz 1986, p. 151 and passim), and *problem solving* (Kaplan 1989, passim; Schooler, Ohlsson, and Brooks 1993).[6]

In the exploration of possible bases for mind popping, I turn first to a phenomenon that has received relatively little attention in recent psychological research: the apparent facilitating role of preconscious mental content and, conversely, the restricting role of conscious material. As an example, consider an experiment by Spence and Holland (1962; see Barber and Rushton 1975 for a replication of their pattern of results). Subjects were presented with the word *cheese* "subliminally" (five separate projections on a screen at approximately 7 milliseconds without a mask in a lighted room) or supraliminally for 2 seconds. They were then presented with a list of ten associates of *cheese* and ten control words, followed by recall. Subjects in the subliminal condition recalled significantly more associated than control words and recalled more associates than did the subjects in the supraliminal group, which showed no difference in the recall of the two kinds of words. Spence and Holland interpret the data as supporting Freud's (1900) notion that preconscious material (recently activated representations) "fans out" over an associative network to a greater degree than conscious material, which shows the "restricting effects of awareness." In other words, activated representations of which we are not aware produce a wider spread of activation than does aware material.

Many instances of mind popping apparently follow periods of incubation. That term has been primarily applied to problem-solving tasks in which the unsuccessful attempts at solution are followed by a pause or delay (filled or not), after which successful solutions are more probable. Explanations of incubation have in common some subset of a list of variables mentioned by Woodworth in 1938, including periodic conscious work on the problem, unconscious work, some version of advertent or inadvertent priming of the correct solution, diminution over time of interference from incorrect solutions, and reduction in fatigue.

Most of the general processes at work in mind popping are similar to those proposed for incubation (Mandler 1994). At the time that the problem is established (prior to the mind-popping event), target structures and candidate responses continue to activate other structures and representations. In the case of mind popping, however, it appears that such activation occurs more easily and fans out more widely than under conditions when active conscious searches are in place. I have argued previously (Mandler 1985a) that conscious problem solving results in waystations that represent progress toward the goal (usually demonstrated in talk-aloud protocols). However, current conscious contents activate their relevant unconscious representations, and this preferential activation of current conscious contents narrows the unconscious material available for further attempts. "Consciousness . . . serves to restrict and focus subsequent pathways by selectively activating those that are currently within the conscious construction" (Mandler 1985a, p. 77). That is the usual method of problem solving; incubation and mind popping provide another method by *not* restricting possible solutions and permitting extensive activations that may lead to a solution.

If dreams and dreamlike states (daydreaming, hypnagogic states) indeed make it possible for us to engage in thoughts that would otherwise be constrained by the reality of the impinging world, then the restricting functions of consciousness play an important role in our daily lives. They prevent us from going too far beyond the bounds of the givens; they prevent, in normal states and normal individuals, fantasy from taking over our transactions with the world. Conversely, poets, artists, creative scientists, and others are able to engage this less restricted world in producing poems, art, and theories.

In the other examples of mind popping, a similar state of affairs occurs. The target is not intentionally sought out and is preconscious; thus, it has the characteristic of fanning out, of engaging wider spreading of activation, more extensive elaboration, and activation. Thus, "thinking" about something else makes it possible for the actual targets to become available for conscious construction.

"Thinking about something else" is the defining characteristic of mind popping. Some target thought comes to mind while one is engaged in some other, usually irrelevant, train of thought. However, there should be similar effects for deliberate retrievals (e.g., following delays in studies of hypermnesia and incubation) if the period preceding the retrieval is filled with material not relevant to the target task. And there is some indication that incubation is more effective when the delay is filled with activities unrelated to the target material (Dorfman 1990; Payne 1987 passim; Smith and Vela 1991).

We would not wish to equate creativity with the chance novelties generated in dreams, though dreams have sometimes been given credit for important creations (Hadamard 1945; Loewi 1953; Poincaré 1905). What is the difference between the weird creatures of our dreams and a true creative act within the kind of mechanism I have proposed? The basic difference is found in Pasteur's dictum that "chance favors the prepared mind." Much of the constructions that arise out of activations that spread without the constraints of reality are due to chance; they are the result of what happens to be available and fitting to an equally happenstance structure. In contrast, the prepared mind is defined by the fact that question posing and problem-relevant structures are in fact primed to assimilate the chance events thrown up by activation. To the extent that the chance events are appropriate to the task at hand, they are likely to be incorporated into the primed structures. In addition, the events that are produced by spreading activation depend on what is active in the first place, which are also likely associations and relations that make reference to the problem at hand (or in mind).

Why does awareness restrict the utilization of unconscious material and thereby the production of novel concatenations? One possible explanation is a relatively simple interference notion. Consider a search process for somebody's name. The immediately obvious conscious contents are replete with the bringing to mind of possible names, of contexts in which one has seen the person, and so forth. All of these incorrect "thoughts" will provide activation to their underlying representations, which in turn will be the dominant preconscious material available for conscious constructions. The result is the well-known but little-researched looping effect, in which the incorrect solutions repeatedly come to mind. Conscious and deliberate processing apparently produces more competition because more material that is similar to the target is generated. But if material totally irrelevant to the task is the primary occupation of conscious constructions, there will be little interference with the mental structure that is initiated by the relevant task, such as, "What is that person's name?" or "What is the right word for that definition?" Repeated search processes and spreading activation can eventually produce the appropriate integration of the correct target item. But note that mind popping in response to difficult problems is not a frequent phenomenon; unfortunately, we do not solve all or most unsolved problems. Another aspect of interference is the restricting character of the surrounding real world. Just as in dreams, the time and space requirements of the waking environment restrict what can be constructed in response to conscious demands. The unconscious activation process, on the other hand, presumably continues without such constraints.

Second, there might be inhibitory processes at work when more than one possible solution is being consciously considered (Rumelhart and McClelland 1982). If an incorrect solution is dominant at any one time or becomes dominant because of conscious preoccupation, the correct solution may well be inhibited, and a reduction in activation may ensue. Again, irrelevant preoccupations will not interfere with the underlying process.

A third possibility is a genuine autonomous restriction of awareness. One should not dismiss the possibility that some states of passive thought approach the sleeping state described by Hobson (1988), in which quasi-random neuronal activity significantly increases. If that can happen in some awake states of passivity, then new elaborations (novel solutions) are more likely to be generated. Such a state of affairs would be very close to the "blind variation and selective retention" approach to problem solving advocated by Campbell (1960). All of these processes may, of course, be operating at different times or at the same time, or some might be specific to certain of the instances of mind popping listed above. Given the multidimensional and overde-termined nature of human thought, that is the most likely conclusion.

Why does a solution come to mind at a particular time? First, the demand for the solution, the question posed, is itself in a continuing high state of activation, and autonomous processes combine this "de-mand" with the newly integrated solution; second is the possibility, always with us, that fortuitous and haphazard events (both extra- and intrapsychic) become cues or primes for the now-readily-accessible solution.

The discussion up to now has been restricted to one possible way in which novel ideas may be constructed—specifically, how they might arise in dreams and in waking states in which the restrictions of reality are reduced. I now turn to a quite different problem: one of the consequences of all or most novel productions and situations. That problem moves us into the realm of emotion and motivation.

The Challenge of Novelty

Novelty often has emotional consequences. We know that most im-mediately from our own and our neighbors' reactions to new fashions, new kinds of music, new foods. We also know from the traditional wisdom of psychology that extinction trials produce emotional reac-tions, that children may react emotionally to strange people and faces. I wish to go beyond these observations and start with an approach to emotions that stresses arousal and evaluation, as exemplified in discrepancy-evaluation theory (Mandler 1975, 1984, 1990). The approach views the construction of emotion as consisting of the combination of cognitive evaluative schemas with visceral arousal (which is perceived as emotional intensity). Together these components are concatenated into a holistic conscious event, the experience of emotion.

The two dimensions of arousal and evaluation respond to the use of emotion in the common language—the notion that emotions represent evaluative cognitions and the assertion that emotions are "hot," implying a gut reaction, a visceral response. Evaluative cognitions— what is good or bad, pleasant or unpleasant, noxious or desirable— provide the quality of the emotional experience, whereas visceral reactions generate its intensity and peculiar emotional and passionate characteristic. Sympathetic nervous system (SNS) arousal not only ensures the hot quality of the emotions but also controls the felt intensity. Recent experimental evidence has shown that the felt intensity of an emotion is a linear function of degree of autonomic (sympathetic) arousal (MacDowell 1991, 1993).

A majority of occasions for visceral (SNS) arousal follows the occurrence of some perceptual or cognitive discrepancy, or the interruption or blocking of some ongoing action. Discrepancies are only a sufficient, not a necessary, condition for sympathetic arousal. Other sources of SNS arousal can and do play a role in emotional experience.

Discrepancies and interruptions depend to a large extent on the organization of the mental representations of thought and action. Within the purview of schema theory, these discrepancies occur when the expectations generated by schemas are violated. This is the case whether the violating event is worse or better than the expected one, and it accounts for visceral arousal on both unhappy and joyful occasions. Discrepancies are also usually involved in cases of conflict— situations in which more than one possible action or thought is possible in response to situational or intrapsychic demands. Pursuing one or the other possibility means abandoning other alternatives, and the general ambivalence displayed in conflicts generates arousal and emotional reactions. Most emotions occur subsequent to such discrepancies because the discrepancy produces visceral arousal. In summary, interruptions, discrepancies, blocks, frustrations, novelties, conflicts, and so forth are occasions for SNS activity (Mandler 1964; MacDowell and Mandler 1989). I concentrate here on the discrepancies produced by novel events and productions.

The very meaning of novelty implies that it is an event, produced by oneself or encountered in the environment, that is discrepant from our previous experience. Depending on the degree of divergence from the expected, novelty will produce varying degrees of SNS arousal. What these conditions will be depends on the kind of novelty encountered. Novelty is not an all-or-none concept, and most of the distinctions among different kinds of creativity that I have listed apply to novelty.

A very frequent evaluation of novelty, when first encountered, is negative. If a situation or event does not fit our expectations of what has occurred in the past or what should be taking place, it will be negatively evaluated. New styles of music and painting, new ways of structuring our social world, new modes of organization are usually greeted with negative evaluations.[7] It may well be adaptive initially to avoid the novel, which is unfamiliar, may be dangerous, and may require new modes of acting and reacting. On the other hand, when is the novel positively valued, as it often can be?

One possible explanation for the search for novelty lies in the positive evaluative state when a novel event or experience can be assimilated into existing schematic structures. The positive effect generated by smooth assimilation would encourage the search for novel but not extremely discrepant situations. Another candidate for the positive coloring of novelty is some evaluative structure that interacts with the novel event. Such structures may be social, as when a novel aspect of a difficult problem is seen as a possible solution, or it may be individual, as with people who seek the novel and find positive value in problem solving, whether cognitive or aesthetic (e.g., the creative individual who seeks out complexity; Dellas and Gaier 1970). Both the creative artist and scientist are part of a cultural tradition that values the novel construction and seeks out novelty. On the other hand, there are social and cultural conditions in which the novel is avoided and considered inappropriate (e.g., in authoritarian societies).

Whether we are an information-seeking species may still be open to argument. A basic preference for the old emerges in children after schemas about the world have been well established, as in stranger anxiety. New information is sought whenever the physical and social world changes and requires new adjustments. In the modern industrial world, we apparently have become novelty junkies, but some very stable preindustrial societies fail to show such a hunt for the novel. It seems premature to generalize our own experience to an assertion about human nature.

The novel, and particularly the creative, event produces discrepancies and discontinuities. New ways of doing and seeing are often seen as destructive and alien. This is most easily demonstrated in the arts, when the new way of seeing or hearing creates strong dissonances in the viewer and hearer. Beethoven's music provides one of many examples. A contemporary critic of the *Eroica* symphony noted that one left the concert hall "crushed by the mass of unconnected and overloaded ideas and a continuing tumult by all the instruments" (cited by Rosen 1971, *p.* 393).

This brings up the question of the role of creative individuals and their actions. The truly creative act, which is both socially and individually creative, will often be seen as destructive of existing values and standards. The artist who breaks new paths and the scientist who creates new theoretical understanding both know that they are destroying or at least undermining existing structures that have been accepted by society and by their peers. In that sense, creative individuals must be able to tolerate the destructive consequences of their creation. If it is seen as aggressive, it will produce one kind of reaction of conflict and competition, but if it is seen not as destructive vis-à-vis others but as "destructive" only of ideas and social and cognitive structures, it may be viewed as a socially desirable rather than as a negative act.[8] Whether such acts will be perceived as negative or positive depends to a large extent on early experiences and perceptions. If we consider nonconformity a necessary concomitant of the creative act, it is not surprising that studies of the personalities of creative individuals have shown them to be nonconforming and accepting of destructiveness (McKinnon 1962; Barron 1968). All of these attitudes will be informed by societal and cultural values to a large extent. A society that sees the creative act as an occasion of competition and aggression will undermine the possibility of seeing the free, creative act as a positive sign of social and personal achievement.

Humans are novelty producers and novelty customers. We produce novelty readily and constantly in dreams but also in daily life. In general, novelty will frequently produce discrepancies and contradictions, which will be the occasion for emotional reactions of varying valences and intensities. The encounter with novel objects, events, tastes, and so forth will also lead to the development or imposition of new values. Changes in values are most likely to occur when contradictions have to be faced.[9] This is to be contrasted with the conservatism of holding to the familiarity and comfort of well-established, habitual schemas. Which of these two roads will dominate in a situation depends on the general schemas that characterize the individual's value system. The outcome of the dialectic between conservatism and change, between the old and the new, is determined by historical and social aspects of the society and the personal history of the individual within that society.

Notes

1. The phenomena of interest have much in common with involuntary (implicit) memories, which psychologists have rediscovered after a century of being preoccupied with memory as a deliberate search or retrieval process.
2. See Mandler (1985b) for a discussion of the distinction among various uses of the concept of goal.
3. Given the longer period involved, these are apparently not just primed events. See Freud (1900) for an extended listing of these "manifest" contents of dreams.
4. On the organized nature of dreams, see also Foulkes (1985 passim).
5. For an earlier discussion of the existing evidence, see Mandler and Kessen (1959, pp. 244–252).
6. I have cited only some representative studies; for more extensive citations and discussions, see Mandler (1994).
7. For a discussion of affect and music, see Gaver and Mandler (1987).
8. For related discussions, see Mandler (1984).
9. See Mandler (1993) for an extensive discussion of the relation between discrepancy and value.

References

Anderson, R. E. (1984). Did I do it or did I imagine doing it? *Journal of Experimental Psychology: General, 113*, 594–613.

Barber, P. J., and Rushton, J. P. (1975). Experimenter bias and subliminal perception. *British Journal of Psychology, 66*, 357–372.

Barron, F. (1968). *Creativity and personal freedom.* Princeton, NJ: Van Nostrand.

Campbell, D. T. (1960). Blind variation and selective retention in creative thought as in other knowledge processes. *Psychological Review, 67*, 380–400.

Cartwright, R. (1990). A network model of dreams. In R. R. Bootzin, J. F. Kihlstrom, and D. L. Schacter (eds.), *Sleep and cognition* (pp. 179–189). Washington, DC: American Psychological Association.

Coslett, H. B., and Saffran, E. M. (1989). Evidence for preserved reading in "pure alexia." *Brain, 112*, 327–359.

Crick, F., and Mitchison, G. (1983). The function of dream sleep. *Nature, 304*, 111–114.

Dellas, M., and Gaier, E. L. (1970). Identification of creativity. *Psychological Bulletin, 73*, 55–73.

Dixon, N. F. (1981). *Preconscious processing.* Chichester: Wiley.

Dorfman, J. (1990). *Metacognitions and incubation effects in insight problem solving.* Unpublished doctoral dissertation, University of California, San Diego.

Findlay, C. S., and Lumsden, C. J. (1988). *The creative mind.* New York: Academic Press.

Finke, R. A., Ward, T. B., and Smith, S. M. (1992). *Creative cognition: Theory, research, and applications.* Cambridge, MA: MIT Press.

Foulkes, D. (1985). *Dreaming: A cognitive-psychological analysis.* Hillsdale, NJ: Erlbaum.

Freud, S. (1900). The interpretation of dreams. In *The standard edition of the complete psychological works of Sigmund Freud* (Vols. 4–5). London: Hogarth Press, 1975.

Gaver, W., and Mandler, G. (1987). Play it again, Sam: On liking music. *Cognition and Emotion, 1*, 259–282.

Goleman, D., Kaufman, P., and Ray, M. (1992). *The creative spirit.* New York: Dutton/ Penguin Group.

Graf, P., and Mandler, G. (1984). Activation makes words more accessible, but not necessarily more retrievable. *Journal of Verbal Learning and Verbal Behavior, 23*, 553–568.

24 George Mandler

Hadamard, J. (1945). *An essay on the psychology of invention in the mathematical field.* Princeton, NJ: Princeton University Press.

Hobson, J. A. (1988). *The dreaming brain.* New York: Basic Books.

Hobson, J. A., Hoffman, S. A., Helfand, R., and Kostner, D. (1987). Dream bizarreness and the activation-synthesis hypothesis. *Human Neurobiology, 6,* 157–164.

Johnson, M. K., and Raye, C. L. (1981). Reality monitoring. *Psychological Review, 88,* 67–85.

Kaplan, C. A. (1989). *Hatching a theory of incubation: Does putting a problem aside really help? If so, why?* Unpublished doctoral dissertation, Carnegie-Mellon University.

Koriat, A., and Feuerstein, N. (1976). The recovery of incidentally acquired information. *Acta Psychologica, 40,* 463–474.

Loewi, O. (1953). *From the workshop of discoveries.* Lawrence: University of Kansas Press.

MacDowell, K. A. (1991, June). *Autonomic (sympathetic) responses predict subjective intensity of experience.* Poster presented at American Psychological Society Convention, Washington, DC.

MacDowell, K. A. (1993). *Representation, arousal, and intensity of experience for expected and unexpected events.* Unpublished doctoral dissertation, University of California, San Diego.

MacDowell, K. A., and Mandler, G. (1989). Constructions of emotion: Discrepancy, arousal, and mood. *Motivation and Emotion, 13,* 105–124.

MacKinnon, D. W. (1962). The nature and nurture of creative talent. *American Psychologist, 17,* 484–495.

Mandler, G. (1964). The interruption of behavior. In E. Levine (ed.), *Nebraska Symposium on Motivation: 1964* (pp. 163–219). Lincoln: University of Nebraska Press.

Mandler, G. (1975). *Mind and emotion.* New York: Wiley.

Mandler, G. (1984). *Mind and body: Psychology of emotion and stress.* New York: Norton.

Mandler, G. (1985a). *Cognitive psychology: An essay in cognitive science.* Hillsdale, NJ: Erlbaum.

Mandler, G. (1985b). Scoring goals. *CC-AI: Journal for the Integrated Study of Artificial Intelligence, Cognitive Science and Applied Epistemology, 2,* 25–31.

Mandler, G. (1990). A constructivist theory of emotion. In N. S. Stein, B. L. Leventhal, and T. Trabasso (eds.), *Psychological and biological approaches to emotion* (pp. 21–43). Hillsdale, NJ: Erlbaum.

Mandler, G. (1992). Toward a theory of consciousness. In H.-G. Geissler, S. W. Link, and J. T. Townsend (eds.), *Cognition, information processing, and psychophysics: Basic issues* (pp. 43–65). Hillsdale, NJ: Erlbaum.

Mandler, G. (1993). Approaches to a psychology of value. In M. Hechter, L. Nadel, and R. E. Michod (eds.), *The origin of values* (pp. 229–258). Hawthorne, NY: Aldine de Gruyter.

Mandler, G. (1994). Hypermnesia, incubation, and mind-popping: On remembering without really trying. In C. Umiltà and M. Moscovitch (eds.), *Attention and performance XV: Conscious and unconscious information processing* (pp. 3–33). Cambridge, MA: MIT Press.

Mandler, G. (in press). Consciousness redux. In J. C. Cohen and J. W. Schooler (eds.), *Consciousness: The Twenty-fifth Carnegie Symposium on Cognition.* Hillsdale, NJ: Erlbaum.

Mandler, G., and Kessen, W. (1959). *The language of psychology.* New York: Wiley.

Marcel, A. J. (1983a). Conscious and unconscious perception: Experiments on visual masking and word recognition. *Cognitive Psychology, 15,* 197–237.

Marcel, A. J. (1983b). Conscious and unconscious perception: An approach to the relations between phenomenal experience and perceptual processes. *Cognitive Psychology, 15,* 238–300.

Nelson, J. I. (1974). Motion sensitivity in peripheral vision. *Perception, 3,* 151–152.

Payne, D. G. (1987). Hypermnesia and reminiscence in recall: A historical and empirical review. *Psychological Bulletin, 101,* 5–27.

Pine, F. (1964). The bearing of psychoanalytic theory on selected issues in research on marginal stimuli. *Journal of Nervous and Mental Diseases, 138,* 68–75.

Poincaré, H. (1905). *Science and hypothesis.* London: Scott.

Rosen, C. (1971). *The classical style.* New York: Viking Press.

Roskos-Ewoldsen, B., Intons-Peterson, M. J., and Anderson, R. E. (1993). *Imagery, discovery and creativity: A cognitive perspective.* Amsterdam: Elsevier.

Rumelhart, D. E., and McClelland, J. L. (1982). An interactive activation model of context effects in letter perception: Part 2. The contextual enhancement effect and some tests and extensions of the model. *Psychological Review, 89,* 60–94.

Schooler, J. W., Ohlsson, S., and Brooks, K. (1993). Thoughts beyond words: When language overshadows insight. *Journal of Experimental Psychology: General, 122,* 166–183.

Smith, S. M., and Vela, E. (1991). Incubated reminiscence effects. *Memory and Cognition, 19,* 168–176.

Spence, D. P., and Holland, B. (1962). The restricting effects of awareness: A paradox and an explanation. *Journal of Abnormal and Social Psychology, 64,* 163–174.

Weiskrantz, L. (1986). *Blindsight: A case study and implications.* Oxford: Clarendon Press.

Woodworth, R. S. (1938). *Experimental psychology.* New York: Holt. Yaniv, I., and Meyer, D. E. (1987). Activation and metacognition of inaccessible stored information: Potential bases for incubation effects in problem solving. *Journal of Experimental Psychology: Learning, Memory, and Cognition, 13,* 187–205.

Chapter 2

Intuitive Antecedents of Insight

Kenneth S. Bowers, Peter Farvolden, and
Lambros Mermigis

The problem of how new knowledge is generated goes back at least to Plato. In his dialogue with Meno, Plato somewhat captiously paraphrases a paradox that Meno has just posed by saying: "I know, Meno, what you mean; but see what a tiresome dispute you are introducing. You argue that a man cannot inquire either about that which he knows, or about that which he does not know; for if he knows, he has no need to inquire; and if not, he cannot; for he does not know the very subject about which he is to inquire" (in Jowett 1937). Plato's extended response to Meno's paradox is that all new knowledge is in fact a recollection of things already learned, perhaps in a previous life. If we elide the reference to past lives and rephrase the basic point in contemporary terms, it might be restated as follows: any novel production or insight must in some sense draw upon what is already known, and what is known must be mnemonically encoded.

Intuition and creativity constitute two important routes to new knowledge, and they are both very dependent on prior mnemonic encodings (Weisberg and Alba 1981). But despite this fundamental similarity, the literatures on creativity and intuition are virtually non-overlapping. Creativity has a literature of its own that is concerned with both creative people and products on one hand (Dellas and Gaier 1970) and with creative processes on the other (Mednick 1962; see also Sternberg 1988). By way of contrast, the psychological literature concerned with intuition has, with some important exceptions (Brainerd and Reyna 1990; Dreyfus and Dreyfus 1986; Hammond et al. 1987; Reber 1989; Simon 1986; Simonton 1980; Westcott 1968), been an appendix to literatures concerned with judgment and decision making under conditions of uncertainty on one hand (Kahneman, Slovic, and Tversky 1982) and with insight in problem solving on the other (Metcalfe and Wiebe 1987).[1]

Creativity and intuition differ in another respect. Creativity by and large implies that a novel form or product has been generated—for example, a sculpture, a sonnet, a sonata—in any case, something that did not exist prior to its creator. Thus, the creator antedates his or her creation. Intuition, on the other hand, implies that some pattern, structure, or organization exists prior to its detection. Accordingly, for intuition, the discerned preexists its discernment. Perhaps this difference between creativity and intuition its one reason that it seems somewhat more natural to speak of creative artists and intuitive scientists rather than the reverse.

The distinction between creativity and intuition is reflected in the nature of the tasks that are used in the two domains. Research on creativity typically involves getting multiple judges to evaluate subjects' responses for their originality (Bowers 1971). Because no one response is preordained as correct, judgments are the only feasible way of evaluating the creativity of response. By way of contrast, research on intuition in the context of problem solving is more likely to use tasks or puzzles with a preordained answer that must be discerned. Interestingly, Mednick and Mednick's (1967) classic research on the Remote Associates Test (RAT) departed from this convention by using single-solution word puzzles to assess creativity. Partly for this reason, the RAT has been criticized as an inappropriate device for assessing creativity (Jackson and Messick 1965). However, research in our laboratory has used RAT-type items to assess intuition, and the same criticism does not apply.

The literature concerning judgment under uncertainty has by and large left intuition looking bereft of value, regarding it as a source of bias and error (Kahneman et al 1982; Nisbett and Ross 1980; Ross 1977). According to this literature, various cognitive heuristics such as availability and representativeness bias intuitive judgment, which is also underinformed by normative considerations such as sample size and regression effects. The upshot of this somewhat pessimistic literature is that when people are asked to make decisions under conditions of uncertainty, we are likely to learn a great deal about the foibles of judgment but little or nothing about whatever was judged. There is much truth to this view, but it must be placed in balance with some of the subtleties of cognition that permit innovation and insight. In general, it can be argued that the literature on judgment under uncertainty regards the cognitive cup as being half empty (at best), whereas intuition in the context of discovery regards the cup as (at least) half full.

The "half-empty" view of cognition is by no means limited to the judgment literature; it extends to cognitive performance generally, as an example shows. In their classic paper, Nisbett and Wilson (1977) recall the string pendulum problem originally conducted by Maier (1931). Subjects in this early investigation were asked to tie together the free ends of two strings that were suspended from the ceiling. The problem was that the two strings were hung so far apart from each other that they could not be reached at the same time. The desired solution involved recognizing that a pair of pliers laying in clear view could serve not only as a tool for grasping but also as a pendulum bob. When tied to one of the strings, the pliers could be swung toward the second one, thereby permitting a subject to hold onto the second string while awaiting the arrival of the first one.

Thirty-seven people who did not solve the string problem in 10 minutes were given an important clue, though it was announced as such: the experimenter "inadvertently" nudged one of the strings into lateral motion. After exposure to this clue, twenty-three subjects solved the problem within 60 seconds. What was at least as interesting, however, is that most of these subjects had no idea that the nudged-string clue had anything to do with their sudden ability to solve the problem. Indeed, many of the subjects denied having seen the string move. Nisbett and Wilson saw this inability of subjects to provide a valid account of their insight as evidence for the foibles of cognition. The implication of this "half-empty" view of cognition is that people who do not understand the actual determinants of their thought and action are likely to behave irrationally.

There is a more benign view of Maier's findings, however. It is well established that consciousness is a limited-capacity mode of information processing (Baars 1988) because people can be conscious of only a few things at once. So although subjects in Maier's experiment may not have consciously noticed the lateral movement of the string (or at least remained unconscious of its influence), they seem nevertheless to have been tacitly informed by it. In other words, people are able to respond productively to information that they do not consciously notice or remember, a possibility that is documented in the literature on priming (Overson and Mandler 1987; Tulving and Schacter 1990) and implicit memory (Schacter 1987) The fact that human cognition is subject to unconscious distortions and biases is balanced by the fact that it can also be tacitly informed (Polanyi 1964). This chapter examines the latter position.

Defining Intuition

We define intuition as the perception of clues to coherence that tacitly activates and guides thought toward an insight or hunch about the nature of the coherence in question. The right-hand panel of figure 2.1 provides a concrete illustration of how intuition, thus defined, works. Pictured there is one of many gestalt closure items that were

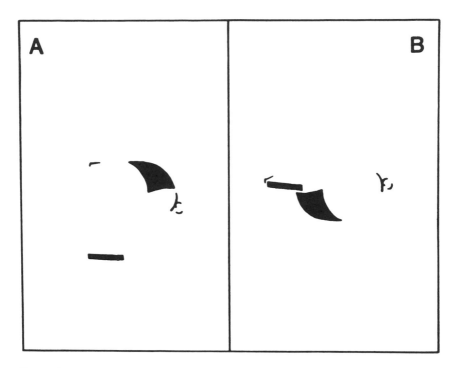

Figure 2.1
A sample item from the Waterloo Gestalt (WGES) test (solution in text)

newly devised for use in our research on intuition (Bowers et al. 1990). Some readers will immediately see the gestalt for what it is, but many will see only black lines and patches. After looking at the gestalt for a little longer, some of these latter people may suddenly see a coherent object emerge from the sundry clues that reflect and finally reveal it. If a few more moments of inspection do not help, perhaps the actual solution will "close" the gestalt: it is a whistle.

What happens in the interval between seeing a confusing array of black patches and lines and seeing them as a whistle? We would like to argue that there is enough "whistleness" in the gestalt to activate incipient thoughts and associations of a whistle (instead of a trombone, say). If and when the idea of whistle is activated sufficiently to become conscious, its pertinence to the gestalt may be recognized in the form of a sudden insight. It follows that a person completely unacquainted with whistles is unlikely to recognize one when it is depicted in a highly schematized form. For such a person, there is nothing in his or her mnemonic network that can be activated by the whistleness of the gestalt. In other words, absent a person's familiarity with whistles, a gestalt of one has no clue value; consequently, the black lines and patches that comprise an unrecognized whistle fall on deaf eyes, as it were.

There is a subtle interplay between conscious and unconscious processes implied by this conceptualization of intuition and insight. The conscious perception of a gestalt stimulus (the black patches and lines) sets into motion a train of processes that are largely automatic and unconscious (Posner and Snyder 1975). Perhaps via spreading activation (Collins and Loftus 1975, Anderson 1983) the whistleness of the gestalt automatically generates relevant memories and associations, including, perhaps, thoughts of a whistle. However, the process of activating the correct word and the process of recognizing it as the solution are separate and distinct, so the fact that "whistle" surfaces into consciousness does not guarantee recognizing it as the solution to the whistle gestalt. This possibility is underscored when a person who has not solved the gestalt is told the answer and even then does not immediately see how it solves the gestalt.

To summarize, there are two conceptually distinct phases in the process of problem solving: (1) an initial, *intuitive phase*, which involves a graded process of activating responses that are stimulated by, and increasingly appropriate to, the available pattern of clues, and (2) an *insight phase*, which involves a conscious recognition, often quite sudden, that a particular response constitutes a potential solution to the problem.

Appreciating the biphasic nature of the model helps to underline how it is not the case that a hypothesis or full-fledged solution occurs unconsciously and then is then simply transferred to consciousness. Rather, the very notion of a hypothesis or solution implies conscious appreciation of how a particular thought or idea organizes or fits the pattern of clues. According to this view, there are no unconscious insights or solutions. By contrast, the automatic, implicit processes that generate a correct response in the first place are not directly represented in conscious experience. Consequently, conscious recognition of a particular response as a viable hypothesis or solution can seem to occur like a bolt out of the blue, despite the largely unconscious precursors of such a realization. The subjective experience of discontinuity so characteristic of this second stage of problem solving is the basis for so-called sudden insight.

In the real world, objects do not come schematized like a gestalt closure. Consequently, there is typically little time and less effort involved in proceeding from the visual clues an object affords to seeing it as a coherent object. With the gestalt closure, however, the process of going from such visual clues to object recognition takes place in slow motion, thereby permitting easier investigative access to this process.

Research Findings

The results of some of our research using different tasks seem to converge on the same basic point: before a solution to a problem is achieved, the mind of the problem solver has been implicitly or tacitly informed by the particulars of the problem. (Some of this research has been previously reported; Bowers et al. 1990.)

Waterloo Gestalt Closure Task (WGES)

On the ordinary gestalt closure task, subjects are presented with a series of gestalt-closure items and asked to solve as many of them as they can. The use of this standard paradigm does not permit assessment of the cognitive processes prior to achieving a solution, so almost by default, the experience of sudden insight that is so characteristic of closing the gestalt becomes evidence for a corresponding discontinuity of the cognitive processes that generated the correct response.

To address this difficulty, we developed a modification of the gestalt closure test, the WGES, that gives us at least some information about whether people closed in on gestalt closure items more gradually than the experience of sudden insight might imply. We had undergraduate art students draw an original batch of gestalt closure items. For each such rendering, they also drew a control stimulus that consisted of the same elements displaced and rotated to generate a pseudo-gestalt, that is, a stimulus configuration that did not reflect a coherent object. The artists were instructed to render the control stimulus aesthetically pleasing. The left-hand panel of figure 3.1 illustrates the control stimulus for the whistle. Pretesting reduced about 130 such pairs of drawings to the 35 to 75 items that were used in five independent samples of subjects ranging in size from 33 to 74.

Subjects in the experiment were asked to look at each stimulus for 5 seconds. During the 8-second interstimulus interval that followed, subjects were asked to do three things: (1) provide a correct answer if possible; (2) in the absence of a correct answer, guess which of the two drawings was a coherent object; and (3) provide a confidence rating from zero (no confidence) to 2 (quite confident) regarding this guess.

Across the five samples, subjects correctly identified 30 to 38 percent of the gestalts. None of these items was included in subsequent analyses because the major question was to see whether people could detect coherence without being able to identify it. The answer was clear: in each of the five samples, subjects selected unsolved but coherent gestalts at above-chance levels. The success rate varied from a low of .56 to a high of .66 ($M = .60$). In other words, in the absence of being able to solve a coherent gestalt, subjects selected the coherent rather than incoherent drawing 60 percent of the time.

One possible explanation of this finding is that people are in touch with the nature of the gestalt's coherence before they can identify it. In figure 3.1, for example, this would mean that subjects are responding to the whistleness of the coherent gestalt before they can see the gestalt as a whistle. There are, however, other possible explanations. Perhaps coherent gestalts are selected by default. This seems especially plausible in a two-choice, forced-choice task in which incoherent gestalts might offend some principle of objectness (Biederman 1987; Schacter, Cooper, and Delaney 1990). Alternatively, perhaps coherent drawings embody preferred aesthetic virtues better than their incoherent counterparts.

If people are in fact informed by the specific nature of the gestalt prior to identifying it, measurable consequences should be forthcoming. For example, absent a solution, the whistle gestalt should activate incipient whistleness and, hence, predispose or prime the response "whistle" on a subsequent test trial. The pseudo-whistle control stimulus should be much less effective in this regard. In a small study, subjects were presented either a genuine gestalt or its pseudo-gestalt counterpart for five seconds. After removing the drawing, we presented a list of four words, one of them the correct solution to the genuine gestalt. Subjects were asked to select which of the words in fact satisfied the genuine gestalt. Across many such sequenced presentations, subjects were able to identify the correct word 52 percent of the time in response to the pseudo-gestalt, considerably above the chance hit rate of 25 percent. Thus, even displaced and rotated elements of a pseudo-gestalt closure item provide differential information about the correct response. However, the genuine gestalts generated a 69 percent hit rate, significantly above the hit rate achieved by control stimuli.

In sum, the coherent gestalts were far better at informing subjects' forced-choice selection of the correct solution-word than were their incoherent counterparts. This result reduces the likelihood that people picked the coherent gestalt by default or that there was some nonspecific feature of coherent gestalts that biased subjects' selection of them. Rather, the specific content (e.g., the whistleness) of an unsolved gestalt seems to have informed subjects' forced choices.

Other, more subtle tests of such priming have yet to be conducted. To illustrate, suppose subjects who were unable to solve the gestalt closure of the whistle were then presented the solution in partial-word form (e.g., whistle as w__stl_). If in fact the unsolved gestalt partially activates the word *whistle*, it should semantically prime (d'Arcais and Schreuder 1987; Tulving, Schacter, and Stark 1982) the correct completion of the word at a higher rate than its pseudo-gestalt counterpart does. Alternatively, would forced responses to unsolved gestalt items be associatively closer to the solution word than are forced responses to its pseudo-gestalt counterpart? These are only two possibilities for exploring the thesis that cognitive processes prior to solving a gestalt are in fact converging toward its solution.

Before leaving this discussion of the WGES, we should note that in four of the five samples run on this task, the more confident that subjects' guesses were, the more likely they were to choose the coherent gestalt. However, even in the subcategory of zero-confidence choices, subjects were correct 57 percent of the time. It is as if subjects' threshold of (forced-choice) coherence detection was lower than the threshold for confidence in their guesses, which was in turn lower than the threshold for actually identifying the coherence. This possibility for multiple thresholds in perception and judgment has previously been raised in the literature on subliminal perception (Cheesman and Merikle 1984) and in previous work on intuition (Simonton 1980). We now turn to other tasks that even more clearly indicate that cognitive processes are tacitly informed by the elements of the problem.

Dyads of Triads Task (DOT)
In this task, subjects are presented with two triads of words. The three words of the coherent triad all have a common associate (many of these items were based on Mednick and Mednick's RAT); the three words of the incoherent triad do not. Subjects are asked to (1) solve the coherent triad; (2) if that proves impossible, select the coherent triad; and (3) provide a confidence rating for this forced-choice selection. From 30 to 60 DOT items were administered to the same five samples of subjects that were run on the gestalt closure task.

Subjects solved from 22 to 32 percent of the DOT items, and again, these solved items were not included in any of the subsequent analyses. In each of the five samples, subjects selected the coherent triad at above-chance levels. The success rate varied from a low of .56 to a high of .60 ($M = .58$). In other words, in the absence of being able to solve a coherent word triad, subjects selected the coherent rather than the incoherent triad 58 percent of the time.[2] There was also a tendency for higher rates of success to be associated with higher confidence, but unlike the gestalt task, the absence of any confidence was associated with chance performance.

One possible understanding of these findings is that the individual clue words of a coherent triad convergently activate their common associate (the solution word) and that this activation, even if insufficient to generate the solution per se, nevertheless informs a forced-choice selection of the coherent triad. It is also possible, however, that people are successful in selecting the coherent word triad by default, sensing the absence of coherence in the incoherent triad rather than its presence in the coherent triad.

The DOT lends itself to internal analyses that effectively precludes the latter interpretation. We belatedly noted that some of the coherent triads were comprised of clue words that were semantically convergent; that is, the solution word was not only a common associate of the three clue words but retained the same meaning with respect to each of these words. For example, the words *goat*, *pass*, and *green* have the word *mountain* as a common associate, and, further, the word *mountain* retains the same semantic meaning with respect to each of the clue words. Word triads of this type are thus semantically convergent. However, consider the clue words *strike*, *same*, and *tennis*. Although each has *match* as a common associate, this solution word changes its meaning in relation to each of the clue words. We refer to this kind of DOT item as semantically divergent.

Each triad was independently rated for the degree of its semantic convergence by five independent judges whose ratings from 0–2 for each item were averaged. We then correlated a triad's degree of semantic convergence with the likelihood that it would be solved ($r = .32$) and the likelihood that it would be selected in the absence of a solution ($r = .44$). In sum, a specific and specifiable character of coherent triads—the degree of their semantic convergence—is related both to the probability of being solved and the probability of being selected (sans solution).

Such an outcome strongly argues against the possibility that subjects select coherent triads by default. It also suggests that semantic activation (Collins and Loftus 1975) of the solution word is the mechanism by which the solution is approached or achieved. Specifically, when the three clue words activate the same semantic address, a resident solution word is likely to answer the puzzle-induced query, or at least acknowledge that it is "home." In the latter case, even though the door to the solution word does not open, its meaning has been activated sufficiently to influence the subjects' forced-choice selection of the coherent triad.

In sum, even more than in the gestalt task, findings from the DOT indicate that prior to the emergence of a solution, there are cognitive processes at work that engender a graded approach to the solution. This is true even when confidence in one's selection is modest, though on the DOT, unlike the gestalt task, the absence of any confidence at all meant that the rate of success did not achieve above-chance levels.

Accumulated Clues Task (ACT)
The WGES and the DOT tasks are structurally similar despite their different content (pictures versus words). The ACT is a verbal task that is structurally quite different from the DOT. In the ACT each of 15 clue words is a low associate of an item's solution word (in a normative sample, most of the clue words occurred five times or less in 1000 responses to the solution word; Arthur 1964). Clues are presented one at a time cumulatively for 15 seconds (at first) and then for progressively less time to 10 seconds (from the tenth clue on). Subjects are obliged to write down a response to each clue word and to indicate when a response seems to represent a viable hunch or hypothesis about the solution of an ACT item. Finally, subjects indicated when they were certain their response was correct. Table 2.1 presents a list of all the words for one ACT item. There were 16 ACT items altogether. The major question addressed by the ACT is this: Do responses to successive clues associatively converge toward the correct hypothesis?

In a sample of 100 subjects, people arrived at a hunch on about the tenth clue ($M = 10.12$, $SD = 4.55$) and were satisfied with the hunch within two more clue words ($M = 1.79$, $SD = .96$). However, the major analyses of the ACT concerned the associative closeness of a subject's responses to an item's solution as a function of the progression of clues. This was accomplished by selecting a subject's responses to four equidistant clues of an ACT item. Subsequently, multiple, indepen-

Table 2.1
Words from an ACT Item with "Fruit" as the Solution

1.	red	9	cocktail
2.	nut	10.	candy
3.	bowl	11.	pie
4.	loom	12.	baking
5.	cup	13.	salad
6.	basket	14.	tree
7.	jelly	15.	fly
8.	fresh	Solution:	Fruit

dent judges rated on a seven-point scale the associative closeness of each response in relation to the item's solution, where 1 indicated very weak associate closeness and 7 very strong associative closeness (no tied ratings were permitted). This procedure was reiterated 96 times, with each ACT item being included six times—twice when it was solved quickly (between 4 and 9 clues), twice with moderate speed (between 9 and 11 clues), and twice when it was solved slowly (between 11 and 16 clues). The judges' ratings for each of a subject's four selected responses to an item were then averaged. These composite ratings were in turn averaged across the 96 iterations, so that we derived an average associative closeness rating for first responses, penultimate responses (the response to a clue prior to the one that generated a correct hypothesis), and responses to two midway, equidistant clues.

There was a linear increase in associative closeness of subjects' responses to the solution of ACT items as a function of clue number (figure 2.2). This increase, of course, differed in slope as a function of whether subjects were fast, moderate, or slow to solve items. How-

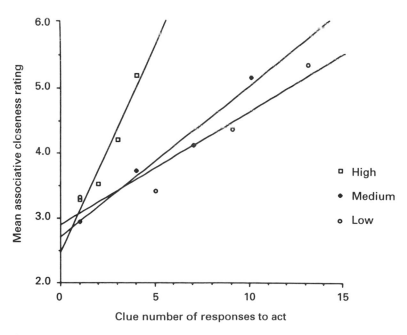

Figure 2.2
Mean associative closeness scores of high, medium, and low intuitive subjects' responses to equi-distant clues of the Accumulated Clues Task (ACT)

ever, when the data were recast as a function of the relative position of the four clues (from 1–4), rather than actual clue number (from 1–16), the increase in the three groups was virtually identical (figure 2.3). In other words, regardless of how quickly or slowly people solved ACT items, their associative approach to the solution remained invariant.

Although people associatively approached the solution to ACT items, they sometimes spontaneously mentioned that the solution seemed to occur quite suddenly. Such metacognitions do not square with evidence for subjects' associative approach to the solution (Metcalfe and Wiebe 1987). Unfortunately, we did not systematically collect subjects' warmth (nearness-to-solution) ratings in this initial study (Bowers et al. 1990), so we were unable to compare their metacognitions of progress on ACT items with an objective index of it. However, evidence from the WGES and the DOT implies that the cognitive processes underlying problem solving are more continuous than the metacognitive experience of sudden insight implies, and it seemed worth pursuing the matter with the ACT.

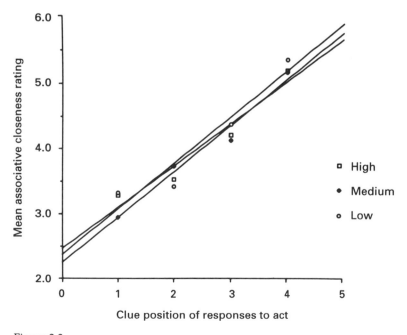

Figure 2.3
Mean associative closeness scores of high, medium, and low intuitive subjects' responses to the *relative* position of clues (regardless of clue number)

Recently Mermigis (1989) ran 20 subjects on 12 ACT items. In addition to providing an obligatory response to each clue, they also provided a warmth rating for each response from 1 to 7, indicating how close they felt the response was to a solution. Both the associative closeness of subjects' responses to the solution and their metacognitive warmth ratings increased significantly from early to late clues. However, following Metcalfe (1986), Mermigis selected a subset of items reflecting nonincremental warmth ratings—that is, items for which ratings increased by 1 or less over the entire series of clues. Even in this subset of items, responses to the penultimate clue are associatively closer to the solution word than were responses to the first clue ($M =$ 3.37 and 3.98 for responses to first and penultimate clues, respectively; $p<.005$). Not surprisingly, however, for the subset of items reflecting incremental warmth ratings (items for which ratings increased by 2 or more from first to penultimate clues), the corresponding increase in associative closeness of responses to the solution words was even larger ($M = 3.07$ and 4.91 for responses to first and penultimate clues, respectively; $p<.0001$). Moreover, the response to the penultimate clue was associatively closer to the solution word in the incremental than in the nonincremental subset of items ($p<.003$).

To summarize, the more objective progress made toward solving the ACT items, the more this progress is reflected in metacognitive warmth ratings. However, even little or no increase in metacognitive warmth from first to penultimate responses is accompanied by some associative progress toward the solution. This latter finding is consistent with findings from the WGES and DOT: even when solutions seem to emerge with discontinuous suddenness, graded rather than discontinuous cognitive processes seem to characterize problem solving.

Partial Word Task (PWOT)
So far, we have examined tasks that have used incomplete pictures— the elements of which serve as clues to the object pictured or word tasks—in which clue words associatively and/or semantically converge onto a solution word. The PWOT is a verbal analogue of a gestalt closure task. Rather than presenting complete words to people, partial words or word fragments are used to see whether they semantically activate the entire word in a graded fashion. This is a particularly interesting possibility, because people who solve such word fragments typically experience the solution as emerging quite suddenly, in a way that is similar to the experience of solving a gestalt closure item. This is true even when the interval between the presentation of the problem and the appearance of the solution is fairly prolonged. Thus, the

PWOT, like the WGES, is an insight task by virtually any standard (Metcalfe and Wiebe 1987).

In his undergraduate honors thesis, Peter Farvolden (1990) utilized the partial word task that was originally used to assess the priming of semantic memory (Tulving, Schacter, and Stark 1982). Table 2.2 presents 6 of 18 partial words used in the present investigation, with their completed counterparts. All of the words occur with relatively low frequency and are either seven or eight letters in length. In each case, a partial word consisted of four letters, and there was only one legitimate word that could complete each word fragment. Forty undergraduates served as subjects in this investigation, and they were seen individually.

In the first part of the investigation, the 18 partial words were presented by the experimenter on 5- by 8-inch flashcards for 30 seconds each. At the end of 20 seconds, subjects were informed that they had 10 seconds to write down either the solution to the word or some other word that occurred to them in the course of trying to solve it. Subjects were specifically told that a nonsolution response need not have any orthographic similarity to the partial word. In fact, to discourage subjects from trying to fit their response to the orthographic features of the partial words, they were falsely informed that some of the partial words could not be completed by an English word, "So, don't get too hung up on trying to find the 'right' answer, because there may not be on." When subjects finished the list of 18 partial words, the words were administered again, this time with the addition of one more letter.

In the second part of the experiment, subjects' incorrect responses to partial words were evaluated. Specifically, we selected incorrect responses to partial words that were subsequently solved when the partial word was enriched by the addition of one more letter. This strategy permits us to address the following question: When a partial

Table 2.2
Six Partial Words and Their Completed Counterparts

Partial Word	Completed Counterpart
_ n _ _ m n _ a	insomnia
a _ _ a _ _ i n	assassin
p o _ _ i w _ _	polliwog
_ n i _ _ _ s e	universe
_ a z _ _ t e	gazette
_ o u _ _ o n	bourbon

word is not solved until it is enriched by an additional letter, is there enough semantic information available in its unenriched edition to generate an incorrect response that is a relatively close associate of the solution?

In order to answer this question, we again used a composite judge technique. Two groups of 15 judges, also undergraduates at the University of Waterloo, each rated half the subjects' responses on scales like the one depicted in figure 2.4.

In this example, the words *arsenal* and *answer* were two responses of a subject to the partial form of the words *assassin* and *insomnia*, respectively. However, in the judgment task, we used synonyms of the partial words, which is why the words *killer* and *sleeplessness* appear in this example rather than *assassin* and *insomnia*. We used synonyms so that judges' ratings could not be influenced by orthographic features of the partial words. Each judge wrote one of the two words at the top-middle of the rating scale into one of the three blanks, with the constraint that there could be only one word per blank. In this example, the word *arsenal* was eventually given a rating of 3 in regard to the word *killer* and a rating of 1 with respect to the control word *sleeplessness*. On the other hand, the word *answer* was eventually given a rating of 2 with respect to both the word *sleeplessness* and its control word, *killer*. Thus, the judgment task permits simultaneous rating of the associative closeness of subjects' responses to a synonym of the original partial word and to a synonym of the control word. The judges' responses for each such item were averaged over judges. This procedure allows us to calculate a mean associative closeness rating of subjects' responses to synonyms of partial words and to corresponding control words.

Overall, an average of 72 percent of partial words were solved with the addition of just one additional letter, and its is this subset of items that were analyzed. There were 74 such items in all; 15 judges made ratings for 37 of the items, and 15 other judges rated the remaining 37

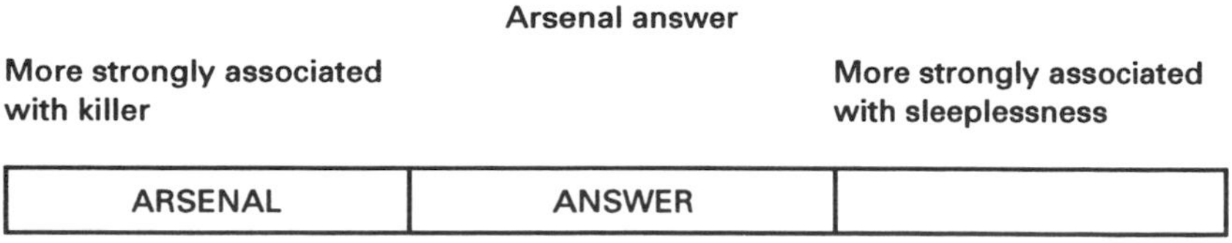

Arsenal answer

More strongly associated with killer		More strongly associated with sleeplessness
ARSENAL	ANSWER	

Figure 2.4
Sample of scale on which judges rated the associative closeness of subjects' responses to PWOT (including a judge's ratings for target and control word)

items. Figure 2.5 presents the results averaged across both sets of judges. Subjects' incorrect responses to partial words were associatively closer to synonyms of the partial words than they were to control words. The results were virtually identical for both samples of judges. In each case, the mean associative closeness for subjects' responses regarding synonyms of the partial words was 2.24; the corresponding mean rating regarding the control words was 1.76. In both cases, the mean differences were significant well beyond the .01 level.

The results of this experiment imply that there is enough semantic information in a partial word to activate relevant semantic information, even if there is not yet enough activation to generate the complete word as a solution. Recall that the partial word task has some claim to being an insight-type task. Accordingly, the fact that incorrect responses to a word fragment are relatively close associates of the solution word implies that even in insight-type verbal problems, there is evidence for a graded process of problem solving. This conceptualization contrasts with the all-or-nothing, perception-like integration of the solution that is favored by advocates of the gestalt view (Ellen 1982; Metcalfe 1986; Scheerer 1963).

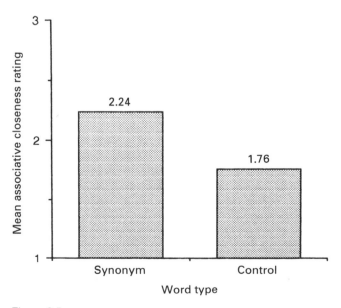

Figure 2.5
Mean associative closeness ratings of subjects' incorrect responses to synonyms of partial and to control words of the PWOT

Individual Differences

An important implication of this conceptualization of intuition is that cognition proceeds from the perception of environmental clues to conclusions about various aspects of the environment (Buchler 1978). When the environment is familiar and information rich, there is little or no experienced gap between seeing an array of clues and seeing them as a whistle, say. However, such gaps do occur when objects in the world are less familiar or are presented in an information-poor fashion. Thus, there is often an experienced gap between perceiving the clues in a gestalt closure item, say, and perceiving the object they reflect and reveal. Historically, there was also a significant gap between perceiving the pattern of clues presented by Rosalind Franklin's crystallographic photographs of the DNA molecule and Watson and Crick's eventual conclusions about the underlying structure that these clues reflected and revealed—the double-helix character of DNA (Watson 1969). Always, however, people use their own mnemonic network to proceed from clues to conclusions about the nature of things. In this sense, cognition is intrinsically intuitive.

Clearly, though, people differ in the degree to which they are intuitive. Sometimes these differences are attributable to differential amounts of experience in a domain of inquiry. For example, it is difficult to be an intuitive physicist without first knowing a lot about physics. However, even people who have similar domain-specific information are likely to differ in how intuitive they are in that domain (Davidson and Sternberg 1984; Simonton 1980). To adapt Jerome Bruner's (1955) wonderful phrase, some people go further (and faster) beyond the given information than other people. This point is made with particular force in a recent biography concerning the implausibly intuitive scientist, Richard Feynman (Gleick 1992).

For technical reasons, the forced-choice data from the DOT and the WGES do not generate reliable individual differences and hence to not lend themselves to documenting individual difference in intuitive ability. However, subjects did differ meaningfully on their ACT performance. Recall that the fewer the clues required to solve an item, the faster it was solved. In addition, we could calculate the number of WGES and DOT items solved. The idea here is that solved items, though uninformative about presolution cognitive processes, potentially tell us about individual differences in intuitive ability. Finally, in four of the five samples that were run, we also administered the vocabulary subtest from the revised Wechsler Adult Intelligence Scale (WAIS-RV) as a measure of intelligence (Wechsler 1981) to assess whether scores on the three intuition tasks were distinct from verbal intelligence.

Table 2.3 presents relevant information for each of the five samples that received the three intuition tasks. The alphas were quite modest for the ACT, partly because this statistic is sensitive to the number of items on the scale, and there were relatively few items presented (each ACT item being very time-consuming). The alphas for the DOT were disappointingly low; those for the WGES were somewhat better. However, there is enough reliability in the measures to conduct correlational analysis on four of the five samples that had all the intuition tasks, plus the WAIS-RV.

These findings shown in table 2.4 indicate that the pattern is more or less the same across all the samples. The ACT and the DOT correlate significantly with each other in all the samples, from a low of .38 to a high of .57 (a low score on the ACT represents greater intuitive ability, so the signs of these correlations have all be changed to reflect the positive relationship between the two variables). The average correlation across the five samples is .46. The internal consistency of the ACT and DOT imposes a theoretical limit of about .66 on the size of the correlation that can be achieved between these two variables. So, the ACT and the DOT correlate with each other at a level that is reasonably close to the limits imposed by their respective reliabilities.

The WAIS-RV also correlates significantly with both the ACT and the DOT in all samples, ranging from a low of .31 to a high of .53. The average correlation of the WAIS-RV with the ACT is .44; with the DOT, the comparable correlation is .41. It is clear that verbal intelligence correlates with the two verbal tasks of intuition almost at the same level as these two tasks correlate with each other.

However, the pattern of correlates of the ACT, DOT, and WAIS-RV with the WGES introduces a complexity into any preliminary conclusion that the ACT and the DOT are simply measures of verbal intelligence. In the largest sample, which generates the most stable correlations, the WGES correlates .08 with the WAIS-RV, while correlating an average of .27 with the ACT and .32 with the DOT. In order to explore this pattern of data more fully, we generated a composite score of verbal intuition by averaging subjects' Z-scores achieved on the ACT and the DOT. The resulting composite of verbal intuition is both more reliable and less encumbered by task-specific variance than either of its components (Nunnally 1978). A multiple correlation was then performed, with the composite of verbal intuition serving as the criterion variable and with WAIS-RV and WGES entered as the first and second predictors, respectively. A multiple R of .59 was generated: 25 percent of the variance was contributed by verbal intelligence, and another 10 percent was contributed by WGES. In this sample at least, not everything that contributes to success on the verbal intuition

Table 2.3
Means, Standard Deviations, and Internal Consistency (α) for the Intuition Tasks and the Vocabulary Subtests of the WAIS-R

Sample	ACT: Average Number of Clues to Correct Hypothesis[a]				DOT: Average Number of Solutions				WGES: Average Number of Solutions				WAIS-RV: Score out of 40	
	No. of Items	M	SD	α	No. of Items	M	SD	α	No. of Items	M	SD	α	M	SD
1 (N = 100)[b]	16	10.12	4.55	.70	60	13.13	5.31	.76	75	24.29	11.72	.91	21.30	7.60
2 (N = 43)	16	9.64	4.47	.56	60	17.23	6.37	.78	75	26.56	12.52	.94	25.19	5.81
3 (N = 72)	8	11.69	3.68	.58	30	8.30	3.22	.56	40	11.86	5.51	.81	22.84	6.09
4 (N = 33)	8	10.72	4.41	.31	30	9.49	2.59	.31	35	13.45	5.40	.77	—	—
5 (N = 60)	10	11.85	4.00	.74	50	15.40	4.41	.58	40	12.68	5.90	.58	23.58	6.44

Note: ACT = Associate Clues Task; DOT = Dyads of Tryads; WGES = Waterloo Gestalt Closure Task.
a. Average mean and standard deviations per item.
b. For this sample only, problems with missing data reduced the sample size for the DOt (N = 87) and the WGES (N = 94).

Table 2.4
Intercorrelations of the Intuition Tasks and the WAIS-RV

	Sample	ACT	DOT	WGES
DOT	1	.38**		
	2	.51**		
	3	.41**		
	4	.57**		
WGES	1	.27**	.32**	
	2	.25	.26*	
	3	.12	.23*	
	4	.09	.16	
WAIS-RV	1	.46**	.37**	.08
	2	.40**	.53**	.32*
	3	.49**	.31**	.05
	5	.44**	.44**	.04

* $p < .05$
** $p < .01$.

composite is a consequence of verbal intelligence. The contributions of the WGES to the prediction of the ACT/DOT composite were somewhat less in the remaining samples (2–5 percent).

Conclusion

Over a variety of tasks, our research has demonstrated that automatic cognitive processes generate a graded approach to solving problems even when a solution seems to surface discontinuously as a sudden insight. These findings challenge the gestalt view of problem solving, which proposes that sudden insight reflects a genuine discontinuity in the underlying perceptual-cognitive processing of information—a more or less spontaneous restructuring of the problem that immediately yields its solution (Metcalfe and Wiebe 1987). Of course, it is possible that other types of problems may yield results that are more in keeping with the gestalt view.

Whatever the task, however, future research in problem solving must contend with the fact that the experience of sudden insight is not in and of itself sufficient grounds for inferring discontinuities in the cognitive processes that underlie problem solving. Rather, there must be some way of assessing cognitive processes prior to achieving a solution and which are independent of whether a solution is finally achieved; depending on metacognitive feelings of warmth is insufficient in this regard. We have seen how the absence of such metacognitions is consistent with discernible progress toward the solution. Alternatively, Metcalfe (1986) has demonstrated rather convincingly that "a strong premonition of solution is liable to be a marker that the wrong answer will follow" (p. 633). So neither the presence nor the absence of such metacognitions suffices to diagnose whether or how much cognitive progress has been made toward a solution. Ingenuity will often be required to find objective indexes of solution proximity, but identifying such measures will permit examination of whether a solution was approached even if it were not achieved and of whether the processes underlying sudden insight are more continuous than discontinuous in nature.

The gradual approach to solving insight-type problems has been explained in terms of semantic activation (Yaniv and Meyer 1987). When people are familiar with the domain under consideration, puzzles activate relevant semantic information. The activation may not be sufficient to achieve a solution, but it may be sufficient to produce a response that is demonstrably close to it. Such activation may also generate feelings of warmth that antedate the appearance of a solution. Presumably when activation is great enough, the correct response crosses the threshold of consciousness, whereupon it is frequently (but not inevitably) recognized as a potential solution. Importantly, the process of activating the correct response and the process of recognizing it as the solution are separate and distinct. This distinctiveness is especially clear when problem clues generate a correct response that is not recognized as the solution.

One important implication of this activation view of intuition is that people cannot be productively intuitive in domains that are unfamiliar to them. Nevertheless, ignorance of the relevant domain may not be the end of the matter, because problem clues may well activate irrelevant information, and hence erroneous "solutions," to the problem at hand. For example, people required to make judgments that presuppose knowledge of base rates, sample sizes, and regression effects are likely to perform badly if they are unfamiliar with such matters; nevertheless, they will do the best they can on the basis of whatever irrelevant considerations are activated by the problem and the available clues.

This last point reminds us that there is a delicate balance between error and discovery. People are seldom at a loss to generate a response to a novel problem or situation. Whether they are satisfied with the response as a viable solution is an entirely different matter. Recognizing the inadequacy of a hypothesis or potential solution is surely a precondition for continued wrestling with the problem—examining it from other points of view and in the light of a variety of background or contextual considerations. In an important sense, a critical stance toward one's mental surfacings is the best safeguard against the inevitability of flawed hypotheses and incorrect solutions. However, intuitive processes that could not generate mistakes could not generate anything new at all, including genuine insight into the nature of things (Bowers 1987; in press). The inevitability of error implies that our cognitive cup is half-empty; the fact that some insights survive critical scrutiny implies that the cup is half-full.

Finally, the above comments regarding error yield one last natural-language distinction between intuition and creativity. The very idea of a mistake implies a standard against which a solution can be assessed and found wanting. In the context of intuition, a particular organization and pattern of clues serves as the standard by which to evaluate whether a proposed solution is correct or mistaken. However, there is no preexisting pattern or organization against which to assess a creative endeavor. Nevertheless, a painting, novel, or invention can succeed or fail, by either very abstract criteria (such as whether something universal is captured in a particular painting) or very concrete criteria (such as whether an invention has commercial value). In sum, it seems somewhat more natural to speak of errors of intuition and insight on one hand, and of failures of imagination and creativity on the other, rather than the reverse—though to be sure, it does not completely violate natural usage to speak of failed intuition or a mistaken creation. Perhaps such subtle and seldom-mentioned distinctions between intuition and creativity as we have raised in this chapter have been at least partially responsible for keeping the research in these two domains so insulated from each other.

Notes

Most of the research reported in this chapter was supported by a generous grant from the Spencer Foundation of Chicago.
1. The psychological literature on intuition differs from the philosophical notion of intuition. The *Oxford English Dictionary* definition of intuition, which reflects this more philosophical view, implies that it involves immediate apprehension of something true without any mediation of consciousness or reasoning. As will become clear shortly, a psychological view of intuition is more concerned with the cognitive processes that antedate and generate insight.
2. It is possible that people sometimes thought of the correct answer, did not recognize it as the solution, and so did not write it down. Their forced-choice decision might nevertheless be informed by the same processes that activated the correct response. This scenario does not compromise our argument that coherence detection can take place in the absence of a solution. It simply underscores the distinction between the automatic generation of a correct response and the conscious recognition of it as the solution.

References

Anderson, J. R. (1983). A spreading activation theory of memory. *Journal of Verbal Learning and Verbal Behavior, 22,* 261–295.

Arthur, A. Z. (1964). *Queens norms for responses to 100 words from the Kent-Rosanoff Word Association Test* (Studies in word association and meaning, National Research Council, Project No. APA0269). Kingston, Ontario.

Baars, B. J. (1988). *A cognitive theory of consciousness.* Cambridge: Cambridge University Press.

Biederman, I. (1987). Recognition-by-components: A theory of human image understanding. *Psychological Review, 94,* 115–147.

Bowers, K. S. (1971). Sex and susceptibility as moderator variables in the relationship of creativity and hypnotic susceptibility. *Journal of Abnormal Psychology, 78,* 93–100.

Bowers, K. S. (1987). Intuition and discovery. In R. Stern (ed.), *Theories of the unconscious and theories of the self* (pp. 71–90). Hillsdale, NJ: Analytic Press.

Bowers, K. S. (in press). Intuition. In R. J. Sternberg (ed.), *Encyclopedia of human intelligence.* New York: Macmillan.

Bowers, K. S., Regehr, G., Balthazard, C., and Parker, K. (1990). Intuition in the context of discovery. *Cognitive Psychology, 22,* 72–110.

Brainerd, C. J., and Reyna, V. F. (1990). Gist is grist: Fuzzy-trace theory and the new intuitionism. *Developmental Review, 10,* 3–47.

Bruner, J. (1955). Going beyond the information given. In H. F. Gruber, K. H. Hammond, and R. Jessor (Eds.), *Cognition: The Colorado symposium* (pp. 41–69). Cambridge, MA: Harvard University Press.

Buchler, J. (1978). *The philosophy of Charles Peirce: Selected writings.* London: Kegan, Paul, Trench, Trubner & Co.

Cheesman, J., and Merikle, P. M. (1984). Priming with and without awareness. *Perception and Psychophysics, 36,* 387–395.

Collins, A. M., and Loftus, E. F. (1975). A spreading-activation theory of semantic processing. *Psychological Review, 82,* 407–428.

d'Arcais, G. B., and Schreuder, R. (1987). Semantic activation during object naming. *Psychological Research, 49,* 153–159.

Davidson, J. E., and Sternberg, R. J. (1984). The role of insight in intellectual giftedness. *Gifted Child Quarterly, 28,* 58–64.

Dellas, M., and Gaier, E. L. (1970). Identification of creativity: The individual. *Psychological Bulletin, 73,* 55–73.

Dreyfus, H. L., and Dreyfus, S. E. (1986). *Mind over machine: The power of human intuition and expertise in the era of the computer.* New York: Free Press.

Ellen, P. (1982). Direction, past experience, and hints in creative problem solving: Reply to Weisberg and Alba. *Journal of Experimental Psychology: General, 111,* 316–325.

Farvolden, P. (1991). *Intuition and early cognitive processes in the solving of partial word puzzles.* Unpublished undergraduate honors thesis, University of Waterloo.

Gleick, J. (1992). *Genius: The life and science of Richard Feynman.* New York: Random House.

Hammond, K. R., Hamm, R. M., Grassia, J., and Pearson, T. (1987). Direct comparison of the efficacy of intuitive and analytical cognition in expert judgment. *IEEE Transactions on systems, man, and cybernetics, SMC-17,* 753–770.

Jackson, P. W., and Messick, S. (1965). The person, the product, and the response: Conceptual problems in the assessment of creativity. *Journal of Personality, 33,* 309–329.

50   Kenneth S. Bowers, Peter Farvolden, and Lambros Mermigis

Jowett, B. (1937). *The dialogues of Plato.* New York: Random House.
Kahneman, D., Slovic, P., and Tversky, A. (eds.). (1982). *Judgment under uncertainty: Heuristics and biases.* Cambridge: Cambridge University Press.
Maier, N. R. (1931). Reasoning in humans. *Journal of Comparative Psychology, 12,* 181–194.
Mednick, S. A. (1962). The associative basis of the creative process. *Psychological Review, 69,* 220–232.
Mednick, S. A., and Mednick, M. (1967). *Examiner's manual: Remote Associates Test.* Boston: Houghton Mifflin.
Mermigis, L. (1989). *The feeling of knowing in insight problem solving.* Unpublished doctoral dissertation, University of Waterloo.
Metcalfe, J. (1986). Premonitions of insight predict impending error. *Journal of Experimental Psychology: Learning, Memory, and Cognition, 12,* 623–634.
Metcalfe, J., and Wiebe, D. (1987). Intuition in insight and noninsight problem solving. *Memory and Cognition, 15,* 238–246.
Nisbett, R., and Ross, L. (1980). *Human inference: Strategies and shortcomings of social judgment.* Englewood Cliffs, NJ: Prentice-Hall.
Nisbett, R., and Wilson, T. D. (1977). Telling more than we can know: Verbal reports on mental processes. *Psychological Review, 84,* 231–259.
Nunnally, J. C. (1978). *Psychometric theory.* New York: McGraw-Hill.
Overson, C., and Mandler, G. (1987). Indirect word priming in connected semantic and phonological contexts. *Bulletin of the Psychonomic Society, 25,* 229–232.
Polanyi, M. (1964). *Personal knowledge: Towards a post-critical philosophy.* New York: Harper Torchbook.
Posner, M. L., and Snyder, C. R. (1975). Attention and cognitive control. In R. Soslo (ed.), *Information processing and cognition: The Loyola Symposium* (pp. 55–85). Hilldale, NJ: Erlbaum.
Reber, A. (1989) Implicit learning and tacit knowledge. *Journal of Experimental Psychology: General, 118,* 219–235.
Ross, L. (1977). The intuitive psychologist and his shortcomings: Distortions in the attribution process. In L. Berkowitz (ed.), *Advances in experimental social psychology 10* (pp. 173–220). New York: Academic Press.
Schacter, D. L. (1987). Implicit memory: History and current status. *Journal of Experimental psychology: Learning, Memory, and Cognition, 13,* 501–518.
Schacter, D. L., Cooper, L. A., and Delaney, S. M. (1990). Implicit memory for unfamiliar objects depends on access to structural descriptions. *Journal of Experimental Psychology: General, 119,* 3–24.
Scheerer, M. (1963). Problem solving. *Scientific American, 208 (4),* 118–128.
Simon, H. A. (1986). The information processing explanation of gestalt phenomena. *Computers in Human Behavior, 2,* 241–255.
Simonton, D. K. (1980). Intuition and analysis: A predictive and explanatory model. *Genetic Psychology Monographs, 102,* 3–40.
Sternberg, R. J. (1988). *The nature of creativity.* Cambridge: Cambridge University Press.
Tulving, E., and Schacter, D. L. (1990). Priming and human memory systems. *Science, 247,* 301–306.
Tulving, E., Schacter, D. L., and Stark H. A. (1982). Priming effects in word-fragment completion are independent of recognition memory. *Journal of Experimental Psychology: Learning, Memory and Cognition, 8,* 336–342.
Watson, J. D. (1969). *The double helix.* New York: Signet.
Wechsler, D. (1981). *WAIS-R Manual.* New York: Psychological Corp.

Weisberg, R. W., and Alba, J. W. (1981). An examination of the alleged role of "fixation" in the solution of several "insight" problems. *Journal of Experimental Psychology: General, 110,* 169–192.

Westcott, M. R. (1968). *Toward a contemporary psychology of intuition: A historical, theoretical, and empirical inquiry.* New York: Holt Rinehart and Winston.

Yaniv, I., and Meyer, D. E. (1987). Activation and metacognition of inaccessible stored information: Potential bases for incubation effects in problem solving. *Journal of Experimental Psychology: Learning, Memory, and Cognition, 13,* 187–205.

Chapter 3

Case Studies of Creative Thinking: Reproduction versus Restructuring in the Real World

Robert W. Weisberg

Life offers many problems for which our textbooks fail to supply solutions. In this way problem situations differ from those in school in which recall is tested by examination questions. We learn many answers in school, but life doesn't ask the right questions. This is where problem solving becomes more basic than memorization.
—N. Maier, Problem Solving and Creativity

From my first day in the lab I knew I would not leave Cambridge for a long time. Departing would be idiocy, for I had immediately discovered the fun of talking to Francis Crick. Finding someone who knew that DNA was more important than proteins was real luck. . . . Our lunch conversations quickly centered on how genes were put together. Within a few days of my arrival, we knew what to do: imitate Linus Pauling and beat him at his own game.
—J. D. Watson, The Double Helix

There has been, in the study of creative thinking, a tension between views that assume that creativity can be explained on the basis of the thinker's applying his or her knowledge to the situation at hand and those that assume that in order to understand how true creativity comes about, one has to deal with the ability to go beyond past experience (for discussion, see Weisberg 1993). Gestalt theorists' development of the closely related concepts of restructuring and insight has been central to the discussion of this issue in the domain of creative problem solving.

In the Gestalt analysis of problem solving, emphasis was placed on the ability to go beyond past experience and produce something new in response to the demands of a problem. This *productive* thinking was contrasted with *reproductive* thinking, which was the application of some previously acquired knowledge to a problem. Productive thinking, which depended on past experience in only the most general way, came about when thinkers analyzed deeply the requirements of the problem and what was available to bring them about (Wertheimer 1982, pp. 49, 236).

It is typical for thinkers to approach a problem reproductively, that is, on the basis of similar problems encountered in the past. This tack will fail, however, with a new problem that is similar to past experience only in superficial ways, or on the surface, and is different from previously encountered problems in its deep structure. Interpreting such a problem through the prism of past experience will by definition lead the thinker astray. In order to solve such a problem, the thinker must abandon the initial approach that stems from past experience and reconceptualize the problem (i.e., restructure the problem) in response to the specific requirements of the problem (Weisberg 1994).

Thus, in the Gestalt analysis of creative thinking as exemplified by problem solving, it was concluded that a reliance on past experience could actually interfere with effective problem solving. This conclusion was based on the assumption that the important problems that confront us demand productive thinking; they require us to change the way of approaching the problem and view it in a new way. The approach based on experience and reproductive thinking would have to be abandoned, and the situation restructured, before progress could take place. This restructuring was assumed to form the basis for insight into the problem (Ohlsson 1984a); that is, the subjective experience of insight is the result of the thinker's restructuring of the situation.

Laboratory demonstrations of such phenomena as problem solving set provided graphic evidence that designing situations in which analyzing a problem on its own terms resulted in excellent performance, whereas past success with similar problems was a hindrance. In these well-known demonstrations, "set" subjects were first given experience solving a series of similar-appearing problems, all of which had the same complicated solution. When they were presented with a similar-appearing problem that could be solved using the set solution or a much simpler one, set subjects often were blind to the simpler solution, while naive subjects saw it immediately. Such results were taken as an analogue of real-world situations, in which it was assumed that experience could also blind thinkers and interfere with efficient performance.

This negative orientation toward the role of experience in creative thinking has gained wide acceptance; it has become standard in writings on creativity to warn would-be creative thinkers that they must be wary of falling victim to experience (Adams 1979; Amabile 1989; Bransford and Stein 1984; deBono 1968). However, there has not been a broad test of this assumption; that is, there has been no attempt to analyze situations in which creative advances have occurred in the world in order to see if those situations have indeed rebuffed initial approaches based on experience. This chapter provides such an analysis. Rather than attempting to broadly and exhaustively summarize case studies in creative thinking, I have selected for discussion several that raise problems for the view that creative thinking comes about because thinkers abandon their ties with the past.

The analysis will show that a number of significant creative accomplishments have come about through continuity with the past (Basalla 1988; Weisberg 1993), that is, reproductively, through the relatively direct application of information from the past to the present situation. Second, when restructuring does occur, it is brought about in more than one way. It can occur through an analysis of the situation, as Wertheimer (1982) proposed, but it also comes about as the result of the thinker's use of external events, which shape the restructuring. In some of these cases, as well, creativity was reproductive.

Continuity, Discontinuity, and Restructuring

Problem solving sometimes requires little more than that the thinker carry out already-known routines, adapting them to the situation at hand. In such a case, solution is based on continuity in thinking, or reproductive thinking; one's knowledge is extended to deal with the new situation. An example is a mathematically knowledgeable subject solving a new problem in long division.

Solving a problem does not always proceed directly from problem presentation to solution generation, however; the initial approach taken by the problem solver may be ineffective, and he or she may have to switch to a new one before progress can be made, in what could be called discontinuity in thinking. Some discontinuities, those of most interest to the Gestalt psychologists, are due to restructuring of problems, or a change in the thinker's representation of the problem (Weisberg in press; Ohlsson 1984b). That is, if we compare the initial solution attempt(s) with the final solution, they must be the result of different analyses of the problem.

These various modes of problem solving can be made clear through the examination of several simple problems:

> 1. A stranger approached a museum curator and offered him an ancient bronze coin. The coin had an authentic appearance and was marked with the date 544 B.C. The curator had happily made acquisitions from suspicious sources before, but this time he promptly called the police and had the stranger arrested. Why?

2. Our basketball team won 72–45 yesterday, and yet not one man on the team scored as much as a single point. How is that possible?

3. Water lilies double in area every twenty-four hours. On the first day of summer, there is one water lily on the lake. Sixty days later, the lake is completely covered with water lilies. On what day is the lake half covered?

The problem representation in problems 1 and 2 consists of the objects in the problem and the relations among them; the solution requires that the thinker devise a scenario wherein the presented events can occur naturally. In more complex problems, such as problem 3, in which the problem solver has to do something, the representation also includes the operators that the thinker has available, in this case, mathematical methods that can be applied to the problem.

In order to determine if a problem is solved through restructuring, we can ask if the solution requires that any of the elements of the representation be changed. In problem 1, solution usually occurs as the result of a discontinuity in thinking but not as the result of restructuring. Most subjects begin by suggesting possibilities such as that the metal of the coin did not look old enough. They typically do not propose the correct solution first: the coin must be fake, because it could not have B.C. as part of the date. The date was available in the problem from the beginning; thus, the discontinuity in this problem came about through the subject's search through alternatives that were available in the initial representation of the problem. Thus, this discontinuity did not depend on restructuring of the problem.

In problem 2, solution requires restructuring because the descriptions of the characters must be changed: our successful basketball team is a women's team. This is also true in problem 3, in which the operator must be changed: most people divide the sixty days by two and propose the thirtieth day as the solution, but since the lilies increase in area geometrically, simple division is not correct. The lilies cover half the pond on the next-to-last day. Problems 2 and 3 require changing the initial structuring of the problem to solve them. If one does not have experience with the appropriate mathematics then the restructuring in that problem would be productive.

Thus, whether a given problem is solved through restructuring depends in part on the way the problem solver approaches it: if a person produces the "insight" solution right away, then the problem in question is not solved through insight, since there is not even a discontinuity in thinking, much less a restructuring (Finke, Ward, and Smith 1992; Weisberg 1994).

Case Studies in Reproductive Creativity

Creativity without Restructuring
In this first set of cases, creative thinking came about through the application of past methods to the present task, that is, reproductive thinking, with some alterations to accommodate past methods to the uniqueness of the present situation. The initial solution attempts and the final product resulted from the same overall analysis of the situation, so no restructuring occurred.

Guernica   Pablo Picasso (1881–1973) is arguably the most influential artist of the twentieth century; his work has had ramifications far beyond the domain of art. *Guernica*, the best known of his works, has been of great symbolic and political importance (Chipp 1988). It was painted in response to the bombing on April 27, 1937, of the Basque town of Guernica, in northern Spain, by the German air force, which was allied with the forces of Franco during the Spanish Civil War. *Guernica* has been taken as a strong antiwar statement, and during World War II it served as the centerpiece for fund-raising activities on the part of supporters of Spanish resistance. In his will, Picasso stipulated that the painting was to stay in New York's Museum of Modern Art until democracy was restored to Spain. Following Franco's death and after considerable diplomatic negotiation, the painting was returned to Spain in 1981, where it has been afforded a position of honor, as a national treasure, with its own display space in the Prado museum in Madrid.

The early sketches for this painting (Chipp 1988), which Picasso kept and labeled with dates of completion, contain basically all the characters in the same relations as the final painting. This large work, painted in monochrome—no color, only black, white, and grays—is dominated in the center by a horse kneeling on the ground, its body pierced by a lance, its head raised in a scream of agony. Above the horse's head is a large light, in the shape of an eye. In the upper right center, a woman holding a lamp leans out of the window of a building on fire. At the left, a large bull stands, his body facing the center of the painting, but his head turning away. In the curve formed by the bull's outline, a mother, her head thrown back in a wide-mouthed scream, holds a dead baby. At the right side of the painting are two more women: a fugitive running into the scene, and one who, clothes afire, falls from the window of a burning building. The broken statue of a warrior lies along the front left of the scene. Although in various sketches some characters are left out, the structure for the painting is clear in the earliest of them.

Chipp (1988) commented on the speed with which Picasso completed the overall conception of *Guernica*, since it was already present in the first day's sketches. One reason for this speed was that the structure was already available from earlier works: many of Picasso's works of the 1930s contain characters similar to those in *Guernica*. Most particularly, the etching *Minotauromachy*, which was done in 1935, contains many of the same characters, and in the same relationships, as in *Guernica*. That is, the structure of *Minotauromachy* was the skeleton on which Picasso constructed *Guernica*, which thus developed in continuity with Picasso's earlier work, without restructuring (Weisberg 1993).

Judged on the basis of its impact on others, *Guernica* is one of Picasso's greatest works, though it was brought about through his reworking of previous work and then-current style rather than through a breakthrough. This work of great importance did not depend on restructuring in its creation.

The Double Helix   Watson and Crick's discovery of the double-helical structure of DNA, perhaps the most important discovery in biology of the twentieth century, also occurred through reproductive thought, without restructuring. As was the case with *Guernica*, they developed the double helix out of an extant idea. (For further discussion of the cognitive aspects of this discovery, see Weisberg 1993; for further information on the facts of the discovery, see Olby 1974; Watson 1968.)

In the fall of 1951, Watson, who had recently received his Ph.D. in genetics from Indiana University and was on a postdoctoral fellowship in Europe to study the chemistry of nucleic acids, joined the Cavendish Laboratory at Cambridge University. There he met Crick, a Ph.D. student. Watson moved to the Cavendish because it had a long history of building molecular models, the avenue he hoped to explore in the analysis of the structure of DNA, which he (and, as it turned out, Crick as well) believed to be the most important question facing biology.

The molecular modeling orientation that attracted Watson and Crick had as its most well-known practitioner Linus Pauling, the world-famous chemist at Cal Tech, who had recently scored a great triumph with a helical model that he proposed for the structure of the protein alpha-keratin, which forms many structures, including hair, horn, and fingernails. Pauling's working methods were of particular interest to Watson and Crick, because proteins are in many ways analogous to DNA: both are long-chain molecules, composed of building blocks, each joined to the next through chemical bonds. The building blocks of protein are the amino acids, while those of DNA are the nucleotides:

a sugar, a phosphate, and one of four nitrogen-rich bases (adenine, cytosine, guanine, and thymine). The double helix of DNA is constructed like a spiral staircase, with two sugar-phosphate chains connected by "rungs" made up of pairs of bases.

The analogy in structure between protein and DNA leads to the possibility that Pauling's methods might be applicable to analysis of DNA, and in the fall of 1951, soon after Watson arrived in Cambridge, he and Crick decided that they would try to build a helical model of DNA. Two specific problems arose in constructing the model: how many helical strands it should contain, and where the bases should be located. The available information did not make clear the quantities or locations of the parts of the molecule, although it was known that the molecule was wider than a single-stranded helix. In Watson and Crick's initial model, there were three strands rather than the correct two, and the bases projected outward from the backbones rather than being between them. The three strands were held together by bonds between magnesium ions.

Soon after Watson and Crick produced the triple helix, they invited a group of researchers from King's College, London, who were carrying out very advanced work on DNA, to see it. One of the members of this group, Maurice Wilkins, was a friend of Crick and had discussed DNA with him many times and with him and Watson after the latter joined the Cavendish. The King's group told Watson and Crick in strong terms that their model surely was incorrect, based on the King's data concerning the amount of water DNA contained, among other things. As well, Rosalind Franklin, one of the King's group, presented some of her reasons for believing that the backbones were on the outside of the molecule, not, as Watson and Crick proposed, on the inside. These criticisms led Watson and Crick to break off work on the triple helix. For almost a year, they did little further work on specific models of DNA, although the structure was never far from the center of their minds. Late in 1952, they began to work again in earnest on the molecular structure of DNA, which led to their development of the correct structure.

Two sorts of information led to the discontinuity from the incorrect triple helix to the correct double helix: information that made it clear that aspects of the triple helix were incorrect and information that made clear various aspects of the correct structure. As one example of rejection of the old, Franklin had argued against magnesium ions' having a role in DNA when she criticized the triple helix, but Watson had not been convinced at that time. In autumn 1952, he tested a sample of DNA for the presence of magnesium and found it did not have any, so the idea then was rejected.

In January 1953, Wilkins showed Watson an x-ray photograph of DNA that Franklin had made but Watson had never seen before. Much additional information was available in this photo, and Watson, who over the last year had developed some expertise in reading x-ray photographs, was able to remember enough to help in their new model building. Wilkins also gave Watson information about some of Franklin's recent results concerning an increase of 20 percent in the length of DNA fibers when they were exposed to high humidity. This information, in conjunction with the data from the new x-ray photo, allowed Watson to deduce that two strands, not three, were involved.

Watson then spent two days building two-strand models with the backbones in the center because he still believed that the bases were on the outside. Two-strand bases-outside models could not be built without the distances between atoms violating important rules of structural chemistry, however, which led a reluctant Watson to abandon the bases-outside configuration.

During the second week of February, Crick received a copy of a research report that contained information concerning the shape of the basic building-block unit of the crystal of DNA (the "unit cell"). This enabled him to deduce that the backbone chains of the DNA molecule ran in opposite directions (were "anti-parallel"), which then allowed him to deduce the pitch of the helix—that is, the angle of the turn of the screw of the helix.

The last part of the puzzle, the pairings of the bases, was resolved in a very quiet way. One morning, Watson came in early and worked on the base pairings, using cardboard models of the bases that he manipulated into various configurations on a table top until he discovered the correct pairings.

There were thus several discontinuities in Watson and Crick's discovery: the change from three to two strands, the change in position of the backbones, and the change from parallel to antiparallel backbone chains. All of these discontinuities came about without restructuring; both alternatives existed as possibilities throughout the work because Watson and Crick had decided that DNA was helical. Once that decision had been made, the rest of their work involved deciding among the alternatives. As one example, the issue of the number of strands was down to two or three; it was not two strands versus an unknown number.

Analogy in Edison's Development of an Electric Lighting System   Many of Thomas Edison's inventions developed through continuity with earlier artifacts, both his own and those of others (Weisberg 1993). One interesting example was his development of a system for delivery of electricity to residential users (Basalla 1988).

After Edison had invented the incandescent light, his next project in the area was to develop an entire system whereby the invention could be made commercially successful. There were at that time two in-place lighting systems (neither one developed by Edison): one using gas lights and the other using electrical arc lights. Gas lights were used mainly for residential lighting, and control was available at each individual light so its brightness could be set independent of any other. The gas fuel was produced elsewhere and was sent to the individual user through gas mains buried in the street.

Edison's electric light bulb was not the first electrical lighting system in operation. Arc lights were already in use, but they were not feasible for residential use. Arc lighting, produced by an electrical spark between carbon rods, was too bright for residential use, was very hot, and produced fumes. In contrast with the gas system, the generating plant was on the premises of the user.

Edison's electric lighting system was based on that used for gas lighting. Edison wrote in his notebooks that he would completely imitate the gas system, replacing gas lighting by electricity. In Edison's electric system, the source of power was remote from the user, and the wires that served to bring the power to the user were underground, in a parallel to the underground gas mains. There were already in place above-ground wiring systems for the telephone and telegraph, but Edison's use of the gas system resulted in his ignoring them, though there were complications in having the wires go beneath the ground. As well, in Edison's electrical system, the individual lights were turned on and off by the user, and the usage of electricity, like that of gas, was metered at the residence. The light bulb in Edison's system was called a burner and was designed to produce the same amount of light as a gas burner.

Conclusions   These cases show that there have been a number of significant creative accomplishments that have occurred on the basis of reproductive thought, that is, without restructuring. In the case of *Guernica,* there was continuity within the creator's own work; in Edison's electric system, the continuity was with the work of others. In the case of DNA, there were discontinuities, with the product changing in significant ways as it was worked on, but the discontinuities did not involve restructuring because the options were available from the beginning within the helical structure of the problem, within which Watson and Crick had chosen to work.

In these cases, then, the world was not resistant to reproductive thinking. A new situation, similar to an earlier one on the surface (DNA and protein; gas residential lighting and electric residential lighting), turned out to be similar on a deeper level as well, so that the analysis of the earlier situation could be transferred to the new situation.

These three case studies are examples of analogical transfer—situations in which information from a previous situation is transferred to a new one that is analogous to the old; the new situation is similar in structure to the old one. Analogical transfer has been extensively studied in laboratory investigations of problem solving (Reeves and Weisberg in press). One first provides problem solvers with information, called the "base" analogue, that can be useful in solving some target problem. The base analogues and target problem share the same underlying structure, although they may be very different on surface details (that is, the objects involved). One then examines how easily problem solvers make use of the base information.

These three cases are examples of near analogical transfer, which is based on common surface elements, such as the base and target's both being large chemical molecules. Remote transfer is based solely on abstract structural similarity, such as the analogy between the solar system and the atom, which have no surface elements in common. Laboratory studies have shown that spontaneous transfer (transfer occurring without informing the subjects that the base is relevant to the target problem) is frequent only when the base and target are similar on the surface. Transfer is very infrequent, and may not occur at all, when the base and target share only abstract structure.

These laboratory results are consistent with data on the use of analogy in real-world creative thinking. In a review of retrospective reports of spontaneous analogical transfer in creative thinking, Perkins (1983) found that remote analogical transfer was almost nonexistent. Dunbar (1994) has moved beyond case studies based solely on historical records and has examined scientific reasoning in what he calls in vivo settings. He has observed scientific research in the scientists' laboratories, in what could be called "on-line" case studies. This allows him to obtain detailed records of the interactions in the labs and to carry out more rigorous analyses than those usually permitted by the historical records used in most case studies.

Dunbar has found that two sorts of analogies are used by the scientists he studied to advance the progress of their work. First, when an experiment was not working, research scientists used what he calls local analogies. An analogy was made to an experiment in a similar research area, and that was used as the basis for changing the experiment. In regional analogies, a less frequent use of analogy, a system of knowledge in one area was mapped to another, to facilitate understanding of the latter. Dunbar found that this usually occurred when scientists were elaborating theories or planning new sets of experiments. He did find some use of remote analogies in the laboratories that he studied, but they served to educate an ignorant individual rather than increase the understanding of the person carrying out the research.

In conclusion, reproductive factors can play important roles in creative thinking. The world is more receptive to the past than students of creative thinking may have believed.

Case Studies of Restructuring
There have been many cases in which creative accomplishment has resulted from restructuring, and in this section I will discuss several in which it occurred as the result of the thinker's exposure to external events. The most dramatic example of this occurs when a specific environmental trigger provides the thinker with the "solution" to his or her problem. These cases are of interest here because they indicate that restructuring does not come about only when the thinker breaks away from the past; in these cases, restructuring may have been based on the use of the past.

The three cases discussed are all from the visual arts, to make their similarities and differences clear. In the first case, Picasso's painting of *Les Demoiselles d'Avignon*, a specific environmental event served as a trigger for a restructuring. In the other two cases, Alexander Calder's mobiles and Jackson Pollock's poured paintings, the restructurings were the result of the artists' incorporation and use of several external events, over significant amounts of time. In these two latter cases, especially, one can argue that the restructuring came about reproductively.

Les Demoiselles d'Avignon   This painting by Picasso, of a group of prostitutes in the parlor of a brothel, exposing themselves to the viewer, was painted in 1907. It has been called the most influential single painting of the twentieth century because of the radical break between it and reality. The women are painted in a grossly distorted way: their faces, which resemble African tribal masks, are darkly colored, striated, and are drawn as if they are made of separate parts; their bodies are sharply angular. These distortions were very different from anything that could be found in the work of Picasso or any of his contemporaries in the Paris art scene early in the century. Furthermore, since Picasso could draw beautifully when he desired to do so, the distortions in this painting serve a purpose: to present the women as they appear. That is, the artist's conception took precedence over perception; he wanted viewers to respond negatively to the women on account of their ugliness (Rubin 1984; Weisberg 1993).

Picasso made and kept many preparatory studies for this painting, of both its overall structure and the individual characters. A comparison of the final version of this work with its earliest manifestations, from Picasso's sketchbooks shows several significant changes over the course of the development of the painting.

The earliest sketches contained seven characters rather than the five in the painting itself: the women were supplemented by two men. The attention of all the people is centered on a man entering on the left. In the final version, the men have been removed, and the attention of the women centers on the viewer, who has become the intruder into their space—the visitor to the brothel. Additionally, versions of this painting in Picasso's sketchbooks, as well as x-ray analyses of the painting itself, show that the faces of the characters were not distorted in the way they are in the final version.

We do not know why Picasso eliminated the men from the painting, but it has been speculated that Picasso reconsidered how best to communicate his intended message (Rubin 1988). The original version of the painting was a relatively straightforward attempt at propaganda: the man in the center of the painting is a customer of the brothel, and the man entering is a medical student (in several preliminary sketches, this man holds a skull in his hand). The message is that the wages of frequenting a brothel can be severe indeed: venereal disease, with the distinct possibility of slow and agonizing death, which was a fear of Picasso at this time. There had been published in Paris photographs of prostitutes in a hospital, in the terminal stages of venereal disease, suffering from large tumors and open abscesses on their faces, and Picasso had spent time in a hospital in Paris while drawing prostitutes. The presence of the medical student thus serves as a warning for the sailor.

As he sketched *Les Demoiselles*, however, Picasso rejected this version and removed the men. In order for the viewer to interpret this original version, he or she needed to know the story Picasso wanted to tell. The final version of the painting requires no knowledge of an anecdotal nature. The distorted appearances of the women are so striking that we respond negatively, and Picasso's message is transmitted. Thus, the change in the structure of the painting may have come from Picasso's analysis of the adequacy of the painting as a communicative device, based on his artistic judgment.

The distortions in the faces of several of the women that so effectively serve to transmit Picasso's message were triggered by a visit Picasso made to an ethnographic museum, where he encountered primitive sculpture. This was not his first visit to the museum, but this time the works he saw stimulated him to distort the faces of three of the women in *Les Demoiselles*. It has been hypothesized that specific masks might have served as models for the changes in the faces of the demoiselles (Rosenblum 1976). However, the faces Picasso painted match no masks present in the museum at that time, so his exposure to the artworks from the South Pacific and elsewhere impressed him with the emotional expressiveness that could be accomplished through primitive means, and he therefore exaggerated several characteristics that had been present in his works about this time, such as striations on faces. Thus, the stimulating effect of the primitive art was through the carrying to a more extreme level of several existing aspects of Picasso's work rather than through the introduction of something completely new.

Calder's Mobiles   In the early 1930s, Alexander Calder (1898–1976), a young American sculptor living in Paris, began to produce a new kind of sculpture, which culminated in his mobiles, abstract or nonrepresentational in format (they neither represent nor contain familiar objects), constructed with a complex framework of wire, and with wind-driven movement as an intrinsic feature. These sculptures were significantly different from earlier works produced by Calder, which had been representational in form. (For information on Calder's development, see Lipman 1989; Marter 1991; Weisberg 1993.)

In April–May 1931, Calder had a solo show in a gallery in Paris. The works displayed were "portraits in wire" (representational works in which the subject's face was "drawn" by Calder's shaping wire) as well as his first abstract works. These were wire and wood sculptures, in which wooden balls and other simple forms were attached to wooden bases using wire. This exhibit marks the point at which Calder's work had taken a radical stylistic turn, and it can serve as a reference point as we attempt to trace the development of the elements in a prototypical mobile (moving abstract sculpture driven by the wind) and determine how each of them came to be present.

Calder's interest in movement began early; he had made action toys as a child and in the 1920s had a contract to design such toys for a toy manufacturer. Also in the 1920s he had created a miniature circus, which provided his first significant success in the Parisian art world. This circus featured figures made of wire and pieces of cloth and wood that could be manipulated so they could do tricks. Calder had also made a wire fishbowl sculpture, with fish that could be moved by turning a crank.

Some of Calder's earliest abstract sculptures were able to move, and some were responsive to the wind. Of the works displayed in the spring of 1931, some could move in a very limited way in response to air currents. Later in 1931, Calder produced abstract sculpture in which more significant movement occurred, in some cases provided by a hand-turned crank, analogous to that used in the goldfish bowl with swimming fish (another example of "near" analogical transfer). He also produced abstract moving sculpture driven by motors.

This mechanical movement, whether from hand cranking or motors, was unsatisfactory to Calder, however, because it was repetitive, so he made some motorized pieces with multiple motors, each driving part of the apparatus, which resulted in more complex and interesting movements. Now the sculpture became very complicated and frequently broke down; also, even with multiple motors, the patterns were still repetitive. These problems led Calder to seek a more unpredictable source of movement, and so he focused on movement produced by air currents, gradually developing sculptures with structures that allowed more complex and unpredictable movements in response to the wind.

The wind-driven movement in Calder's mature mobiles developed from the primitive responsiveness to wind in the early abstract sculptures. This use of movement was an extension of the movement in his earlier works and could be viewed as the most current focus of Calder's lifelong interest in movement and mechanisms. The use of wire as a framework for the mobiles was also continuous with Calder's early works; he had used wire as his medium of preference for many years, creating figures of many types, ranging from wire portraits, to the crank-driven goldfish bowl, to variations on classical themes.

Calder's early work was representational in style, so the abstract works displayed in 1931 represent a restructuring. There is evidence that Calder's exposure to the work of other artists was important in triggering his turn to abstraction. In 1930, Calder visited the studio of the well-known abstract painter Mondrian, whose work was severely geometric in structure, with white canvases divided into rectangular blocks by black lines, with some of the blocks painted with primary colors. Mondrian's entire studio, which included his living area, was decorated in this style, with rectangles of color hung on white walls. Immediately after his visit to Mondrian's studio, Calder began to paint in an abstract style very similar to Mondrian's. He soon returned to sculpture, a form with which he felt more comfortable, but now producing abstract sculpture containing geometric forms, mainly painted black and white, with an occasional primary color.

The forms in some of Calder's abstract works also resemble those in the works of Miró, another influential artist in Paris about that time, who produced abstract sculpture. Thus, the restructuring of Calder's sculpture style came about through his adaptation of components of the styles of others.

Jackson Pollock's Poured Paintings   Jackson Pollock's (1912 1956) paintings in the late 1940s formed one of the cornerstones for the development of the abstract expressionist movement in the United States. These works are abstract, constructed out of swirling lines of paint, with no structure except for the rhythmic patterns produced by the lines of paint. The paint was not applied with a brush; rather, Pollock splashed, dripped, and poured the paint on the canvas, which allowed the application of unbroken lines of paint, without the continuous pausing to replenish a brush. (For further discussion and examples, see Landau 1989; Rubin 1967; Weisberg 1993.)

Pollock's earliest works, however, were realistic paintings of American country scenes, strongly reminiscent of the work of his first teacher, Thomas Hart Benton, a well-known American artist of the 1930s who painted many large-scale murals depicting the grandeur of ordinary American life. Pollock later came under the influence of John Graham, a charismatic painter and art theorist who introduced many young American artists in New York in the 1930s and 1940s (including Calder) to the most recent developments occurring in Europe. Graham was especially impressed with Picasso's works, and much of Pollock's work in the 1930s looks like Picasso's of that time. Graham believed that primitive art allows the unconscious to add to the emotional content of a painting and thus viewed Picasso's incorporation of primitive art in his works as very important.

Pollock became very familiar as well with the work and theories of the surrealists, a group of European painters who had fled to New York just before World War II and were interested in the direct expression of the unconscious in works of art. The surrealists attempted to use dream imagery as the basis for paintings, and they developed what they called "automatic" techniques in an attempt to break away from conscious control of artistic production. In one such technique, called "The Exquisite Corpse," a piece of paper was passed among participants; each wrote one word on it and then folded it over so that the word could not be seen. The resulting "sentence" was then read and interpreted by the players. It was thought that the juxtaposed words of individuals would approach the freedom of thought without conscious constraints. (The title of the game derived from an accidental juxtaposition of words that occurred in an early session.) Pollock and fellow artists also participated in visual forms of this game; each participant would draw part of an image, fold the paper, and pass it to the next artist.

Pollock's interest in automatic techniques deepened as a result of his study with Stanley William Hayter, a graphic artist and teacher who moved from Paris to New York during World War II. Hayter discussed with Pollock the ideas of Paul Klee, a Swiss-born painter whom Pollock was familiar with from his contact with the surrealists. One of Klee's most important ideas concerned automatic drawing, in which one allows the drawing instrument to move without attempting to control it so as to produce specific objects. Hayter's own works were abstract in style, and his teachings emphasized Klee's notions concerning automatic elements of drawing. Pollock's engravings made at Hayter's studio show strong similarities to Hayter's.

As a result of these experiences, Pollock came to believe that painting should attempt to express the unconscious directly, and not necessarily represent objects realistically. By the mid-1940s, he had moved from the realism of his earliest work, through a Picasso-like style, to a surrealist-influenced abstract style. This restructuring in subject matter came about through outside influences, over a long period of time.

The second restructuring in Pollock's career, pouring as a technique for automatic painting, developed out of two sets of earlier experiences with pouring paint on canvas. Pollock was first exposed to pouring paint during his participation in a workshop organized in 1936 in New York by the Mexican muralist David Siqueiros in which Siqueiros and other young artists explored new techniques for painting, among them nontraditional methods of applying paint, such as airbrushes, and pouring and dripping. Siqueiros in 1936 painted *Collective Suicide*, a nonrepresentational work, by pouring paint on a wooden panel laid on the floor and using sticks to flick paint onto the surface. Siqueiros encouraged such techniques on projects that the participants worked on in the workshop.

During the winter of 1942–1943, Pollock and several other young American painters met with Roberto Matta Echaurren, a young surrealist artist, to see each other's work, discuss issues of interest, and experiment with automatic techniques. During this period, Pollock and his fellow artists practiced these techniques; one painting was produced as a collaboration when Pollock and two other artists experimented with pouring of paint.

That antecedents for the components of Pollock's mature style can be traced does not mean that Pollock only appropriated the ideas of others. As did Picasso and Calder, Pollock undoubtedly used what was available but then went beyond what had been done before, in several ways. The various surrealist techniques were used by them to produce only initial ideas for a work of art, which the artist could then elaborate in more traditional ways into a finished work. In Pollock's mature style, the pouring technique itself served to produce the painting. As well, Klee's and Hayter's use of automatic drawing was on a much smaller scale than that developed by Pollock. Perhaps because of his admiration for the wall-sized murals of Benton, his first teacher, and for the works of others, Pollock was interested in working on a large scale. He therefore had to go beyond automatic drawing, because the technique did not work on large canvas.

Over a number of years, Pollock developed pouring into a technique that he could use, the consequences of which he understood. He could plan compositions because he knew what was going to happen when he began a gesture. In his mature works, Pollock was not experimenting with spilling and pouring; he was using these techniques for painting.

Reproductive Restructuring: Conclusions   These three case studies have made clear the role of external factors in restructuring. The time scales of the three cases are different, but the underlying processes are similar. In the distortions in *Les Demoiselles*, there was an acute change, triggered by the single event of Picasso's visit to the museum. Calder's shift to abstraction also had an acute trigger—his visit to Mondrian's studio—but exposure to the works of other artists also contributed. In Pollock's case, the change from brushing to pouring took place over a longer period of time, with pouring only gradually emerging as a true technique over a number of years.

Pollock's restructuring had a reproductive basis; he took ideas from others and only gradually shaped them to meet his needs. In his development of this most radical innovation, Pollock never rejected the past. Nor did Calder: his abstraction too was derived from that of others; he could never have restructured his style without exposure to the works of others.

Productive Thinking: On Going beyond Past Experience

In his discussion of productive thinking, Wertheimer (1982) made it clear that he did not believe that it occurred independent of past experience. Rather, the important issue for him was how the thinker chose which past experience was relevant to the new situation and how the thinker reorganized this experience to deal with the situation.

However, brief consideration of an example of restructuring discussed by Wertheimer shows that he gave past experience a much less important role in restructuring than these cases lead one to conclude.

Wertheimer believed that problem analysis itself could provide the impetus for restructuring and that nothing further was needed in the way of specialized knowledge. A classic example of restructuring coming about through problem analysis is seen in his report of how a young girl solved the problem of determining the area of a parallelogram. The child had already been shown how to calculate the area of a rectangle by counting the number of small squares that could be fit inside it. Of course, placing squares inside the parallelogram was impossible, since the lack of right angles made it impossible for the squares to fit completely:

> Given the parallelogram problem, after she had been shown briefly how to get at the area of the rectangle, she said, "I certainly don't know how to do *that*." Then after a moment of silence: "This is *no good here*," pointing to the region at the left end; "and *no good here*," pointing to the region at the right. "It's troublesome, here and here." Hesitatingly she said: "I could make it right here . . . but . . ." Suddenly she cried out, "May I have a pair of scissors? What is bad there is just what is needed here. It fits." She took the scissors, cut the figure vertically, and placed the left end at the right. (Wertheimer 1982, p. 49)

Although this child knew how to use scissors, she had never been taught to cut a parallelogram to construct a rectangle in order to calculate area. Thus, although she had no specific knowledge, she was able to analyze the difficulty that faced her, go beyond her experience and create something new.

In comparing this example with the cases previously discussed in this chapter, it is obvious that there are differences concerning the specificity of experience. In Wertheimer's example, the girl did not have to know anything in order to solve the problem. This was not true in the case studies; the advances could not have occurred without specific experiences. For example, Pollock surely could not have developed his pouring style simply by thinking about how he could express his unconscious impulses on a large scale (assuming that he could have gotten to that point in his career by himself). He needed to know about the surrealists and Klee and to have been exposed to others' experiments with pouring and splashing paint. Although it cannot be measured directly, there seems to be a large difference between Wertheimer's example and what happens in reality, which raises questions as to whether such an example serves as a microcosm of real-world situations.

Case Studies of Creativity: Conclusions

The first conclusion to be drawn from this chapter is that the mechanisms underlying creative thinking are not simple or uniform. It is incorrect to assume first that all creative advances are the result of restructuring (i.e., of "productive" thinking), since several creative advances have been the result of reproductive thinking, in which the past directly served the present. These case studies indicate that emphasis on the negative influences of experiences on creative thinking is at the very least overstated. Laboratory demonstrations of problem-solving set are not useful analogies for the real-world situations in these cases, because there the world was not resistant to experience. Although nothing was said in this chapter in the way of defining creativity, the three studies reviewed in the first section of the chapter are of unqualified creativity; *Guernica* is the most renowned of Picasso's works, and the double helix of DNA has been of revolutionary impact in biology. Therefore, the reproductive nature of the creative advances in these cases cannot be dismissed because the cases do not qualify as being the result of creative thinking.

Second, it should also not be assumed that when creative thinking does result in restructuring of a situation, it always occurs as the result of productive thinking (independent of the past or in rejection of the past). Finally, although by definition creative thinking produces novelty, it should not be assumed that it does so by rejecting what has been done before. Rather, creative thinking moves beyond what has been done only slowly, and when it does, it is more as a modification of the past than rejection of it.

References

Adams, J. (1979). *Conceptual blockbusting* (2d ed.). New York: Norton.

Amabile, T. (1989). *Growing up creative: Nurturing a lifetime of creativity.* New York: Crown.

Basalla, G. (1988). *The evolution of technology.* New York: Cambridge University Press.

Bransford, J. D., and Stein, B. S. (1984). *The IDEAL problem solver.* New York: Freeman.

Chipp, H. B. (1988). *Picasso's "Guernica": History, transformations, meanings.* Berkeley: University of California Press.

deBono, E. (1968). *New think.* New York: Basic Books.

Dunbar, K. (1994). How scientists really reason: Scientific reasoning in real-world laboratories. In R. J. Sternberg and J. Davidson (eds.), *The Nature of insight.* Cambridge, MA: MIT Press.

Finke, R. A., Ward, T. B., and Smith, S. M. (1992). *Creative cognition: Theory, research, and applications.* Cambridge, MA: MIT Press.

Landau, E. G. (1989). *Jackson Pollock*. New York: Abrams.

Lipman, J. (1989). *Calder's universe*. Philadelphia: Running Press.

Maier, N. R. F. (1970). *Problem solving and creativity: In individuals and groups*. Belmont, CA: Wadsworth.

Marter, J. M. (1991). *Alexander Calder*. Cambridge: Cambridge University Press.

Ohlsson, S. (1984a). Restructuring revisited. I. Summary and critique of the Gestalt theory of problem solving. *Scandinavian Journal of Psychology, 25,* 65–78.

Ohlsson, S. (1984b). Restructuring revisited. II. An information processing theory of restructuring and insight. *Scandinavian Journal of Psychology, 25,* 117–129.

Olby, R. (1974). *The path to the double helix*. Seattle, WA: University of Washington Press.

Perkins, D. N. (1983). Novel remote analogies seldom contribute to discovery. *Journal of Creative Behavior, 17,* 223–239.

Reeves, L., and Weisberg, R. W. (in press). Models of analogical transfer in problem solving. *Psychological Bulletin.*

Rosenblum, R. (1976). *Cubism and twentieth-century art*. New York: Abrams.

Rubin, W. (1967). Jackson Pollock and the modern tradition. *Art Forum, 5,* 14–22.

Rubin, W. (1984). Picasso. In W. Rubin (ed.), *"Primitivism" in 20th century art* (Vol. 1, pp. 241–343). New York: Museum of Modern Art.

Watson, J. D. (1968). *The double helix*. New York: Signet.

Weisberg, R. W. (1993). *Creativity: Beyond the myth of genius*. San Francisco: Freeman.

Weisberg, R. W. (1994). Prolegomena to theories of insight in problem solving: Definition of terms and a taxonomy of problems. In R. J. Sternberg and J. Davidson (eds.), *The Nature of insight*. Cambridge MA: MIT Press.

Wertheimer, M. (1982). *Productive thinking* (enl. ed.). Chicago: University of Chicago Press.

Chapter 4

Productive Problem Solving

Roger L. Dominowski

The distinction between doing something old versus doing something new to solve a problem has long been associated with Gestalt views on problem solving. These researchers emphasized novel instances of problem solving, considering them to be more interesting and to involve additional explanatory concepts. In his studies of problem solving by chimpanzees, Kohler (1976) wanted to observe their behavior in situations requiring them to use new or nonobvious means to achieve a goal. In the problems he presented, the objective (usually a piece of fruit) could not be attained by direct approach. Rather, the chimpanzees had to employ novel, indirect means—taking a detour route, using a stick, positioning and climbing on a box, or putting two short sticks together to make one long enough to reach the goal. It is worth noting that the chimpanzees not only had to engage in activities that were novel in the presented context but also had to overcome their habitual tendency to use direct approach to the objective.

Maier (1940) contrasted habitual directions, which result in reproducing old solutions, with new directions, which give rise to new combinations of experiences. The experiences may well be familiar, but the combination is new. Maier argued that reproducing old solutions could be accounted for by memory and associative processes but that producing new combinations required an additional factor, a direction that is established in the problem situation and controls memory integration.

One of the examples Maier used to illustrate his argument concerned the two-string problem. In this problem, the individual is asked to tie together the ends of two strings, each of which has one end fastened to the ceiling with the other end just reaching the floor. The strings are separated enough so that by taking hold of one string, a person will be unable to reach the other string; hence, the problem is to obtain a string that is out of reach. Maier noted that most attempts at solution depended on habitual directions—for example, using an object to extend one's reach or tying something to the end of a string to make it functionally longer. One solution, however, involves a change in meaning, a new direction. In the pendulum solution, the subject ties a small object of appropriate weight (e.g., pliers) to the end of one string and then initiates the swinging back and forth of the weighted string. By holding the other string and waiting for the swinging string to come close enough to be grasped, the problem is effectively solved. Multiple meaning changes are involved; for example, rather than the person going to the needed string, the string comes to the person; the pliers, rather than being seen as a tool, must be seen as a weight. For Maier, the change in meaning accompanying the production of a new combination constituted the experience of insight. He also stressed that production of the pendulum solution was not simply a result of past experience. Rather, he remarked that giving people experience with a pendulum prior to presenting the two-string problem had proved ineffective.

Kohler (1969), in his final comment on thinking, presented a view quite similar to Maier's argument. Kohler distinguished ordinary thinking from productive thinking, the latter involving a change in mental representation. He noted that prior learning is required not only to solve problems but also to understand the nature of problems that one confronts. Although some problems might be solved by nothing more than recall and application of prior learning, other instances of problem solving—productive thinking—require something more. Kohler argued that all problem solving concerns awareness of relations and that productive problem solving involves awareness of new relations among problem components. Understanding of these new relations, according to Kohler, is what is meant by insight. He further asserted that particular relations arise only when the person's attention is directed to their appearance, thus implying that the emergence of new relations depends on contextual influences. Kohler believed that instances of productive thinking ranged from the solution of simple problems to great achievements, such as scientific discoveries.

Wertheimer (1982) criticized computationally oriented training procedures for their lack of useful transfer and argued for emphasis on productive thinking that is based on structural understanding. According to his characterization of productive thinking, (1) the problem must be viewed as a whole rather than piecemeal, (2) gaps or disturbances must be dealt with structurally, (3) internal structural relations must be sought, and (4) operations must be considered in relation to their role in overall structural change. This partial list illustrates the strong emphasis that Wertheimer gave to grasping the internal structure of a problem situation as the central component of productive thinking. He further noted that an initial, incorrect view of the situation can prevent the person from seeing the real structure of the situation and what must be done to close the gaps in the structure. An initial view, he noted, might be vague; in that case, solution would require mainly that the situation be clarified. He contrasted this circumstance with one requiring a "radical transformation from first to second view." The transition from an inadequate view to a fundamentally different, more appropriate structural view is associated with insight. Wertheimer applied similar analyses to puzzles, school mathematics, discoveries by Galileo and Einstein, social situations, and more, leaving no doubt that he viewed his principles of productive thinking as applicable to creative achievement on small and grand scale.

These views share several convictions: (1) a distinction must be made between solving problems by familiar means versus problem solving that requires doing something new; (2) changing views of problem structure is a central component of producing new solutions, an activity called productive thinking; and (3) similar phenonema occur in both simple and highly regarded instances of productive thinking. This shared view has stimulated research on a number of tasks typically labeled insight problems. Although there are obvious surface differences among the insight problems that have been used by various investigators, three shared features do seem to apply: (1) no specialized knowledge is required (or the problem is well within the competence of those to whom it is given), (2) some form of new response is required for solution, and (3) a change in view of the problem is required for solution. Before examining points (2) and (3) and focusing on performance on insight problems, two related issues will be considered.

First, are insight problems different? At the outset it must be stated that no problem can be unconditionally characterized as an insight problem. The reason is that, for any problem, one could in principle teach the solution to a person before presenting the problem, which would make success in problem solving a matter of recall. Thus, reference to an insight problem must be taken to mean that for the typical or appropriate problem solver, a task has the three insight features noted. The use of *insight problem* can be seen as a kind of shorthand.

The Gestalt psychologists clearly considered insight problems to be different from problems that can be solved by reproductive means. Solving insight problems, they proposed, involved restructuring and changes in meaning. It is important to note that a comparable distinction between insight and noninsight problems is made by modern theorists. According to Anderson (1993), typical problem solving requires applying some method in a fixed problem space. Anderson also recognized an alternative, that problem solving sometimes involves a change in the problem space, and he commented that such instances of problem solving are considered to be (more) insightful. Kaplan and Simon (1990) made a similar distinction, noting that only some problems—insight problems—require a change in representation for their solution. Greeno, Magone, and Chaiklin (1979) distinguished between problems that require the construction of new problem spaces and those that do not.

A reasonable consensus exists for designating problems that require a change in representation as insight problems and for distinguishing such problems from others that lack this requirement. This distinction can be made while leaving open questions such as how the changes occur or in what ways theoretical accounts of insight problem solving will differ from those for noninsight problems. A clear implication is that there will be some difference. Representation should be treated broadly, as equivalent to interpretation, and representation should concern the whole problem or its significant aspects. Moving from state to state in, say, the disc transfer problem, does not qualify as a change in representation in the present sense. A further implication of the focus on changing representation is that the change will be from a more familiar interpretation that is suggested by the problem presentation to a more novel interpretation. A problem solver's initial representation of a problem is strongly influenced by the way in which the problem is presented. The organization and cuing features of the problem presentation will favor a particular representation, which will most often elicit the familiar and ordinary aspects of the knowledge relevant to interpreting the problem. If the problem requires a change in representation, it follows that the required representation must be more novel and contrary to the influence of the problem as presented. In short, a change in representation is highly likely to be from familiar to new, just as initially proposed by the Gestalt psychologists.

This characterization of insight problems is primarily definitional. There are also reports of empirical differences between insight and noninsight problems. Metcalfe and Wiebe (1987) had problem solvers rate their perceived nearness to solution ("warmth") during work on different problems. Their essential finding was that changes in warmth ratings over working time showed different patterns for traditionally labeled insight problems versus noninsight algebra problems. For insight problems, warmth ratings exhibited abrupt changes just prior to solution, a pattern consistent with a process of restructuring. Although Weisberg (1992) has raised some objections to Metcalfe and

Wiebe's findings and interpretations, the basic fact remains that their procedures yielded different data for insight and algebra problems. Schooler, Ohlsson, and Brooks (1993) used insight and noninsight problems comparable to those used by Metcalfe and Wiebe and found that requiring problem solvers to verbalize disrupted performance only for insight problems. The theoretical implications of this finding will be discussed later; the relevance of the result here is to demonstrate another empirical difference between insight and noninsight problems.

The second issue is whether solving insight problems is creative. Creative ideas are frequently defined in terms of their novelty and usefulness (or appropriate satisfaction of some quality criteria). Research tasks used to assess creative production are ordinarily rather ill defined, allowing many responses of varying originality and quality. Novelty is associated with statistical infrequency, and quality or appropriateness is sometimes difficult to judge because of vagueness in the relevant criteria, especially for more artistic endeavors. From this perspective, questions might be raised about the relevance of solving insight problems to creativity. Clearly, the solution to an insight problem meets the appropriateness criterion (because a problem is solved), but this would be true of any problem solution. But insight problems have fixed, known solutions, so wherein lies the novelty?

There are two ways in which solving insight problems can be said to involve novelty. First, the idea required for solution often is itself less frequent than others that might be elicited. If an object must be used to achieve the goal, an unusual use of the object is required; if a particular meaning of a word or phrase is required, it is the less familiar, less dominant meaning that is needed. Thus, a degree of statistical infrequency often characterizes insight problem solutions.

The second and more general aspect of novelty stems from the requirement (by definition) to overcome the interpretation fostered by the problem presentation and to adopt a new, more structurally appropriate representation. Overcoming convention and generating a new understanding of a situation is considered to be an important component of creativity. For example, Gilhooly and Green (1989) cite the difficulty of abandoning habit-bound ways of thought as a major obstacle to creative work. In discussing their IDEAL (identify, define, explore, act, look and learn) cycle of problem solving, Bransford, Sherwood, and Sturdevant (1987) point out that "the creative person who reenters the IDEAL cycle will often redefine a problem in a way that suggests simpler and more workable strategies" (p. 168).

Perkins (1981) suggested that although the solutions to puzzle-like insight problems have no significance themselves, the processes involved in achieving them are much the same as those used in producing more celebrated insights. Later, Perkins (1990) argued against ideational fluency as an account of creative thinking and stressed the importance of certain patterns of thinking. One of these, called problem finding, includes pursuing changes in direction and reformulations of problems. Similarly, Sternberg and Lubart (1992) include redefinition of problems as a critical component in their theory of creativity. These researchers found that performance on problem redefinition was strongly correlated with creativity scores on tasks such as drawing, writing short stories, and solving creative science problems. Both Sternberg and Lubart (1992) and Perkins (1990) cite evidence indicating that problem-reformulation measures predict real-world creative production. Finding a new and productive interpretation of a situation is just one component in creativity, but it serves to link solving insight problems with creative thinking.

Obstacles to Solution

Problems of any sort might fail to be solved for a variety of reasons; overloading short-term memory and failure to retrieve needed information from long-term memory are frequently cited sources of failure. What we seek here, however, are causes of failure that are of particular relevance to insight problems. Before considering some of these obstacles, I will first comment on a view that implies no differences between insight and other problems. Weisberg (1992) has proposed that all problem solving consists of repeated cycles of retrieval of information from long-term memory and attempts to apply that information. Similarly Keane (1989), in devising a model to account for certain phenomena of insight problem solving, assumed that everybody has (in long-term memory) all of the condition-action plans to produce solutions. According to the model, failure to solve occurs because the right plan is not accessed.

   As noted earlier, knowledge—information in long-term memory—is important for representing problems as well as for finding solutions, but restricting problem solving to memory retrieval is at best incomplete, for several reasons. The approach fails to distinguish between problems requiring a change in representation and those lacking this requirement. Also, a problem solver might be required to find new relations among previously unconnected ideas (Collins et al. 1975; Maier 1940). Novel situations require converting declarative knowledge into action plans, and the conversion process can be error prone (Anderson 1987). There are insight problems for which it seems that little more than thinking of the appropriate meaning of a critical term is required for solution. In these circumstances, the relevant questions concern what prevents successful retrieval and how the needed meaning is eventually achieved. There is no reason to expect that all insight problems will have the same sources of difficulty. Although the problems share certain characteristics, they also differ in multiple respects, at least some of which affect solution difficulty. Some of the major obstacles to solution will now be considered.

Functional Fixedness
Object-use insight problems require an ordinary object to be used in a relatively unusual fashion in order to reach a solution. For example, the two-string problem requires tying together two strings suspended from the ceiling, far enough apart so that a subject cannot hold one and reach the other. The problem is often structured so that the subject must tie a small electrical relay (or pliers) to the end of one string, set the weighted string swinging like a pendulum, go to and grasp the second string, and wait for the first string to swing close enough to be retrieved. Other problems of this type require using pliers as a pair of legs for a small flower stand, using the blade of a screwdriver to complete a small electrical circuit, or using a small box as a platform for a candle by tacking the box to a cork wall. The underlying concept of functional fixedness is that ordinary ideas block thinking of unusual ideas. The basic demonstration of functional fixedness is to show that emphasis on an object's usual function impairs thinking of the required unusual use. Two paradigms have been used: *transfer of fixedness*, which refers to a two-stage paradigm in which one employs the object in its usual function just before encountering a problem requiring an unusual use, and *perceptual fixedness*, which refers to the object's serving its usual function when the problem is presented.

Transfer of fixedness has been studied using a two-object procedure. For example, the problem solver might first use a small relay to complete an electrical circuit and then be given the two-string problem with both the relay and a small switch available. The basic finding is that solvers tend to use the switch in the two-string problem if they have used the relay in its usual function (Adamson and Taylor 1954). Prior, ordinary use is assumed to lead to encoding the object in terms of properties relevant to its usual function, thus decreasing the chances of the object's being seen as suitable for the novel use. The two-object procedure has two weaknesses that limit its impact. First, it can be argued that the introduction of the second object at problem presentation creates a demand to use it, the first object already having been used. Second, the second object provides a perfectly acceptable solution to the problem (the first object would be no better), so the phenomenon seems to involve preference more than solution obstacles.

Transfer of fixedness has also been investigated with a single object that is first used in its usual function and then is the only or most suitable object available to solve the problem. With this procedure, one can ask whether the first, ordinary use impairs solving the problem. Duncker (1945) used this procedure with several different objects and problems and did indeed find impairment of solutions. Transfer of fixedness occurs only in one direction; that is, prior use of an object in an unusual way has no effect on then using it in its ordinary function (van de Geer 1957). Also, the effect fades over time (Adamson and Taylor 1954). Finally, the effect disappears if the first, ordinary use occurs in a context different from the problem context requiring an unusual use (Duncker 1945). It makes sense that the transfer effect would be limited. The first use serves to activate temporarily a particular meaning for the object; the activation diminishes with a change in context or the passage of time.

Perceptual fixedness appears to be a stronger effect. Presenting a problem with a critical object serving its usual function noticeably impairs using the object in an unusual way. For example, the box-candle problem requires tacking a small box to a wall or door as a platform for a candle. If the box is empty when problem materials are presented, the problem is easy, but the problem proves quite difficult when the box is filled with the tacks (Glucksberg and Weisberg 1966). Duncker (1945) studied both perceptual fixedness and transfer of fixedness, finding greater impairment in the perceptual fixedness cases. The two cases differ in multiple ways, all of which might plausibly affect difficulty. With perceptual fixedness, (1) the usual function exists in the problem situation and will persist unless some action is taken, (2) the usual function exists independent of the person's activity (e.g., boxes contain, corks stop up bottles, without one doing anything at the current time), and (3) the critical object is typically part of a larger perceptual-functional complex.

It is not clear whether the effect occurs at the functional or attentional level. That is, does the presence of the ordinary function prevent thinking of an unusual use for the object, or does the problem solver fail to notice the object when it serves its ordinary role as part of a meaningful complex? The basis of the effect is functional, in that the object must serve a meaningful, ordinary function for impairment to occur; for example, having a string hold up an old piece of cardboard does not retard using the string to solve a problem (Scheerer 1963). Yet drawing the problem solver's attention to the object with perceptual cues (e.g., labeling the object) eliminates the effect (Duncker 1945;

Glucksberg and Weisberg 1966). These findings, together with problem solvers' comments, support the idea of an attentional effect.

The matter is complicated by a related finding (Maier and Janzen 1968). The two-string problem was used, with variation in the objects made available. No perceptual manipulation was involved; in the simplest case, a single object lay on a table. The focus was on the functional values of the objects and how these are related to use of the objects in the problem. To illustrate, both an ordinary ruler and a bar of soap are suitable as weights needed for the pendulum solution. A ruler's major function is measurement and line drawing, but it is also commonly used to extend one's reach and hook an object in order to retrieve it. In the problem, the ruler was too short to be used successfully in this way. The soap's usual function, washing, is irrelevant to the problem setting. Compared to the ruler's being the only object available, there were more pendulum solutions, produced more quickly, when the soap alone was available. Surely the problem solvers noticed the object in this setting, so the implication is that the existence of a contextually relevant, competing function impairs thinking of an unusual use for an object.

Functional encoding and attentional deficiencies are not incompatible and can both contribute to fixedness. Object-use problems are modest in scope, but they nonetheless illustrate how overcoming initial interpretations can be critical to problem solving. In particular, perceptual fixedness is a special case of a more general phenomenon: that solutions are blocked by the initial structure of the problem situation.

Inappropriate Organization
A fundamental fact about problem solving is that performance is affected by the way in which a problem is presented. The implication is that a problem solver's representation of a problem is strongly determined by the initial structure of the situation. This influence is not intrinsically harmful. The prompted representation might be correct, with the problem concerning how to proceed within that problem space. There are two ways in which the initial presentation might impair problem solving, and these must be distinguished. First, there might be induced a representation that allows the solution to be achieved but that makes doing so difficult because of high strain on short-term memory, inference making, or record keeping (Schwartz 1971; Simon and Hayes 1976). Second, the first representation might make solving impossible, so that a change in interpretation is necessary for solution. This circumstance characterizes insight problems.

To impair problem solving, the initial problem situation must be organized but wrongly structured. To the extent that the initial situation is disorganized, it serves as a baseline against which to compare different types of organization. As noted in the discussion of perceptual fixedness, the box-candle problem is quite easy when the problem materials are presented in an unorganized fashion, scattered on the table. But when the box contains tacks, providing a meaningful but inappropriate perceptual organization, the problem proves difficult. Comparable manipulations have been employed with anagram (scrambled-word) problems. The anagram letter string must be rearranged to spell a word, so the initial ordering is always wrong. It may vary in its organization, however, and more structured anagrams are more difficult to solve. For example, anagrams that are easier to pronounce, because they conform more to the structural rules for English words, are more difficult to solve. Compare *lurof* to *rlfuo*; the former is easier to pronounce, and such anagrams are generally harder to solve (either can be rearranged to make *flour*). In addition, practice at pronouncing letter strings, which makes them easier to pronounce, makes them harder to solve when presented as anagram problems (Dominowski 1969). As a special case of this effect, anagrams that are themselves words (e.g., given *night*, find *thing*) are more difficult than nonword anagrams (Ekstrand and Dominowski 1968; Fink and Dominowski 1974). Note that there is no task requirement to attend to the pronounceability or meaning of the anagram string; indeed, one would be better off ignoring such features. The implication is that the cuing aspects of the problem presentation in conjunction with the knowledge base of the problem solver lead to automatic encoding of selected features of the situation.

There is a considerable variety of problems that elicit interpretations that will prevent solution. One such problem is that nine-dot problem (figure 4.1). The Gestalt analysis (Scheerer 1963) was that the dots would be seen as forming a square with line-drawing attempts then restricted to the area of the square; this approach cannot lead to solution. Empirically, most solution attempts are confined to the area of the square, and this problem is quite difficult for college students (Lung and Dominowski 1985). To solve this problem, one must change from a representation of drawing lines inside the square to a representation of extending and intersecting lines outside the are of the dots. It has sometimes been argued (Weisberg and Alba 1981) that the concept of insight (restructuring) requires that extending lines must lead immediately and inevitably to solving the problem. This argument is misleading. A task analysis of the nine-dot problem clearly shows that changing one's representation (from inside to outside the

Figure 4.1
The nine-dot problem. Connect all dots by drawing four straight lines without lifting the pencil from the paper or retracing any line.

dots) is not all that must be done to solve the problem. Given that one extends lines, it remains necessary to find the right lines to draw, in the right order, to complete the solution. Empirically, extending lines leads to solution about two-thirds of the time (Lung and Dominowski 1985). Extending lines is just part of the complete solution; this fact in no way diminishes the importance of the necessity of changing one's representation of the problem or of any phenomena associated with the change (Ohlsson 1992).

Box 4.1 contains several insight problems that have multiple differences though each, in some sense, tends to elicit an initial interpretation that prevents solution. Problem A typically leads to a variety of attempts to calculate an answer, whereas the precise question, "Which will be closer when they meet?" requires no computation as the two bikes must be equidistant from any point when they meet. The first reading of problem B seems to make a solution impossible; only when one realizes that *married* has two possible meanings and that the *man* could be a minister does a solution appear. Problem C usually elicits the incorrect answer, no, and resists solution as long as the problem solver interprets *4th of July* as a holiday; reinterpreting the phrase as simply a date leads directly to the correct answer, yes.

Problem D tends to yield *30 days* as a wrong answer. This problem, in contrast to those such as the bicycle problem, does require calculation in some sense. Problems like this one might not be well captured by the definition of insight problems proposed here—that they require a change in representation. Given tasks like problem D, people tend to calculate an answer, which in a broad sense is appropriate; they choose a wrong format for calculating. These tasks do, however, meet other proposed criteria for insight problems: they are likely to produce an impasse (Schooler, Ohlsson, and Brooks 1993), and the initial re-

Box 4.1
Examples of insight problems

A. Al starts biking at the beginning of Shoreline Road and continues north toward Gull Beach, averaging 5 miles per hour. An hour later, Dave starts biking at the same place and heads north on the same route, averaging 10 miles per hour. It is 25 miles from the beginning of Shoreline Road to Gull Beach. Which bike is nearer to Gull Beach when they meet?

B. A man who lived in a small town in the United States married twenty different women of the same town. All are still living, and he never divorced any of them. In this town, polygamy is unlawful, yet he has broken no law. How could this be?

C. Calendars made in England do not show Lincoln's birthday, of course. Do these calendars show the 4th of July? Explain your answer.

D. Water lilies double in area every 24 hours. At the beginning of the summer there is one water lily on the lake. It takes 60 days for the lake to become covered with water lilies. On what day is the lake halfway covered?

sponses fail to consider the full structure of the problem (Wertheimer 1945). For example, comparing the answer "30 days" to the problem information leads to the inference that the lake would be covered in 30 days, which is clearly inconsistent with the information given. Although such problems meet some proposed criteria for insight problems, they might represent a problem type with distinct properties.

Inadequate representations of insight problems seem to stem from relatively superficial processing of initial problem information; this characterization includes tasks like the water lilies problem. Inadequate representations can lead to either of two outcomes: a wrong answer or no answer. Producing any answer can effectively terminate problem solving, but failure to produce an answer ought to stimulate continued effort (until one simply gives up). Some problems allow solution attempts to be evaluated clearly (e.g., the nine-dot problem), but in other cases self-evaluation can be difficult if one has wrongly interpreted the problem (e.g., the 4th of July problem). Given that problems can encourage inadequate representations, what factors influence the degree of impairment? Are the obstacles minor or serious? Let us consider some alternatives.

Inadequate Monitoring
The initial organization of an insight problem will suggest an inappropriate representation. If that leads to an incorrect answer, perhaps all that is involved is a failure to check one's answer against all the problem information. The implication is that the error is minor, one

that could be readily corrected, if only the problem solver engaged in better monitoring. Dallob and Dominowski (1992) investigated this possibility using insight problems that are known to yield overt, incorrect answers (e.g., problems A, C, and D in box 4.1). They presented a number of such problems; when wrong answers were given, they told the problem solvers that their solutions were incorrect and asked them to provide another answer. If initial wrong answers were due merely to inadequate monitoring, then informing people of their answers' inadequacy should lead to rechecking of problem information, correction of the initial assumption, and production of the correct answer. In a number of instances, error feedback led to correct solutions—an additional 30 percent solutions for the bicycle and 4th of July problems. This suggests that some wrong answers result from superficial processing and weak monitoring, so that people find it easy to alter their answers when evaluations are provided for them. For some problems, however, error feedback was completely ineffective (e.g., for the water lilies problem), implying that more serious deficiencies are involved. Even when error feedback helped, the improvement was not universal; 40 percent of subjects failed to solve the bicycles problem after error feedback. The implication is again that more serious obstacles are involved.

In another study (Dallob and Dominowski 1993), the attempt was made to draw problem solvers' attention to the critical items in a problem statement. If wrong interpretations stem from superficial processing and if drawing attention to certain items will yield more careful processing, then highlighting critical terms should improve performance. Such manipulations involve the assumptions that one has identified the critical information and that highlighting that information will yield different processing. In some cases, highlighting information assumed to be critical did facilitate solutions (e.g., highlighting *when they meet* for the bicycle problem), yet a substantial number of failures persisted.

These results resemble the findings of Maier and Casselman (1970), who attempted to construct easier versions of a number of insight problems. In each case, they made an analysis of the likely source of difficulty (supported by observations of people attempting to solve the problems) and tried to find a way to reduce that obstacle. They used a more heterogeneous set of problems and modifications, and only in a few instances were they able to increase solution rates. With such manipulations, it is always possible that the key component has not been identified; alternatively, failures to solve might be based on more than inadequate attention or monitoring.

Fixation

In many circumstances, people exhibit fixation, persisting in an inappropriate representation of the situation for an extended period of time. Sometimes initial misrepresentations can readily be altered on the basis of error feedback; sometimes such feedback does not help. For some problems, people make repeated attempts within the same interpretation (all lines within the square in the nine-dot problem), failing repeatedly. For other problems, people do very little, apparently stymied.

Why is there such persistence in pursuing wrong approaches to a problem? Why don't people change to a different approach? One possible reason is that they lack some knowledge required for solution. Researchers regularly assume that no knowledge gap exists because of the ordinary nature of solutions to insight problems. At least one researcher has checked this assumption. P. I. Dallob (personal communication, July 7, 1993), using problems like those in box 4.1, found that when people gave a wrong answer after error feedback, telling them that their second answers were wrong and asking for a third answer did not help. Indeed, most failures to solve after one or two cycles of error feedback were either failures to respond or nonsensical answers apparently given to avoid saying nothing (Dallob and Dominowski 1992). To assess unsuccessful solvers' relevant knowledge, she gave them a series of aids to see if they could generate the solutions with some help. In virtually all cases, subjects demonstrated that they had the knowledge needed to comprehend the solution. The reason for failure lies elsewhere.

To account for fixation, Weisberg and Alba (1981) proposed that the problem space generated by the initial representation might be so large that people are unable to explore it completely in the time they are allowed. If so, they would neither change to a different approach nor solve the problem (because the first problem space is inappropriate). There is, however, no support for this proposal. Unsuccessful solvers have been found to switch approaches, quit, or repeat old wrong attempts (if they are required to keep responding) long before they have exhausted all possibilities in their first problem space.

Burke (1970) suggested that persistence in a wrong approach will be directly related to the approach's nearness to success. He observed attempts to solve the hat rack problem, in which people are asked to build a structure, sufficiently stable to hold a man's overcoat, at a specified point in the room. They were given two sticks 1 inch by 1 inch, each 4 to 5 feet long, and a C clamp to work with; an overcoat was available for testing constructions. The solution to this problem involves clamping the two sticks together so they can be wedged between the floor and ceiling, with the clamp also serving as the coat hook. Burke, however, was interested in incorrect approaches, which include balance attempts—leaning the two sticks against each other (e.g., in a slightly distorted X shape) and joining them with the clamp—and base attempts—with one stick lying on the floor with the other vertical (an inverted T shape) and the clamp joining them at floor level. Base structures are not stable enough to work, but they are far more stable than balance structures and thus nearer to success. Burke found that people trying balance structures tended to abandon them in less than 5 minutes, whereas almost half of the subjects trying base solutions persisted with them for more than 10 minutes. The near-success principle could account for some prolonged wrong approaches, but it can apply only when solvers are actively trying alternatives. Fixation accompanied by no response or repetition of old responses that have failed requires another concept.

Consider the idea that the existence of the initial representation blocks the formation of a second representation. Perhaps the basis of fixation lies in the nature of encoding processes. As noted by Ohlsson (1992), at any time we are ordinarily aware of only one interpretation of the information presented to us, and the process of forming a representation occurs automatically and implicitly (Scheerer 1963). Context effects are powerful influences on interpretation. In the case of insight problems, the initial problem information is structured to encourage a particular (and wrong) interpretation. The problem solver reaches an initial representation with ease and without awareness of how that representation was formed.

Consider an alternative case. Suppose one has deliberately constructed a representation of a problem (as does occur with some tasks; see, e.g., Schwartz 1971). Presumably because the person knows how the representation was built up, the process could be unpacked and modified, if doing so were desired. But if the representation was formed on a largely implicit basis, what does one do? To what extent can deliberate activity modify an implicitly formed interpretation? What kinds of actions will be effective? In everyday life, people perceive and interpret scenes, actions, all sorts of events automatically, taking things as they present themselves. If there are heuristics that can be used to modify representations, perhaps many people are unaware of them and are thus more likely to be stuck with their first interpretation.

How Solutions Occur

The solution to an insight problem might occur in either of two circumstances: with or without an event external to the problem solver's precipitating a solution. The first circumstance is exemplified by the giving of hints, which we will briefly consider before turning to the more complex case of unaided solutions.

Effects of Hints

A hint is some piece of information provided to a problem solver during work on a problem. Ordinarily, a hint is relevant to the problem and is provided with the intention of assisting solutions (although misleading hints are possible). It is a new element in the situation; its effect on behavior depends on its relation to the problem solver's ongoing activity and its relation to alternative solution approaches.

Burke, Maier, and Hoffman (1966) provided a good example of the effects of hints on solving insight problems. They employed the hat rack problem and compared two hints: a clamp hint, stating that in the solution the coat hangs on the clamp, and the ceiling hint, stating that the ceiling is part of the construction in the solution. Among their findings, they noted that a hint changes behavior only when it is inconsistent with the ongoing approach; for example, the clamp hint does not lead to abandoning balance solutions. The ceiling hint leads to much faster solutions because it is inconsistent with more incorrect approaches than is the clamp hint (which often first produced changes from base to balance attempts).

These researchers also studied the timing of hints, based on the idea that a hint given after the person has adopted a problem representation might have less impact than one given at the outset, when it is part of the information used in creating the initial representation. They obtained results supporting this idea, but subsequent research, although replicating the overall effects of hints, did not confirm any consistent effect of the timing of hints (Dominowski and Jenrick 1972; Maier and Burke 1967).

A hint, or any other new element introduced into the problem situation, might trigger a new problem representation. The new interpretation might lead to a solution, quickly or slowly, or it too might be inappropriate. In any case, the source of the change is known. But how do problem solvers change representations on their own?

Changing Representations: Heuristics and Spreading Activation

Kohler (1969) offered the following comments about solving insight problems without outside help: "In the solution of a problem, I said, we suddenly become aware of new relations, but these new relations appear only after we have mentally changed, amplified, or restructured the given material. . . . For the most part, we do not produce such sudden structurings intentionally, but rather find ourselves suddenly confronted with their emergence" (pp. 153–154). He concluded that some brain processes must assume new forms that are the basis of our seeing new relations. Although he attributed the critical events to brain processes outside of awareness, he did insist that restructurings would occur only after the problem material had been thoroughly examined. Duncker (1945) described a number of heuristic methods that he considered to be critical to restructuring and solution, including analysis of the problem material, of the goal, and of the conflict present in the situation. In his view, reformulations of a problem were mediated by general heuristic methods. Duncker seems to assign greater importance to deliberate use of analytical methods as a means of producing new representations, compared to Kohler's view.

Recently, considerable attention has been given to *spreading activation* as the process underlying insightful solutions. In Ohlsson's (1992) theory of insight, the initial representation of a problem includes the problem situation, or givens, and the solution criterion, or goal. The representation serves as a memory probe; activation spreads from the knowledge structures encoding the situation and goal to related knowledge structures. Activation weakens over time and is shared among the links over which it spreads. The spread of activation is an unconscious, automatic process. Recall that, in Ohlsson's theory, the formation of a representation is also an implicit process.

If the initial representation does not activate the knowledge needed for solution, the problem solver will eventually reach an impasse. What to do? Ohlsson states, "We cannot exert volitional control over the spread of activation. . . . The only way to change the pattern of activation is to change the source nodes from which it is spreading" (p. 12). In short, a new representation must be generated. Ohlsson describes three mechanisms that could yield restructuring. *Elaboration* enriches a representation, adding information either by noticing previously ignored aspects of the situation or recalling facts from long-term memory. *Reencoding* involves rejecting one or more aspects of a representation and then creating a new and possibly incompatible interpretation (e.g., changing from encoding the box as a container to seeing it as a platform, in the box-candle problem). The third mechanism, *constraint relaxation*, operates on the goal representation, dropping a constraining assumption (e.g., that lines must stay within the dots in the nine-dot problem). The new representation allows new operators to be activated, possibly leading to a solution.

Ohlsson makes several additional points about restructuring. Because both forming representations and spreading activation occur outside consciousness, a problem solver cannot directly control them. In addition, the person will have difficulty verbalizing what is hap-

pening. Although the restructuring mechanisms can result from deliberate efforts by the problem solver, there is no way to know in
advance which activities will be successful or which aspects of a representation should be altered. Thus, success might be difficult to
achieve, and the problem solver will be unable to anticipate a solution
(recall Metcalfe and Wiebe's 1987 findings on feelings of warmth).
Ohlsson views reaching an impasse as a simple consequence of working on novel problems, something that will happen, or not happen,
in an unpredictable fashion. He does not consider the occurrence of
impasses to be related to problem-solving skills. With respect to overcoming impasses, he does not appear to be optimistic.

Schooler, Ohlsson, and Brooks (1993), employing this theoretical
approach in studying the effects of verbalization on insight problem
solving, found that thinking aloud during problem solving reduced
solutions to insight problems but had no effect on solving noninsight
problems. Their explanation of this finding was that verbalizing disrupted representation formation and spreading activation, processes
that are critical to solving insight problems, occur outside awareness
and are nonreportable. In contrast, verbalizing about solving noninsight problems should not be disruptive because solutions to these
problems do not depend on nonverbalizable processes. The additional
finding, that subjects did not benefit from an instruction to try an
alternative approach if they felt they were stuck, was taken as further
support for the idea that the crucial processes in solving insight problems are automatic and not under volitional control. There is little
opportunity left for deliberate activity by the problem solver to play a
role.

Before presenting some positive information about the role of heuristics, I will offer some comments about the emphasis on automatic
processing and spreading activation. It is assumed that activation
spreads from the nodes in the problem representation to related
knowledge structures. In the case of insight problems including critical
words having multiple meanings (e.g., *married* in the minister problem), why doesn't activation spread to the multiple meanings when
the word is encoded? Surely the several meanings of a word are related
knowledge structures, as are the features of objects that might be
relevant to different functions. Regarding the effects of verbalization,
it is not clear how verbalization could directly affect spreading activation, a process assumed to be automatic and outside awareness.
Once underway, activation presumably would continue to spread. A
more plausible alternative is that verbalization is likely to redirect the
person's attention to readily verbalizable content (as noted by
Schooler, Ohlsson, and Brooks 1993), changing the input to represen-

tational processes. The representational processes themselves would not be changed. Finally, although much attention has been given to spreading activation, the concept might not be doing much theoretical work. In Ohlsson's (1992) theory, spreading activation follows restructuring; the issue remains how restructuring takes place.

What about heuristic processes—deliberate activities by the problem solver that might facilitate restructuring? Duncker (1945) emphasized heuristic processes and gave examples of their use gleaned from subjects' protocols. Recently, Kaplan and Simon (1990) studied the attainment of insight with the mutilated checkerboard problem. Imagine an 8 by 8 checkerboard from which two diagonally opposite corner squares have been removed, and imagine placing dominoes on the board so that each domino covers two vertically or horizontally (but not diagonally) adjacent squares. The problem is to show how one can cover the board with 31 dominoes or to prove that it cannot be done. The task can be done with pencil and paper. Typically, initial attempts involve drawing in dominoes in various patterns, trying to find an arrangement that will work. In fact, the task is impossible. The simplest explanation is that, with alternate squares colored differently (black and white), diagonally opposite squares will be the same color, and each domino will cover one square of each color. Removing diagonally opposite squares will leave 32 squares of one color and 30 of the other color. After covering 30 black-white pairs of squares with 30 dominoes, the remaining task is to cover two squares of the same color with one domino. It cannot be done. Initially subjects focus on the numbers of squares and dominoes, whereas the solution requires changing to a representation that reflects the alternation of squares of two types (black and white).

The important aspects of Kaplan and Simon's results are that they had people think aloud while working on the problem, the protocols yielded a wealth of information about what problem solvers were doing, and fast and slow solvers were found to differ in their use of heuristics. Fast subjects noticed more aspects of the problem situation and a greater variety of invariant features. They focused more on perceptual invariants—for example, that squares are of two types, that each domino covers one square of each type, and that diagonally opposite squares are of the same type. These findings imply that heuristic processes play a key role in arriving at a better representation and solving the problem. There are many differences between the situations and methods used by Kaplan and Simon and by Schooler, Ohlsson, and Brooks, precluding meaningful comparison. The circumstances under which heuristic processes do or do not contribute to restructuring have yet to be identified.

Learning to Solve Insight Problems

Can people become better able to overcome poor representations and find solutions to insight problems? The issue is not whether one can be taught to solve any particular problem but whether some skill might be developed that would enable greater success on a range of problems. The nature of insight problems presents a dilemma for skill development. The usual path to expertise is through extensive training in a domain, acquiring domain-specific procedures to produce solutions to problems readily that have, in fact, become familiar (Anderson 1987). But insight problems contain an element of novelty, have varying content, and can present different obstacles; such features imply that improvement will be difficult.

In Ohlsson's (1992) view, impasses will occur when working on insight problems, but unpredictably. The processes leading to restructuring and solution are automatic and subject to little control by the problem solver. The chances that some beneficial skill might be acquired seem poor. This view is similar in tone to the disappointed conclusions reached by earlier researchers who were unable to facilitate or predict performance on insight problems (Burke and Maier 1965; Duncan 1961). There have been some positive results, however.

One issue is whether performance on insight problems is related to any problem-solving abilities. Jacobs and Dominowski (1981) found that success on a collection of object-use insight problems was correlated with scores on the Gestalt Transformations Test, which requires the person to select objects having parts that can be used to satisfy stated requirements (e.g., that a bicycle has a useful part if one needs a hose). Dallob and Dominowski (1993) found that success on a set of insight problems like those in box 4.1 was correlated with scores on both the Gestalt Transformations Test and the Remote Associates Test. Items on the latter test require that a fourth word be generated that is associated with each of three presented words (e.g., given *blue*, *rat*, and *cottage*, produce *cheese*). These findings suggest that at least some more general abilities are involved in solving insight problems, thus providing a possible basis for skill development.

A more direct issue is whether people show any improvement in solving insight problems. Lung and Dominowski (1985) found greater success on the nine-dot problem following practice on other dot-connecting problems requiring lines to be extended beyond the dots, especially when instructions to follow a line-extending strategy were included. Jacobs and Dominowski (1981) noted improved performance over a series of object-use insight problems (each problem involving a different critical object and different novel use). Wicker and associates (1978) assessed performance on a mixed set of insight problems, finding that practice on other insight problems combined with reformulation training led to the greatest success in transfer. In reformulation training, subjects were shown the solution for each practice problem and the false assumption to be overcome, and they were encouraged to work continually on reformulating their views of the problems to be sure that they were not defining the problem too narrowly or making an unnecessary assumption. This treatment was much stronger than the brief instruction that Schooler, Ohlsson, and Brooks (1993) found to be unhelpful.

These studies indicate that people can improve performance on insight problems. In each case, the improvement was modest in amount or in scope, but the training effort was also modest. These efforts lend some support to a focus on heuristics in trying to increase insightful behavior. More comprehensive, heuristic-based training schemes could be implemented and evaluated; their success would clarify the role of heuristics in achieving insightful solutions, as well as provide an estimate of the degree to which productive thinking can be nurtured.

References

Adamson, R. E., and Taylor, D. W. (1954). Functional fixedness as related to elapsed time and to set. *Journal of Experimental Psychology, 47,* 122–126.

Anderson, J. R. (1987). Skill acquisition: Compilation of weak-method problem solutions. *Psychological Review, 94,* 192–210.

Anderson, J. R. (1993). Problem solving and learning. *American Psychologist, 48,* 35–44.

Bransford, J. D., Sherwood, R. D., and Sturdevant, T. (1987). Teaching thinking and problem solving. In J. B. Baron and R. J. Sternberg (eds.), *Teaching thinking skills: Theory and practice.* New York: W. H. Freeman.

Burke, R. J. (1970). Nearsuccess and solution persistence in individual problem solving. *Journal of General Psychology, 82,* 133–138.

Burke, R. J., and Maier, N. R. F. (1965). Attempts to predict success on an insight problem. *Psychological Reports, 17,* 303–310.

Burke, R. J., Maier, N. R. F., and Hoffman, J. R. (1966). Functions of hints in individual problem-solving. *American Journal of Psychology, 79,* 389–399.

Collins, A., Warnock, E. H., Aiello, N., and Miller, M. L. (1975). Reasoning from incomplete knowledge. In D. G. Bobrow and A. M. Collins (eds.), *Representation and understanding.* New York: Academic Press.

Dallob, P. I., and Dominowski, R. L. (1992). *Erroneous solutions to verbal insight problems: Fixation or insufficient monitoring?* Paper presented at the meeting of the Western Psychological Association, Portland, Oregon, April.

Dallob, P. I., and Dominowski, R. L. (1993). *Erroneous solutions to verbal insight problems: Effects of highlighting critical material.* Paper presented at the meeting of the Western Psychological Association, April.

Dominowski, R. L. (1969). The effect of pronunciation practice on anagram difficulty. *Psychonomic Science, 16,* 99–100.

Dominowski, R. L., and Jenrick, R. (1972). Effects of hints and interpolated activity on solution of an insight problem. *Psychonomic Science, 26,* 335–338.

Duncan, C. P. (1961). Attempts to influence performance on an insight problem. *Psychological Reports, 9,* 35–42.

Duncker, K. (1945). On problem-solving. *Psychological Monographs, 58* (Whole No. 270).

Ekstrand, B. R., and Dominowski, R. L. (1968). Solving words as anagrams: II. A clarification. *Journal of Experimental Psychology, 77,* 552–558.

Fink, R. S., and Dominowski, R. L. (1974). Pronounceability as an explanation of the difference between word and nonsense anagrams. *Journal of Experimental Psychology, 102,* 159–160.

Gilhooly, K. J., and Green, A. J. K. (1989). Learning problem-solving skills. In A. M. Colley and J. R. Beech (eds.), *Acquisition and performance of cognitive skills.* Chichester, UK: Wiley.

Glucksberg, S., and Weisberg, R. (1966). Verbal behavior and problem solving: Some effects of labeling in a functional fixedness problem. *Journal of Experimental Psychology, 71,* 659–664.

Greeno, J. G., Magone, M. E., and Chaiklin, S. (1979). Theory of constructions and set in problem solving. *Memory and Cognition, 7,* 445–461.

Jacobs, M. K., and Dominowski, R. L. (1981). Learning to solve insight problems. *Bulletin of the Psychonomic Society, 17,* 171–174.

Kaplan, C. A., and Simon, H. A. (1990). In search of insight. *Cognitive Psychology, 22,* 374–419.

Keane, M. (1989). Modelling problem solving in Gestalt "insight" problems. *Irish Journal of Psychology, 10,* 201–215.

Kohler, W. (1969). *The task of Gestalt psychology.* Princeton, NJ: Princeton University Press.

Kohler, W. (1976). *The Mentality of apes.* New York: Liveright. (Originally published 1925).

Lung, C. T., and Dominowski, R. L. (1985). Effects of strategy instructions and practice on nine-dot problem solving. *Journal of Experimental Psychology: Learning, Memory, and Cognition, 11,* 804–811.

Maier, N. R. F. (1940). The behavior mechanisms concerned with problem solving. *Psychological Review, 47,* 43–53.

Maier, N. R. F., and Burke, R. J. (1967). Influence of timing of hints on their effectiveness. *Psychological Reports, 20,* 3–8.

Maier, N. R. F., and Casselman, G. C. (1970). Locating the difficulty in insight problems: Individual and sex differences. *Psychological Reports, 26,* 103–117.

Maier, N. R. F., and Janzen, J. C. (1968). Functional values as aids and distractors in problem solving. *Psychological Reports, 22,* 1021–1034.

Metcalfe, J., and Wiebe, D. (1987). Intuition in insight and noninsight problem solving. *Memory and Cognition, 15,* 238–246.

Ohlsson, S. (1992). Information-processing explanations of insight and related phenomena. In M. T. Keane and K. J. Gilhooly (eds.), *Advances in the psychology of thinking* (Vol. 1). London: Harvester-Wheatsheaf.

Perkins, D. N. (1981). *The mind's best work.* Cambridge, MA: Harvard University Press.

Perkins, D. N. (1990). The nature and nurture of creativity. In B. F. Jones and L. Idol (eds.), *Dimensions of thinking and cognitive instruction.* Hillsdale, NJ: Erlbaum.

Scheerer, M. (1963). Problem-solving. *Scientific American, 208,* 118–128.

Schooler, J. W., Ohlsson, S., and Brooks, K. (1993). Thoughts beyond words: When language overshadows insight. *Journal of Experimental Psychology: General, 122,* 166–183.

Schwartz, S. H. (1971). Modes of representation and problem solving: Well evolved is half solved. *Journal of Experimental Psychology, 91,* 347–350.

Simon, H. A., and Hayes, J. R. (1976). The understanding process: Problem isomorphs. *Cognitive Psychology, 8,* 165–190.

Sternberg, R. J., and Lubart, T. I. (1992). Buy low and sell high: An investment approach to creativity. *Current Directions in Psychological Science, 1,* 1–5.

van de Geer, J. P. (1957). *A psychological study of problem solving.* Haarlem: Uitgeverig De Toorts.

Weisberg, R. W. (1992). Metacognition and insight during problem solving: Comment on Metcalfe. *Journal of Experimental Psychology: Learning, Memory, and Cognition, 18,* 426–431.

Weisberg, R. W., and Alba, J. W. (1981). An examination of the alleged role of "fixation" in the solution of several "insight" problems. *Journal of Experimental Psychology: General, 110,* 169–192.

Wertheimer, M. (1982). *Productive thinking.* Chicago: University of Chicago Press. (Originally published 1945).

Wicker, F. W., Weinstein, C. F., Yelich, C. A., and Brooks, J. D. (1978). Problem-reformulation training and visualization training with insight problems. *Journal of Educational Psychology, 70,* 372–377.

Chapter 5

The Ineffability of Insight

Jonathan W. Schooler and Joseph Melcher

Language can become a screen that stands between the thinker and reality.
That is the reason why true creativity often starts where language ends.
Arthur Koestler, *The Act of Creation.*

We often cannot say from where a creative idea came. Such insights can seem to pop into mind, as if from nowhere. This ineffable quality of creativity has frequently elicited mystical views. The ancient Greeks believed that creativity occurred only by the grace of the muses, and to this day many people attribute their creative inspiration to religious or mystical sources. Scientific reactions to the phenomenologically elusive character of creativity have taken two general forms. Many theorists developed approaches to creativity that rely heavily on unconscious processes (Koestler 1964; Simonton 1988). Others attempted to dismiss the elusiveness of creativity altogether and suggested that creative processes are fully accessible and not qualitatively different from other forms of reasoning (Perkins 1981; Weisberg 1986). Researchers who dismiss the importance of the nonreportable aspects of creativity seem to feel that accepting such processes promotes the enigma of creativity and interferes with the successful investigation of the basic cognitive processes on which creativity must be based (Weisberg 1986).

Far from closing the door on creativity, the hypothesis that creativity involves nonreportable processes leads to a number of fruitful research pursuits. First, the nonreportability of creative processes suggests a rather intriguing hypothesis about the possible effects of language on creativity: if certain creative processes cannot be adequately captured in words, then attempting to articulate such processes may actually be disruptive. In fact, recently Schooler, Ohlsson, and Brooks (1993) have produced evidence supporting this claim. Second, although the suggestion that some creative processes cannot be articulated necessarily constrains the informativeness of self-reports, it does not eliminate their value. Comparing self-reports of tasks that vary in their hypothesized use of creative nonreportable components may be helpful specifically because they can help to reveal what is absent from the self-reports of creative processes. Finally, the suggestion that creative processes cannot be fully articulated does not imply that they must remain mysterious. Indeed, there are other nonreportable processes, such as those associated with perception and memory retrieval, that are accepted components of modern theories of cognition (e.g., pattern recognition, spreading activation). One way to examine the role of such processes is to use an individual differences approach to determine the correlation between performance on tasks requiring creativity and tasks involving the nonreportable processes hypothesized to be associated with creativity. Using these approaches, we can begin to confront the enigma of creativity scientifically without denying its phenomenological ineffability.

In our view, many discussions of creativity have been hampered not only because their subject matter is so elusive but also because the domain of creativity is conceived so broadly. Virtually any thought activity can in principle involve components that could be described as creative. Discovering an important new mathematical theorem certainly requires creativity, but so may figuring out where you left your keys this morning. It seems clear that the processes that contribute to these two examples of creativity differ markedly. Rather than considering the entire spectrum of creative processes, we focus on one of its components, insight, defined as the sudden solution to a problem that one has been working on without any sense of progress. The relationship between insight and creativity has been of some contention. Some argue that insight is the central component of creativity (Taylor 1988), while others suggest that it has no importance (Weisberg 1986). However, as Tardif and Sternberg (1988) note, "The majority view falls somewhere in between with 'flashes of insight' discussed as a small but necessary component of the creative process" (p. 430). If insight represents only a small portion of the full creative process, it nevertheless constitutes one of the major sources of ineffability with which discussions of creativity have grappled. Thus, if we want to explore the unreportable aspects of creativity, it makes sense to begin with insight.

Theoretical Characterizations of Insight

Over the years, there have been many records of individuals' experiencing sudden and profound realizations about problems for which they perceived themselves to be at an impasse. Readers familiar with the creativity literature have probably read (ad nauseam) tales of Archimedes sitting down in his bath and suddenly realizing water displacement as a technique for measuring the volume of the king's crown and Poincaré stepping on a bus and abruptly recognizing the relationship between Fuchian functions and non-Euclidian geometry.

To add a fresh anecdote to the list, a front-page article in the *New York Times* on February 18, 1993, reported a medical student's (Yung Kang Chow) account of how he came to invent a technique that appears to be the first successful method for eliminating the AIDS virus from human cells in the test tube and also preventing the infection of healthy cells. Chow challenged the medical dogma that the treatment value of combining drugs is due to the fact that each drug attacks the disease at a different stage in the life cycle. His insight was that multiple drugs might work together at a single stage of the virus's life cycle.[1] This insight occurred to him as he reflected on his adviser's query about why patients could develop a resistance to each of two drugs and yet still benefit from their combination. Chow conveys the exhilarating surprise he experienced when he suddenly realized the misdirection of medical dogma and the implications of his alternative perspective: "I was reading during dinner, which is a bad thing to do . . . but I had to because I had so much to do that evening. I was thinking of ways to explain the phenomenon, and the idea just came to me in an instant. It was an inspiration, almost like 'Eureka', I was ecstatic jumping up and down and telling my wife that I think this was the most exciting thing I ever came up with because right away I realized the implications of the work."

This example has many of the classic qualities of insight discoveries. First, an impasse in solving the problem is produced because of the existence of unwarranted assumptions. A second quality, not necessary for insight solutions but often postulated to be helpful, is that the solver has sufficient but not excessive experience with the problem, thereby being less entrenched in the unwarranted assumption (Ellen 1982; Luchins 1942). Chow speculated, "Perhaps by virtue of being a graduate student and not having learned much medicine yet, I had much more naive insight into the problem." Finally, the solution appeared suddenly with no warning, instantly transforming Chow from worriedly eating his dinner to jumping up and down ecstatically. The suddenness of anecdotal insights may in some cases be exaggerated (Perkins 1981) but their persistent recurrence makes them difficult to dismiss. Moreover, researchers have also developed laboratory analogues of these discoveries using puzzle problems that elicit solutions possessing the same suddenness as that reported in the anecdotes of creative discoveries (Metcalfe and Wiebe 1987).

The suddenness of insight solutions has prompted many theorists to postulate a role of unconscious, and hence unreportable, processes. Accordingly, dismissing the possibility that the solutions truly come out of nowhere (as is often the phenomenological experience) means that the critical processes leading to insights are outside awareness. Many speculations regarding the nature of these unreportable processes were developed prior to the cognitive era of psychology and thus included terms and constructs that can seem rather imprecise to those steeped in the cognitive tradition. Indeed, the obscure quality of early approaches to insight may in part account for why some cognitive theorists have attempted to dismiss prior claims that insight relies on important nonreportable processes. Cognitive theorists who have considered the nonreportable aspects of insight as an issue worthy of explanation have sought to avoid the vagueness that plagued their predecessors by defining the issue using basic cognitive constructs. In so doing, these approaches have recast the valuable ideas of past approaches. Generally modern approaches have been largely successful in adopting the useful elements from past approaches. However, at least one useful idea from the past seems not to have made the cut: some insight processes, by virtue of their nonreportability, may actually be disrupted by language. We now turn to a brief review of past and current approaches to insight and then discuss our attempts to salvage this abandoned notion of the potential negative effects of language on insight.

Pre–Information Processing Approaches
Pre–information processing approaches to insight explored a number of overlapping elements of insight: the notions of restructuring, context-induced mental set, unconscious idea recombination, and the suggestion that more than merely inconsequential to insight, language, and logic might actually impair the insight process.

Restructuring   Gestalt theorists argued that insights often involve restructuring the problem in a manner similar to the classic perceptual figure-ground reversals (such as the Necker cube or the vase-face illusion) (for a review see Ohlsson 1984). Restructuring was conceived of as involving a global shift in one's perspective of the problem, such that the solver initially sees the problem one way but in an entirely different light the next moment. Drawing parallels between problem solving and perception, the Gestaltists further suggested that such restructurings or perspective shifts followed principles comparable to the notions of "good form" used to account for perceptual organization. The unsolved problem was seen as creating unacceptable gaps that the brain naturally tried to close by restructuring processes (Wertheimer 1959). Although the Gestalt tradition never adequately articulated the precise mechanisms by which restructuring occurred, they did note a number of conditions that they viewed as most likely to lead to restructuring. First, it was critical that the problem solver devote sufficient concentration to the problem to enable a holistic representation whereby the problematic gaps would emerge. Second, although effort was required to establish the perception of gaps that lead to restructuring, the actual restructuring process itself was believed to be passive and nonconscious, thus accounting for the surprise quality of the insight.

Context-Induced Mental Set   A related theme in historical treatments of insight that also emerged from the Gestalt tradition was the view that the context of a problem could fixate subjects into adhering to particular unwarranted assumptions, thereby preventing the consideration of alternative approaches. Duncker (1945) used the term *functional fixedness* to convey the idea that when people perceived objects in the context of their standard functions, they assumed the objects must be used in their usual manner. Fixedness thereby made individuals unable to consider an atypical application of the object, for example, using a tool as ballast for a pendulum in order to tie two strings together. Discussions of the mechanisms involved in producing the insight that can occur when subjects overcome such context-induced fixations often emphasized the importance of nonreportable components. For example, Maier (1931) asked subjects to report retrospectively their solutions to the two-string problem in which they had been given a seemingly accidental hint by the experimenter. Subjects who could report the stepwise construction of the solution also reported the hint and its effect on their problem solution, but subjects who reported the solution as having arrived in a flash of insight gave no evidence of being aware of the hint. Others, such as Koestler (1964), Poincaré (1952), and Wallas (1926), suggested that new approaches could result from an incubation period in which the subconscious searched for new combinations of ideas. It should be noted, however, that not all of the precognitive theorists claimed that putting a problem aside necessarily elicited complex, unconscious processes. Some suggested that a break simply facilitated the forgetting of inappropriate approaches (Woodworth 1938).

Unconscious Idea Recombination   A third component of a number of the original approaches to insight followed from anecdotal reports of important scientific and mathematical discoveries involving the sudden connection of diverse ideas. Such claims led theorists to speculate that the unconscious may combine and recombine previously unrelated ideas. Poincaré (cited by Koestler 1964) expressed this view using the analogy of ideas as atoms hooked to a wall, some of which become loosened when individuals initially think about a problem. During incubation, these loosened ideas become detached and recombine: "During a period of apparent rest and unconscious work certain of them are detached from the wall and put into motion. They flash in every direction through space . . . like the molecules of gas in the kinematic theory of gases. Then their mutual impacts may produce new combinations" (p. 165). Poincaré observed that such combinations typically would be of no value but occasionally would produce fruitful results whose aesthetic quality would be appreciated by the unconscious and therefore delivered to consciousness. Similar theories of unconscious idea recombination were proposed by Wallas (1926), Hadamard (1954), Koestler (1964), and others, all sharing the basic view that insight results from the sudden appearance in consciousness of ideas that had been recombined in the unconscious. These theories differed primarily with respect to the specific mechanisms of recombination and in particular the degree to which the unconscious was guided by intelligent versus random processes.

The Constraint of Language on Insight   The suggestion that insight does not rely on the language and logic that mediates conscious thought led some of the original insight theorists to speculate that these elements of consciousness might in fact impede insight. For example, Koestler (1964) suggested that language and logic served as "constraints which are necessary to maintain the discipline of routine thoughts but may become an impediment to the creative leap" (p. 169). With respect to language he further noted that "words are a blessing which can turn into a curse. They crystallize thought; they give articulation and precision to vague images and hazy intuitions. But a crystal is no longer fluid" (p. 173). Koestler argued that the price of language's ability to crystallize thought is that it can prevent distant connections. The remedy for this constraint of language is the unconscious, in which "more primitive levels of mental organization are brought into activity" (p. 169). According to Koestler, by ignoring the laws of logic and language that constrain conscious thought, the unconscious is capable of bringing together thoughts that would be too rigidly distinct to be connected consciously. Similar views regarding the constraints of language were also noted by others. For example, Hadamard (1954) vehemently asserted, "I insist that words are totally absent from my mind when I really think . . . and I fully agree with Schopenhauer when he writes, 'thoughts die the moment they are embodied in words'" (p. 75). While these authors' discussions of the nonlanguage-based process that leads to insights may seem imprecise in the context of modern information processing views, the basic premise that conscious thought, and in particular language, may restrict creative leaps represents a hypothesis of some merit. Nevertheless, perhaps because this view was often tied to some of the most fanciful discussions of insight (Koestler 1964) it was left out of many of the subsequent information processing views of insight.

Information Processing Views of Insight
The enigmatic unconscious processes that have historically been proposed to account for insight may have discouraged serious information processing theorists from tackling this sticky issue. In addition to its historical association with questionable theories of the unconscious, as Ohlsson (1993) observed, the construct of insight is also somewhat of a challenge to the information processing view that problem solving represents the stepwise implementation of symbol manipulation. In the light of these difficulties, a number of the initial information processing examinations of insight were conducted in an effort to dismiss all of its alleged elusive qualities. We briefly review these information processing repudiations of insight and then consider cognitive approaches that have taken a more sympathetic view of insight.

The Dismissal of Insight   Weisberg (1986) and Perkins (1981) provide forceful arguments for dismissing the view that insight is distinguished from other types of problem solving by its sudden appearance and reliance on nonreportable processes. Weisberg rejects the involvement of unreportable cognitive processes in creativity by challenging the anecdotal evidence on which the early claims of such processes were based. Drawing on evidence that providing subjects with hints to the solution to so-called insight problems does not bring about immediate success, he further denounces the suggestion that insight involves global and sudden shifts in perspectives and argues that insight problem solving encompasses the same incremental steps used in other types of problems. He concludes that "there seems to be very little reason to believe that solutions to novel problems come about in leaps of insight. At every step of the way, the process involves a small movement away from what is known" (p. 50).

Perkins (1981) shares Weisberg's skepticism that insight problem solving differs from other types of problem solving and further advocates the view that elements of insight problem solving are readily reportable. He based his conclusion in part on an analysis of subjects' retrospective reports of how they solved an insight puzzle problems (specifically problem C used in our studies, see box 5.1 later in this chapter). Perkins observed that whereas some subjects retrospectively reported leaplike experiences, the majority reported solving the problems in a more piecemeal, stepwise fashion. Because these verbal reports reflect subjects' underlying processes, Perkins further suggests, there should be no concern that language might interfere with the solving of so-called insight problems.

Reconceptualizing Insight Constructs Using Current Theories of Cognition
Although a number of information processing approaches have sought to dismiss insight as a distinct type of problem solving, other approaches manage to reconceptualize many of the earlier aspects of insight theorizing within a modern cognitive framework.

Restructuring. Current conceptualizations of problem restructuring focus on the notion that insight solutions may require shifting to a new problem space (Ohlsson 1984). In other words, the difficulty in many insight problems is to find a representation of the problem that enables it to be readily solved. Using protocol analysis for an extremely difficult insight problem (the mutilated checkerboard), Kaplan and Simon (1990) found evidence that subjects spent most of their time searching for an appropriate way to represent the problem. Once the correct representation was found, the solution followed quickly.

With respect to the mechanisms involved in restructuring, Kaplan and Simon suggest that the re-representation of problems involves a memory search for a new problem space comparable to that involved in searching within a problem space. Others, however, recovered the Gestalt view of the importance of perception. For example, Ellen (1982) suggests that the suddenness of insights makes them especially akin to figure-ground reversals in which "elements at one moment are seen as one unity, at the next moment, another unity appears with the same elements" (p. 324). Still others, such as Ohlsson, propose that either memory search or perceptual reencoding may be involved, depending on the problem.

Context-induced mental set. The notion that the context of a problem can cause subjects to adhere to false assumptions has also been incorporated into current cognitive conceptualizations of insight. In modern terms, fixedness is conceptualized as excessive activation of inappropriate operators—that is, the knowledge and actions that one attempts to use to solve the problem (Ohlsson 1993). From this perspective, one benefit of an incubation period is that it enables the activation to dampen, thereby increasing the likelihood that other, more useful operators will be accessed on subsequent attempts (Simon 1986; Smith and Vela 1991). Empirical support for this view was recently provided by Smith and Blankenship (1989) using a paradigm in which subjects were given insightlike problems with either helpful or misleading hints. Smith observed a benefit of incubation only for subjects who received the misleading hints, suggesting that the main benefit of the incubation period was to enable the decay of activation of the misleading hint.

Unconscious idea recombination. Even the suggestion that insight may entail unconscious search processes for new combinations has made its way into some of the current cognitive conceptualizations. In this case, unconscious search and combinations are viewed as consequences of spreading activation. Accordingly, activation of ideas during problem solving may spread to related concepts. With sufficient activation, critical operators may rise above the threshold of awareness and become available to solve the problem. Such unconscious spreading activation mechanisms have been incorporated into a number of theories of insight (Langley and Jones 1988; Ohlsson 1993; Yaniv and Meyer 1987) and have even received some empirical support. For example, Bowers and associates (1990) and Bowers (1991) looked at the attempted responses provided by subjects who were unable to generate the correct solution to "insight-like" problems such as recognizing distant semantic associates (e.g., What word relates to both *arsenic* and *shoe*?) and solving anagrams. Bowers observed that incorrect guesses often had some semantic relationship to the correct solution, indicating that solution-relevant information was being activated and implying that this subawareness activation may have contributed to the solving of the problem. Bowers and associates concluded, "The suddenness with which insights sometimes occur thus represents an abrupt awareness of a mental product or end state generated by more continuous, sub rosa cognitive processes" (p. 95).

Constraints of language. Although there is debate about the role of nonreportable processes in current conceptualizations of insight, nonreportable processes are centrally involved in a number of current theories. Moreover, even some of the theorists who reject the possibility of nonreportable search mechanisms acknowledge that nonreportable processes may play an important role in insight. As Simon (1966) observed, "The subconscious plays a major role in modern theories of motivation, emotion and psychopathology. There is no a priori reason, then, to assign the problem-solving process to the conscious rather than the unconscious" (p. 30). Despite current theorists' advancement of previous claims that insight may involve nonreportable processes, they generally have not taken their predecessors' further step of suggesting that language might actually interfere with insight. For example, Simon, one of the central architects of cognitive approaches to problem solving, acknowledges a role of subconscious processes in insight. Nevertheless, in other writings, he strongly asserts that verbal reports, when properly elicited, should not impair performance other than possibly slowing it down slightly (Ericsson and Simon 1984). As we shall see, current faith in the nonreactivity of language is open to question, which in turn reopens the door for earlier suggestions that language may disrupt insight.

Empirical Demonstrations of the Disruptive Effects of Language

Recently, we and others have been finding evidence that verbalization can interfere with a variety of tasks hypothesized to involve nonreportable processes.

A natural starting place for examining nonverbal thought is face recognition. As the philosopher Polanyi (1967) noted: "I shall reconsider human knowledge by starting from the fact that we can know more than we can tell. . . . Take an example. We know a person's face, and can recognize it among a thousand, indeed a million. Yet we usually cannot tell how we recognize a face. So most of this knowledge cannot be put into words" (p. 4). The clear nonreportability of much of the information involved in recognizing faces suggests that if verbalization can disrupt nonreportable processes, then face recognition is a sensible place to look for evidence for such verbal disruption. Consistent with this view, Schooler and Engstler-Schooler (1990) observed that verbalizing the appearance of a previously seen face markedly interfered with subjects' ability to recognize that face from an array of similar ones. Additional studies supported the interpretation that verbalization may emphasize verbalizable attributes of the stimulus while overshadowing the critical nonreportable information necessary for optimum performance. For example, visualization was found to have no negative effects on face recognition; however, verbalization was found to disrupt the recall of other nonreportable stimuli (color) while marginally improving performance on a readily reportable stimulus (a spoken statement). Similar disruptive effects of verbalization have been observed in a variety of other domains hypothesized to rely on nonreportable processes or information, including taste judgments (Wilson and Schooler 1991), aesthetic evaluations (Wilson et al. 1993), visual imagery (Brandimonte, Hitch, and Bishop 1992), and implicit learning (Fallshore and Schooler 1993). Of greatest relevance here are a recent series of studies examining the effects of verbalization on insight problem solving.

Schooler, Ohlsson, and Brooks (1993) compared the effects of concurrent, nondirected verbalization on subjects' ability to solve insight and noninsight problems. The insight problems were comparable to the "aha" type of problems used by other investigators of insight (see table 5.1). The noninsight problems were comparable to the logic problems used in the analytic section of the Graduate Record Examination and used by other researchers comparing insight to noninsight problems (Metcalfe and Wiebe 1987). (For ease of reference we will henceforth refer to these noninsight problems as analytic problems.) The main result of this series of studies was that concurrent verbalization markedly impaired insight problem solving while having no effect on the solving of analytic problems of comparable difficulty.

A number of possible interpretations of the disruptive effects of verbalization on insight were considered. For example, verbalization might consume processing resources that otherwise would have been available for the problem-solving effort (Russo et al. 1989). This explanation predicts that performance on noninsight problems of comparable difficulty should also be reduced by verbalization, a prediction that turned out to be unfounded. A related alternative explanation for the effect of concurrent verbalization is that it slows problem solving without qualitatively altering it. However, there was no difference between the solution times of insight problems in the verbalization and control conditions. A final possibility was that subjects, when thinking aloud, were reluctant to reveal to the experimenter that they perceived themselves to be on the wrong track and hence continued with the wrong approach in order to avoid the appearance of seeming inconsistent or scattered. To investigate this possibility, subjects in one of the experiments were given a hint that described the "mind-sets" associated with insight problems. These subjects were advised that some of the problems were of this nature and suggested that when they felt they were working on such problems they should try approaching the problem from a new perspective. Two minutes into each problem, the experimenter reminded them of this hint. Even with this strong encouragement to consider alternative approaches, the negative effect of concurrent verbalization was maintained, suggesting that subjects were not simply sticking with the inappropriate approach in order to follow the potential implicit demand to maintain a consistent approach to the problem.

In the absence of a compelling alternative explanation and in the light of the variety of other demonstrations that nonreportable processes can be vulnerable to verbalization, these findings were interpreted as being most compatible with the hypothesis, first suggested by the early insight theorists, that language can disrupt nonreportable processes that are critical to achieving insight solutions. It must be conceded, however, that this study did not report any direct evidence that insight problem solving involved nonreportable processes, other than the fact that the insight problems were uniquely susceptible to verbalization. Since the publication of this study, we have uncovered additional direct evidence supporting the suggestion that our subjects were more reliant on nonreportable processes when they solved insight as compared to analytic problems. This evidence emerged from careful examination of the contents of subjects' protocols.

A Comparison of Insight and Analytic Problem-Solving Protocols

Readers may wonder what we might expect to find in the protocols of subjects' solving insight problems if, as we claim, the processes leading to insight are truly nonreportable. Nevertheless, even if the processes associated with insight problem solving are nonreportable, we still may be able to see by-products of these processes in subjects' self-reports. More important, if protocols of insight problem solving differ from those associated with analytic problems with respect to the degree to which they provide information about the steps subjects used to reach their solutions, then this observation in itself would provide evidence that insight problems do not rely on the reportable processes associated with other types of problems.

Our specific predictions regarding differences between insight and analytic problem-solving protocols were based on some of the previously mentioned characterizations of the difference between these two types of problems. To recap, insight and analytic problem solving can be conceptualized as differing with respect to the degree to which their solutions rely on a stepwise set of logical arguments. According to this view, analytic problems entail a series of incremental arguments, each building on the previous one and leading ultimately to a solution. In contrast, insight problems elicit an initial impasse in which subjects are unaware of making any progress as they struggle simply to determine the right approach to tackle the problem. Ultimately, we hypothesize that nonreportable memory and perceptual processes provide a new view of the problem that leads to sudden solutions. This characterization makes some rather specific predictions about differences between the two sets of protocols. Analytic problems would be expected to involve greater use of logical arguments, the bricks and mortar on which solutions to these problems are built. Insight problem solving's greater reliance on nonreportable processes suggests that subjects should be more likely to pause while trying to solve insight as compared to analytic problems. Insight problems would also be expected to contain more metacognitions, reflecting subjects' struggle to find the right general approach for solving the problem.

In addition to differences in the overall frequency of different types of problem-solving components, our characterization also suggests predictions about the correspondence of protocol elements with actual performance. If, for example, the use of logical argumentation is critical for analytic but not insight problem solving, then argument usage should be relatively more predictive of success on analytic as compared to insight problems. Additionally, if the critical components to the solution of insight problems are nonreportable, then there should be little in the contents of subjects' reports that will predict their success. Indeed, the one attribute that might be predictive of success on insight problems is the frequency with which subjects stopped verbalizing and allowed the nonreportable process to proceed unhampered.

Method/Coding Scheme
In order to test these predictions, we transcribed the "think-aloud" protocols of the 40 verbalization subjects who participated in experiment 4 of Schooler, Ohlsson, and Brooks (1993).[2] The six problems that subjects attempted to solve (three insight and three analytic) are presented in box 5.1. Each transcript was exhaustively coded according to a set of categories whose development was guided by the literatures on protocol analysis (Chi 1992; Ericsson and Simon 1984; Ohlsson 1990), noninsight problem solving (Chi et al. 1989; Chi and VanLehn 1991; Voss et al. 1983), insight problem solving (Ohlsson 1993), and mental modeling (Collins and Gentner 1987). The coded segments were defined as thought units—the smallest coherent or complete statements (whole or partial sentences). Definitions for the final set of coding categories are presented in box 5.2. The first section of the table defines the three categories that we predicted would distinguish insight from analytic problems; we had no particular predictions for the other categories.

Three persons coded the 40 protocols in a consistent two-step process. First, the raters worked through two protocols together. Second, the raters separately coded a third protocol, exhaustively compared their codings, and resolved discrepancies through discussion. Step 2 was repeated once again, by which time the prediscussion interrater agreement had reached 85 percent. (This value is likely to be a conservative estimation for the remaining protocols because we later collapsed a number of the more subtle category distinctions.)

Box 5.1
Insight and Analytic Problems used in Experiments 3 and 4

Insight problems

A. Show how you can make the triangle point downward by moving only three of the circles:

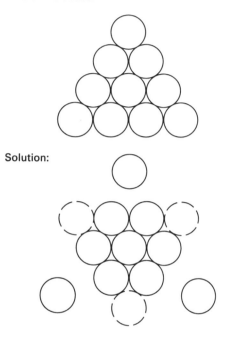

Solution:

Figure 5.1
Diagram and solution for the "triangle" problem

B. A prisoner was attempting to escape from a tower. He found in his cell a rope that was half long enough to permit him to reach the ground safely. He divided the rope in half and tied the two parts together and escaped. How could he have done this?

C. A dealer in antique coins got an offer to buy a beautiful bronze coin. The coin had an emperor's head on one side and the date 544 B.C. stamped on the other. The dealer examined the coin, but instead of buying it, he called the police. Why?

Analytic problems

D. Three cards from an ordinary deck are lying on a table, face down. The following information (for some peculiar reason) is known about those three cards (all the information refers to the same three cards):

Box 5.1
(continued)

To the left of a Queen, there is a Jack
To the left of a Spade, there is a Diamond
To the right of a Heart, there is a King
To the right of a King, there is a Spade

Can you assign the proper suit to each card?

E. The police were convinced that A, B, C, or D had committed a crime. Each of the suspects made a statement, but only one of the statements was true:

A said, "I didn't do it."
B said, "A is lying."
C said, "B is lying."
D said, "B did it."

Who is telling the truth? Who committed the crime?

F. There are four coins—two heavier coins of equal weight and two lighter coins of equal weight—all distinguishable in appearance or by touch (you cannot tell them apart by looking at them or holding them). How can you tell which coins are the heavy ones and which coins are the light ones in two weighings on a balance scale? (You may use the scale only twice.)

Using Fisher's (1991) computer program we obtained the frequency of category occurrence for each subject by problem type. The statement frequencies of each subject's insight and analytic protocols were then converted into a percentage of the total number of coded elements that each subject's protocol contained for that problem type. So, for example, a subject who made 12 MOVE statements during the course of 240 coded statements would have 5 percent MOVEs for the particular type of problem.

Table 5.1 shows the percentages for each problem-solving category. Comparison of the relative preponderance of different categories in the insight and analytic problems, collapsed across hint conditions, revealed a number of differences consistent with our predictions. Before discussing these differences, however, we should note that in many respects the usages were quite similar for insight and analytic problems. The rank orders of elements were very similar for the two problem types as indicated by a Spearman rank order correlation of .95 between insight and analytic problems. The absence of relative rank order differences for these various statement elements suggests that there are certain basic problem-solving characteristics that generalize between insight and analytic problems. Nevertheless, exami-

Box 5.2
Definitions of Protocol Coding Categories

Categories predicted to distinguish the two types of problems

ARGUMENT: Any kind of reasoning, logic, propositional (e.g., if-then statements), or means-ends analysis.

METACOGNITION: Self-reflective comments about the subject's problem-solving progress, technique, perspective, impasses, etc.

PAUSE: Breaks in verbalization lasting between 5 and 15 seconds (after 15 seconds, the experimenter prompted subjects to continue verbalizing their thoughts).

Other statement elements

REREAD: Verbatim rereading of all or a part of the problem, there were two types:

1. Reread premise: Reread a single problem premise, constraint, or goal.
2. Reread entire: Reread the entire problem.

REHEARSE: Any attempt to state, draw, rehearse, etc., some aspect of the problem or its status, a large proportion of rehearses were paraphrases of the problem elements or their premises.

MOVE: To assign a new physical position or categorical name to a problem element. Subjects often prefaced moves with "maybe" or "you could" or "assume that." Also, to state hypotheticals for the purpose of argumentation.

RECALL: To retrieve relevant world knowledge from memory.

QUESTION: To ask a question other than the nominal problem question. There were two types:

1. Asking oneself a question.
2. Asking the experimenter a question.

SOLUTION: The actual or presumed solution. The subject had to announce it as such unless it was clear from the context. There were three types:

1. Correct solutions.
2. Incorrect solutions (including partial solutions).
3. Solve-not (subject failed to solve a problem during the allotted time of 6 minutes).

FEEDBACK (from the experimenter): To inform subjects of incorrect solutions (often noting the reason the proffered solution was incorrect) or the need to adhere to problem constraints. Feedback was also given in response to direct questions from the subject.

MISCELLANEOUS: Otherwise uncodable fragments, such as inaudible statements, mumbling, or incomplete fragments of thought.

Table 5.1
Percentages of Protocol Problem-Solving Elements with Predicted Differences

	Insight Problems	Analytic Problems
ARGUMENT	12.05	19.85
METACOGNITION	8.09	2.89
PAUSE	4.70	2.58
Other elements		
REREAD	14.93	29.97
REHEARSE	19.27	17.93
MOVE	8.89	5.88
RECALL	1.03	0.04
QUESTION-SELF	2.11	0.97
QUESTION-EXPERIMENTER	4.48	2.04
SOLUTION-INCORRECT	5.08	2.92
FEEDBACK	11.38	7.25
MISCELLANEOUS	5.82	4.40
Totals[a]	97.83	96.72
Total elements	3,333.00	4,668.00

a. Totals are less than 100 percent because they do not include the terminal states (correct solutions, failure-to-solve, or, in the HINT condition, the "hints").

nation of the relative usage of specific statement elements that we hypothesized differentiate these two types of problems provides compelling evidence that despite a superficial similarity in approaches, insight and analytic problem solving also differ in significant ways.

Differences between the Statement Elements of Insight and Analytic Problems
With respect to the elements that characterize analytic problems, we had one central prediction: that these problems, by virtue of their reliance on a step-by-step logical solutions, would include a greater incidence of logical arguments than insight problems. Consistent with this prediction, we found that analytic protocols contained a significantly greater proportion of arguments (logic, or means-ends analysis) as compared to insight protocols ($t(39) = -4.50$, $p < .001$).[3]

A second characteristic of analytic problem protocols also points to the step-by-step structure and solution process associated with these problems. Compared to insight protocols, the analytic protocols were associated with a significantly greater proportion of statement elements involving rereading the problem ($t(39) = -8.73$, $p < .01$). Although we had not explicitly predicted this difference, this finding is consistent with the suggestion that analytic problems are distinguished from insight problems with respect to their requirement to be solved in a series of steps. Accordingly, after subjects solved one step in an analytical problem, they may have needed to reread the problem in order to help determine the next step. In the case of insight problems, a step-by-step strategy may have been less appropriate, and so such solve-and-review strategies occurred less often.

We had two predictions regarding the types of statement elements that would characterize insight problem solving. First, because insight problems are hypothesized to involve a greater reliance on nonreportable processes, we predicted that they would be more likely to elicit pauses. Comparison of the relative incidence of pauses for the two types of problems supported this prediction. Subjects paused more while solving insight problems than during analytic problems. A paired t-test showed that the difference was significant ($t(39) = 2.91$, $p < .01$). Our second prediction was that insight problems, by virtue of the nonreportability of their processes, their likelihood to induce impasses, and their requirement to shift perspectives, would be more likely than analytic problems to elicit metacognitive statements. As with pauses, we found a significant difference in the predicted direction, with metacognition means of 8.09 percent and 2.89 percent for insight and analytic problems, respectively ($t(39) = 5.41$, $p < .01$).[4]

In order to get a deeper understanding of the nature of the differential probability of reporting metacognitive statements, we further divided the metacognitive statements into six subcategories (box 5.3).[5] The results of this analysis were generally consistent with our predictions. Insight subjects were more likely to indicate that they were at

Box 5.3
Definitions for Metacognition Subcategories

IMPASSE: Subject specifically states that he or she is unable to make further progress.

STRATEGY DESCRIPTION: Subject states what strategy he or she was using or had tried to use.

PERSPECTIVE SHIFT: Subject explicitly notes that he or she is exploring a different approach.

NONREPORTABILITY: Subject states that it is difficult or impossible to verbalize what he or she is thinking.

COMPETENCE: Subject evaluates his or her ability to solve (or not solve) the problem.

OTHER: Otherwise unclassifiable metacognitions.

an impasse with metacognitions such as "I just can't imagine . . . ,"
"I don't think I can solve it at all, no matter how much time I had,"
and "I am just wondering where to go from here." There were an
average of 1.8 impasse statements per subject during insight problems
as compared to just 0.3 during analytic problems ($t(19) = -3.71$, $p <$
.0001). Also consistent with our predictions, insight protocols tended
to be more likely to contain nonreportability statements, that is, reports that subjects were having difficulty articulating their thoughts.
For example, one subject exclaimed while working on an insight problem, "there is nothing that's going through my mind that's really in
any kind of—that's in a verbal fashion. Another subject noted, "There
is not a whole lot I can say about this while I'm trying to figure it out."
Still another subject exclaimed, "I know I am supposed to keep talking
but I don't know what I am thinking." There were an average of only
.05 nonreportability statements per subject in the analytic protocols
as compared to .70 such statements for insight problems. A paired
t-test indicated that the difference was significant ($t(19) = -2.02$,
$p = < .03$, one tailed).

   We had also predicted that while solving insight problems, subjects
would be more likely to mention their attempts to shift perspectives
as, for example, a subject who said, "I could look at it from different
angles"; another volunteered "OK, I'm going to look at it a different
way then." Although these occurred numerically more often in the
insight condition, the respective frequencies were too low (four for
insight, two for analytic) to be significant.

Statement Elements as Predictors of Success
Although comparing the overall frequency of different types of statement elements helps to characterize the differences between the approaches that subjects take to solving insight and analytic problems,
such a comparison has a fundamental limitation. The fact that subjects
incorporated particular statement elements in their protocols does not
in itself indicate that those elements necessarily contributed to their
problem solutions. Indeed, it is our contention that little of what
subjects said in the case of the insight problems had anything to do
with the actual processes that elicited the solutions. To get at the actual
utility of different statement elements, it is helpful to examine the
degree to which the existence of these elements was predictive of
successful problem solving. Accordingly, if a particular type of problem element is useful for a particular type of problem, then subjects
who are more likely to use that problem element should tend to be
more successful.

Before discussing this analysis, we briefly review our predictions. With respect to analytic problems, given our contention that the key to their solutions lies in progressive processes of logical reasoning, it follows that the frequent use of logical arguments should be predictive of successful solutions. In the case of insight problems, the claim that verbalization has little to do with solving these problems predicts that there should be very little in the content of these problems that would be predictive. One element that might be predictive, however, is the frequency of pauses, with subjects who were more likely to pause potentially being more likely to concentrate on, or otherwise to access more effectively, nonreportable processes.

Our results (table 5.2) were generally in keeping with the predictions. In the case of analytic problems, the percentage of subjects' statement elements that were coded as arguments was strongly correlated with the number of problems that they solved ($r = .57$, $p < .01$). In contrast, in the case of insight problems, there was no correlation between arguments and problem success ($r = .08$, $p > .60$).

A second unique predictor of analytic problems was percentage of reread statements. The percentage of rereading was inversely predictive of subjects' success on analytic problems ($r = -.44$, $p < .01$). In other words, the more successful subjects spent a lower percentage of effort on rereading premises, suggesting that subjects who were able to maintain the premises of a problem in working memory may have been less likely to confuse the steps involved in analytic problems. For insight, there was a much lower, nonsignificant correlation between rereading and performance ($r = -.13$, $p > .40$).

Table 5.2
Correlations (Pearson's r) between Selected Protocol Categories and Number of Correct Solutions

	Problem Type	
	Analytic N = 40)	Insight (N = 39)
ARGUMENT	.57**	.08
METACOGNITION	−.09	.01
PAUSES	−.04	.20
REREADS	−.44**	.13
REHEARSE	.09	−.18
MOVE	.17	.38*[a]
MISCELLANEOUS	−.35*	−.05

a. $r = .20$ ($p > .05$) when the triangle problem is omitted from this analysis.
* $p < .05$.
**$p < .01$.

In the case of insight problems, our prediction that very little in the protocols would be diagnostic of success was borne out by the dearth of significant predictors. There was a slight trend for subjects who paused more tending to be more successful ($r = .20$, $p < .11$, one-tailed), with not even a hint of this trend for analytic problem solving ($r = -.04$). There was an unexpected correlation between performance and the number of MOVEs that subjects used on average to solve insight problems ($r = .37$). However, examination of the incidence of MOVE statements for insight problems indicated that virtually all of the MOVE statements were associated with the triangle problem in which subjects had to reconfigure the circles in a triangle (see problem A in box 5.1). Because this problem can be solved by trial and error, it seems likely that making more moves may have simply increased subjects' likelihood of stumbling onto the solution. Indeed, when this problem was omitted from the analysis, MOVEs were no longer predictive of insight solution success (table 5.2).

Although these findings are generally consistent with the claim that the useful elements of analytic problem solving are not of value for insight problems, there is a possible alternative interpretation: subjects solving insight problems do in fact use the same processes as those used by analytic problems, but the time course of the application of those processes is simply too fast to be revealed in concurrent verbalization protocols. Using retrospective reports, Perkins (1981) suggested that subjects solving insight problems engaged in series of logical steps, each happening so quickly that they may seem to occur as a single leap (Ohlsson 1993). Although retrospective reports are somewhat suspect because subjects may have inferred post hoc steps that they did not actually take, this speeded reasoning view might be used to dismiss some of our findings. Accordingly, if the critical logical steps in insight problem solutions happen too quickly to be reported, then our assessment of the actual number of logical steps used by insight subjects may not be accurate, and consequently, it is not surprising that we found no correlation between the frequency of logical arguments and insight solutions. This reasoning, although potentially sound, implies a prediction that was not supported by the data. Specifically, if we assume that insight and analytical problem solving involve comparable logical reasoning processes—that are more quickly implemented during insight problems—then it follows that subjects' logical reasoning with analytic problems should be predictive of their performance with the insight problems. Because subjects in our experiment solved both types of problems, it was possible to address this question. As it turned out, their use of logical arguments while solving analytic problems was not at all correlated with their performance on the insight problems ($r = .07$), even though this argumentation was highly correlated with analytic problem solving ($r = .57$). The lack of a correlation between argument usage for analytic problems and success with insight problems is particularly interesting in view of the overall correlation between success on the two types of problem ($r = .45$, $p < .01$). It would seem the successful subjects effectively drew on distinctly different processing strategies for insight versus analytic problems: argumentation for analytic and some other nonreported process for insight problems. We will return to the possible factors that may account for individual differences in insight and analytic problem solving.

Summary
In short, our protocol analysis suggests that the factor that distinguishes whether problems are vulnerable to verbalization is whether they elicit straightforward and logical problem-solving strategies. When subjects are faced with problems that they can solve logically, as in the case of the standard analytic problem, they can verbally report the stepwise arguments necessary to solve the problem, and they are unimpaired by verbalization. In contrast, when solving insight problems, subjects are less likely to draw on logical arguments and more likely to attempt to make metacognitions reflecting their inability to progress following standard logical means. This relative lack of reliance on reportable processes may therefore make them vulnerable to verbalization.

The analysis provides direct evidence for the logical processes used by analytic problem solvers and the lack of such processes in insight problem solving. By inference, these findings support the importance of nonreportable processes for solving insight problems; however, they are less revealing regarding the precise nature of those unreportable processes. The protocol analysis suggested that metacognitive considerations such as overcoming impasses were important. However, the manner in which such impasses are overcome was not clear. In the following section, we report a preliminary study that attempted to explore these hypothesized nonreportable processes.

Individual Differences and Insight

An individual-differences approach can often offer a first step in establishing the component processes involved in a skill. The basic logic of this approach is that if process A is involved in a particular skill B, then performance on tasks involving process A should be predictive of tasks requiring skill B. There have been countless applications of

the individual-differences approach in identifying the processes associated with intelligence (Hunt, Lunneborg, and Lewis, 1975); however, relatively little research has used this approach to identify the
processes associated with insight problem solving.

There have been a few examinations of the factors that correlate
with insight, but the conclusions that can be drawn from these are
quite limited. A number of researchers failed to find any correlates
with insight performance (Burke and Maier 1965; Maier and Burke
1966; Raaheim and Kaufmann 1972). However, these researchers used
only a single insight problem (Maier's 1945 hat rack problem), thereby
greatly attenuating their statistical sensitivity, not to mention constraining the generalizability of any results. Other researchers have
found reliable predictors of insight, although again the implications
of these findings are limited. For example, Jacobs and Dominowski
(1981) observed significant correlations between performance on different insight problems and further found that performance on insight
problems was correlated with performance on the Gestalt Transformation Test (a measure of subjects' ability to figure out unusual uses
for objects). Although this finding provides some validity to the notion
that insight may tap a measurable skill, it does not do much to explain
that skill since the items on the task are themselves quite similar to
insight problems. For example, one of the items asks subjects to decide
which of the following objects would be most appropriate to use in
lubricating a friction point: water, pencil, bottle of ink, eraser, or
dictionary. The answer is the pencil (graphite can be used as a
lubricant).

In addition to these difficulties, the past published studies of the
correlates of insight problem solving have typically omitted a critical
control, the inclusion of analytic problems. In the absence of an analytic problem control, a correlation between insight problem solving
and other individual-differences measures may suggest a factor that
is unique to insight problem solving, or it may simply correspond to
a general problem-solving skill. In order to determine the processes
that are unique to insight, it is necessary to examine the relationship
between individual-differences measures and both insight and analytic problem-solving ability.

In the following study, we (Schooler, McCleod, Brooks, and Melcher
1993) examined the correlation between a variety of different measures
and both insight and analytic problem solving in an effort to illuminate
the nonreportable processes that appear to mediate insight problem
solving. As a starting place, we considered the three elements of
insight that have repeatedly appeared in both the early and recent

discussion of insight: restructuring, context-induced fixedness, and unconscious search.

The basic premise of the Gestalt approach to restructuring was that insight involves a process, analogous to perceptual pattern recognition, whereby individuals find a new, more complete representation of the problem. The measure that taps this characterization was not immediately obvious. After some reflection, we opted for the task of recognizing out-of-focus pictures (Bruner and Potter 1964). This task requires pattern recognition, and it also elicits the phenomenological experience of a sudden shift in perspective; one moment you have no idea what the object is, and the next moment it is obvious.

Recognizing out-of-focus pictures also provided us with the opportunity to test a second element of many theories of insight: the notion that insight problems require one to overcome a set produced by the context of the problem. Bruner and Potter (1964) observed that exposure to extremely out-of-focus pictures impairs subjects' ability to recognize mildly out-of-focus versions of the same picture. The interpretation of this result is that viewing a very blurred picture causes subjects to adopt inaccurate interpretations (comparable to a false set), which can then interfere with their later recognition of the picture. In our study, we attempted to examine the role of this induced set by generating a difference measure corresponding to the difference between subjects' recognition of moderately out-of-focus pictures that were presented either in isolation (single presentation) or preceded by very out-of-focus versions of the same picture (serial presentation). If the set hypothesized to be elicited by seeing very out-of-focus pictures corresponds to a general susceptibility to context-induced set and if insight solutions are hampered by a similar process, then the difference between subjects' identification of singly and serially presented pictures may be predictive of insight performance. That a susceptibility to context-induced set might hamper insight problem solving also suggested the applicability of one of the most widely used individual difference constructs: field dependence. Measures of field dependence, most notably the embedded-figures test and the rod and frame test, have been shown, under a large number of different situations, to reveal the degree to which an individual's judgment is influenced by context (for a review see Witkin et al. 1962). Indeed, some unpublished research suggests that it may be correlated with performance on at least one insight problem (Harris, cited by Witkin 1971). If insight problems require subjects to ignore the implicit context of a problem and seek out some alternative perspective, then field dependence might well prove a reliable predictor of the ability to solve various insight problems.

If, as many theories have suggested, insight draws on the process of extensive unconscious memory search, then one might expect that memory search ability might be correlated with insight problem-solving performance. In order to explore this hypothesis we used the following measures that require extensive memory search:

1. Remote associates: This measure gives individuals three distant associates, such as *salt, deep, foam,* and requires them to retrieve a fourth word that relates to all three words (*sea*).

2. Category instance generation: This speeded task requires subjects to generate an instance of a category given only the first letter (e.g., fruit—*P*).

3. Anagrams; This task requires subjects to search for a word that corresponds to a rearrangement of the presented words (e.g., *mhnua = human*).

In addition to these three measures of abilities hypothesized to be associated with insight, we also included some more general measures of intellectual ability, including mathematical ability (Math SAT), verbal ability (Verbal SAT, Vocabulary), spatial ability (mental rotation task), and general intellectual curiosity (need for cognition). These measures enabled us to distinguish general intellectual abilities from those hypothesized to be more specifically required for insight problem solving.

Method
Fifty-one subjects were given a battery of measures during 2-hour sessions. Subjects were run in groups ranging from one to eight individuals. The measures were 8 insight problems, 8 analytic problems, and out-of-focus picture identification task of 10 out-of-focus pictures presented with slide projector (5 pictures were presented singly and 5 were preceded by very out-of-focus versions of the same picture), the Group Embedded Figures Test (Witkin et al. 1971), a standard vocabulary test, 40 single-solution anagrams drawn from two sources (Gilhooly and Johnson 1978; Tresselt and Mayzner 1966), 32 remote associates problems drawn from Bowers and associates (1990), 40 category completion items modeled after Freedman and Loftus (1971), a mental rotation test (Hunt, Davidson, and Lansman 1981), and the need-for-cognition scale (Cacioppo and Petty 1982). Subjects were given a consent form asking their permission for us to obtain their SAT information.

Results and Discussion
The correlation matrix of all measures are presented in table 5.3. Because our central interest was to determine the factors that distin-

Table 5.3
Individual Difference Correlates of Insight and Analytic Problem Solving

	INS	ANAL	PIC	PICDIF	EMB	CAT	ANAG	REM	VOC	ROT	NEED	SATV	SATM
Problem-Solving type													
Insight (INS)	1.00												
Analytic (ANAL)	.36*	1.00											
Restructuring													
Out-of-focus pictures (PIC)	.45**	.21	1.00										
Context-induced set													
Out-of-focus difference (PICDIF)	.14	.02	.18	1.00									
Embedded figures (EMB)	.41**	.18	.35*	.14	1.00								
Memory retrieval													
Categorization (CAT)	.25	.38*	.29	.11	.360	1.00							
Anagrams (ANAG)	.25	.40*	.33*	.23	.46**	.54**	1.00						
Remote associates solved (REM)	.37*	.54**	.24	-.03	.46**	.49**	.55**	1.00					
General abilities													
Vocabulary (VOC)	.36*	.36*	.39*	-.11	.19	.53**	.47**	.55**	1.00				
Mental rotation (ROT)	.26	.13	.19	.16	.10	-.16	.09	.01	-.14	1.00			
Need for cognition (NEED)	.21	.14	.23	.02	.37*	.22	.29	.43*	.36*	-.18	1.00		
Verbal SAT[a] (SATV)	.17	.24	.36*	-.01	.06	.46*	.26	.52**	.84**	-.01	.42**	1.00	
Math SAT[a] (SATM)	.20	.36*	.10	.09	.16	.44**	.27	.35*	.50**	.13	.26	.61**	1.00

Note: Correlations are based on $N = 51$.
The first two columns are presented in boldface in order to draw attention to the most important correlations—those between the various individual difference measures and the Insight and Analytical problem types.
a. Correlations are based on $N = 40$.
*$p < .05$.
**$p < .01$.

guish insight and analytic problem solving, we consider correlates of these two abilities in turn.

Predictors of Insight Problem Solving   Although the patterns that emerged were somewhat complex, at least some measures associated with all three of the hypothesized components of insight proved to be predictive of insight performance.

Our first predicted element of insight performance was perceptual restructuring, which we measured by examining subjects' ability to recognize out-of-focus pictures. This ability turned out to be the single best predictor of insight performance (table 5.6), suggesting that restructuring may play an important role in insight problem solving.

The second element of insight problem solving investigated was overcoming context-induced set. We used two measures to examine this construct: the difference between sequentially and singularly presented pictures, and field dependence. With respect to the former measure, we replicated earlier findings that moderately out-of-focus pictures preceded by very out-of-focus versions were more difficult to recognize than moderately out-of-focus pictures that were presented alone. Mean performance scores for sequential and single picture recognition were 1.59 and 2.77, respectively ($t(50) = -5.786, p < .01$). This suggests that the sequence manipulation did produce some type of disruptive set; however, when we took the difference between scores on these two versions of the task in order to derive a measure of "susceptibility to set," we found that performance on this value was not correlated with insight performance. While this may serve as some evidence against the hypothesis that context-induced set constrains insight, we must be cautious in interpreting this null result, particularly because this measure also proved to be uncorrelated with all other measures. Indeed when insight performance was correlated with a validated measure of sensitivity to context (field dependence), a strong positive correlation emerged (the greater the score on the embedded figure test, the lesser one's degree of field dependence). Thus, the hypothesis that insight requires overcoming context-induced set garnered some support.

The third element of insight examined was memory retrieval—the ability to engage in extensive memory search. Consistent with our predictions, subjects' ability to find remote associates was correlated with their insight performance. However, the other two measures of memory search (category instance generation and anagrams) proved to be unpredictive. Indeed all three of these measures turned out to be more predictive of analytic performance than insight performance. Although the findings provide only minimal evidence for the memory search component of insight, we note in hindsight that we may not have used measures that fully capture the memory search requirements of insight problems.

Of the general measures of intellectual ability, only vocabulary was significantly correlated with insight problem solving. This finding suggests that whereas some general knowledge may be useful for insight solutions, insight problem solving is distinct from general intellectual functioning. It is also of interest that insight was only marginally correlated with spatial ability. One less interesting interpretation of the results could follow from the fact that a few of the insight problems involved diagrams and thus had spatial characteristics. Accordingly, it could be that the spatial ability required by a few of the insight problems could have been responsible for the correlations between insight and the embedded figures and out-of focus picture recognition tasks, both of which also involve spatial information. However, the fact that these factors were predictive of insight performance even when spatial ability was partialed out ($r = .37$ and $.42$, respectively) argues against this interpretation.

Predictors of Analytic Problem Solving   While there was a significant correlation between insight and analytic problem solving, it is quite notable that the factors that predicted performance on the two types of problems were generally different. Embedded figures and out-of-focus pictures, the two measures that were most strongly correlated with insight problem solving, were not significantly correlated with analytic problems. Moreover, anagrams, categorization, and Math SAT scores, which were not significantly correlated with the insight problems, were significantly correlated with the analytic problems. This differential pattern of findings suggests once again that the two types of problems draw on qualitatively different processes. Some of the factors that were uniquely predictive of analytic problem solving follow directly from our previous characterization. For example, performance on the math SAT requires the same type of logical step-by-step process that we associated with analytic problems. Other factors that we did not predict to correlate with analytic problem solving nevertheless make some sense in hindsight. The three memory retrieval measures all correlated quite highly with noninsight problem-solving performance as well as with each other. It thus seems quite reasonable to speculate that these three measures all tap some general ability to retrieve verbal information. The previous protocol analysis suggested that analytic problems put a sizable demand on subjects' ability to maintain verbal information. This was indicated both by the high frequency with which subjects needed to reread the problems and by the negative correlation between rereading the problem and successful solutions. It thus seems reasonable to speculate that the sizable correlation between the various memory retrieval measures and analytic problem solving reflected the role of verbal working memory skills (Daneman and Carpenter 1980; Just and Carpenter 1992) required for maintaining the verbal information necessary for solving analytic problems.

The suggestion that analytic problems put unique demands on verbal working memory raises the possibility that the verbal memory measures used in this study may have correlated with insight and analytic problems for different reasons. Insight problems may correlate with verbal memory measures because of their demand for real-world knowledge. In contrast, analytic problem solving may correlate with verbal memory measures because such measures also tap the verbal working memory abilities necessary to maintain and manipulate information. This speculative characterization could be empirically tested by examining the correlation of working memory measures with insight and noninsight problem solving. If analytic problem solving particularly draws on verbal working memory, then verbal working memory measures should correlate more with analytic problem solving than insight problem solving. Such a hypothesis must be considered merely speculative at this time, but it might be well worth exploring.

Summary
This individual-differences analysis provided some hints as to the nonreportable processes associated with insight. Both perceptual restructuring, as measured by the ability to recognize out-of-focus pictures, and the ability to overcome context-induced set, as measured by performance on the embedded-figures task, were highly correlated with insight performance but insignificantly correlated with analytic performance. In contrast, analytic problem solving was particularly correlated with other tasks that can be solved in a step-by-step manner (e.g., math SAT and anagrams) as well as verbal memory measures that may reflect the potentially unique working memory demands of analytic problems.

Conclusions

Our empirical investigations provide some support for a number of historical speculations about the ineffable nature of insight. Research investigating the effects of verbalization on insight and analytic processes (Schooler, Ohlsson, and Brooks 1993) suggests that there is some truth to past suggestions that insight may be hampered by language. Analysis of the protocols generated in that study supported the historic view that verbalizable logical thinking, so central to analytic problem solving, is of relatively little use in achieving insights. Finally, our individual-differences study provided evidence for at least two of the three nonreportable processes identified in historical discussions of insight: restructuring process comparable to perceptual pattern recognition and avoiding context-induced mental sets. Furthermore, the fact that the two measures most correlated with insight performance were perceptual in nature provides some support for early Gestalt claims that the nonreportable processes involved in insight may be analogous in some respects to those involved in perception.

Although this work is generally consistent with the view that insight involves unique nonreportable processes, it also suggests that insight and analytic problems share significant qualities. The verbalization research indicated that although insight and analytic problems are differentially vulnerable to verbalization under normal conditions, the analytic problems can become impaired by verbalization when subjects are encouraged to think of them as potential insight problems. The protocol analysis showed that although the two problem types differ in the frequency with which they elicit different types of statement elements, most statement elements were applied to both types of problems. Finally, the individual-differences study suggested that although insight and analytic problems are differentially correlated with a number of variables, they also share correlations with other variables and indeed are somewhat correlated with each other. Thus, it seems inappropriate to conclude that insight and analytic problems involve an entirely distinct set of mental processes. Rather, it seems more reasonable to suggest that they may share some processes but not others. Indeed, the semioverlapping nature of the processes involved in insight and analytic problems may help to explain some of the difficulties that subjects can have solving these problems. For example, the demand to think out loud may induce subjects to draw on analytic problems-solving processes such as explicit logical argumentation, even if such elements are not useful, simply because they are readily verbalized. A misapplication of metacognitive processes required for insight to analytic problems may similarly account for the disruptive effects of the "insight hint" on analytic problems (see 2–4). In short, insight and analytic problem solving may overlap relatively more with respect to the types of processes that subjects attempt to use and relatively less with respect to the processes that ultimately end up being useful.

The research discussed in this chapter suggests that the nonreportability of insight need not impede efforts to begin to characterize the processes that distinguish insight from analytic problem solving. In closing, we briefly speculate about worthwhile directions for future research on this topic. With respect to the disruptive effects of verbalization on insight, it would be quite useful to manipulate the insight problems components systematically in order to isolate the elements of insight problem solving that are disrupted by verbalization. For example, it may be that verbalization primarily disrupts the search for alternative problem approaches (restructuring). Alternatively, verbalization may prevent subjects from disregarding the initial context-induced approach (overcoming set). These alternatives might be teased out by identifying problems that differentially elicit these hypothesized problem components, and examining their relative vulnerability to verbalization. With respect to the protocol analysis research, it may be helpful to compare in more detail the specific reasoning used in individual problems. We took the approach of exhaustively coding and quantifying all statement elements at a relatively coarse level of analysis. This quantitative approach helped to demonstrate the generality of the basic factors that distinguish the two types of problems but at the expense of more qualitative analyses of a few protocols. Such qualitative analyses can be quite informative (Chi and VanLehn 1991) by leading to inferences about complex reasoning operations. For example, it is possible that a very fine grained analysis of analytic problems could reveal that they may sometimes require little insights in order to move from one step to the next, thus helping to account for the overlapping nature of the two types of problems. With respect to the individual-differences approach to characterizing the two types of problems, we suggest that future research might try more sophisticated measures for revealing the search component hypothesized to be associated with insight. Langley and Jones (1988) suggest that memory "indexing" is a critical component of the memory search required by insight problem solving. Memory indexing involves relating the elements of a problem to existing knowledge structures in a manner that optimizes the likelihood that activation can spread in useful directions. It seems likely that simple semantic searches that were required by our measures did not tap memory indexing ability and therefore may not have reflected this critical component of the memory search required for insight problems. Future research might profitably explore the relationship between memory indexing and insight performance by examining the correlation between insight problem solving and other measures that more directly draw on memory indexing ability, such as the ability to recognize analogies between the deep structure of two superficially different problems (Gick and Holyoak 1980).

In addition to pursuing the specific approaches documented here, future insight research might also begin to apply recent advances in other domains that examine nonreportable cognitive processes. For example, research on dissociating conscious from automatic processes (Jacoby, Ste Marie, and Toth in press), subliminal perception (Merikle and Reingold 1990), implicit learning (Reber 1989), and implicit memory (Schacter 1987) may offer other paradigms by which to study insight. Neuropsychological developments in localizing brain function may also prove useful. For example, a recent priming study using brief stimulus presentations to the right and left visual fields suggests that activation in the right hemisphere may spread more broadly than in the left, that is, to more distant associates (Beeman et al. in press). This finding raises the possibility that the spreading activation to divergent concepts, which has been hypothesized to be involved in insight problem solving, may be localized to the right hemisphere. Since the right hemisphere is also associated with a number of other properties related to insight, including nonverbal cognition (Milner 1971), visual-spatial processing (Kosslyn 1987), appreciating humor (Foldi, Cicone, and Gardner 1983), and recognizing the multiple interpretations of metaphor (Winner and Garnder 1977), empirical investigations of the relationship between hemispheric function and insight and analytic problem solving seem worthwhile.

We endorse future efforts to uncover the ineffable elements of insight while acknowledging a concern that naturally arises from the implications of our endeavor. In analyzing insight, are we in effect attempting to pin down verbally the very process that we have shown to be hampered by verbal analysis? Might our effort to understand insight require the specific operations that hinder it? We cannot rule out the possibility that, by becoming excessively analytic about the insight process, we may have limited ourselves in a manner comparable to what verbalization did to the subjects in our study. We note, however, that our approach to studying insight involved a relatively straightforward logical analysis, drawing on the type of reasoning that readily lends itself to verbalization. While this analytical approach has allowed us to make real progress on the topic, we must concede that there is little in this chapter that can be characterized as a true insight about insight. Toward this goal, we might profitably draw on Poincaré's advice that "to invent, one must think aside." Insight may be like a faint star, best seen when kept slightly away from the center of focus. While definite progress can be made when insight is examined directly, perhaps the true insights about insight will occur if, as we study other aspects of human cognition, we keep insight in the corner of our eyes.

Notes

The research described in this chapter was supported by a grant to the first author from the National Institute of Mental Health. Many thanks to Carolanne Fisher for her kindness in providing a copy of her Protocol Analyst's Workbench (PAW) software, which was instrumental in supporting this analysis. Thanks also to Aspasia Rigopoulou, who suffered with J.M. through the grueling process of coding the protocols and whose comments helped sharpen the definitions. Stellan Ohlsson provided useful feedback and encouragement along the way. Micki Chi and Carmi Schooler provided advice and comments on earlier versions of the chapter. Marte Fallshore, Steve Fiore, and Mary-Jo Nelum-Hart all provided helpful suggestions. Thanks to Bob Ryan for giving so freely of his statistical expertise. Kevin Brooks ran subjects and coded protocols.

1. Since we wrote this chapter, more recent reports suggest that Chow's original study contained some flaws that bring into question its conclusions. Nevertheless, after some deliberation we opted to keep this example; even if it ultimately turns out not to be valid, it remains a fine instance of an insight in the sense that it suggested a highly plausible alternative view that had not been previously considered. In addition, while there has yet to be a fully successful implementation of Chow's basic insight—that multiple drugs may operate by targeting the same, as opposed to different stages in a diseases' growth cycle—this alternative approach has also yet to be ruled out completely.

2. In this experiment half of the subjects received a "mind-set hint" describing insight problems and suggesting that such problems might require them to overcome a "mind-set" and find an alternative approach. This hint had no effect on insight problem solving (replicating Olton and Johnson 1976) but reduced verbalization subjects' performance on the noninsight problems. In interpreting this unexpected result, Schooler, Ohlsson, and Brooks (1993) speculated that the hint manipulation may have caused subjects to treat analytic problems more like insight problems, thereby increasing their vulnerability to verbalization. This hypothesis was reflected by some mild differences in the analytic problem protocols of hint and no-hint subjects. However, because the effects of insight hints on noninsight problem solving is not the focus of our concern, we will limit to a few brief notes our discussion of the mild effects of these hints on subjects' protocols.

3. Arguments constituted 23.26 percent of analytic problem statements in the no-hint condition as compared to 16.44 percent in the hint condition ($t(38) = 1.63$, $p < .06$, one-tailed). This marginally significant difference is consistent with the suggestion that the insight hint caused subjects to treat analytic problems more like insight problems.

4. Metacognitions constituted 2.19 percent of analytic problem statements in the no-hint condition as compared to 3.60 percent in the hint condition ($t(38) = 1.63$, $p < .06$, one-tailed). This marginally significant finding is also consistent with the suggestion that the insight hint caused subjects to treat analytic problems more like insight problems. Additional evidence that subjects in the hint condition were treating analytic problems as if they were insight problems is suggested by the content of their metacognitions. For example, one subject speculated, "But I might be in a mind-set, I don't know." Another exclaimed, "I'm in a mind-set," while rapping the table. Still another said, "All right, all right. The first thing I'm thinking is that—this is what it is—an insight question."

5. Because of the influence of the hint on subjects' metacognition, we limited the analysis of metacognitions to the 20 no-hint protocols.

References

Bowers, K. S. (1991). How sudden insight and how can we tell? Paper presented at symposium, Annual American Psychological Society Meeting.

Bowers, K. S., Regehr, G., Balthazard, C., and Parker, K. (1990). Intuition in the context of discovery. *Cognitive Psychology, 22,* 72–110.

Brandimonte, M. A., Hitch, G. J., and Bishop, D. V. M. (1992). Influence of short-term memory codes on visual image processing: Evidence from image transformation tasks. *Journal of Experimental Psychology: Learning, Memory and Cognition, 18,* 157–165.

Bruner, J., and Potter, M. (1964). Interference in visual recognition. *Science, 144,* 424–425.

Burke, R. J., and Maier, N. R. F. (1965). Attempts to predict success on an insight problem. *Psychological Reports, 17,* 303–310.

Cacioppo, J. T., and Petty, R. E. (1982). The need for cognition. *Journal of Personality and Social Psychology, 42,*(1), 116–131.

Chi, M. T. H. (1992). *A practical guide to content analysis of verbal data: A reflection of knowledge representation.* Washington, DC: Office of Educational Research and Improvement, National Center on Student Learning, U.S. Department of Education.

Chi, M. T. H., Bassok, M., Lewis, M. W., Reimann, P., and Glaser, R. (1989). Self-explanations: How students study and use examples in learning to solve problems. *Cognitive Science, 13,* 145–182.

Chi, M. T. H., and VanLehn, K. A. (1991). The content of physics self-explanations. *Journal of the Learning Sciences, 1,* 69–105.

Collins, A., and Gentner, D. (1987). How people construct mental models. In D. Holland and N. Quinn (eds.), *Cultural models in thought and language.* Cambridge, UK: Cambridge University Press.

Daneman, M., and Carpenter, P. A. (1980). Individual differences in working memory and reading. *Journal of Verbal Learning and Verbal Behavior, 19,* 450–466.

Duncker, K. (1945). On problem solving. *Psychological Monographs, 58.*

Ellen, P. (1982). Direction, past experience, and hints in creative problem solving: A reply to Weisberg and Alba. *Journal of Experimental Psychology: General, 111,* 316–325.

Ericsson, K. A., and Simon, H. A. (1984). *Protocol analysis: Verbal reports as data.* Cambridge, MA: MIT Press.

Fallshore, M., and Schooler, J. W. (1993). Post-encoding verbalization impairs transfer on artificial grammar tasks. In *Fifteenth Annual Meeting of the Cognitive Science Society,* Boulder, CO: Cognitive Science Society.

Fisher, C. (1987). Advancing the study of programming with computer-aided protocol analysis. In G. Olson, E. Soloway, and S. Sheppard (eds.), *Empirical studies of programmers: Second workshop.* Norwood, NJ: Ablex.

Fisher, C. (1991). *Computer-aided protocol analysis.* Unpublished doctoral dissertation, Carnegie-Mellon University.

Foldi, N. S., Cicone, M., and Gardner, H. (1983). Pragmatic aspects of communication in brain damaged patients. In S. J. Segalowtitz (ed.), *Language functions and brain organization.* New York: Academic Press.

Freedman, J. L., and Loftus, E. F. (1971). Retrieval of words from long-term memory. *Journal of Verbal Learning and Verbal Behavior, 10,* 107–115.

Gick, M., and Holyoak, K. (1980). Analogical problem solving. *Cognitive Psychology, 12,* 306–355.

Gilhooly, K. J., and Johnson, C. E. (1978). Effects of solution word attributes on anagram difficulty: A regression analysis. *Quarterly Journal of Experimental Psychology, 30,* 57–70.

Hadamard, J. (1954). *An essay on the psychology of invention in the mathematical field.* New York: Dover.

Hunt, E. B., Davidson, J., and Lansman, M. (1981). Individual differences in long term memory access. *Memory and Cognition, 9*(6), 599–608.

Hunt, E., Lunneborg, C., and Lewis, J. (1975). What does it mean to be high verbal? *Cognitive Psychology, 7,* 194–227.

Jacobs, M. K., and Dominowski, R. L. (1981). Learning to solve insight problems. *Bulletin of the Psychonomic Society, 17*(4), 171–174.

Jacoby, L. L., Ste Marie, D., and Toth, J. P. (1993). Redefining automaticity: Unconscious influences, awareness and control. In A. D. Baddeley and L. Weiskrantz (eds.), *Attention, selection, awareness and control: A tribute to Donald Broadbent.* Oxford: Clarendon.

Just, M. A., and Carpetner, P. A. (1992). A capacity theory of comprehension: Individual differences in working memory. *Psychological Review, 99*(1), 122–149.

Kaplan, C. A., and Simon, H. A. (1990). In search of insight. *Cognitive Psychology, 22,* 374–419.

Koestler, A. (1964). *The act of creation.* New York: Dell.

Kosslyn, S. M. (1987). Seeing and imagining in the cerebral hemispheres: A computational approach. *Psychological Review, 94,* 148–175.

Langley, P., and Jones, R. (1988). A computational model of scientific insight. In R. J. Sternberg (ed.), *The nature of creativity: Contemporary psychological perspectives* (pp. 177–201). Cambridge: Cambridge University Press.

Luchins, A. S. (1942). Mechanization in problem solving: The effect of Einstellung. *Psychological Monographs, 54*(6, Whole No. 248).

Maier, N. R. F. (1931). Reasoning in humans. II. The solution of a problem and its appearance in consciousness. *Journal of Comparative Psychology, 12,* 181–194.

Maier, N. R. F. (1945). Reasoning in humans: III. The mechanisms of equivalent stimuli and of reasoning. *Journal of Experimental Psychology, 35,* 349–360.

Maier, N. R. F., and Burke, R. J. (1966). Test of the concept of "availability of functions" in problem solving. *Psychological Reports, 19,* 119–125.

Merikle, P. M., and Reingold, E. M. (1990). Recognition and lexical decision without detection: Unconscious perception? *Journal of Experimental Psychology: Human Perception and Performance, 16*(3), 574–583.

Metcalfe, J., and Wiebe, D. (1987). Intuition in insight and noninsight problem solving. *Memory and Cognition, 15,* 238–246.

Milner, B. (1971). Interhemispheric differences and psychological processes. *British Medical Bulletin, 27,* 272–277.

Nisbett, R. E., and Wilson, T. D. (1977). Telling more than we can know: Verbal reports on mental processes. *Psychological Review, 84,* 231–259.

Ohlsson, S. (1984). Restructuring revisited: I. Summary and critique of the Gestalt theory of problem solving. *Scandinavian Journal of Psychology, 24,* 65–78.

Ohlsson, S. (1990). Trace analysis and spatial reasoning: An example of intensive cognitive diagnosis and its implications for testing. In N. Fredericksen, R. Glaser, A. Lesgold, and M. Shafto (eds.), *Diagnostic monitoring of skill and knowledge acquisition* (pp. 251–296). Hillsdale, NJ: Erlbaum.

Ohlsson, S. (1993). Information-processing explanations of insight and related phenomena. In M. Keane and K. Gilhooley (eds.), *Advances in the psychology of thinking*. London: Harvester-Wheatsheaf.

Olton, R. M., and Johnson, D. M. (1976). Mechanisms of intuition in creative problem solving. *American Journal of Psychology, 89,* 617–630.

Perkins, D. N. (1981). The mind's best work. Cambridge: Cambridge University Press.

Poincaré, H. (1952). Mathematical discovery. In *Science and method* (pp. 46–63). New York: Dover Books.

Polanyi, M. (1967). *The tacit dimension.* Garden City, NY: Doubleday.

Raaheim, K., and Kauffman, G. (1972). Level of activity and success in solving an unfamiliar problem. *Psychological Reports, 30,* 271–274.

Reber, A. S. (1967). Implicit learning of artificial grammars. *Journal of Verbal Learning and Verbal Behavior, 5,* 855–863.

Reber, A. S. (1989). Implicit learning and tacit knowledge. *Journal of Experimental Psychology: General, 3,* 219–235.

Russo, J. E., Johnson, E. J., and Stephens, D. L. (1989). The validity of verbal protocols. *Memory and Cognition, 17,* 759–769.

Schacter, D. L. (1987). Implicit memory: History and current status. *Journal of Experimental Psychology: Learning Memory, and Cognition, 13,* 501–518.

Schooler, J. W. (1989). *Verbalization can impair the non-verbal components of visual memories.* Paper presented at the 30th Annual Meeting of the Psychonomic Society, November, Atlanta, GA.

Schooler, J. W., and Engstler-Schooler, T. Y. (1990). Verbal overshadowing of visual memories: Some things are better left unsaid. *Cognitive Psychology, 22,* 36–71.

Schooler, J. W., McCleod, C., Brooks, K., and Melcher, J. (1993). [Individual differences in solving insight and analytical problems.] Unpublished data.

Schooler, J. W., Ohlsson, S., and Brooks, K. (1993). Thoughts beyond words: When language overshadows insight. *Journal of Experimental Psychology: General, 122,(2),* 166–183.

Simon, H. A. (1966). Scientific discovery and the psychology of problem solving. In *Mind and cosmos: Essays in contemporary science and philosophy*. Pittsburgh, PA: University of Pittsburgh Press.

Simon, H. A. (1986). The information processing explanation of Gestalt phenomena. *Computers in Human Behavior, 2,* 241–255.

Simonton, D. K. (1988). Scientific genius: A psychology of science. Cambridge: Cambridge University Press.

Smith, S. M., and Blankenship, S. E. (1989). Incubation effects. *Bulletin of the Psychonomic Society, 27*(4), 311–314.

Smith, S. M., and Vela, E. (1991). Incubated reminiscence effects. *Memory and Cognition, 19,* 168–176.

Tardif, T. Z., and Sternberg, R. J. (1988). What do we know about creativity? In R. J. Sternberg (eds.), *The nature of creativity: Contemporary psychological perspectives.* Cambridge: Cambridge University Press.

Taylor, C. W. (1988). Various approaches to and definitions of creativity. In R. J. Sternberg (eds.), *The nature of creativity: Contemporary psychological perspectives.* Cambridge: Cambridge University Press.

Tresselt, M. E., and Mayzner, S. (1966). Normative solution times for a sample of 134 solution words and 378 associated anagrams. *Psychonomic Monograph Supplements, 1*(15), 293–298.

Voss, J. F., Greene, T. R., Post, T. A., and Penner, B. C. (1983). Problem-solving skill in the social sciences. In G. H. Bower (eds.), *The Psychology of Learning and Motivation: Advances in Research Theory*. New York: Academy Press.

Wallas, G. (1926). *The art of thought*. London: J. Cape.

Weisberg, R. W. (1986). *Creativity, genius and other myths*. New York: W. H. Freeman.

Wertheimer, M. (1959). *Productive thinking*. New York: Harper & Row.

Wilson, T. D., and Schooler, J. W. (1991). Thinking too much: Introspection can reduce the quality of preferences and decisions. *Journal of Personality and Social Psychology, 60*, 181–192.

Wilson, T. D., Lisle, D. J., Schooler, J. W., Hodges, S. D., Klaaren, K. J., and Lafleur, S. J. (1993). Introspecting about reasons can reduce post-choice satisfaction. *Personality and Social Psychology Bulletin, 19*, 331–339.

Winner, E., and Garnder, H. (1977). The comprehension of metaphor in brain-damaged patients. *Brain, 100*, 717–729.

Witkin, H. A., Dyk, R., Faterson, H. F., Goodenough, D. R., and Karp, S. A. (1962). *Psychological differentiation*. New York: Wiley.

Witkin, H. A., Oltman, P. K., Raskin, E., and Karp, S. A. (1971). *A manual for the embedded figures test*. Palo Alto, CA: Consulting Psychologists Press.

Woodworth, R. S. (ed.). (1938). *Experimental psychology*. New York: Henry Holt.

Yaniv, I., and Meyer, D. E. (1987). Activation and metacognition of inaccessible stored information: Potential bases for incubation effects in problem solving. *Journal of Experimental Psychology: Learning, Memory, and Cognition, 13*, 187–205.

Chapter 6

Fixation, Incubation, and Insight in Memory and Creative Thinking

Steven M. Smith

Creative thinking does not involve a specific, unitary cognitive process but rather is seen in more general patterns of cognition (Finke, Ward, and Smith 1992). Indeed, the same can be said for many domains of study in cognitive psychology, such as memory, categorization, meta-cognition, or comprehension. Each of these consists of multiple inter-dependent processes; none can adequately be described as a single cognitive process. This chapter takes a broad view of cognition, characterizing certain aspects of creative thinking, including fixation, incubation, and insight experiences, in terms of patterns of simpler cognitive processes. The description is also relevant for similar phenomena in problem solving and memory.

In problem solving, work on a task that is not immediately completed may reach an impasse. In such cases, it is often useful to put the task aside momentarily, returning to it after a delay, when a solution quite suddenly and unpredictably may arise. This pattern of cognition—initial work, impasse, delay, and sudden insight—describes three of Wallas's (1926) four stages of problem solving: preparation, incubation, and illumination. This pattern also describes a common progression of events in recall: interference, recovery, and reminiscence. This chapter proposes that the same underlying mechanisms can account for both of these patterns.

Patterns of Cognition

Searching within a Plan versus Restructuring

Memory retrieval, problem solving, and creative thinking can all involve a constructive search: rather than being simply retrieved as previously stored units, memories and ideas can be constructed from retrieved elements in the course of systematic searches of memory. Bartlett (1932) and Thorndyke (1977), among others, have shown that memories are not passively recorded and replayed in their original form; rather, they are reconstructed from fragments of knowledge, with the reconstruction following a plan, such as a schema or a script (Schank and Abelson 1977). Thus, you might retrieve the knowledge of what you ate for dinner six Sundays ago by reconstructing the needed information from landmarks in memory. The reconstruction could retrieve the same needed information in different ways, such as by thinking back day by day, using common knowledge of what you always eat on Sundays, or focusing on an important memory that you know was near in time to the needed target knowledge and working from there. Problem solving and creative thinking also involve a constructive search, flexibly piecing together fragments of retrieved knowledge according to a guiding structure. This point of view acknowledges the importance of retrieval and the use of prior knowledge in creative thinking, but it also views the structuring of the retrieved elements as important.

The structuring of retrieved elements is done according to a plan (Miller, Galanter, and Pribram 1960), a term used here for convenience to refer to any generalized knowledge structure, such as a script or a mental model. If a known plan is retrieved as a unit stored in memory and used to guide thinking, the process is reproductive rather than creative because known solutions are not novel. For example, a formula for converting degrees Celsius to degrees Fahrenheit can be stored as a unit and used reproductively. If a new plan is constructed from known elements, then one can deal flexibly with unfamiliar problems. For example, solving a Remote Associates Test (RAT) problem (Smith and Blankenship 1991), in which the solution is a single word that is associated with each of three test words (e.g., *apple-family-house*), may require construction of a new plan from the elements of the problem and long-term knowledge. An example of a plan for solving RAT problems is shown in figure 6.1.

In addition to the construction of plans, creative thinking requires the construction of ideas or solutions. Recall targets (the targets of memory searches), problem solutions, and creative ideas are constructed by two different methods: searching within a plan and structuring (or restructuring) plans. Searching within a plan refers to thinking that is guided by sets of rules. This type of thinking typically constructs targets and solutions incrementally or in a stepwise fashion. Structuring, on the other hand, refers to selecting a known plan or constructing a plan from pieces of knowledge. The structured plan then guides subsequent thinking and searching until or unless another plan is constructed.

When memory is searched within a plan, it is done as an iterative process that involves alternate probing and monitoring of memory. A probe is an assembled set of elements of information used to search

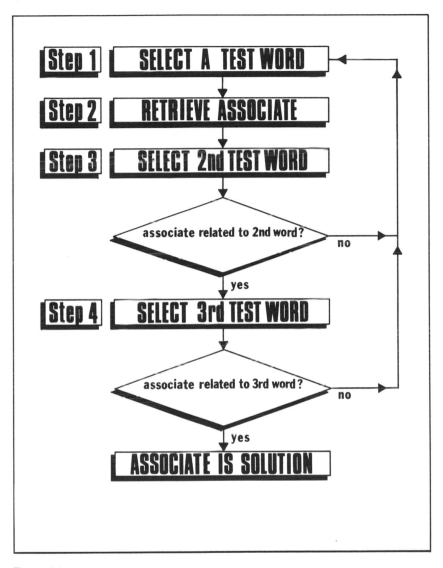

Figure 6.1
A simple plan for solving Remote Associates Test (RAT) problems, beginning with three
test words (e.g., *Apple, Family, House*)

memory, with each element of the probe functioning as a cue that activates information in long-term memory. Inclusion of an element in a probe can be intentional or automatic. The knowledge activated by a probe can then be monitored and analyzed, and the monitored elements can be included in a succeeding probe. When a plan is instantiated, it guides processing by determining the cues contained in successions of probes. Each time a probe results in the activation of knowledge that satisfies the needs or constraints of a problem as defined by the instantiated plan, the plan's activation is renewed, thereby stabilizing the instantiated plan. Persistence at searching within a plan depends on whether such work is successfully satisfying needs or constraints.

A Plan-Determined Road Map
This general theory can provide some insight into the mental searches involved in recall, problem solving, and creative thinking by representing the search as a road map, an abstract spatial representation of various sets of elements in consciousness. The road map is not meant as a mental construction but rather as a stepwise plot of places, whereby each place represents a probe or a set of activated elements. Steps along the road map represent knowledge states that could potentially be visited, beginning with the representation of a problem and progressing toward the representation of a solution in a problem-solving space.[1] As elements fluctuate into and out of the activated set of information, the moment-to-moment record of its contents correspond to placement and movement on the map.

The road map, or problem-solving space, is an abstract structure determined by an activated plan and is relevant only to that plan. Places on a road map that can be visited, the rules that determine movement on the map, and the constraints and needs satisfied by searching the map are all relative to that instantiated plan. Movement downward corresponds to fulfilling needs or constraints of an activated plan, and the connections between places represent operations allowable by the plan—that is, changing, according to the rules of an activated plan, from one set of activated elements to a new set, constitutes searching within a plan, the goal of which is to move down the road map far enough to reach a target solution. Figure 6.2 shows part of a road map for solving the RAT problem apple-family-house.

Subgoals also constitute plans. When a subgoal of a plan is activated, it acts as any other plan in that it has a set of needs or constraints and a set of allowable operations. Subgoal needs and operations can be independent of those of the superordinate plan. Conflict may arise when a need of a subgoal is satisfied at the expense of a need or

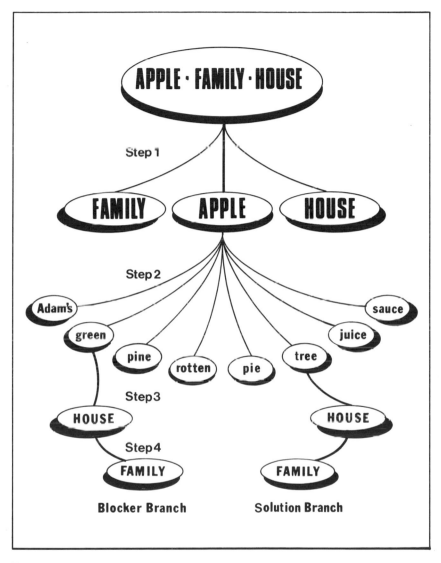

Figure 6.2
A roadmap of a constructive search for the apple-family-house RAT problem. Each step fulfills a need or constraint of the plan. In this case the associate retrieved at step 1 can determine whether the intended solution (tree) or a blocker (green) is retrieved. The blocker branching fails to meet the criterion for a solution because *green* is not related to the test word *family*. The solution (tree) branching satisfies the criterion.

constraint of the superordinate plan. This possibility will be discussed shortly in terms of abandoning a plan or subgoal.

A plan has goals that must be satisfied before it can be successfully exited. A quest to satisfy any subgoal also constitutes execution of a plan; completion of any plan might satisfy only one subgoal of some superordinate plan. Each time a subgoal is satisfied, the superordinate plan is reinforced, meaning that it will continue to be activated for a longer time (even in the absence of future subgoal completion) and that it will be learned better, thereby making it more likely to be activated again for later tasks. The persistence resulting from longer activation can be said to stabilize the plan.

Metacognitive Monitoring
Metacognitive monitoring of work toward the goals of an instantiated plan can yield information to be used for projection into the future. For example, predictions of eventual completion at a task or feelings of imminent success can be based on a variety of sources, one of which includes the constraints or needs that have been met in the course of searching within a plan. The extent to which the needs of a plan have been satisfied or the rate at which those needs have been satisfied may be used to determine predictions, such as feelings of knowing (FOK), tip of the tongue (TOT), or "warmth" (nearness-to-solution) predictions in problem solving, that are sometimes requested by researchers of metacognitive monitoring (Metcalfe 1986b; Metcalfe and Weibe 1987; Smith 1994a).

Metacognitions of impending problem solutions or memory retrievals can be inferred from the amount of work accomplished relative to planned goals or solutions. Such metacognitions are often predictive of impending success. Use of a plan that cannot produce a solution (e.g., the *green* branch of the map in figure 6.2), however, may also result in feelings of impending success. These illusory feelings of warmth may be falsely inferred from progress toward an anticipated type of solution for which there is no token. In the *apple-family-house* RAT problem, if the word *green* is retrieved (figure 6.2), it will produce a subjective feeling of warmth because it satisfies some of the needs of a problem solution by combining successfully with two of the three test words (*green-apple* and *green-house*). This pattern is a recipe for fixation, defined as a counterproductive adherence to a plan or a target solution.

Implicit Fixation
The elements or cues that are included in a probe are determined by several factors, including recent experiences, permanent knowledge,

recently primed knowledge, and contextual information, such as incidental environmental cues or influential verbal cues. Cues can be intentionally or implicitly included in a probe. A cue intentionally included in a probe at one point in an iterative search process may be implicitly included in subsequent probes due to the cue's recency or its association with contextual cues. For example, on the *apple-family-house* RAT problem, one might initially include a control element in probes that lead one to search for two-word phrases that end with a test word, such as *dog-house, green-house,* or *white-house,* rather than phrases that begin with test words, such as *house-fly, house-guest,* or *house-arrest.* This initially intentional inclusion may become an implicit assumption as the search for solutions continues. The intentional inclusion of cues in a probe allows thinking to be guided by plans, and the implicit inclusion of cues allows a selective set of information to be primed or foregrounded, creating a set or a context that can be used to interpret and resolve ambiguities and to generate expectations. The effort required to keep implicit cues activated is very small, freeing attention for more demanding tasks.

Repetition priming effects, according to this point of view, occur because recent experience of a target, such as a word that solves a fragment, anagram, or RAT problem, increases the chances that the correct elements will be implicitly included in probes. By the same token, if elements that correspond to dead-end branchings of a plan's road map (such as *green* in the *apple-family-house* problem) are primed, then the chances of finding a correct solution are diminished, and the time to reach a solution should be increased. This pattern describes a negative priming effect; that is, performance on a task is worse because of priming.

A cue that is implicitly included in a probe may lead to continued fixation, and without awareness of what is preventing a successful search, one may have great difficulty discovering where one has erred. If the goal is not reached, the search process is repeated until either success is finally achieved or sufficient failures discourage further probes. Therefore, one may adopt a stopping rule that discontinues a search after a set number of search attempts have failed to satisfy any unsatisfied needs or constraints (Raaijmakers and Shiffrin 1980; Rundus 1973). Once a search has been stopped, an instantiated plan or subgoal may become destabilized, making it possible for other plans or subgoals to become activated.

Destabilization
Activated plans must be stabilized to remain activated. An activated plan competitively prevents activation of other plans if the needs and

constraints of the active plan continue to be satisfied. Destabilization, and a resultant loss of activation, can occur for many reasons. One is that an activated plan may reach a dead-end on its road map; that is, work within a plan may not continue to progress toward its intended goal beyond a certain point. The number or duration of failures to progress could be used as a criterion for deciding whether to stop or to persist at a plan. When an activated plan cannot produce its intended goal (the plan's road map dead-ends and cannot get to its intended goal), eventual success depends on abandoning the inappropriate plan. Particularly relevant here is the persistence and abandoning of inappropriate plans, patterns of cognition that are proposed to underlie fixation and incubation in memory and problem solving.

A second reason that a plan may destabilize is that conflicts among the goals or needs of interacting plans may be unavoidable and unresolvable. For example, if the major goal of law enforcement is to reduce crime and a subgoal is to arrest criminals, then arranging to entrap people by luring them into committing crimes would cause a conflict. Entrapment would serve the subgoal by increasing arrests but conflict with the more basic goal of reducing crime because it would cause crimes to occur.

In these two situations, the major impediment is not necessarily with the overall plan; the conflict may occur with only one particular branching of the plan's road map. Without abandoning a plan entirely, one can often return to a previous branching and choose another route that may avoid such conflicts. This backing-up strategy still constitutes searching within a plan because thinking is still guided by the activated plan. Backing up requires selectively eliminating or inhibiting the elements in probes that represent the dead end or conflicting branchings and then searching down other branchings of a plan's road map.

Selective elimination of probe elements requires an awareness that those elements are being included in probes. For example, solving a mystery may begin with a clue that leads to a dead end. Intentionally dropping the first clue, one may then try another lead. It may not be possible, however, selectively to eliminate elements that are implicitly or automatically included in probes. In creative problem-solving situations, these blocks are called "implicit assumptions" that prevent successful ideas (Adams 1974).

Restructuring as Changing Plans
Once a plan is abandoned, a new plan may be activated. This process is called restructuring because a new cognitive structure is instantiated. The term *restructuring* (Dominowski, chap. 4; Metcalfe 1986a; Schooler and Melcher, chap. 5) has been used to refer to a rapid

perceptual-like reformulation or reconceptualization of a problem, causing a solution to burst suddenly into consciousness. According to this definition, not all restructuring should result in a flash of insight; a newly adopted plan may construct solutions in a slow, incremental fashion.

Insight experiences occur when restructuring yields a knowledge state in which many, or perhaps all, of the important constraints or needs of a problem are suddenly satisfied. In the case of deeper insights, solutions may be suddenly seen to apply to many other problems besides the one at hand. Rapid emergence of information into consciousness increases confidence in the reliability or appropriateness of the retrieved information (Kelley and Lindsay 1993). Thus, the rapid activation of a new plan, or restructuring, causes the extreme confidence in insight experiences.

Problems in which insight experiences can occur are those in which (1) an inappropriate plan is initially used and (2) the information readily at hand makes a solution obvious once an appropriate plan is activated. The reason that the obvious solution is not initially seen is that a likelier but inappropriate plan is initially instantiated. Information can be readily at hand because of physical clues that are present, because of a "prepared mind" (Mandler, chap. 1), or both. For novices, such as subjects in typical psychology experiments, this situation can be approximated with insight problems (Dominowski, chap. 4; Metcalfe 1986b; Schooler and Melcher, chap. 5) that provide all the necessary clues but lead the subject initially astray by fixating subjects on inappropriate plans. Historically significant insights can occur when a prepared mind restructures a traditional approach to a problem; insights such as agriculture, nongeocentric astronomy, or that diseases can be caused by bacterial infection may seem very obvious in retrospect, yet these ideas clearly eluded earlier fixated approaches to the problems that they solved.

Phenomena Explained

Several phenomena that have been observed, including various forms of fixation or blocking, incubation or recovery, and insight experiences, can be parsimoniously explained in essentially the same way.

Fixation
Fixation, a counterproductive adherence to a target or an approach, may occur because of memory blocking. In terms of the road-map metaphor, fixation and related forms of blocking are explained as a wrong turn in the search process that prevents one from finding an

intended target. A tendency to retrieve blockers rather than targets can have deleterious effects on performance in a number of different cognitive tasks. These tasks include so-called memory phenomena, such as classic interference (Barnes and Underwood 1959), output interference (Rundus 1973), TOT tasks (Jones 1989), and blocking in indirect memory tasks (Smith 1993a). In addition to noting some fixation effects in memory studies, I will also briefly review some recent studies of fixation in creative problem solving.

Fixation in Memory Tasks   Classic retroactive and proactive interference findings have been explained as response competition; correct targets are not retrieved (i.e., they are blocked) if similar items in memory are retrieved instead. The elements in a probe that differentiate retrieval of a target from retrieval of a blocker map onto different branchings in a road map guided by a recall plan.

Output interference, or blocking of recallable targets, can occur when part of the search set is provided as retrieval cues (Rundus 1973). Similar output interference effects may be caused in free recall, when a subject retrieves some targets from a search set; the initially recalled items block recall of the rest of the search set.

Another memory phenomenon that appears to be caused, at least in part, by memory blocking is the TOT state (Jones 1989). Although some TOT reports clearly occur for reasons other than retrieval blocking (Koriat and Lieblich 1974; Schwartz and Metcalfe 1992; Smith 1994a), there is abundant evidence that retrieval blocking is often associated with TOT states (Jones 1989; Jones and Langford 1987; Reason and Lucas 1984; Smith 1991, 1994a). Blocking words are often reported in conjunction with TOT experiences (Reason and Lucas 1984), and TOTs are increased when words related to correct targets are given at recall (Jones 1987; Jones and Langford 1987; Smith 1991). As with the interference effects noted, the TOT blocking phenomenon can be explained in terms of searching inappropriate branchings of the road map representing a recall plan.

The interference or blocking effects in memory tasks noted so far have been demonstrated using direct tests of memory, which rely heavily on explicit, intentional remembering. Indirect tests, such as word fragment completion (Tulving, Schacter, and Stark 1982), are better measures of implicit remembering, or remembering without awareness (Richardson-Klavehn and Bjork 1988; Schacter 1987). Studies of implicit memory have found that word fragments are more likely to be completed if the solutions have been recently primed (Tulving, Schacter, and Stark 1982), even when subjects do not appear to be aware that recent memory is benefiting performance.

In a recent study (Smith 1993c) I examined the hypothesis that recent primes could negatively affect word fragment completion; the experiment was a test of implicit fixation. On an incidental task, subjects saw a number of words, some of them related to subsequent word fragment completion problems. Some of the related words were solutions to fragments (positive primes), as in typical repetition priming studies. Others, however, were orthographically similar to fragment solutions but could not be used to solve the similar fragments (blockers, or negative primes). Table 6.1 contains four items that showed both positive and negative priming.

In comparison to the proportion correctly completed following unrelated primes (.69), performance after positive primes was elevated (.83), and performance following negative primes was decreased (.53). This negative priming or blocking effect may constitute implicit fixation, implicitly diverting searches down dead-end branchings of a retrieval plan. If experimentally induced fixation can occur without one's awareness, then naturally occurring factors, such as implicit assumptions, might also cause fixation. Many more empirical studies of implicit blocking will be needed before more definitive conclusions can be drawn.

Fixation in Creative Problem Solving   The blocking or fixation effects noted in memory tasks can also be seen in problem-solving tasks, including creative problem solving. A classic case of fixation caused by recent priming is the *Einstellung* or mental set effect demonstrated by Luchins and Luchins (1959). In those studies, subjects would see a long sequence of problems, each of which could be solved by plugging given numbers into a formula. After many of the problems, subjects learned to reapply the formula on each successive problem. At the end of the list, however, a problem was given that could not be solved by the learned formula (referred to as the "set" or *Einstellung*

Table 6.1
Word Fragments and Corresponding Primes

Fragment	Type of prime		
	Blocker	Solution	Unrelated
L _ D _ E R	LEADER	LADDER	MEMBRANE
A N _ T O _ Y	ANCHOVY	ANATOMY	SHERIFF
I N _ R T _ _	INVERTED	INERTIA	UNIVERSE
L E _ T _ R E	LETTER	LECTURE	TEQUILA

Source: Smith 1993.

solution) but that could be solved by a much simpler formula. The difficulty that the subjects had with the critical problems can be explained in terms of the road map of the plan guiding problem solving. The set solution represents a dead-end branching, different from the correct solution.

RAT problems, which have been used as a test of creativity (Mednick 1962), have also been used to demonstrate fixation or negative priming effects (e.g., Smith and Blankenship 1991). For example, when the negative primes *green-apple* and *green-house* were given on an incidental task prior to solving RAT problems, the corresponding RAT problem *apple-family-house* was less likely to be solved (the correct answer is *tree*, which makes the phrases *apple-tree*, *family-tree*, and *tree-house*). Priming phrases with the word *green* led searches down an inappropriate branch of the problem-solving plan, preventing discovery of the correct solution (Figure 6.2).

Fixation in Creative Idea Generation   Ideas for approaches to creative problems often occur in a less than complete form, such as a pre-inventive idea (Finke 1990) or a mental model. The initially generated ideas can then be considered and developed further toward a creative solution or product. Some creative problem-solving methods, such as brainstorming, focus on idea generation, emphasizing novelty, quantity, diversity, unusualness, and imaginativeness.

To study creative idea generation experimentally, my colleagues and I have used a novel idea generation technique (Jansson and Smith 1991; Smith, Ward, and Schumacher 1993; Ward in press, chap. 7). In these studies subjects are asked to design as many new ideas as possible for, for example, a spillproof coffee cup, a creature from an inhabited planet similar to Earth, or a toy. The subjects are instructed that existing objects are not allowed and that they must draw and describe new ideas they have never before encountered. Most college students are surprisingly imaginative and prolific in these studies, sketching several creative ideas within a brief span of time.

What has especially interested us in these experiments are the often limiting or fixating effects of prior experience on creative idea generation. As in the memory and problem-solving tasks, we have looked at negative priming effects. In one set of studies, we asked subjects to generate as many new toys or as many new extraterrestrial creatures as possible in 20 minutes (Smith, Ward, and Schumacher 1993). Each idea was sketched and labeled on a separate page. Half of the subjects briefly viewed three example toys or creatures prior to the generation task; the control group saw no examples. In all three experiments, the ideas that subjects generated after seeing examples were far more likely than the control group to contain the features of the example toys (i.e., used a ball, involved high physical activity, used electronic devices) and creatures (had four legs, antennae, and a tail).

These consistent results indicate that creative thinking, which often involves generation of divergent ideas, can be restricted if priming draws the generative search down common branchings of a plan's road map. Furthermore, even when the subjects were told to create new ideas that would be as different as possible from the examples, their ideas still conformed to the examples. The fact that subjects, when instructed, could not escape the conformity effects caused by the briefly seen examples suggests that the restriction of ideas was involuntary or unintentional.

A similar conformity effect caused by recent priming was reported by Jansson and Smith (1991), who gave mechanical engineering design problems to students and professional designers. The problems required subjects to sketch and describe as many new ideas as possible for objects, such as spillproof coffee cups, measuring cups for the blind, or biomechanical measuring devices. They too found that ideas conformed to examples that were shown in advance. Even when a faulty feature of the example was forbidden in the instructions, subjects' designs still contained the forbidden feature much more often than was seen in control subjects' designs. This design fixation, a restriction in the creativity of designs caused by adherence to an example, was also reported by engineers as a common problem in professional design settings.

Incubation and Contextual Fluctuation
Different probes may result in the retrieval or activation of different elements in memory. Of particular importance here is that one probe may lead to a target in memory, a solution to a problem, or a creative idea, whereas another probe may lead only to failure. Furthermore, the contents and direction of a probe may be context sensitive. Because different contexts are represented by different sets of activated elements in consciousness, a problem or memory cue presented in two different contexts may be represented by different probes (Smith 1994b). Therefore, if a problem presented in one context becomes fixated, trying the problem in a new context may lead to success if the new context induces a problem representation that avoids fixation.

When the activated set of elements in consciousness fluctuates over time, such that more fluctuation occurs when more time passes (Bower 1972), then time passage is associated with contextual change. The same problem is more likely to be approached differently if more time passes between two attempts at a problem because greater contextual change is likelier to have occurred. If a constructive search has become fixated, then contextual or temporal changes may lead to a probe that is different from the fixated one and therefore has a greater chance of succeeding than a probe similar to the fixated one.

This idea, which I have proposed elsewhere (Smith, 1994b; Smith and Blankenship 1991), provides a theoretical basis for incubation effects, defined as a situation in which initial attempts at a task fail and greater improvement in problem solving or memory can be seen when retesting occurs after a delay rather than immediately. According to this explanation, incubation occurs primarily in situations in which initial fixation blocks one from remembering or solving a problem. If a retest is attempted when fixated elements are still active in consciousness, then solutions and targets will remain blocked. But if a retest occurs after a delay or in a changed context, the problem may be represented differently, increasing the chances of success.

This pattern describes incubation as a dissipation of fixation. Correct answers or approaches to problems may become temporarily inaccessible when competing material causes fixation, but after an incubation interval, the correct answers and approaches are predicted to be less inaccessible.

Although this pattern of interference and recovery was originally intended to characterize retroactive interference, essentially the same pattern can be adapted to the domains of output interference and reminiscence, TOT retrieval failures and resolution of such states, and fixation and incubation in problem solving. Approaches to incubation, TOT resolution, and reminiscence have typically been constructive, explaining the progress that leads to solutions and retrieval targets. In contrast, the proposed theory treats these phenomena as cases in which cognitive fixation is overcome.

Recovery from Retroactive Interference   Patterns of interference have long shown that a well-learned response will decrease in accessibility when a competing response becomes stronger (Barnes and Underwood 1959). Such interference diminishes with longer retention intervals, giving rise to spontaneous recovery, an increase in accessibility of the original response that had suffered from interference. Mensink and Raaijmakers (1988) modeled this phenomenon, based on a system that increases contextual fluctuation with longer retention intervals. In terms of the present theory, the contextual fluctuation allowed by the recovery period made probes less likely to retrieve interfering responses.

Recovery from Output Interference   If recall is blocked by output interference as it is by retroactive interference, then recovery from output interference should also show and incubation effect. Output interference has been theorized to occur because of part-list cues (Rundus 1973) or because of items initially retrieved in free recall (Roediger 1974). If an initial free recall attempt is constrained by output interference, then reminiscence (recalling information on a second test after failing to recall it on an initial test) should be greater after an incubation period.

Smith and Vela (1991) reported three experiments that found incubated reminiscence effects; that is, reminiscence was greater following a delayed retest of free recall as compared to an immediate retest. Incubated reminiscence effects were not diminished when a difficult distractor task was given during the incubation time, indicating that the effects were not due to conscious memory searches conducted during the incubation period. Also, the incubated reminiscence effects Smith and Vela observed occurred primarily in the first minute of the retest, which is consistent with the idea that incubation time helps one avoid fixation by creating a new mental set.

Recovery from TOT States   Retrieval blocks can occur because material that is similar to the correct target is highly accessible. For example, TOT states often appear to result from retrieval of incorrect words or names that are similar to the correct target (Reason and Lucas 1984). In a test of the blocking hypothesis, Smith (1991) gave subjects a list of named imaginary animals (TOTimals) to learn and then tested them on the names. The level of TOTs reported was found to be greater when an incorrect TOTimal name was supplied with the retrieval cues. In another study, Balfour and Smith (1993) found that TOTs observed in response to general knowledge questions increased when subjects attended to the meaning of blocker words that were related to the recall targets.

If TOTs often represent retrieval blocks, then are such blocks better resolved after an incubation interval? Consistent with this possibility are data reported in a diary study by Burke and coworkers (1991), who found that TOTs that were not resolved within 2 minutes often took hours or days to resolve. An experimental study by Smith (1991) using the TOTimals examined incubation effects for unrecalled items in TOT states. Subjects were given two recall tests for each TOTimal name. The second recall test was given either immediately after the first or delayed by an incubation interval. For items not recalled in the first attempt, few were resolved if the retest was given immediately; only 9 percent of TOT items were resolved on the immediate retest. More

TOT resolutions (43 percent) occurred when the retest followed an incubation interval.

Recovery from Implicit Fixation   An experiment reported by Smith (1993) was described in which negative priming was found in word fragment completion, a task often used in tests of implicit memory. Smith, Carr, and Tindell (1993) hypothesized that this implicit blocking, like output interference and TOTs, should be diminished after an incubation interval. Following negative priming and initial attempts at fragments, unsolved word fragments were retested, either immediately or after a filled incubation interval. An incubation effect was observed; more fragments that were initially unsolved were resolved on the retest if the retest was delayed rather than immediate.

Recovery from Fixation in Problem Solving   Paradigms similar to the already described memory tasks have also been used to show incubation effects in problem solving (Smith and Blankenship 1989, 1991). That is, following negative priming, problems were tested, and initially unsolved ones were retested, either immediately or after an incubation interval. Incubation effects in problem solving were observed in four experiments that used picture-word puzzles (Smith and Blankenship 1989) and in three experiments that used RAT problems (Smith and Blankenship 1991).

Insight Experiences
Incubation effects, by definition, depend on the resolution of memory or problem-solving impasses. These resolutions of problems may occur very suddenly and unexpectedly, either during some unrelated or unstructured activity (Mandler, chap. 1), or when returning to a problem after a hiatus. This sudden resolution of a problem when an idea bursts into consciousness is called illumination or an insight experience.

Questions about the existence of insight, its nature, and definitions of insight problems have been debated in recent years (Metcalfe and Weibe 1987; Smith 1994b; Weisberg and Alba 1981). One approach to distinguishing between insight and noninsight problems is to examine the metacognitions that accompany work on a problem (Metcalfe and Weibe 1987). This metacognitive approach clearly emphasizes the primacy of conscious experience in insight phenomena. In several experiments Metcalfe and her colleagues (Metcalfe 1986a, 1986b; Metcalfe and Weibe 1987) have found that subjects' predictions of impending success showed an incremental pattern in solving noninsight problems, as compared with a sudden "catastrophic" increase just prior to solutions of insight problems.

Typical work on noninsight problems reflects searching within a plan. If metacognitions of impending success are based on satisfying the needs of an activated plan and the needs of the plan are being satisfied incrementally, then it follows that warmth ratings should increase incrementally, as Metcalfe (1986b) reported. Work on insight problems may begin with incremental progress down an inappropriate plan's road map. If so, then corresponding incremental increases in warmth ratings on insight problems would end in failures, which is exactly the result Metcalfe and Weibe (1987) reported. Insight experiences, according to this explanation, are sudden and unexpected because they involve finding a new plan or cognitive structure once the initial fixated plan becomes destabilized.

Summary

The proposed theory conceptualizes cognition at a relatively macroscopic level. When activated plans guide thinking, the plans' rules determine the types of solutions and targets that are anticipated and the knowledge states that can potentially be constructed en route to solutions. A plan's potential knowledge states can be plotted as a road map in which the plan's needs and constraints are satisfied as one travels from one knowledge state to another, searching within the plan's domain. Fixation is a counterproductive adherence to a branching of a plan's road map, or to an entire plan, and can be particularly problematic if elements that correspond to fixated branchings and plans are implicitly included in probes when memory is searched. Metacognitions of impending success at a task are inferential judgments based on the needs of a plan that are satisfied relative to an anticipated solution. Satisfying needs stabilizes plans and encourages their persistence, whereas failures to satisfy needs destabilize plans, threatening their activation. Restructuring refers to selection or construction of a new plan when a previous one is destabilized.

An insight experience takes place when restructuring and satisfying needs of the new plan occur rapidly. If fixation has occurred and a search has become stuck in a dead-end branching of a road map, incubation can contribute to insight experiences because time passage allows the elements in consciousness to fluctuate. Because a fixated branching is determined by a set of activated elements, that dead end is less likely to be reconstructed once the active elements have fluctuated. Avoiding or escaping dead ends can improve the chances that previously blocked plans will be activated, increasing the likelihood of activating a successful plan. Contextual changes and challenges of probe contents can help destabilize fixated plans or branchings.

Predictions

Several principles and hypotheses can be derived from the theory proposed here.

1. A single explanation, recovery from blocks, can explain phenomena in episodic recall, semantic recall, implicit memory, problem solving, and creative thinking. Therefore, analogues of phenomena such as fixation, incubation, and insight should be observed in all of these domains.

2. Fixation can be implicit. The findings of negative priming in word fragment completion (Smith 1993; Smith, Carr, and Tindell 1993) suggest, but do not prove, that blocks can operate beyond one's awareness. Given the recent proliferation of methods designed to study memory without awareness (Richardson-Klavehn and Bjork 1988; Schacter 1987), it seems reasonable that it should be possible to study implicit fixation. Findings of implicit fixation would provide an empirical basis for the notion that problem solving and creative idea generation can be blocked or restricted because of implicit assumptions.

3. Fixation is sensitive to incidental contextual influences. Given the proposed interference and recovery theory of fixation and incubation, a way to reduce retrieval blocks should be to shift contexts. Context-dependent memory has been reliably shown to occur even for incidental manipulations of environmental contexts (Smith 1988). Contextual cuing is the most commonly known type of context-dependent memory, showing that contextual reinstatement helps to cue memories acquired in a context. The most robust context effects, however, have been findings that interference is reduced when target sets are acquired in separate contexts (Smith 1988). Therefore, shifting from a fixated context is predicted to increase incubation effects by reducing the interference that causes fixation. This theory also predicts that memory for fixation material should be poorer if tested in an altered context.

4. Metacognitions of impending success at recall or problem solving are predictive of success when solutions are achieved according to plans but are not predictive when solutions or resolutions require restructuring. Therefore, a sense of imminent success can be illusory on insight problems or other situations that require nonobvious approaches. If blocks are induced, as with a negative priming procedure, subjects should be more inclined to use inappropriate plans initially.

Therefore, it is predicted that resolutions of initial memory and problem-solving failures will show an insight pattern when the failures are caused by blocks.

5. Becoming aware of elements that are being implicitly included in probes and challenging probe contents may be a way to escape fixation. One way to approach the task of becoming aware of implicitly included cues in a generative search is to try to reconceptualize the problem in more general or abstract terms. For example, paraphrasing the problem as given or as understood may help one to focus on the more general meaning of the problem. Creative generation tasks (Smith, Balfour, and Brown 1994; Ward in press, chap. 7) should be ideal for studying how to challenge one's implicit assumptions because subjects appear to impose their own conceptual constraints in such tasks and because it is possible to induce such constraints experimentally with negative priming procedures.

Conclusion

The perspective discussed in this chapter provides a general, macroscopic view of cognition. Many theories, particularly computational ones, have focused on microcognitive levels of explanations. Although an understanding of cognition clearly depends on microscopic theories, it is also important to get a larger point of view if we are to understand an issue as complex as creativity, which depends on the interaction of many cognitive activities.

The explanation of incubation provided here describes a memory mechanism other than spreading activation that can account for an increase in accessibility over time of a problem solution or a blocked memory. Alterations of the encoding context, caused by physical contextual changes, changes in tasks or situations, or time-dependent fluctuations of one's mental set, lead to a problem representation that is different from a prior fixated one. A different representation is therefore more likely to produce a solution or the target of a memory search and could lead to creative ideas that had been previously blocked by fixated thinking. This is essentially the same theory that has been used to explain recovery from retroactive interference (Mensink and Raaijmakers 1988). Therefore, an underlying memory representation can explain incubation effects, whether or not spreading activation also can cause incubation.

Another advantage of the perspective described in this chapter is that it resolves apparent conflicts between ideas about insight versus incremental progress in problem solving. The same theory can explain how incremental progress on problem solving or memory retrieval can be made and metacognitively monitored, how fixation can occur and lead to illusory incremental patterns of warmth, and how insight experiences can occur.

Finally, consistent with the aim of a creative cognition approach, the theory makes predictions about both creativity (e.g., enhancing incubation with contextual manipulations; awareness and challenging of probe elements) and memory (e.g., metacognitions about impending recall).

Notes

The work reported in this chapter was supported by NIMH grant R01 MH4473001.
1. This idea of a hierarchical branching representation of a problem-solving or planning space is related to ideas described by many others, such as Newell, Shaw, and Simon (1962).

References

Adams, J. L. (1974). *Conceptual blockbusting*. Stanford, CA: Stanford Alumni Association.

Balfour, S. P., and Smith, S. M. (1993, April). *A demonstration of meaning-related blocking in the tip-of-the-tongue phenomenon*. Paper presented at the meeting of the Midwestern Psychological Association, Chicago.

Barnes, J. M., and Underwood, B. J. (1959). "Fate" of first-list associations in transfer theory. *Journal of Experimental Psychology, 58*, 97–105.

Bartlett, F. C. (1932). *Remembering*. Cambridge: Cambridge University Press.

Bower, G. H. (1972). Stimulus sampling theory of encoding variability. In A. W. Melton and E. Martin (eds.), *Coding processes in human memory*. Washington, DC: Winston.

Burke, D., MacKay, D. G., Worthley, J. S., and Wade, E. (1991). On the tip of the tongue: What causes word finding failures in young and older adults? *Journal of Memory and Language, 30*, 237–246.

Finke, R. A. (1990). *Creative imagery: Discoveries and inventions in visualization*. Hillsdale, NJ: Erlbaum.

Finke, R. A., Ward, T. B., and Smith, S. M. (1992). *Creative cognition: Theory, research, and applications*. Cambridge, MA: MIT Press.

Jansson, D. G., and Smith, S. M. (1991). Design fixation. *Design Studies, 12* (1), 3–11.

Jones, G. V. (1989). Back to Woodworth: Role of interlopers in the tip-of-the-tongue phenomenon. *Memory and Cognition, 17*, 69–76.

Jones, G. V., and Langford, S. (1987). Phonological blocking in the tip of the tongue state. *Cognition, 26*, 115–122.

Kelley, C. M., and Lindsay, D. S. (1993). Remembering mistaken for knowing: Ease of retrieval as a basis for confidence in answers to general knowledge questions. *Journal of Memory and Language, 32*, 1–24.

Koriat, A., and Lieblich, I. (1974). What does a person in a "TOT" state know that a person in a "don't know" state doesn't know? *Memory and Cognition, 2*, 647–655.

Luchins, A. S., and Luchins, E. H. (1959). *Rigidity of behavior*. Eugene, OR: University of Oregon Press.

Mednick, S. A. (1962). The associative basis of the creative process. *Psychological Review, 69*, 220–232.

Mensink, G., and Raaijmakers, J. G. W. (1988). A model for interference and forgetting. *Psychological Review, 95,* 434–455.

Metcalfe, J. (1986a). Feeling of knowing in memory and problem solving. *Journal of Experimental Psychology: Learning, Memory, and Cognition, 12,* 288–294.

Metcalfe, J. (1986b). Premonitions of insight predict impending error. *Journal of Experimental Psychology: Learning, Memory, and Cognition, 12,* 623–634.

Metcalfe, J., and Weibe, D. (1987). Intuition in insight and non-insight problem solving. *Memory and Cognition, 15,* 238–246.

Miller, G. A., Galanter, E., and Pribram, K. H. (1960). *Plans and the structure of behavior.* New York: Holt, Rinehart, and Winston.

Newell, A., Shaw, J. C., and Simon, H. A. (1962). The process of creative thinking. In Gruber, H. E., Terrell, G., and Wertheimer, M. (eds.), *Contemporary approaches to creative thinking.* New York: Atherton Press.

Raaijmakers, J. G. W., and Shiffrin, R. M. (1980). SAM: A theory of probabilistic search of associative memory. In G. H. Bower (ed.), *The psychology of learning and motivation: Advances in research and theory* (Vol. 14). New York: Academic Press.

Reason, J. T., and Lucas, D. (1984). Using cognitive diaries to investigate naturally occurring memory blocks. In J. Harris and P. E. Morris (eds.), *Everyday memory actions, and absent mindedness* (pp. 53–70). New York: Academic Press.

Richardson-Klavehn, A., and Bjork, R. A. (1988). Measures of memory. *Annual Review of Psychology, 39,* 475–543.

Roediger, II. L., III (1974). Inhibiting effects of recall. *Memory and Cognition, 2,* 261–269.

Rundus, D. (1973). Negative effects of using list items as recall cues. *Journal of Verbal Learning and Verbal Behavior, 12,* 212–218.

Schacter, D. L. (1987). Implicit memory: History and current status. *Journal of Experimental Psychology: Learning, Memory, and Cognition, 13,* 501–518.

Schank, R. C., and Abelson, R. (1977). *Scripts, plans, goals, and understanding.* Hillsdale, NJ: Erlbaum.

Schwartz, B. L., and Metcalfe, J. (1992). Cue familiarity but not target retrievability enhances feeling-of-knowing judgments. *Journal of Experimental Psychology; Learning, Memory, and Cognition, 18,* 1074–1083.

Smith, S. M. (1988). Environmental context-dependent memory. In G. Davies and D. Thomson (eds.), *Memory in context: Context in memory* (pp. 13–33). New York: Wiley.

Smith, S. M. (1991, November). *Tip-of-the-tongue states and blockers with imaginary animals as targets.* Paper presented at the meeting of the Psychonomic Society, San Francisco.

Smith, S. M. (1993). *Fixation in memory and problem solving.* Address presented at the Weiskrantz Symposium on Memory, Baylor University, Waco, TX.

Smith, S. M. (1994a). Frustrated feelings of imminence: On the tip-of-the-tongue. In J. Metcalfe and A. Shimamura (eds.), *Metacognition: Knowing about knowing.* Cambridge, MA: MIT Press.

Smith, S. M. (1994b). Getting into and out of mental ruts: A theory of fixation, incubation, and insight. In R. Sternberg and J. Davidson (eds.) *The nature of insight.* Cambridge, MA: MIT Press.

Smith, S. M., Balfour, S. P., and Brown, J. M. (1994). Effects of practice on TOT states. *Memory, 2,* 31–49.

Smith, S. M., and Blankenship, S. E. (1989). Incubation effects. *Bulletin of the Psychonomic Society, 27,* 311–314.

Smith, S. M., and Blankenship, S. E. (1991). Incubation and the persistence of fixation in problem solving. *American Journal of Psychology, 104,* 61–87.

Smith, S. M., Brown, J. M., and Balfour, S. P. (1991). TOTimals: A controlled experimental method for observing tip-of-the-tongue states. *Bulletin of the Psychonomic Society, 29* (5), 445–447.

Smith, S. M., Carr, J. A., and Tindell, D. R. (1993, April). *Fixation and incubation in word fragment completion.* Paper presented at the meeting of the Midwestern Psychological Association, Chicago.

Smith, S. M., and Vela, E. (1991). Incubated reminiscence effects. *Memory and Cognition, 19* (2), 168–176.

Smith, S. M., Ward, T. B., and Schumacher, J. S. (1993). Constraining effects of examples in a creative generation task. *Memory and Cognition, 21,* 837–845.

Thorndyke, P. W. (1977). Cognitive structures in comprehension and memory of narrative discourse. *Cognitive Psychology, 9,* 77–110.

Tulving, E., Schacter, D. L., and Stark, H. A. (1982). Priming effects in word fragment completion are independent of recognition memory. *Journal of Experimental Psychology: Learning, Memory, and Cognition, 8,* 336–342.

Wallas, G. (1926). *The art of thought.* New York: Harcourt.

Ward, T. B. (in press). Structured imagination: The role of category structure in exemplar generation. *Cognitive Psychology.*

Weisberg, R. W. (1986). *Creativity: Genius and other myths.* San Francisco: W. H. Freeman.

Weisberg, R. W., and Alba, J. W. (1981). An examination of the alleged role of "fixation" in the solution of several "insight" problems. *Journal of Experimental Psychology: General, 110,* 169–192.

Yaniv, I., and Meyer, D. E. (1987). Activation and metacognition of inaccessible stored information: Potential bases for incubation effects in problem solving. *Journal of Experimental Psychology: Learning, Memory, and Cognition, 13,* 187–205.

Chapter 7

What's Old about New Ideas?

Thomas B. Ward

Accident. As the locomotive on the Paterson Railroad, with a train, composed of transportation and passenger cars, was approaching the depot at Paterson, on Monday evening, an axle of the leading transportation car gave way, which overturned that and the next car, and threw the third off the track. The locomotive and passenger cars remained upon the track uninjured, though the passengers felt a shock by the concussion. Mr. Speer, the conductor of transportation, a very industrious and sober man, was seated on the car at the break, and unfortunately was crushed to death under the load.
American Railroad Journal, *1835.*

What factors contributed to Mr. Speer's untimely death, and what can an understanding of those factors tell us about the nature of creative and productive thought? Certainly there is an immediate cause—the breaking of the axle and the resultant derailing of the train cars—but there is a subtler and more pertinent cause as well. Note that Mr. Speer was riding *on* the car, not *in* it, and that none of the passengers, who were inside, was seriously hurt. Mr. Speer was a victim of a convergence of design flaws that required conductors to ride on the outside of cars that were easily derailed. Those flaws reveal important constraints on creative thought and exemplify the phenomenon I have called structured imagination (Ward in press).

Structured imagination refers to the fact that when people use their imagination to develop new ideas, those ideas are heavily structured in predictable ways by the properties of existing categories and concepts. This is true whether the individuals are inventors developing new artifacts, writers generating ideas for works of fiction, scientists speculating about life on other planets, or everyday people fantasizing about a better world.

Importantly, structured imagination entails more than the simple fact that new ideas are influenced by existing knowledge. Clearly, ideas do not arise in a vacuum, and there is a trivial sense in which we must always rely on some type of stored information when we develop any new idea. What could we use other than existing knowledge that we retrieve, draw inferences from, combine in novel ways, and so forth? An important aspect of structured imagination, however, is that the exact features of old ideas that are retained in new ideas are readily predictable from the general principles of categorization and from the particular information people have stored as part of specific category representations.

In this chapter, I will develop several themes relevant to structured imagination. The first is that basic research on the noncreative aspects of categorization can be used to help explain which features of old ideas are most likely to be retained in new ones. This is important, because without a principled way of predicting the likely properties of imagined entities, we run the risk of either failing to notice important aspects of their structure or identifying obvious but trivial ones.

A second theme is that there is an important distinction between novel ideas being structured by existing concepts and those ideas being unimaginative or uncreative. Most ideas that would be judged as highly creative are, nevertheless, structured in predictable ways by existing knowledge (see Finke, chap. 13, and Weisberg, chap. 3, for related ideas). Novelty most often manifests itself within a definite structural framework. Consequently, a complete understanding of creative functioning must include an assessment of both what is new and what is old about new ideas. Structured imagination considers both.

A related theme is that structured imagination can have good consequences, as well as bad ones. Although constraints on creativity, as in the case of early railroad car designs, are often thought of as deleterious, sometimes it is very useful to retain attributes of old ideas when new ideas are being developed. Particularly in recurring engineering problems, for instance, it may be useful to retain well-tested approaches.

A final theme is that it may be possible to overcome some of the constraining effects of structured imagination while retaining necessary or useful properties of older ideas. Specifically, by considering broader knowledge structures (Murphy and Medin 1985) and the processes of structural alignment that guide appropriate feature mappings in categorization and similarity judgment (Medin, Goldstone, and Gentner 1993; Markman and Gentner 1993), it may be possible to determine which attributes one ought to abandon and which attributes ought to be retained.

Structured Imagination in the Real World

As a real-world example of structured imagination, early designs for railway cars were heavily influenced by the properties of the most common vehicle of the day, the stagecoach. In fact, the first railroad passenger cars were little more than stagecoaches with wheels designed to fit on the tracks (White 1978). Like stagecoaches, they contained compartments for the passengers and running boards on which conductors could stand. They had no central aisles through which conductors might safely walk. Similarly, freight or transportation cars, of the type Mr. Speer was riding on, were designed so that conductors had to ride on the outside.

In addition, like stagecoaches, early railroad cars were mounted on two sets of two wheels with a single axle for each set. This meant that if one of the often-unreliable axles broke, the car had a high probability of toppling or derailing (White 1978). Finally, as was true of stagecoaches, the brakes were located on the outside and were operated by a conductor who was seated well above the ground on the front of the car. These factors, which reflect a clear structuring of a new product by the properties of existing products, all conspired to throw Mr. Speer to his death.

The early stagecoach-type models of passenger cars were supplanted relatively quickly in the United States by designs with aisles, but they continued to be used in Europe into the twentieth century. Even in the United States there was some resistance to including a central aisle, based on the concern that it might become one long spittoon (Latrobe 1868). In addition, brakemen continued to fall from their precarious perches on freight cars, 12 feet off the ground, even into the late 1880s. In 1886, for instance, 72 trainmen were killed in falls from cars in Massachusetts, New York, and Michigan alone (*Railroad and Engineering Journal*, 1887).

Clearly, designs for early railroad cars included features from earlier types of vehicles that were inappropriate for the new task. Yet we would not consider their developers to be unimaginative people. On the contrary, many would be considered visionaries who foresaw the importance of the railroad as the transportation of the future long before most people took the idea seriously. In fact, the railroad itself was a revolutionary means of transportation that fundamentally altered the way people traveled in the nineteenth century. What this suggests is that even highly creative individuals and the ideas they develop are susceptible to the constraining influences of structured imagination.

In addition, although the stagecoach-based designs presented some safety problems, they allowed rail travel. By retaining some features of earlier vehicles, designers did not have to start from scratch. Thus, there were some benefits and some drawbacks in the structured imagination that affected early railroad car design.

Weisberg's description (chap. 3) of Edison's idea for an electric lighting distribution system provides another interesting case that illustrates the good and bad aspects of patterning new ideas after old ones. Edison's reliance on the gas distribution system as a model for an electric light system was extremely helpful in providing the basic idea, but it also led to his reliance on the problematic procedure of running wires underground, just as gas mains ran underground.

Structured Imagination in the Laboratory

Although interesting and thought provoking, the historical case of railroad car design does not allow a careful examination of the cognitive principles involved in structured imagination. We cannot go back and reconstruct the thought processes involved, examine the knowledge base of the developers, or, in retrospect, experimentally control their approaches to the design task. We do know that many of the developers had previously made carriages. Thus, they were intimately familiar with the designs of stagecoaches, and their railroad car designs directly reflected that knowledge. To get closer to the cognitive structures and processes involved, however, it is helpful to bring the phenomenon into the laboratory.

In the laboratory paradigm I have developed to examine structured imagination, individuals are asked to generate a novel exemplar of a category that would be appropriate to an imaginary setting. In one set of experiments, I asked subjects to imagine, draw, and describe the kinds of animals that might exist on other planets. Although there are important differences between imaginary animals and railroad cars, and between the goals of experimental subjects and real-world inventors, the basic processes by which a person imagines a new life form ought to be similar to those involved in imagining a new artifact. Thus, the studies can provide important generalities about the way people develop new ideas. In addition, because most people have well-developed ideas about animals, the studies can provide information from a larger sample to complement the analyses on the specialized knowledge of smaller but more creative samples. The results of the laboratory studies thus far indicate that imaginary animals are heavily structured in ways that are directly predictable from what we know about the general principles of noncreative categorization and about people's animal categories in particular (Ward in press).

A Framework for Predictions and a Null Hypothesis

Some of the general principles that govern categorization, as revealed in noncreative categorization tasks, are (1) that people agree on the attributes that are characteristic of typical category members (Ashcraft 1978; Tversky and Hemenway 1984), (2) that the typicality of category exemplars can vary with the context (Barsalou 1987), (3) that people are sensitive to correlations between attributes (Rosch 1978), and (4) that much of categorization is guided by the broad, naive theories that people hold about the workings of the world and by processes of structural alignment that help to determine the most relevant features and feature matches (Markman and Gentner 1993; Medin, Goldstone, and Gentner 1993; Murphy and Medin 1985).

Beyond these general principles of categorization, there are specific things we know about people's animal categories that can be used to predict exactly how their imagined animals will be structured. For example, when people list the properties they believe to be characteristic of animals on earth, they regularly list eyes and other sense organs, and legs and other appendages (Ashcraft 1978; Hampton 1979; Tversky and Hemenway 1984). Clearly, these properties are central to the "earth animal" concept. Further, although people do not spontaneously list bilateral symmetry as a property of animals, it is clear that the attributes they list are not isolated entities but rather parts of larger, coherent, symmetric wholes (Tversky and Hemenway 1984; Ward in press). In addition, attribute listing studies reveal that knowledge about correlated properties is central to people's "animal" category representations. Examples include the knowledge that feathers co-occur with wings and that scales co-occur with fins. Finally, when people judge that two creatures are members of the same specific animal category, they require that the creatures match in terms of shape and parts, but they allow considerable variation in size (Ward et al. 1989).

Taken together, the results from traditional research on the noncreative aspects of categorization lead us to expect that imagined animals will have standard sense organs and appendages arranged into symmetric wholes, that certain attributes will co-occur often, that members of the same imagined species will share the same basic shape and parts but may vary in size, and that broader knowledge and structural alignment processes will have an influence on the creatures that people imagine. It is not just that imaginary animals will be influenced by existing knowledge; rather, the mapping of properties from the earth animal category onto the imagined entity will be predictable from what we know about noncreative aspects of categorization.

It is important to note, however, that there is no reason in principle why animals on other planets would have to resemble animals on earth, and there is nothing in the task description that requires people to access their earth animal categories in developing their imaginary creatures. They could tap into any existing knowledge base, such as breakfast cereals or rock formations, to get an idea for the general shape of their creatures, and each person could access something different. Even if they were all compelled to access the animal category, there is no reason they would have to use typical exemplars and characteristic properties of earth animals or be influenced by the same type of structural alignment that guides noncreative categorization; they could use more exotic animate properties, and they could vary the standard mapping principles.

Thus, there is a meaningful null hypothesis stating that imagined animals will not bear the specific predicted relations to real earth animals. Failure to find the predicted relations could occur if creativity is inherently unpredictable and idiosyncratic, if it is predictable but based on different processes and structures than ordinary cognition, or if it emerges from divine inspiration or some other unobservable source.

Note also that the structured imagination predictions are about the natural or default tendencies that people will follow due to the nature of category structures and processes. These default tendencies determine the paths along which imaginative ideas are most likely to be guided. They do not represent absolute constraints that can never be overridden.

Mapping of Basic Properties

Despite the infinite variety of imagined creatures possible, the college students I tested developed creatures with highly predictable properties (Ward in press). Across four experiments, the vast majority of imagined animals possessed attributes that are characteristic of typical animals on earth, such as symmetry, appendages (e.g., legs), and sense organs (e.g., eyes), exactly the attributes predicted from traditional attribute listing studies. Examples of some of the creatures are shown in figure 7.1. Note also that those creatures tend to have typical numbers and locations of sense and appendages. Thus, they are highly similar to earth animals in many important and predictable ways. Just

Figure 7.1
Examples of imaginary animals produced by college students in Ward (in press)

as railroad passenger cars retained the characteristic features of stagecoaches, these imaginary animals retained the characteristic features
of earth animals.

When I asked these students to generate a second member of the
same imaginary species, they developed creatures that matched the
first in shape, sense organs, and appendages but often explicitly varied
from it in size. When I asked them to generate a member of a different
imaginary species, they most often developed a creature that varied
from the first in shape, senses, and appendages but not explicitly in
size (Ward in press, experiment 1). In addition, only when subjects
were developing a second member of the same species did they explicitly vary gender. In other words, subjects varied some attributes
more within species and other attributes more between species.

The relative likelihood of subjects' including particular attribute variations within and between species was highly predictable. The pattern indicates that people apply to the imaginary domain "animals on another planet" the same principles that structure their existing animal categories (e.g., that members of the same basic category should have the same shape and parts). More subtly, the fact that subjects explicitly mentioned size and gender variations less often across two imaginary species than within a single imaginary species indicates that imagination may be influenced by a structural alignment process similar to that characterizing noncreative categorization (Markman and Gentner 1993; Medin, Goldstone, and Gentner 1993). Specifically, to explain how people are able to judge category membership or determine similarity in noncreative tasks, it appears necessary to have some sort of alignment process by which an individual could determine which attributes of one object to compare with which attributes of another object, and which attributes should receive the most attention.

Presumably the alignment process is guided by broader knowledge frameworks. For instance, consider a comparison between a bull and a goose. How similar are they, and should they be assigned to the same category? One broad knowledge framework might tell us to compare the bull's legs to the goose's legs and to count this as a difference in terms of "number of legs." An alternate relational framework might lead to an alignment of the bull's legs with the goose's wings as a mismatch on the dimension "means of movement." Broader knowledge might also lessen the salience of the sex difference in this comparison but heighten it in the within-species comparison between a bull and cow or a gander and a goose.

To extend this notion of structural alignment to the creative domain, the same type of broader knowledge framework appears to decrease the importance of sex differences across different imaginary species and highlight them within an imaginary species. Gender comparisons are made more salient within than across species, whether in the real or imaginary realm.

Evidence for the role of structural alignment also comes from two other observations. First, the fact that the component parts of the imaginary creatures were organized into symmetric wholes indicates that the normal relationships that hold between component attributes of earth animals were mapped onto the imaginary ones. Subjects did not, for instance, develop creatures with a leg and an arm on the upper body and another leg and arm on the lower body, although there is no reason that such an arrangement is impossible or unimaginable.

Second, subjects did not alter the standard relationships that exist, for earth animals, between the appearance of an attribute and its normal function. For instance, subjects did not typically include structures shaped like legs that were intended to extract visual information. Instead they preserved the normal mappings between structures and functions that are true for animals on earth. The fact that these types of relational information are preserved in imaginary creatures indicates that some type of structural alignment process is at work. Rather than mapping the relations across two existing entities as in noncreative categorization, however, relations are apparently projected from an existing category onto a novel frame.

Presumably a similar structural alignment process contributed to the relative placement of various stagecoach features on newly designed railroad cars. For instance, the relative positioning of the entrances on the sides of the vehicles was preserved, a feature that was sensibly linked to the single compartment design that included two facing seats, each going the full width of the car. Thus, the inclusion of particular features seems to reflect the mapping of a broader relational structure rather than just individual isolated properties. The novel feature of front and rear entrances, which would have been more compatible with a central aisle running the length of the vehicle, would have been part of a different relational structure.

Correlated Attributes

Imagined animals are also influenced by the known attribute correlations that characterize existing categories of earth animals. For instance, subjects who were told that the novel creature was feathered were more likely to produce imaginary animals with wings and beaks, and those told it had scales were more likely to produce creatures with fins and gills, relative to subjects given no information about its attributes (Ward in press, experiment 2). Consistent with these findings, subjects who were told the creature was feathered were more likely to report that they had relied on exemplars of birds in developing their imaginary animal, whereas those who were told that the creature had scales were more likely to report that they had relied on fish. This suggests that many subjects pattern their imaginary animal after specific instances of typical earth animals and that typicality varies with the context, much as it does in noncreative tasks (Barsalou 1987). Similarly, and predictably, railroad car designers relied on other land vehicles of the day rather than, for example, water vehicles.

Considering the Imaginer's Intent

One important difference between the imaginary animal studies and the case of railroad car design is that the college students did not have to be concerned with any real-world constraints. We might have expected them to develop ideas that were less constrained, yet they seemed no less influenced by existing knowledge than were railroad car designers who had to develop products that would work in a particular setting. Structured imagination, then, appears to be a very general phenomenon that emerges even when there are minimal constraints.

Is it possible that the college students were responding to a perceived demand to produce sensible creatures? Did they impose constraints on their thinking because they believed that they were supposed to? This seems unlikely because they developed highly structured creatures even when asked to use their wildest imagination and not to be concerned about generating something that would be believable to others (Ward in press, experiment 4).

Novelty Embedded within Structure

The amount of innovation included in imagined animals appears to be greatly constrained by subjects' prior conceptions of animals on earth, but there was also novelty in their creations. For instance, although almost all individuals included standard sense and appendages, many also included variations on the sense (e.g., several eyes at the ends of long tentacles) and unusual appendages (e.g., wheels for mobility). Thus, they were being innovative within the structured constraint of including certain central features. Again, this highlights the fact that structure and innovation are not incompatible and that new creations should be assessed in terms of both what is old and what is new. In fact, truly useful creativity may reflect a balance between novelty and a connection to previous ideas (Finke, chap. 13).

Senses and appendages can be thought of as central or context-independent attributes (Barsalou 1982) that will almost always be present any time the concept of animal is instantiated, whether for a real or imaginary setting. These central attributes may derive their importance to the concept from the mere fact that most typical animals have them, or from their link to the broader understanding that living things would generally benefit from being able to sense their environment, move, and manipulate objects. In either case, however, they provide the framework, or figurative skeleton, upon which novel variations can be built or a kind of characteristic theme on which variations can be played. For instance, although one may nearly always develop a creature with some visual sense, one might also develop some novel and exotic variation on that sense.

In the present case, the central attributes were predicted from traditional attribute listing tasks, and such tasks might be used to generate predictions for the central properties of other domains that would be expected to extend to imaginary settings. For instance, "handle" might be listed as an attribute of most tools, and most imaginary tools would be expected to have handles. One caveat is that subjects may not list all of the attributes that are truly central to a category because they represent implicit assumptions that are "too obvious" to mention (e.g., that animals are bounded solids). As an alternate procedure, transformation and discovery paradigms, such as those used by Keil (1989), may help to reveal what people consider to be essential about different types of categories. Again, those essential properties would then form the framework upon which imaginary entities from that domain would be constructed. Thus, research on basic aspects of cognition can inform us about what to expect in creative tasks.

There is sometimes an apparent conflict between work on creativity that emphasizes the rejection of prior knowledge and the development of novel reconstructions (Dominowski, chap. 4) and that which emphasizes the use of standard knowledge structures that underlie the emergence of creative ideas (Weisberg, chap. 3). My view is that there is merit in both of these positions; creative ideas are most often a mix of new and old, and there is value in attempting to assess the unchanging, underlying frameworks and the variations that are developed within them. This is consistent with Boden's (1991) and Schank and Cleary's (chap. 10) suggestions that the creativity of a product should be judged with respect to something. In the present case, that something is the central features of a category that will ordinarily form the framework on which novelty is imposed. In extreme cases, a creative leap may involve a rejection of a central feature, but even that would represent a deliberate consideration of the feature and why it might be essential.

Using Broader Knowledge: Novelty and Appropriateness

The findings from the imaginary animal studies reveal a pattern in which college students develop certain novel variations on highly structured central attributes. However, they were not asked to develop creatures that could survive in any particular environment, so it is not possible to assess the appropriateness of the variations they introduced. Because the creativity of a product is often judged in terms of novelty and appropriateness, it is useful to try to assess the latter in structured imagination studies.

To examine the appropriateness of subject's novel variations and, more generally, their use of broader knowledge frameworks, I asked college students to generate animals that would be adapted to specific novel environments (Ward in press, experiment 3). Some of the subjects in that study were told about a furry creature that lived on a molten planet with only a few islands of solid rock. The clear survival demand on this planet was safe travel from one island to the next. To meet this demand, many of the students developed flying creatures (figure 7.2). However, they were not birdlike creatures as would be expected if these subjects had retrieved exemplars of typical birds. Rather, the only resemblance to birds was that they had wings, which suggests that subjects used general knowledge of how animals might adapt to environments to construct novel flying creatures.

The subjects in this study also included interesting variations on the senses that were adapted to the planetary conditions. For example, one student developed a creature with a visual mechanism that would allow it to detect cooler prey against the hotter background of the planet. The adaptation was novel, appropriate, and, once again, grounded in the central attribute of a visual sense.

Structured Imagination in Science Fiction and Speculative Science

One concern with the laboratory studies described thus far is that the subjects were college students who developed their ideas in less than an hour. Perhaps college students are not the most imaginative group to sample, and perhaps an hour is not enough time to generate truly exotic ideas that escape the bonds of structured imagination.

To extend the idea of structured imagination to a more extreme case, I have examined the types of creatures developed by science fiction writers. One difficulty in doing a study of this type is isolating a reasonably large and representative sample of depictions of such creatures, but an interesting approximation to such a sample is found in *Barlowe's Guide to Extraterrestrials* (1979). The book contains depictions of 50 creatures from some of the most noted science fiction writers that were chosen for inclusion because they were challenging to the imagination. There is little doubt in casually examining these creatures that they are highly imaginative and they were developed by creatively gifted writers and artists. However, a careful examination reveals that approximately three-fourths of these creatures are symmetric and have standard eyes and legs (Ward in press, experiment 5). Again there is

Figure 7.2
Examples of nonbirdlike creatures developed by college students in Ward (in press) who were asked to imagine furry creatures on a mostly molten planet

a distinction between a product's being structured and being creative. The innovations are embedded within a highly predictable framework.

The science fiction literature does contain some amazing creations that violate the properties of symmetry, senses, and appendages. For example, Piers Anthony's *Polarian* is a teardrop-shaped creature with no obvious standard appendages or sense organs. A number of authors have also developed creatures with no obvious form or even clear external boundaries. Others have overcome the idea that members of the same species must resemble one another in shape, appendages, and sense organs. For example, in Donald Moffitt's *Cygnan* species, the male is simply a tiny parasite that lives on the body of the female. (Only metaphorically are the parasitic males of this imaginary species similar to some of their human counterparts.) Importantly, however, these types of exotic creations are the exceptions to the general trend.

Some scientists also speculate that life on other planets, particularly intelligent life, has properties very similar to life on earth. For example, Frank Drake, a noted astronomer involved in the Search of Extraterrestrial Intelligence (SETI) project, speculates that intelligent life in other parts of the universe resembles human life. In fact, the SETI project itself is based on the idea that intelligent life elsewhere is similar enough to us that it will communicate in ways very similar to the way we communicate.

Overcoming or Controlling the Structuring of New Ideas

An important aspect of the creative cognition approach is that by identifying the process associated with more innovative outcomes, it may be possible to enhance (or inhibit) creative functioning. Any time a person develops a new idea, it will be based to some extent on recalled information; however, the exact manner or form in which information is recalled may affect the likelihood of a creative outcome.

There are intuitive, empirical, and theoretical reasons for believing that people will be more innovative, as judged by deviations from characteristic category attributes, if they begin the task of imagining a new entity by considering a highly abstract characterization of what properties the entity ought to possess rather than if they begin by retrieving and modifying a specific known entity. Intuitively, for example, a person who retrieved a dog would seem to have a greater chance of producing an animal with two eyes located symmetrically in the head than would a person who considered the more abstract idea that a creature must have some means of extracting information from its environment.

Empirically, subjects who report basing their creations on specific earth animals produce less innovative creatures than those who report considering more abstract and general ideas, such as what type of environment the creature might inhabit (Ward in press). For example, in experiment 2, 26 percent of the former and 41 percent of the latter developed creatures that had some novel variation on the senses; nevertheless there were no differences between these groups in the tendency to include standard senses and appendages. There are thus limits to the amount of innovation that will be observed even when people rely on abstract information.

In addition, Smith, Ward, and Schumacher (1993) had subjects design novel animals and toys. Subjects in the Examples condition were given three specific examples of previous designs prior to generating their own creations; those in the Control condition were not. Those in the Examples condition were significantly more likely to include properties of the examples. For instance, the example animals all had tails; 37 percent of creatures produced in the examples condition of experiment 1 had tails, compared to only 15 percent in the Control condition. This conformity to properties of the examples occurred even when subjects were instructed to make their creatures as different as possible from the examples (experiment 3). Jansson and Smith (1991) found a similar result with engineering students and professional engineers who were given the task of designing new objects, such as bicycle racks and spillproof cups. Thus, having a specific model available appears to inhibit creativity, whether that model is self-generated, as in the case of Ward's subjects who reported retrieving specific exemplars, or experimenter presented, as in Smith, Ward, and Schumacher and Jansson and Smith.

Extending these ideas even further into the engineering domain, there is suggestive evidence that a process of accessing abstract information can lead to greater innovation than the more typical engineering approach of basing new products on specific existing objects. Condoor, Brock, and Burger (1993), for example, have argued that one problem in traditional approaches to design problems is that engineers too quickly choose a single specific preexisting solution to form the basis for a new solution. This is particularly problematic for situations in which innovation is required. Perhaps this is what designers of early railroad cars did.

Condoor, Brock, and Burger (1993) describe a function structure development approach they have used in design classes with mechanical engineering students. In that approach, students are encouraged to begin with an abstract definition that will identify the real needs in a design task. This is intended to prevent a premature fixation on any one specific previous solution. For example, students might think of a task of designing a brake system for a new vehicle as one of transferring the kinetic energy of the vehicle to some other energy state rather than converging immediately on a specific example, such as disc brakes. Condoor, Brock, and Burger note that their students have developed many designs that have been judged to be highly innovative, even by the experts in the field who have been attempting to develop solutions to the same problems. The implication is that novices using an abstraction procedure are at least as successful as experts who typical use an approach more reliant on specific prior solutions.

Theoretically, there are several ways to account for the relative advantage of abstraction. First, one can describe design problems, which require the development of some new entity, as having unspecified start states (Goel and Pirolli 1989). The consequence is that people must seek additional information, either from external sources or by way of retrieving prior knowledge, and many foreclose on a single related prior example from memory that provides a quick but nonoptimal problem representation (Condoor, Brock, and Burger 1993). Because design often precedes production in real-world situations, any problems with a selected example may not become obvious until well into the design process, when individuals are strongly committed to patterning the new entity after that idea. Designers can then become fixated on the properties of initially retrieved ideas even when they might result in a less than optimal solution, because those properties are truly essential to the operation of that particular fixating example, the designer believes them to be essential, or the designer fails to consider whether they are essential. Abstraction, done in advance, would allow assessments of essential properties prior to making these commitments.

A somewhat different theoretical account relies on the notion of retrieval blocking (Smith this volume; Smith, Ward, and Schumacher). The heightened accessibility of an initially retrieved or presented example (or its component attributes) makes alternative examples or attributes less accessible or retrievable. By moving to a more abstract representation, one may be able to lessen the dominance of any one instance and better equate the accessibility of other items. One may then be able to retrieve an alternative item, perhaps a less typical one, or synthesize a novel item from the abstract principles.

In effect, by going back up in a hierarchy, one may be able to go back down a different path toward an alternate solution, in the process both overcoming unwanted attributes and noticing potentially helpful ones that were otherwise inaccessible. For example, Edison could not see that above-ground wires from the arc lighting system could be used because they were part of a different branching from the higher-level node of distribution systems than he was using.

This notion that abstraction allows access to alternative ideas is also reflected in Martindale's suggestions (this volume) about generalization gradients. Activation of specific examples may correspond to a steep gradient around a single entity, whereas activation at a more general level in a hierarchy could allow a shallower gradient, with more specific-level items becoming available.

A third view of the value of abstraction is that it can aid in restructuring a problem representation. By moving to a more abstract description of the problem, it may be possible to clarify the goals, what is needed to achieve them, and the nature of the elements available in the problem situation. This approach can also make explicit any underlying assumptions that might otherwise inhibit a creative solution. By making such assumptions explicit, one may be able to challenge them to destabilize the current problem representation (Smith this volume) or drop, negate, or otherwise modify them to achieve creativity that alters the original structure of a domain (Boden 1991). If the assumptions remain implicit, they may not be overcome

Interestingly, even if one negates an assumption to achieve a more creative solution, one can still be said to have made use of the existing knowledge embodied in that assumption. Thus, even when new ideas seem to reflect an abandonment of earlier ideas, they may still be structured by the earlier knowledge, analogous to the way a stubborn child's behavior may be structured by being exactly the opposite of what parents request.

Practical advice for developing creative ideas sometimes includes suggestions consistent with this idea of explicitly considering central properties. For example, Ochoa and Osier (1993) advise prospective science fiction writers to consider the typical properties of animals on earth, such as symmetry, senses, and means of locomotion, and some possible variations on those properties. Presumably by making such properties explicit, one can either develop interesting variations or perhaps even reject a property entirely.

Related to this third view of abstraction is the general idea that categories are represented and must be understood within broader knowledge frameworks (Murphy and Medin 1985). Those frameworks, along with structural alignment processes, provide needed information about which attributes are essential and which are expendable. Because creative products should be useful and not just novel, such frameworks may also aid creative functioning. Just as these broader frameworks and alignment processes provide important guidance to various cognitive processes (Markman and Gentner 1993; Medin, Goldstone, and Gentner 1993; Murphy 1988), they can provide similar guidance for developing innovative ideas that still maintain a meaningful link to earlier ideas that exhibit what Finke (chap. 13) refers to as structural connectedness. Just as good analogies maintain higher-order relations (Gentner 1983) and are influenced by pragmatic concerns (Holland et al. 1986), so too might creative ideas be influenced in positive ways by such factors. By this categorization-based view, abstraction works by identifying what must be retained and what should be abandoned, thus fostering the development of novel and appropriate ideas. Again the assumptions in the broader frameworks should be made explicit to facilitate such guidance.

The Path of Least Resistance

Elsewhere, I proposed a path-of-least-resistance model, which stated that the default approach in tasks of imagination is to access a specific known entity or category exemplar and pattern the new entity after it (Ward in press). This provides the imaginer with an easy first approach and is most likely to be used when there are few constraints to be satisfied. Moving to a more abstract representation, making central, implicit assumptions explicit, and synthesizing a new entity from abstract principles requires more cognitive effort and is likely to occur only when constraints must be satisfied or motivation is high.

The path-of-least-resistance model assumes that category representations include specific exemplars that are embedded within broader knowledge frameworks, which give the exemplars their categorical coherence. It also states that truly useful, creative innovations that are novel and appropriate to a task are more likely (though not guaranteed) to occur when individuals access broader knowledge structures than when they simply retrieve exemplars. The exemplars are seen as largely static, uninterpreted entities, in contrast to the dynamic and flexible information in broader knowledge structures. Although one might randomly vary attributes of retrieved exemplars, without the guidance provided by access to broader structures, there is little chance of those novel variations' being appropriate for a given task. Thus, to the extent that individuals have access to well-developed explanatory frameworks, they are in a position to modify existing designs or develop new ones.

A Caveat

There is no guarantee that a focus on more abstract principles will lead to greater innovation. The inclusion of old characteristic features in new exemplars could result from retrieving exemplars or consulting broader knowledge frameworks. For example, if we ask engineers and nonengineers to design a new cover for an access aperture ("manhole") it is likely that both groups will produce round covers. For nonengineers this would occur because most exemplars of manhole covers they have encountered and could retrieve are round. In contrast, engineers might produce round designs because their broader knowledge tells them that circles have the optimal strength-shape relationship; they recognize why manhole covers tend to be round an also understand that it is the same reason that windows in airplanes tend to be round. The prime advantage that engineers would have is that their greater domain knowledge would allow them to consider more reasonable alternatives if they make their assumptions explicit.

Relation to Traditional Creativity Topics

Fixation
Much work in creativity has been concerned with the idea that people sometimes become fixated and fail to achieve creative solutions to problems. For example, when people fail to see that a pair of pliers can be used as a weight for a pendulum, they are exhibiting functional fixedness, and they do not achieve a solution to the "two-string" problem (Dominowski, chap. 4). Structured imagination relates to this type of fixedness by way of its focus on the central attributes of objects that are projected onto new situations. This focus on central features is similar to Barsalou's (1982) distinction between context-independent properties that form the core meanings of concepts and context-dependent properties that are typically activated only under particular conditions.

The central features can be thought of as part of the typical initial approach to a problem. When the concept is thought about, those features will be implicitly included. In the case of imaginary animals, the central features appear to be senses and appendages, which may reflect that two essential features of animals are extraction of information and movement. For artifacts, the most essential feature is their function. When the function of an artifact is changed, its category identity is changed (Keil 1989). Thus, unless they are viewed at a more abstract level, people's active representations of artifacts, such as pliers, will almost always be dominated by the central feature of their typical function. Once the insightful solutions are discovered (e.g., using pliers as a pendulum weight), such features may be judged as unnecessary baggage. Presumably the same features that are found to be central in traditional categorization tasks and in structured imagination tasks will result in fixation if they conflict with the solution to a particular insight problem.

Restructuring
The concept of restructuring has been central to the topic of creativity and is mentioned by several contributors to this book (Dominowski, Schooler and Melcher, Smith, and Weisberg). Although the exact definition may vary from one researcher to the next, restructuring generally refers to a change in the way a person views a problem. The implication is that a person has either failed to develop a structure or initially structured the problem the wrong way and must somehow find a better way to organize the components of the problem and their relations to one another. Are there basic principles that can be used to guide restructuring? I believe that one such principle is to describe a problem in its most abstract form.

Summary and Conclusions

Research on structured imagination has helped to delineate the specific ways in which properties of existing concepts are projected or mapped onto new entities (Ward in press). In so doing it contributes to our understanding of how people generate ideas. It is clear that many of the factors that influence noncreative categorization also influence creative or imaginative phenomena. Central attributes, as determined by their frequency of association to a known category, their link to broader knowledge frameworks, and their role in structural alignment processes, and as identified by attribute listing and other traditional tasks, play a key role in the development of new ideas.

The results show the clear value of relying on traditional work in cognitive psychology to understand creativity. We can begin to identify the likely underlying framework on which innovations will be possible, and by identifying what is unlikely to change, we are in a better position to understand what is likely to change and in what way. More generally, this work leads to a synthesis of previous positions on creativity. Rather than focusing primarily on what is new or what is old about new ideas, research on structured imagination focuses on both.

At the same time, by studying imagination, we can identify how standard models of categorization fall short and must be expanded to account for creative phenomena. For example, because they have focused primarily on category decision making, most traditional categorization models have not specified exactly how an individual would imagine or generate a novel instance of a category. One possibility, suggested by work on structured imagination, is that the same types of representations used for making category decisions (e.g., stored exemplars) are used as the starting point for a novel exemplar (Ward in press). The work also suggests that a mixed representation, involving specific exemplars embedded in broader organizing frameworks, may be necessary to account for imaginative use of category information.

By focusing on the predictive power and the shortcomings of traditional categorization models, research on structured imagination typifies the creative cognition approach (Finke, Ward, and Smith 1992). Theoretical and empirical advances from traditional cognitive science are used to understand creative phenomena, and an examination of the creative aspects of human functioning provides new insights about the nature of standard cognitive processes and structures.

References

Ashcraft, M. H. (1978). Property norms for typical and atypical items from 17 categories: A description and discussion. *Memory and Cognition, 6,* 227–232.

Barlowe, W. D., and Summers, I. (1979). *Barlowe's guide to extraterrestrials.* New York: Workman Publishing.

Barsalou, L. W. (1982). Context-independent and context-dependent information in concepts. *Memory and Cognition, 10,* 82–93.

Barsalou, L. W. (1987). The instability of graded structure: Implications for the nature of concepts. In U. Neisser (ed.), *Concepts and conceptual development: Ecological and intellectual factors in categorization* (pp. 101–140). Cambridge: Cambridge University Press.

Boden, M. (1991). *The creative mind: Myths and mechanisms.* New York: Basic Books.

Condoor, S. S., Brock, H. R., and Burger, C. P. (1993, June). *Innovation through early recognition of critical design parameters.* Paper presented at the meeting of the ASEE, Urbana, IL.

Finke, R. A., Ward, T. B., and Smith, S. M. (1992). *Creative cognition: Theory, research, and applications.* Cambridge, MA: MIT Press.

Gentner, D. (1983). Structure-mapping: A theoretical framework for analogy. *Cognitive Science, 7,* 155–170.

Goel, V., and Pirolli, P. (1989). Motivating the notion of generic design within information-processing theory: The design problem space. *AI Magazine, 10,* 19–36.

Hampton, J. A. (1979). Polymorphous concepts in semantic memory. *Journal of Verbal Learning and Verbal Behavior, 18,* 441–461.

Holland, J. H., Holyoak, K. J., Nisbett, R. E., and Thagard, P. R. (1986). *Induction: Processes of inference, learning, and discovery.* Cambridge, MA: MIT Press.

Jansson, D. G., and Smith, S. M. (1991). Design fixation. *Design Studies, 12,* 3–11.

Keil, F. C. (1989). *Concepts, kinds, and cognitive development.* Cambridge, MA: MIT Press.

Latrobe, J. H. B. (1868). *The Baltimore and Ohio Railroad: A personal recollection.* Baltimore: Sun Book and Job Printing.

Markman, A. B., and Gentner, D. (1993). Splitting the differences: A structural alignment view of similarity. *Journal of Memory and Language, 32,* 517–535.

Medin, D. L., Goldstone, R. L., and Gentner, D. (1993). Respects for similarity. *Psychological Review, 100,* 254–278.

Murphy, G. L. (1988). Comprehending complex concepts. *Cognitive Science, 12,* 529–562.

Murphy, G. L., and Medin, D. L. (1985). The role of theories in conceptual coherence. *Psychological Review, 92,* 289–316.

Ochoa, G., and Osier, J. (1993). *Writer's guide to creating a science fiction universe.* Cincinnati: Writer's Digest Books.

Rosch, E. (1978). Principles of categorization. In E. Rosch and B. Lloyd (eds.), *Cognition and categorization* (pp. 28–36). Hillsdale, NJ: Erlbaum.

Smith, S. M., Ward, T. B., and Schumacher, J. S. (1993). Constraining effects of examples in a creative generation task. *Memory and Cognition, 21,* 837–845.

Tversky, B., and Hemenway, K. (1984). Objects, parts, and categories. *Journal of Experimental Psychology: General, 113,* 169–193.

Ward, T. B. (in press). Structured imagination: The role of category structure in exemplar generation. *Cognitive Psychology.*

Ward, T. B., Vela, E., Peery, M. L., Lewis, S., Bauer, N. K., and Klint, K. (1989). What makes a vibble a vibble: A developmental study of category generalization. *Child Development, 60,* 214–224.

White, J. H. (1978). *The American railroad passenger car.* Baltimore: Johns Hopkins University Press.

Part II

Visual and Computational Approaches to Creative Cognition

Chapter 8

Static Patterns Moving in the Mind

Jennifer J. Freyd and Teresa M. Pantzer

Some simple static patterns like arrows and triangles can produce a compelling sense of directionality (figure 8.1). In this chapter we explore the possibility that the phenomenal sensation of directionality is based on a dynamic mental representation (Freyd 1987, 1993). Results from three experiments suggest that memory for the position of static arrows and triangles is sometimes distorted in the direction that the pattern appears to point, as if the arrow or triangle moved in the mind. Then, using the Geneplore model of creativity (Finke, Ward, and Smith 1992) as our framework, we consider the possibility that dynamic representations may underlie creative processes. The dynamic properties of static form may influence both the generative and exploratory aspects of creative invention

Consider the static patterns in figure 8.1. The isosceles triangle appears to point to the right. Even the equilateral triangle appears to point in one particular direction at any one time, although it is multistable over time (Attneave 1968). Attneave and later Palmer and Bucher (Palmer 1980; Palmer and Bucher 1982) investigated the basis of this multistability and found that cues that define the axis of symmetry seem to disambiguate the triangle. In this chapter we raise three related but different questions: (1) why do some static patterns, like triangles, point at all, (2) what does this phenomenon of "pointing" tell us about *mental representation,* and (3) what implications does our theory of representation have for creative thought? We propose that the phenomenon of pointing in perception is based on a perceptual interpretation of directionality and that this interpretation is implemented by a *dynamic mental representation* (Freyd 1987, 1993). After reporting on the results of experiments that provide support for this hypothesis, we consider the implications our theory of mental representation has for the role of dynamics in creative visual synthesis.

We conclude by suggesting that dynamic representations are the medium of creative visual synthesis. Following the Geneplore model of Finke, Ward, and Smith (1992), we consider the possibility that the

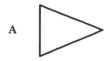

Figure 8.1
The isosceles triangle (A) appears to point to the right, in the direction of its smallest angle. The equilateral triangle without biasing cues (B) is ambiguous in direction of pointing. The equilateral triangle with axis-aligned stripes (C) appears to point to the right.

dynamic properties of static form may influence both the generative and exploratory aspects of creative invention. This possibility may help explain some of the subjective reports subjects make about their own creative processes. When interpreting "preinventive forms" during the generative phase of creative invention, for instance, subjects often report that they imagine using the forms or interacting with them in dynamic ways (Finke 1990). Some of this dynamic interaction may result directly from the dynamic mental representations underlying the perceived directionality of static forms.

Dynamic Mental Representations

We briefly describe an experiment on the mental representation of static patterns that led to the notion of dynamic mental representations. Freyd (1983) tested the hypothesis that the perception of still things, in this case photographs, might involve representation of dynamic information. In particular, people might perceive implicit motion when presented with pictures of frozen motion; in this case, perceiving implicit motion could mean the movement an object would undergo were it to be unfrozen. Using pairs of before-and-after pictures taken from action scenes, individual stills were presented to subjects tachistoscopically. Subjects were instructed to look at one picture and hold it in memory, and then to view a second picture and decide as rapidly as possible whether the second frame was same as or different from the first. They were shown the pairs in either real order or backward order. Subjects took longer to indicate correctly that the second frame was different when the pair was in real-world temporal order.

Freyd's theory of dynamic representations has been heavily influenced by results from studies of representational momentum (Finke, Freyd, and Shyi 1986; Finke and Shyi 1988; Freyd and Finke 1984, 1985; Freyd and Johnson 1987; Freyd, Kelly, and DeKay 1990; Hubbard 1990; Hubbard and Bharucha 1988; Kelly and Freyd 1987; Verfaillie and d'Ydewalle 1991). In one representational momentum experiment, subjects were presented with a static figure in a sequence of orientations sampled from a possible path of rotation (Freyd and Finke 1985). Subjects were instructed to remember the third orientation they saw and were presented with a fourth orientation that was either the same as or different from the third. Test orientations were varied parametrically around "True-Same." Freyd and Finke found a generally symmetric unimodal distribution of "Same" responses centered not on True-Same but on a forward rotation from True-Same. That is, subjects showed a forward shift in memory for position.

Studies like these led Freyd to develop the idea that some mental representations might be dynamic. Toward the aim of specifying what a dynamic representation might be, she proposed two criteria, the first relevant for this chapter: a dynamic mental representation is one in which time is represented, using Palmer's (1978) terminology, "intrinsically." That means that time is represented with some of the same inherent structure as real-world time. For a representation to be dynamic, at least two aspects of the temporal dimension in the world must also be consequences of the inherent structure of the representing dimension: the temporal dimension must be directional, because time goes forward, and it must be continuous, because between any two points of time, another point of time exists.

We now propose that directionality is not only a necessary characteristic of dynamic representations but, more important, that perceived directionality depends on representational dynamics. Further, we theorize that perceived directionality depends on representational dynamics even when the directionality relates to a nontemporal dimension, such as a spatial dimension. Thus, we propose that the perceived directionality of a pattern depends on an underlying dynamic mental representation of it (Freyd 1987). In particular, we suggest that the representation of directionality for a given dimension is accomplished by representing change along that dimension in a particular direction. This suggestion leads to the hypothesis that memory for the position of a static pattern with clear directionality will be

ARROW

AIRPLANE

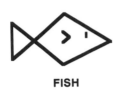

FISH

Figure 8.2
The stimulus patterns used in experiment 1

distorted in a predictable way: The remembered position will be further along the directional dimension, just as memory for position is distorted in the direction of implied motion in static photographs (Freyd 1983) and in representational momentum (Freyd and Finke 1984; Hubbard and Bharucha 1988; Kelly and Freyd 1987). Thus, if a pattern "points" rightward, we predict that memory for the position of the figure will be shifted to the right.

Experiment 1

Our goal for experiment 1 was to establish a memory distortion using a simple static pattern that conveys directionality. We also hoped to get some qualitative evidence that patterns varying in strength of directionality would result in memory shifts that were correspondingly weak or strong. We chose a rightward-facing arrow as our highly directional static pattern and also included two additional patterns, schematic drawings of a fish and an airplane, also rightward facing (figure 8.2).

In each trial subjects were presented with one of the three patterns, centered on the screen. After a 500-ms stimulus duration and a 750-ms retention interval, subjects were presented with the same pattern in one of seven equally likely test positions. Three test positions were slightly to the left of center, three were slightly to the right of center, and one was centered. Subjects were asked to indicate whether the test position was the same as or different from the to-be-remembered pattern. Our dependent measure of interest was the number of same responses for each of the seven test positions. Since the arrow was rightward facing, we predicted that subjects would make more errors for arrows positioned to the right of center than to the left of center. We predicted similar but weaker asymmetry in the number of same responses for the fish and airplane.

Method

Subjects   Eleven subjects recruited from the Cornell University community were paid for their participation in this experiment. Subjects in each of the experiments reported in this chapter were informed about the hypotheses and designs of the studies only after completion of the experimental session. No subject participated in more than one of the reported experiments.

Stimuli   A computer-controlled vector-plotting HP graphics display screen was used to present stimuli. Figure 8.2 displays the three static patterns used in this experiment. Each pattern had a standard position, which was horizontally centered on the screen. Test positions consisted of identical patterns displaced horizontally -3, -2, -1, 0, 1, 2, or 3 mm to the right. The seven different test positions were presented equally often. The first pattern was always presented with a 500-ms stimulus duration, followed by a 750-ms retention interval in which the graphics screen was blank. The test pattern remained on the screen until the subject made a response. There were three pattern conditions corresponding to the three different static patterns. Test patterns were always the same shape as the to-be-remembered patterns and varied only in position on the screen.

Procedure   Subjects were run individually in a session that lasted approximately 45 min. After reading an instruction sheet, each subject completed a block of 21 practice trials, followed by a block of 210 experimental trials. The block of 21 practice trials included one example of each trial type (formed from three pattern conditions in seven test positions). The block of 210 experimental trials was composed of 10 replications for each of the 21 trial types. Trials within each block were randomly ordered for each subject. Subjects, sitting at a comfortable viewing distance from the screen, initiated each trial by press-

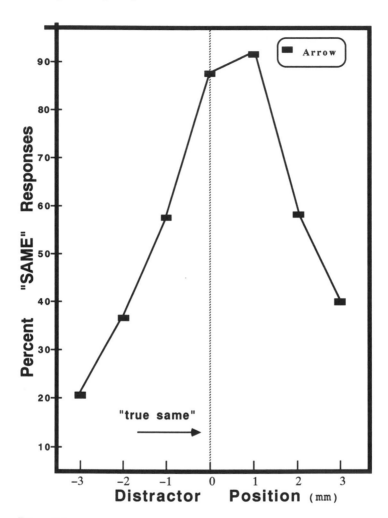

Figure 8.3
The mean percentage of "same" responses given for each distractor position plotted
separately for each of the stimulus patterns used in experiment 1

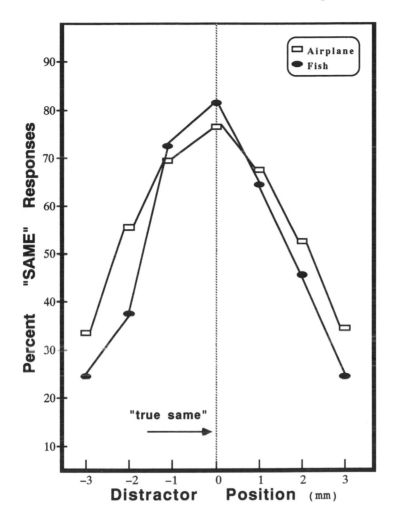

Figure 8.3
(*continued*)

ing a foot pedal and concluded each one by pressing one of two response buttons held in each hand (right for "same" and left for "different"). They were instructed to respond "same" only when the test position was exactly the same as the to-be-remembered position and encouraged to respond as quickly and accurately as possible.

Accuracy Criteria   Data for individual subjects were first evaluated for overall accuracy. For all experiments reported in this chapter, we had preset accuracy criteria for individual subjects, established in order to increase the accuracy of our estimates of memory shifts. We required that the accuracy rate for the True-Same position by 50 percent or greater (averaged across all conditions) and that the mean accuracy rate combined for the two most extreme distractor positions be 50 percent or greater (also averaged across all conditions). For experiment 1 we excluded one subject for failing to meet the accuracy requirement.

Results and Discussion
Figure 8.3 displays the results averaged across subjects for each of the three pattern conditions. As predicted, subjects were more likely to respond "same" for arrow test positions that were to the right of center than those to the left of center. Indeed, there were more "same" responses for the arrow test position 1 mm to the right than for the True-Same position. No such asymmetry is apparent in the results for the fish and airplane patterns.

For the studies reported in this chapter, we did not use quadratic regression (Freyd and Finke 1985) to estimate individual subject shifts for use in significance tests. The regression analyses produced estimated memory shifts that were larger than the largest test position for a few subjects in a few experiments, because those subjects showed such a strong bias for the forward test positions. A parabolic fit for data in which the peak of the parabola is outside the range of the data is highly unstable. We therefore used an alternative method of estimating the memory distortions; following Faust (1990) we calculated arithmetic weighted means using the number of same responses for each test position. A shift of 0.0 would be expected if there was no memory distortion; a shift of -1.0 would correspond to 1 mm to the left; a shift of $+1.0$ would correspond to 1 mm to the right.

A one-way ANOVA using the weighted means revealed a main effect for pattern condition (arrow, fish, or airplane) ($F(2,18) = 11.05$; $p < .001$). We used t-tests to evaluate whether the weighted means were significantly different from 0 for each of the three pattern conditions. As predicted, the shifts were significantly to the right for the arrow ($t(10) = 4.14; p < .005$). Neither the airplane nor the fish pattern reached significance (t of less than 1.0 in both cases).

Experiment 2

Experiment 1 demonstrated that a rightward-pointing arrow induces memory shifts toward the right. We interpret these memory shifts as arising from a dynamic representation, such that memory for the arrow's position changes over time in the direction that the arrow points. In representational momentum experiments, memory shifts are induced by showing a figure in a sequence of static positions such that movement is implied. Our interpretation of the memory shift discovered in experiment 1 for a static arrow predicts that the directionality of a static pattern should influence the magnitude of memory shift if used in a representational momentum experiment. In experiment 2 we used the arrow in a representational momentum experiment to test the hypothesis that the memory shift should be greater when the arrow direction is consistent with the direction of implied movement than when the arrow direction is inconsistent with the direction of implied movement.

A drawback of experiment 1 is that leftward-pointing arrows were not presented to subjects. In experiment 2 we counterbalanced arrow direction as well as direction of movement.

Method

Subjects   Twelve University of Oregon undergraduates enrolled in an introductory psychology class received credit toward a course research requirement by participating in this experiment. All subjects met the accuracy criterion (as described for experiment 1).

Apparatus and Stimuli   The apparatus was the same as in experiment 1. The stimuli were arrows presented in a sequence of three positions such that horizontal movement was implied by the sequence. In the Consistent condition, the arrow direction and the direction of implied movement were the same (for half the trials, the arrow pointed left and the direction of implied motion was left; for the other half of the Consistent trials, the arrow pointed right and the direction of implied motion was right). In the Inconsistent condition, the direction that the arrow pointed was at odds with the movement implied by the sequence of positions (for half the trials, the arrow pointed to the left and the implied movement was to the right; for the other half of the

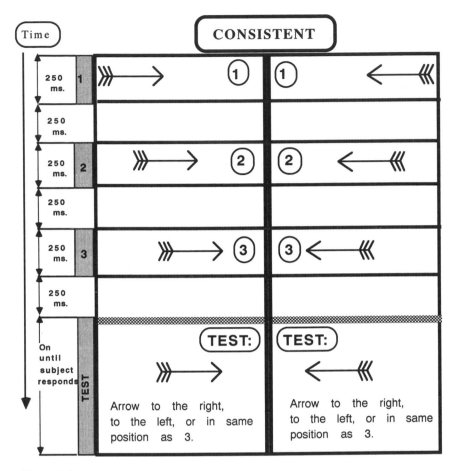

Figure 8.4
Schematic depictions of the Consistent and Inconsistent conditions used in experiment 2

Inconsistent trials, the arrow pointed to the right and the implied movement was to the left). The stimuli are depicted in figure 8.4.

The rightward arrow was the same as the arrow used in experiment 1. The leftward arrow was a mirror reflection of the rightward arrow. Each arrow was presented in three positions on the screen, followed by a test position. The third position was always centered on the screen. For movement to the right, the first position of the arrow was 2.6 mm left of center. The second position was 1.3 mm left of center. For movement to the left, the arrow was presented

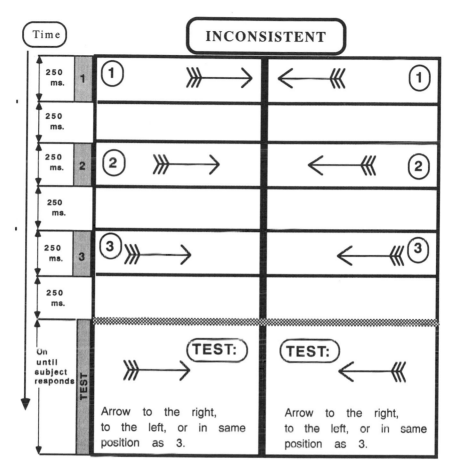

Figure 8.4
(*continued*)

2.6 mm right of center, followed by 1.3 mm right of center. The seven test positions were the same as those used in experiment 1.

The first three arrows were presented with 250-ms stimulus durations, separated by 250-ms interstimulus intervals. The retention interval between the third arrow and the test position was 250 ms. The test arrow remained on the screen until the subject made a response.

Procedure   Subjects completed a practice block of 28 trials and then a block of 280 experimental trials, formed from 1 replication and 10 replications, respectively, of each of 28 trial types. The 28 trial types

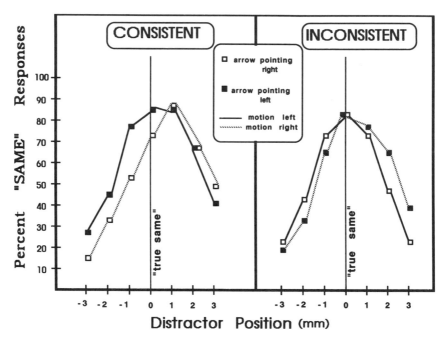

Figure 8.5
Results for experiment 2

were composed of two consistency conditions (Consistent or Inconsistent), each of which had two nested conditions such that the direction of implied motion and the direction that the arrow pointed were counterbalanced times seven distractor positions. The 28 practice trials and the 280 experimental trials were randomly ordered for each subject.

Accuracy Criteria   We applied the same accuracy criteria as described for experiment 1. All 12 subjects met the criterion for experiment 2.

Results and Discussion
Figure 8.5 displays the percentage of "same" responses for the Consistent and Inconsistent conditions, averaged across subjects. Positive distractor positions are in the direction of the implied movement; negative distractor positions are in the opposite direction. Combining across all conditions there was a significant shift of $+.29$ mm ($t = 3.10$; $p = .01$). In other words, we found a significant representational momentum effect.

As predicted, when the directionality of the static pattern is consistent with the implied movement, the magnitude of the memory shift is greater than when the directionality of the static pattern is inconsistent with the implied movement. Averaged across subjects, the estimated memory shift of .39 mm for the Consistent trials is significantly larger than the shift of +.19 mm for the Inconsistent trials ($t(11)$ = 1.99; p = .036, one-tailed). This means that, as predicted, the static configuration of the stimulus (the arrow direction) affected the magnitude of the memory distortion induced by the movement implied by a sequence of positions.

In experiment 1 we found that memory for the position of a rightward-pointing arrow was distorted to the right. In experiment 2 we used arrows in a representational momentum paradigm and found that when the arrow's directionality was consistent with the implied motion, the memory shift was greater than when the arrow's directionality was inconsistent with the implied motion. We interpret these results as supportive of our hypothesis that the perceived directionality of static figures is based on a dynamic mental representation.

Experiment 3

One limitation of the first two experiments is that the stimulus pattern used, an arrow, has a conventional meaning that may evoke a dynamic representation. Specifically, arrows are often used to indicate movement in a particular direction. In experiment 3 we attempted to generalize our claim about the directionality of static forms by using patterns that do not have a conventional meaning related to movement: an equilateral triangle and three isosceles triangles varying in width (figure 8.6). Attneave (1968) noted that at any one moment, an equilateral triangle appears to point in a particular direction, although the directionality is multistable. Later, Palmer (1980; Palmer and Bucher, 1982) discovered that the addition of stripes inside the triangle biases the particular interpretation of directionality. If the stripes are orthogonal to one side of the triangle, the triangle appears to point in the direction defined by the axis of symmetry.

In experiment 3 we looked for a relationship between the pointedness of a triangle and magnitude of the memory shift. We varied pointedness by varying the narrowness of the triangle. We assumed that the narrower the triangle, the more it would seem to point. (This assumption would break down as the triangle became so narrow as to appear as a straight line.) We used the four triangles displayed in figure 8.6 in two tasks. In the rating task, subjects were asked to indicate in which direction each triangle pointed and then to give a

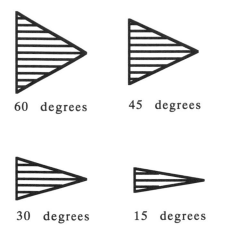

60 degrees   45 degrees

30 degrees   15 degrees

Figure 8.6
The 60-, 45-, 30-, and 15-degree triangles used in experiment 3

rating from 1 (barely pointing) to 10 (strongly pointing). For the memory task, a different group of subjects were given the standard Same-Different task.

Method

Subjects   Twenty-nine members of the University of Oregon community volunteered to participate in the rating task used in experiment 3. Of those 29 subjects, 12 had previously participated in a pilot study using triangles; the remaining 17 subjects were completely new subjects. Twenty-five additional University of Oregon undergraduates enrolled in an introductory psychology class received credit toward a course research requirement by participating in the memory task used in experiment 3.

Rating Task   Figure 8.6 shows the triangles used in both the rating and memory tasks. For the rating task, each triangle was printed (using a computer-controlled laser printer) on a separate sheet of paper. Subjects were then individually presented with each of the four triangles in a random order. Upon presentation of each triangle, subjects were asked to answer two questions: (1) In what direction is the triangle pointing? (2) On a scale of 1 to 10 (10 being very strongly and 1 being very weakly), how strongly is the triangle pointing in that direction? Subjects gave their responses verbally.

Memory Task   The apparatus was the same as in experiments 1 and 2. On each trial, subjects were presented with one of four triangles for 250 ms, followed by a 500-ms retention interval, followed by the same pattern in one of nine test positions. The four triangles (60, 45, 30, and 15 degrees) are displayed in figure 8.6. The vertical edge of the triangles was centered on the screen. The nine test positions ranged from −4 to 4 mm in 1-mm steps around the True-Same position. Subjects were run individually. After reading an instruction sheet, each subject completed a block of 36 practice trials, followed by a block of 540 experimental trials. The block of 36 practice trials included one example of each trial type (formed from four pattern conditions in nine test positions). The block of 540 experimental trials was composed of 15 replications for each of the 36 trial types. Trials within each block were randomly ordered for each subject. All other aspects of the procedure were the same as for experiments 1 and 2.

Accuracy Criteria   We applied the same accuracy criteria as we had for experiments 1 and 2. To our surprise, only 17 of the 25 subjects we tested met the criteria. Because these criteria were preset, we will report results for only these 17 subjects. However, because we were concerned about disregarding the data from so many subjects, we also performed a complete set of statistical tests on the data for all 25 subjects. The results were qualitatively the same for the larger group of subjects as for those who met the accuracy criterion. More important, all results that were significant in one case were also significant at approximately the same level in the other.

Results and Discussion

Rating Task   We first considered the responses to question 1 about the direction each of the four triangles appeared to point. All 29 subjects indicated that they thought the 45-, 30-, and 15-degree triangles pointed to the right. Twenty-six subjects indicated that the 60-degree (equilateral) triangle pointed to the right. One subject was not sure in which direction the 60-degree triangle pointed; one subject indicated that he thought that the 60-degree triangle pointed down; and the remaining subject indicated that it pointed up.

We next considered the responses to question 2 about the degree to which the triangle pointed in a given direction for the 26 subjects who indicated that all four triangles appeared to point to the right. Figure 8.7 shows the average rating for each of the four triangles. We performed a two-way ANOVA in which subject experience was a be-

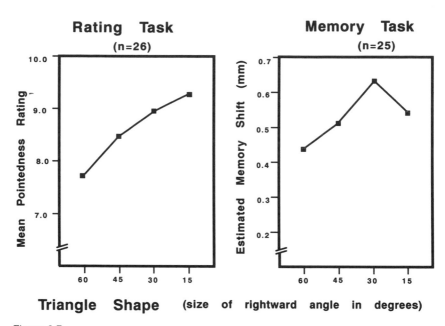

Figure 8.7
Results for experiment 3

tween-subject factor with two levels (10 subjects were previously in a pilot study using triangles and were thus considered experienced; 16 subjects were inexperienced), and triangle shape was a within-subject factor with four levels. The ANOVA revealed no main effect of subject experience ($F(1,24) = .005; p = .95$) and no interaction between subject experience and triangle shape ($F(3,72) = .65; p = .59$). As predicted, however, triangle shape led to significantly different pointedness ratings ($F(3,72) = 13.81; p < .001$).

Memory Task   Figure 8.7 also displays the average weighted means for the memory task for each of the four triangles. Memory for the position of the triangles was significantly shifted rightward for each of the four triangles, including for the 60-degree (equilateral) triangle ($t(16) = 2.08; p < .05$, one-tailed). A one-way ANOVA revealed a main effect for triangle shape ($F(3,48) = 3.91; p < 0.05$).

The fact that there was a significant shift for the equilateral (60-degree) triangle is important because it is the least arrow-like of the four triangles and thus the triangle for which it seems especially unlikely that any shifts in memory depend on a conventional interpretation of the stimuli. However, one limitation of experiment 3 is that the predicted memory shifts for the triangles were all toward the right. Perhaps shifts to the right reflect a tendency to misremember the position of triangles toward the right, independent of the biasing cues. In a separate experiment we used identical stimuli to those used in experiment 3 except that the triangles had no internal stripes to bias direction of pointing. Thus, the 60-degree triangle was an ambiguous equilateral triangle (Attneave 1968). If there is a general tendency to misremember objects to the right, we should see some indication for rightward shifts with these stripeless triangles. Fifteen additional subjects participated. The procedure was the same except that the retention interval was 250 ms instead of 500 ms. The shifts we measured were negative (-0.16, -0.25, -0.26, and -0.11, for the 60-, 45-, 30-, and 15-degree triangles, respectively), that is, toward the left but not significantly so. A one-way ANOVA revealed no significant effect for triangle shape ($F(3,42) = 1.46$; $p > .20$), suggesting that without the biasing stripes, even the isosceles triangles are fairly ambiguous pointers.

In this experiment we found that memory for the position of an equilateral triangle is shifted in the direction it appears to point. This finding can be compared with a study by Bucher and Palmer (1985) in which they attempted to bias perceived pointing of an equilateral triangle by showing the triangle moving in a particular direction. They hypothesized that movement could define an axis of symmetry, which would then determine the direction of pointing, and found that movement aligned with the axis of symmetry (that is, parallel to a possible direction of pointing) effectively biased pointing, but movement aligned with a side of the triangle (that is, perpendicular to a possible direction of pointing) produced no such effect. Further, for the axis-aligned movement, pointing was more effectively facilitated in the same direction of motion than in the reverse direction of motion, which they interpreted as a response-compatibility effect. In other words, Bucher and Palmer's strongest biasing condition was exactly the same direction of motion that we find predicts shifts in memory for position of a static triangle. They argued that their results were consistent with the hypothesis that symmetry determines perceived pointing; we suggest that their results are also consistent with our interpretation of the phenomenon of pointing (and these interpretations are not mutually exclusive): that it depends on an underlying dynamic mental representation.

General Discussion

Summary
In experiment 1 subjects were asked to look at a rightward-pointing arrow, a static pattern that has compelling directionality, and after a brief retention interval were asked to make a same-different judgment. The same arrow was presented in one of seven locations centered around True-Same. We found a clear shift to the right, the direction in which the arrow points. Based on the results from experiment 1, we wondered whether the directionality of the static arrow was powerful enough to affect the memory shift induced by a standard representational momentum paradigm. We tested this possibility in experiment 2 by comparing trials in which the direction of the arrow was consistent with the direction implied by the sequence of positions with inconsistent cases in which the static configuration was at odds with the direction implied by the sequence of positions. We found that the directionality of the arrow had a clear and strong effect on the magnitude of representational momentum, suggesting that both the directionality of the arrow and the implied movement in representational momentum tap into the same dynamic representation. In experiment 3 we looked for a relationship between the pointedness of a triangle and the magnitude of the memory shift. We varied pointedness by varying the narrowness of the triangle. The results from a rating task verified our assumption that the narrower the triangle was, the more it appeared to point. Results from the memory task were also consistent with this assumption, in that the shifts were generally larger for the narrower triangles. We found a significant shift even for the equilateral triangle. Thus, even with a stimulus that has no known semantic association with movement, we nonetheless see a memory shift consistent with an underlying dynamic representation.

Implications for Aesthetics
These three experiments go beyond our previous work on the dynamics of static forms because we used static patterns that do not imply, in any obvious way, real-world dynamics. In comparison, Freyd's (1983) study investigating memory for photographs used stimuli that were specifically chosen because an action was frozen in the snapshot. Similarly, the representational momentum experiments (Freyd and Finke 1984; Kelly and Freyd 1987) all used a sequence of static positions sampled from a possible real-world transformation. Even the studies by Freyd, Pantzer, and Cheng (1988), looking at memory for highly stable scenes, employed a depiction of the disruption of equilibrium to induce a memory shift.

The proposal that static form alone, without virtue of representing likely real-world transformations, can induce a representation of dynamics is compatible with a theory of visual aesthetics proposed by Arnheim (1974, 1988). Arnheim (1988) points out, for instance, that Matisse's *La Danseuse* (which does not directly represent a common object or scene) manages through form alone to create a powerfully dynamic image. We predict that where Arnheim notes dynamics in art, most observers would more readily experience directionality, or even "pointing," within the static picture. We also predict that where Arnheim notes dynamics in static art, observers have systematic shifts in memory for position of the form in the direction of pointing. Freyd (1993) hypothesized that memory shifts occur in between recurring eye fixations on points of dynamic interest such that the observer is repeatedly experiencing representational surprise at the discrepancy between the remembered and the experienced reality of a dynamic element. In turn, this representational surprise might relate to aesthetic excitement. McKeown and Freyd (1992) have confirmed that memory shifts can occur for static art.

Dynamic Representations as Medium for Creative Cognition
While creative artists exploit the potential to invoke a dynamic representation with static art, dynamic representations likely have an even more general role in cognition and creative cognition. Finke, Ward, and Smith (1992) suggest that the study of basic cognitive processes and of creativity are naturally interdependent pursuits. Our consideration of dynamic representations would thus inform the investigation of creative cognition by establishing foundational aspects of mental representation. Specifically, we propose that dynamic mental representations are employed during creative thought. At the same time, creative processes may ultimately shape the direction of the dynamic representations. For instance, creative cognition might determine the *path* of motion (Finke and Freyd 1989).

Finke, Ward, and Smith (1992) propose the Geneplore model of creativity, which consists of two processing stages: a *generative* phase, in which mental representations called "preinventive structures" are constructed, followed by an *exploratory* phase, in which these structures are explored for possible interpretations. Finke, Ward, and Smith (1992) apply this model to a variety of domains of invention, including visual synthesis. We suggest here that the dynamic properties of static objects will have an important role in both the generative and exploratory phases of creative invention.

Figure 8.8
A pattern (croquet) created from the letter *T*, the number *8*, and the letter *P* in an experiment on creative visual synthesis (Finke and Slayton 1988). We suggest that the angle of the *T* implies movement, which helps define the *T* as a croquet mallet; this illustrates the potential role of dynamics in creative visualization and interpretation.

Generative Phase   We propose that if components such as preinventive structures are highly directional, this will lead, first, to a greater ease of mental synthesis. If the components are dynamic, they may lend themselves more easily to movement and other transformations. Second, it will lead to constraints on creative combinations. For instance, some combinations might be more likely than others due to the inherent dynamics of the stimuli. Finke (1990) has noted that when they interpret preinventive forms, subjects often report that they imagine using the forms or interacting with them in dynamic ways, in order to gain insight into how best to interpret the forms. Some of this dynamic interaction may result directly from the dynamic mental representations underlying the perceived directionality of static forms.

Exploratory Phase   Just as pattern goodness affects how easily one might recognize an emergent pattern in imagery (Finke, Ward, and Smith 1992, p. 53), the emergent dynamic properties of creative combinations may influence interpretation. Consider the creative visual synthesis produced by a subject in Finke and Slayton (1988), illustrated in figure 8.8. Would the subject's interpretation of the pattern as depicting the game of croquet have been as likely if the mallet were in a stable position? In other cases, the nature of the dynamics might suggest particular interpretations by virtue of knowledge of kinds of motion. For instance, aspects of directionality and pointedness may suggest animacy (Freyd 1992). Animals are directional; they tend to move in the direction in which they point. Freyd and Miller (1992) have shown that representational momentum shifts are greater for animate-appearing shapes moving in a forward direction than for the same shapes moving backward. Knowledge of likely motion based on static shape, whether croquet mallet or animal, is likely to inform creative interpretation.

At a more abstract level, we speculate about some of the ways that dynamic representations may shed light on creative process.[1] Many creative ideas have an apparent dynamic quality; they flow forward in time, constantly evolving and revealing new implications. They seem to have a conceptual momentum all their own. Most of these ideas seem to move more naturally in certain conceptual directions than others. Further, once they emerge, creative ideas often mask earlier ideas and beliefs. This may be analogous to the way memories for previous positions are pushed forward in time. In other words, the creative process may have a kind of directionality to it, with consequences somewhat like those for the temporal directionality of representational momentum; there is, in some sense, no going back to an earlier state. Fiction and poetry writers, filmmakers, and composers may well exploit this sort of conceptual momentum, just as painters may exploit the more perceptual processes of dynamic representations and representational momentum. The observer of the artistic creation is, in essence, expected to extrapolate into the future from any given point in the creative product, and thus artists' job is, in part, to invoke creative processes in the observer.

Future Research and Conclusion
The results reported here suggest a number of research directions. In future studies, researchers could vary the dynamic nature of the component parts used in mental constructions to test the role of dynamics in the generative phase of creative thought. Similarly they could examine the role of implied dynamics in arriving at novel pattern interpretations in the exploratory phase of creative discovery. Eventually it would be interesting to extend this line of research to nonvisual forms of creative cognition.

An additional direction for future research is to investigate the role of directionality in other sorts of patterns. A possibility we have considered is to use ambiguous patterns such as the duck-rabbit pattern shown in figure 8.9. It would be interesting to determine if subjects would misremember the position of the pattern in a direction consistent with the interpretation they have for the pattern. That is, if the pattern appears to be a rabbit, we would predict a memory shift in the direction the rabbit seems to be facing, but vice versa for the duck. This also raises the possibility that underlying dynamics may play a role in the interpretation of ambiguous figures.

In the meantime, our results are supportive of the hypothesis that perceived directionality is based on a dynamic representation. This is further evidence for the critical role of time in mental representation. To the extent that dynamic representations are fundamental to every-

Figure 8.9
Three ambiguous patterns (from left to right: duck/rabbit, goose/hawk, duck/squirrel) that change directionality with interpretation

day cognition, we would expect to learn that dynamic representations are fundamental to creative thought (Finke, Ward, and Smith 1992). In particular, the dynamic properties of mental representation may influence both the generative and exploratory aspects of creative invention.

Notes

This chapter is dedicated to the late Fred Attneave in fond memory of his curiosity, inspiration, and creativity. The empirical research was supported by NSF Presidential Young Investigator Award BNS-8796324 and NIMH grants R01-MH39784 and K02-MH00780 awarded to Freyd. We thank Andrea Sprute for her help with data collection and analysis and Jill Christman, Ron Finke, Doug Hintzman, Roger Shepard, and the editors of this book for helpful comments on the project and manuscript. Please address correspondence to Jennifer Freyd, Department of Psychology, University of Oregon, Eugene, OR, 97403 or to jjf@dynamic.uoregon.edu.
1. We are indebted to the editors of this book for their creative suggestions captured in this paragraph.

References

Arnheim, R. (1974) *Art and Visual Perception (The New Version)*. Berkeley: University of California Press.

Arnheim, R. (1988) Visual dynamics. *American Scientist, 76*, 585–591.

Attneave, F., (1968). Triangles as ambiguous figures. *American Journal of Psychology, 81*, 447–453.

Block, J. R., and Yuker, H. E. (1992). *Can you believe your eyes?* New York: Brunner/Mazel Publishers.

Bucher, N. M., and Palmer, S. E. (1985). Effects of motion on perceived pointing of ambiguous triangles. *Perception and Psychophysics, 38*, 227–236.

Faust, M. E. (1990). *Representational momentum: A dual process perspective.* Unpublished doctoral dissertation, University of Oregon.

Finke, R. A. (1990). *Creative imagery: Discoveries and inventions in visualization.* Hillsdale, NJ: Erlbaum.

Finke, R. A., and Freyd, J. J. (1989). Mental extrapolation and cognitive penetrability: Reply to Ranney, and some other matters. *Journal of Experimental Psychology: General, 118,* 403–408.

Finke, R. A., Freyd, J. J., and Shyi, G. C.-W. (1986). Implied velocity and acceleration induce transformations of visual memory. *Journal of Experimental Psychology: General, 115,* 175–188.

Finke, R. A., and Shyi, G. C.-W. (1988). Mental extrapolation and representational momentum for complex implied motions. *Journal of Experimental Psychology: Learning, Memory, and Cognition, 14*(1), 112–120.

Finke, R. A., and Slayton, K. (1988). Explorations of creative visual synthesis in mental imagery. *Memory and Cognition, 14,* 112–120.

Finke, R. A., Ward, T. B., and Smith, S. M. (1992). *Creative cognition: Theory, research, and applications.* Cambridge, MA: MIT Press.

Fodor, J. A. (1983). *The modularity of mind.* Cambridge, MA: MIT Press.

Freyd J. J. (1983). The mental representation of movement when static stimuli are viewed. *Perception and Psychophysics, 33,* 575–581.

Freyd, J. J. (1987). Dynamic mental representations. *Psychological Review, 94,* 427–438.

Freyd, J. J. (1992). Dynamic representations guiding adaptive behavior. In F. Macar, V. Pouthas, and J. Friedman (eds.), *Time, action and cognition: Towards bridging the gap* (pp. 309–323). Dordrecht: Kluwer Academic Publishers.

Freyd, J. J. (1993). Five hunches about perceptual processes and dynamic representations. In D. E. Meyer and S. Kornblum (eds.), *Attention and performance XIV: Synergies in experimental psychology, artificial intelligence, and cognitive neuroscience— A silver jubilee* (pp. 99–120). Cambridge, MA: MIT Press.

Freyd, J. J., and Finke, R. A. (1984). Representational momentum. *Journal of Experimental Psychology: Learning, Memory, and Cognition, 10,* 126–132.

Freyd, J. J., and Finke, R. A. (1985). A velocity effect for representational momentum. *Bulletin of the Psychonomic Society, 23,* 443–446.

Freyd, J. J., and Johnson, J. Q. (1987). Probing the time course of representational momentum. *Journal of Experimental Psychology: Learning, Memory, and Cognition, 13,* 259–268.

Freyd, J. J., Kelly, M. H., and DeKay, M. (1990). Representational momentum in memory for pitch. *Journal of Experimental Psychology: Learning, Memory, and Cognition, 16,* 1107–1117.

Freyd, J. J., and Miller, G. F. (1992) *Creature motion.* Paper presented at the Thirty-third Annual Meeting of the Psychonomic Society, St. Louis, November 13–15.

Freyd, J. J., Pantzer, T. M., and Cheng, J. L. (1988). Representing statics as forces in equilibrium. *Journal of Experimental Psychology: General, 117,* 395–407.

Hubbard, T. L. (1990). Cognitive representations of linear motion: Possible direction and gravity effects in judged displacements. *Memory and Cognition, 18,* 299–309.

Hubbard, T. L., and Bharucha, J. J. (1988). Judged displacement in apparent vertical and horizontal motion. *Perception and Psychophysics, 44,* 211–221.

Kelly, M. H., and Freyd, J. J. (1987). Explorations of representational momentum. *Cognitive Psychology, 19,* 369–401.

McKeown, D., and Freyd, J. J. (1992) Dynamic aspects of static art. Poster presented at the 1992 convention of the American Psychological Society, San Diego, June.

Palmer, S. E. (1978). Fundamental aspects of cognitive representation. In E. Rosch and B. B. Lloyd (eds.), *Cognition and categorization* (pp. 259–303). Hillsdale, NJ: Erlbaum.

Palmer, S. E. (1980). What makes triangles point: Local and global effects in configurations of ambiguous triangles. *Cognitive Psychology, 12,* 285–305.

Palmer, S. E., and Bucher, N. M. (1982). Textural effects in perceived pointing of ambiguous triangles. *Journal of Experimental Psychology: Human Perception and Performance, 8,* 693–708.

Verfaillie, K., and d'Ydewalle, G. (1991). Representational momentum and event course anticipation in the perception of implied periodical motions. *Journal of Experimental Psychology: Learning, Memory, and Cognition, 17,* 302–313.

Chapter 9

Scientific Discovery and Creative Reasoning with Diagrams

Peter C.-H. Cheng and Herbert A. Simon

Scientific discovery is a highly creative human endeavor well worth studying as an example of creative cognition. There is substantial research interest in the nature of the processes of scientific discovery in cognitive science, many empirical investigations have been undertaken, and numerous computational models have been constructed. Langley and associates (1987) have argued that scientific discovery can be viewed as problem solving by heuristic search, and in a series of simulation programs they have shown how laws can be discovered inductively under this conception. Cheng (1992a) reviews the many different computational discovery systems that now exist, and Shrager and Langley (1990) and Zytkow's (1992) books describe a broad selection of the recent and current computational research. The empirical work has studied how subjects make discoveries in different simulated discovery environments (Klahr and Dunbar 1988; Qin and Simon 1990; Schunn and Klahr 1992). Gorman (1992) considers the empirical studies from the perspective of falsification in discovery.

Although much has been learned about the processes of scientific discovery, there are aspects that still remain to be examined, one of them the role of multiple representations and diagrammatic representations. Shepard (1978, 1988) describes many examples of creative imagery from the history of science and considers some of the developmental factors that may be associated with the power of imagery. Computational models and empirical work have tended to focus on discoveries made with a single non-diagrammatic knowledge representation despite the ubiquity of diagrams in scientific reasoning and discovery and the wide acknowledgment of the need to examine the role of diagrammatic representations (Langley et al. 1987; Shrager and Langley 1990; Cheng 1992a). Research on multiple representations and diagrams in discovery is still rather novel, though there has been significant progress on reasoning with diagrammatic representations more generally (Novak 1977; Larkin and Simon 1987; Larkin 1989;

Koedinger and Anderson 1990; Tabachneck 1992; Qin 1992; Narayanan 1992). With respect to discovery, Shrager (1990) has produced a computer program that uses diagrammatic and propositional representations as two different modalities that are grounded on sensory experience to demonstrate his theory of commonsense perception. Theory formation in this view employs processes that work within and between the different modalities to compare and combine information in the different representations.

Our own work has investigated the role of discovery with diagrams in early physics. Cheng (1992b) demonstrates the computational benefits that Galileo achieved in his kinematic discoveries with diagrams over a more conventional approach using algebraic equations. Galileo made many important discoveries, but we noted that he never arrived at the principle of conservation of momentum. We were curious as to whether this was because, dealing only with gravitational force on a single body, he never had to introduce the concept of mass; or because the algebraic and diagrammatic methods he employed did not lead readily to the statement of momentum conservation. To satisfy our curiosity, we examined the reasoning methods of Huygens and his contemporaries and found that their diagrammatic methods were quite similar to Galileo's, but also quite conducive to inferring the law of conservation of momentum. Cheng and Simon (1992) show how it was easier for those early physicists to discover the conservation of momentum using diagrams than to induce the law directly from numerical data.

This chapter describes our continuing investigation of the role of discovery with diagrams in early physics by presenting a system that performs law induction using one-dimensional diagrams. The system is called HUYGENS and although we do not like to claim that HUYGENS gives a specific description of the thought methods of the scientist, Huygens, it does at least at a qualitative level give some indication of the way in which diagrammatic representations shaped thought early in the seventeenth century.

We first give some examples of the creative use of diagrams in scientific discovery and reasoning from the history of science. Then as a further step toward understanding the role of diagrams in discovery, we consider the basis for one-dimensional diagrammatic law induction. The regularity spotters, operators, and heuristics used by the HUYGENS diagrammatic law induction program are considered and one of its simulations of a discovery described. The limitations of one-dimensional diagrammatic law induction are discussed and the possibilities of diagrammatic discovery are considered more generally.

Reasoning and Discovery with Diagrams

Diagrams are useful to scientists trying to make discoveries for several reasons. At a general level, multiple representation gives the scientist the possibility of switching to an alternate representation when an impasse is reached. Diagrams have certain properties that often give them advantages over other representations. They can facilitate problem solving by reducing the amount of computation required to search for relevant information and by reducing the effort required for recognizing appropriate operators or inference rules (Larkin and Simon 1987). Further, they permit perceptual inferences to be made more easily than with their more difficult logical counterparts (Larkin 1989).

Consider Galileo's kinematic discoveries described in his *Two New Sciences* (1974). All the propositions described here are from the third section of that book. The 30th proposition considers the following situation: Given inclined planes, ramps, running between two parallel vertical lines (figure 9.1), what inclination of the plane will give the quickest time of descent? This will be called the "quickest descent" problem. The acceleration of the ball increases with greater inclination. However, the total distance to be travelled also increases. The problem is to find when the two effects combine to produce a minimum. Galileo considered this problem after he had discovered his law of free fall (the second proposition), but he did not approach the problem by trying to apply the law directly to the situation. Rather, he used a diagrammatic approach involving the sixth proposition, known as Galileo's theorem (Drake 1978).

Galileo's theorem is concerned with the times of descent along inclined planes within a vertical circle. Figure 9.2 shows inclined planes running from points on the circumference of a circle to the lowest point in the circle and planes running to the circumference from the highest point. The times of descent on all such inclined planes

Figure 9.1
Quickest descent problem—proposition 30

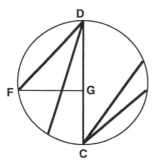

Figure 9.2
Galileo's theorem—proposition 6

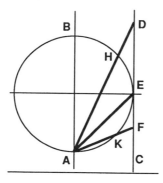

Figure 9.3
Solution to quickest descent problem

are equal, which Galileo proves from the law of free fall and the geometry of circles (by relating the law's square relation between distance and time to the mathematical description of circles as the sum of two squares). The way Galileo solved the quickest descent time problem was to combine figures 9.1 and 9.2, giving figure 9.3. The circle has been drawn with a radius equal to the distance between the parallel lines with its bottom at the point of intersection of all the inclined planes. From Galileo's theorem it immediately follows that the times of descent along the inclined planes within the circle are equal; $t_{EA} = t_{HA} = t_{KA}$. However, as the inclined planes DA and FA are longer than HA and KA, their times of descent must be greater than times for HA and KA. Therefore, the descent time between the verticals along the incline EA is the shortest; the inclination is 45 degrees.

Although it is quite feasible to do, there is no record that Galileo attempted to solve the problem by the direct application of his various laws of motion using a more conventional mathematical approach. However, it is interesting to consider what is involved under that approach because the contrast shows the ingenuity of Galileo's diagrammatic solution. A general inclined plane is represented by the triangle DAC (figure 9.4). The time of descent down the plane is given by the fifth proposition on uniform velocity motion from the *Two New Sciences*;

$$t_{DA} = d_{DA} / V_{DA} , \tag{9.1}$$

where t, d, and V are time, distance, and mean speed, respectively. The mean speed is equal to the maximum speed at the end of the descent, $Vmax$, divided by two, thus:

$$t_{DA} = 2 \cdot d_{DA} / Vmax_{DA} . \tag{9.2}$$

Galileo's law of free fall relates the time, t, for descents down an inclined plane to the vertical distance, h, traveled,

$$h_{ST} / h_{SY} = t_{ST}^2 / t_{SY}^2 , \tag{9.3}$$

where the subscripts refer to different parts of the descent from rest. The terminal velocity at the end of an inclined plane is thus proportionate to the square root of the height of the plane, so

$$t_{DA} = 2 \cdot d_{DA} / \sqrt{h_{DC}} , \tag{9.4}$$

where h is the height. From Pythagoras's theorem, the length of the inclined plane can be replaced by its height and the horizontal component of its length, giving

$$t_{DA} = 2 \cdot \sqrt{(d_{AC}^2 + h_{DC}^2)} / \sqrt{h_{DC}} . \tag{9.5}$$

The final step is to find the relation between h_{DC} and d_{AC} that yields the minimum value of t_{DA}. There are various ways to do this but none is straightforward and simple; for example, it is possible to reason directly about the values of numerator and denominator of equation 9.5 as h_{DC} varies. The solution corresponds to an angle of the plane of 45 degrees, where $h_{DC} = d_{AC}$.

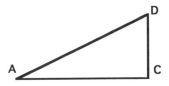

Figure 9.4
Simple inclined plane

The conventional mathematical approach is more complex than the diagrammatic approach, because the bulk of the reasoning centers around the abstract equations expressing kinematic laws. Four laws were combined to find equation 9.5, which requires further difficult reasoning to determine the minimum time. Under the diagrammatic approach, the minimum time was found by spotting the line that did not extend beyond the circumference of a circle, a simple piece of perceptual reasoning. Cheng (1992b) has modeled various Galilean kinematic discoveries under the diagrammatic and the conventional mathematical approaches, including this example, and has shown that the diagrammatic approach often requires less computation than the conventional approach.

In the following sections the discovery of more complex laws using diagrams is considered. First, we explore the diagrams that the early physicists may have used to discover the conservation of momentum.

Conservation Laws as One-Dimensional Diagrams

The momentum of a body is the product of its mass and velocity. For two bodies colliding in one dimension, the momentum conservation law is usually written as an equation,

$$m_1 \cdot U_1 + m_2 \cdot U_2 = m_1 \cdot V_1 + m_2 \cdot V_2 , \qquad (9.6)$$

where, m_1 and m_2 are the masses of the two bodies, U_1 and U_2 are their velocities before collision, and V_1 and V_2 their velocities after collision. If energy is also conserved in the collisions then the following energy conservation equation holds simultaneously;

$$m_1 \cdot U_1^2 + m_2 \cdot U_2^2 = m_1 \cdot V_1^2 + m_2 \cdot V_2^2 . \qquad (9.7)$$

However, it is possible to encode the two laws in a diagrammatic form that embraces both equations; three examples are shown in the first row of figure 9.5. The top line of the left diagram shows that body 1 comes in from the left and impacts body 2, which is initially stationary. Body 1 is bigger than body 2, as shown by the middle line. The bottom line shows that both bodies travel off to the right. The speeds of the bodies are in proportion to the lengths of their respective lines. The center diagram shows a collision where the bodies approach from opposite directions with equal speeds, but depart with different speeds in opposite directions, because the masses have different magnitudes. The right diagram shows that when the ratio of the initial speeds, U_1/U_2, is equal to the inverse of the ratio of their masses, m_2/m_1, then the final speeds for each body are the same as before collision, but the bodies' directions are reversed.

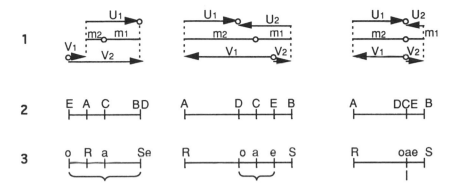

Figure 9.5
One-dimensional momentum conservation diagrams

Notice that the total lengths for initial and final velocity lines are equal, that is:

$$U_1 - U_2 = V_2 - V_1 \tag{9.8}$$

This relation can be simply derived from equations 9.6 and 9.7. The lines for the masses are drawn end to end with their total length equal to the length of the $U_1 - U_2$ line. The structures of the laws are such that the ends of the lines, shown by the small circles, must always lie in a straight vertical or diagonal line. Huygens and Wren presented similar diagrams to the Royal Society of London when they first described the law of the conservation of momentum (Hutton, Shaw and Pearson 1804). In Huygens's diagrams, row 2 in figure 9.5, A and B are the two bodies, their velocities before impact are denoted by the lines AD and BD, the velocities after impact by EA and EB, and the masses of A and B by BC and AC [sic], respectively. In the diagrams, the lengths of DC and CE are always equal. Wren's diagrams, row 3 in figure 9.5, are essentially the same, except for differences in notation and the fact that Wren explicitly states that the diagrams are reversible; that is, either Ro and So or Re and Se can indicate the initial velocities, with eR and eS or oR and oS the final velocities, respectively.

Some of the points about the potential advantages of diagrammatic representations can be seen with these diagrams. For example, different configurations of collisions may be distinguished when velocities of the balls have different signs, are equal, unequal, or are zero. How many different configurations exist? This is not a simple problem working directly from equations 9.6 and 9.7, but using the diagrams it is simple to answer. For instance, when the masses are equal there

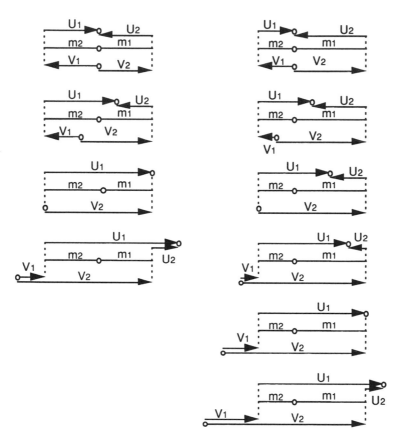

Figure 9.6
Configurations of collisions

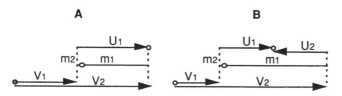

Figure 9.7
Collisions in which the ratio of mass tends to infinity

are four configurations (figure 9.6). Huygens and Wren provided such series of diagrams in their expositions (Hutton, Shaw, and Pearson, 1804). Further, it is possible to do simple quantitative reasoning and reasoning about extreme cases with these diagrams, using the fact that the small circles in diagrams must always lie in a straight line, vertically or diagonally (row 1, figure 9.5). Figure 9.7A shows what happens when a stationary ball (m_1) is hit by another (m_2) as the ratio of their masses tends to infinity. The maximum speed (V_2) that the stationary ball can attain after the collision is just two times that of the first ball (U_1). Similarly, figure 9.7B shows what happens when two balls approach with equal speeds from opposite directions as the mass of one tends toward infinity compared to the other. The maximum speed of the smaller ball after impact (V_2) is three times its initial speed (U_2).

There are several different ways in which the conservation of momentum may have been discovered. One possibility is that the law was discovered in a theoretical fashion by derivation from energy conservation and considerations of invariance of motion relative to Galilean transformation of coordinates (Barbour 1989). A second possibility is that the law was induced from sets of numerical data gathered in experiments. This method of discovery is quite feasible, as demonstrated by several systems that have modeled the discovery of the principle of momentum conservation (BACON.5, Langley et al., 1987; ABACUS, Falkenhainer and Michalski 1986). These systems find the law by searching a space of algebraic relations among the variables using the numerical data. A third possibility also considers that the law was induced from experimental data but using diagrams rather than working directly with algebraic equations. Cheng and Simon (1992) have modeled the discovery in this manner and have shown that it would have been easier for Huygens and Wren to have made the discovery by using diagrams than by the conventional mathematical methods available at the time.

The HUYGENS System

Cheng and Simon's (1992) system simulated the discovery of the conservation of momentum using one-dimensional diagrams, but some of its heuristics were specific to the structure of the conservation law problem, specifically, the heuristics to deal with the two independent variables (V_1 and V_2). Here a more general system for one-dimensional diagrammatic law induction is described. Known as HUYGENS, it considers one diagram for each set of experimental data obtained from a single experimental test (Cheng 1991). Variables are represented as line segments on the number line. The length of a line segment (line, for short) is in proportion to the magnitude of the value of its variable, and the orientation, positioning, and relative sizes of lines encode different algebraic relations between the variables. HUYGENS operates by constructing diagrams from sets of data using diagrammatic operators. A group of diagrams is generated by applying the same sequence of operators to the sets of data. Relations that really exist are manifested as patterns common to all the diagrams in a group and it is the job of regularity spotters to find such patterns. When a pattern is found, an algebraic law is simply inferred from the regularity and the particular operators used to generate the diagrams. HUYGENS employs cycles of regularity spotting and operator application.

Operators
The job of the diagrammatic operators is to construct or modify diagrams so that they encode different relations between the variables. Tables 9.1 and 9.2 show the diagrammatic operators that are required in the cases of discovery modeled so far. (Other operators may be needed in other cases of discovery.) Various conventions are used when drawing the diagrams. The number line is assumed to increase toward the right. The lines in the diagrams are considered to lie on the number line, but for clarity they are drawn with vertical separation. When appropriate, the origin of a line is indicated by an o and its point of interest (interest point) by an x. An interest point is the end of a line; its position depends on the magnitude of the variable, and is determined by the data. Where appropriate, construction points are also marked by a | (a construction point is an intermediate point identified and used by operators in the construction of a line). The lines are labeled with symbols for their variables. HUYGENS's internal

Table 9.1
Elementary Operators

Name	Operator		Relation
PLOT	x	$o\!\!\xrightarrow{\ x\ }\!\!x$	—
ADD	$o\!\!\xrightarrow{\ x_1\ }\!\!x$ $o\!\!\xrightarrow{\ x_2\ }\!\!x$	$\underline{\ x_1\ }\ \underline{\ x_2\ }$ $o\!\!\xrightarrow{\ x'\ }\!\!x$	$x' = x_1 + x_2$
SUBTRACT	$o\!\!\xrightarrow{\ x_1\ }\!\!x$ $o\!\!\xrightarrow{\ x_2\ }\!\!x$	$\underline{\ x_1\ }$ $\underline{\ x_2\ }$ $o\!\!\xrightarrow{\ x'\ }\!\!x$	$x' = x_1 + x_2$
NEGATE	$o\!\!\xrightarrow{\ x\ }\!\!x$	$x\!\!\xrightarrow{\ x_1\ }\!\!o$	$x' = -x$

Table 9.2
Normalization Operators

Name	Operator	Relation
NORMALIZE		$x' = (y_2/y_1)x$
NORMALIZE-ADD-1		$x' = \dfrac{y_1 + y_2}{y_1} x$
NORMALIZE-ADD-2		$x' = \dfrac{y_1}{y_1 + y_2} x$
NORMALIZE-MINUS-1		$x' = \dfrac{y_1 - y_2}{y_1} x$
NORMALIZE-MINUS-2		$x' = \dfrac{y_1}{y_1 + y_2} x$

representations of the lines take the form of triples of numbers for the origin, the interest point, and the construction point, if applicable. These triples are stored together in lists corresponding to diagrams, and diagrams are themselves stored together in lists to form groups. The overall organization of the data is equivalent to the structure of the diagrams, as if they were drawn on paper.

An internal representation that is even closer to real diagrams (marks on paper) could be employed. For example, the lines and markers for the different points could be held in a bit map. The operators could be modified to generate lines in such a format, and the regularity spotters modified to look for points on such lines. However, the operators and spotters would be functionally equivalent to those currently possessed by HUYGENS but would make the implementation more complex, without contributing anything further to the analysis. HUYGENS nevertheless uses a simple routine to convert the sets of number triples into real lines for display in its output trace.

Values of various attributes for each variable or line are recorded by HUYGENS and initially given as part of the input to the system. The

attributes considered are the *type* (whether a line stands for an independent or dependent variable), the *property* of the line (e.g., velocity
or temperature) and the *status* of the line (whether or not it is a new
line just generated by an operator). The properties of new lines are
inherited from the original lines in a manner appropriate to each
operator employed.

Table 9.1 shows four elementary operators. The PLOT operator
takes a variable, X, and draws a line with a length in proportion to
the magnitude of X. All the origins of all the lines drawn by PLOT are
at the same arbitrary position on the number line. The opposite end
of a line is its interest point, because its location depends on the
magnitude of X. The ADD operator finds the sum of two variables,
X_1 and X_2, that have the same dimensionality by redrawing their lines
end to end. The total length may be considered as a new variable or
term, X', representing the sum of X_1 and X_2. The SUBTRACT operator
finds the difference between the two variables, X_1 and X_2, having the
same dimensionality, by redrawing the X_2 line with its interest point
coinciding with the interest point of X_1. The length of the new line in
between the origins, X', equals the difference between X_1 and X_2. The
NEGATE operation makes the inverse of a variable by redrawing its
line with the interest point on the opposite side of the origin. ADD,
SUBTRACT, and NEGATE assign to the new lines they generate the
same property as the original lines.

The five normalization operators (table 9.2) are used to incorporate
variables standing for more than one type of property into a diagram.
They all require a pair of variables, Y_1 and Y_2, for one type of property,
P_y, and a single variable, X, for some other property, P_x. X is taken as
the datum against which the other variables are standardized. NOR-
MALIZE is the simplest and works by redrawing Y_1 with its length
equal to X, and then redrawing Y_2 in proportion to Y_1. A new term,
X', for property P_x is obtained with a value equal to X times Y_2/Y_1.
The other normalization operators are similar to NORMALIZE, but
they take the sum (or difference) between Y_1 and Y_2 and use Y_1+Y_2,
Y_1-Y_2, or Y_1 alone as the basis for standardization of X.

The application of an operator usually reduces, and never increases,
the number of lines in a diagram. Each operator generates a new line
standing for a variable or a term that expresses a potential relation
among the variables for the old lines (e.g., the third column of tables
9.1 and 9.2). Groups of diagrams are generated by different sequences
of operators. A sequence of operators that successfully encodes a
regularity in the data will produce the same pattern in every diagram
in its group. Determining whether any relations really exist by looking
for such patterns is the job of the regularity spotters.

Regularity Spotters
The regularity spotters look for patterns that are common to every diagram in a group. The spotters examine the interest points in the diagrams, because these reflect any patterns that are present in the data. Tables 9.3 and 9.4 present regularity spotters required in the cases of discovery so far modeled.

The precise spotters (table 9.3) look for exact patterns in diagrams. The EQUAL regularity spotter identifies when two lines are equal in length in every diagram in a group. The relation inferred is that Z_1 is equal to Z_2. The CONSTANT regularity spotter identifies when the difference between two variables is a constant for all the members of a group. The MEAN spotter identifies when a variable has a magnitude equal to the mean of the two others, for every diagram in a group. When regularity is found, the relation can be written as an equation with appropriate symbols for the variables (column 3).

Table 9.4 presents two more regularity spotters. They are relative spotters that seek patterns based on the relative lengths of lines rather than their exact lengths. The BETWEEN spotter identifies when a

Table 9.3
Precise Regulatory Spotters

Name	Pattern	Relation
EQUAL		$Z_1 = Z_2$
CONSTANT		$C = Z_1 - Z_2$
MEAN		$Y = (X + Z)/2$

Table 9.4
Relative Regulatory Spotters

Name	Pattern	Relation
BETWEEN		$X > Y > Z$ or $X < Y < Z$
NEGATIVE		$X > 0$ and $Y > 0$ or $X > 0$ and $Y > 0$

variable always has a magnitude between those of two others, in any order. The NEGATIVE spotter identifies when a pair of lines has interest points on opposite sides of a common origin. The main use of the relative spotters is in heuristics that suggest when different operators may be appropriate to consider.

The regularity spotters look for patterns across pairs or triplets of lines in each diagram in a group. How the pairs and triplets are chosen for consideration and how the regularity spotters suggest the use of certain operators are considered next.

Heuristics

HUYGENS needs heuristics to limit the size of the search space of diagrams. There are various places where appropriate heuristics are employed (table 9.5).

First, when HUYGENS is looking for a common pattern within all the diagrams from a particular group, pairs and triplets of lines have to be identified for the regularity spotters. Rather than consider all combinations of pairs and triplets, HUYGENS uses a strategy that takes into account the type, property, and status attributes of the lines. Different combinations of the attributes are considered by the SELEC-TION-BY-ATTRIBUTE heuristic: status and property, type and property, and property alone. For each combination, HUYGENS finds the total number of pairs and triplets that can be generated when the lines have matching (non-nil) values for the specified attributes. For ex-

Table 9.5
Huygen's Heuristics

Heuristic	Action
SELECTION-BY-ATTRIBUTE	Select the most reasonable number of pairs and triplets of lines by considering those that match under different combinations attributes.
DEPENDENT-PROPERTY-FOCUS	Choose pairs and triplets of lines that have the same property as the independent line(s).
PREFER-PRECISE-SPOTTERS	Give regularities found by the precise spotters a higher priority than those found by the relative spotters.
SPOTTER-OPERATOR-MATCH	Specific particular operator(s) when a particular regularity has been found.
DEFAULT-OPERATORS	When no regularities have been found, try the ADD and SUBTRACT operators on the selected pairs.

ample, when the type and property combination is considered, only lines in a diagram standing for the same property and that are exclusively independent or dependent variables are taken as potential pairs or triplets. The set of pairs and triplets chosen is the one that has the greatest number of pairs plus triplets not exceeding the number of lines in the diagram.

All three attribute combinations consider the same property of the lines because it is not valid to compare quantities for different properties. The status and property combination is included because it is worthwhile looking for patterns among new lines that have just been generated. The type and property combination is included because it is sensible to consider the independent lines together before complicating matters with the inclusion of the dependent lines. The property attribute alone is included in case the other combinations do not yield any pairs or triplets.

Before applying the regularity spotters to the pairs and triplets of lines, HUYGENS attempts to focus the spotters on those pairs and triplets whose lines have the same property as the dependent line the (DEPENDENT-PROPERTY-FOCUS heuristic). The simple rationale being that it seems sensible to seek relations for lines with the same property as the dependent line(s) before making things more complex by considering lines with other properties.

Regularity spotters are then applied to the selected pairs and triplets of lines to find any patterns that are common to all the diagrams in a group. The PREFER-PRECISE-SPOTTERS heuristic gives priority to the precise regularity spotters, because they identify exact relations between the lines. If on a particular cycle HUYGENS finds a group of diagrams with a precise regularity and another with a relative regularity, then only the precise group is considered in the next cycle. Depending on the regularity found and whether there are further lines to consider HUYGENS will apply different operators (the SPOTTER-OPERATOR-MATCH heuristic). When a precise regularity is found and there are no other lines left in the diagrams to be considered, HUYGENS states that a law was found. However, when a precise regularity is found and lines remain, HUYGENS will apply the normalization operators, using the regularity found as the basis for standardization.

For example, when the CONSTANT regularity spotter is true and there are remaining lines, HUYGENS will use the distance found (C in table 9.3) as the basis against which to compare the remaining lines when applying the normalization operators. The two relative spotters are considered if no precise regularities are found. When a relative regularity is found, the SPOTTER-OPERATOR-MATCH heuristic suggests that particular operators may be appropriate. For example, suppose the BETWEEN regularity holds for three variables, A, B and C, so that B is always between A and C. Now, if other variables need to be considered, NORMALIZE-ADD-2 is a good choice, with the difference between A and C as the basis for standardization (X in table 9.2). The new term formed by this normalization operation will always be between the ends of A and C, so it is likely to be directly related to B.

The possibility exists that no regularity will be found in a group of diagrams. In such cases HUYGENS will apply the ADD and SUBTRACT operators to the selected pairs as a default. This is the DEFAULT-OPERATORS heuristic.

Simulation of a Discovery
Here we consider HUYGENS's simulation of the discovery of the conservation of momentum.

The data given to HUYGENS for the conservation law problem are shown in table 9.6. The first row in figure 9.8 shows the lines given to HUYGENS as input, based on the data. In the first collision, case 1, body 1 comes in from the left and impacts body two, which is initially stationary. Body 1 has twice the mass of body 2, so both move off to the right at different speeds. Case 2 is a collision in which the bodies approach from opposite directions at equal speed, body 1 from the left and body 2 from the right. The bodies depart at different speeds and in opposite directions, because the masses are different. In the third case the bodies are moving from left to right both before and after the collision. In the collision, body 1 loses speed and body 2 gains speed.

The simulation of the discovery involves five cycles of regularity spotting and operator application. In the first cycle, the pairs of variables that were chosen by the SELECTION-BY-ATTRIBUTE heuristic were (m_1, m_2), (U_1, U_2) and (V_1, V_2), but these were narrowed to the

Table 9.6
Momentum Conservation Law Data

Symbol	Property	Type	Case 1	Case 2	Case 3
m_1	Mass	Independent	2	1	3
m_2	Mass	Independent	1	2	1
U_1	Velocity	Independent	3	3	3
U_2	Velocity	Independent	0	-3	1
V_1	Velocity	Independent	1	-5	2
V_2	Velocity	Independent	4	1	4

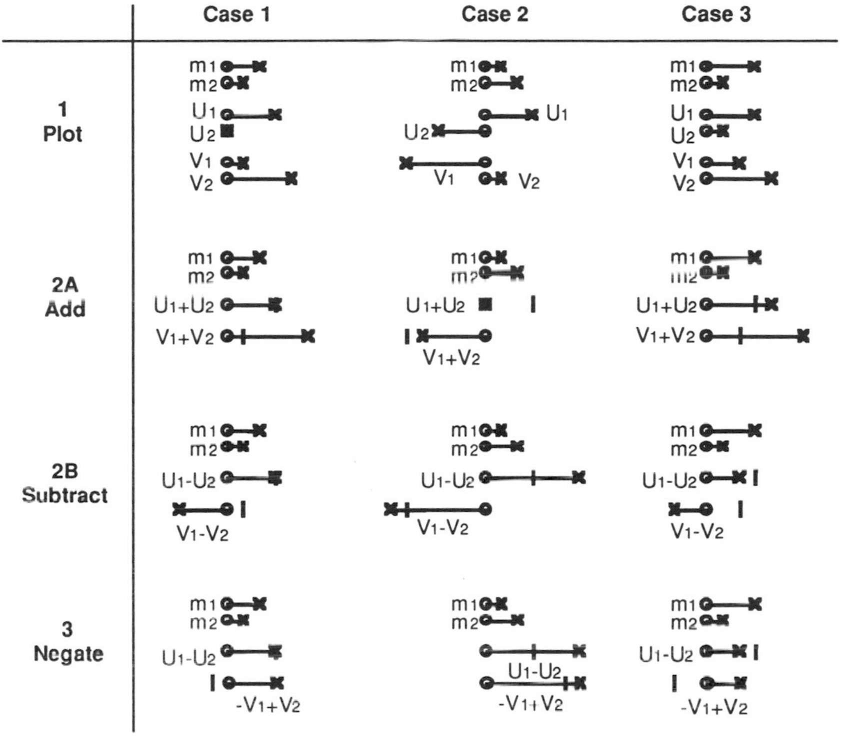

	Case 1	Case 2	Case 3
1 Plot	m_1, m_2, U_1, U_2, V_1, V_2	m_1, m_2, U_1, U_2, V_1, V_2	m_1, m_2, U_1, U_2, V_1, V_2
2A Add	m_1, m_2, U_1+U_2, V_1+V_2	m_1, m_2, U_1+U_2, V_1+V_2	m_1, m_2, U_1+U_2, V_1+V_2
2B Subtract	m_1, m_2, U_1-U_2, V_1-V_2	m_1, m_2, U_1-U_2, V_1-V_2	m_1, m_2, U_1-U_2, V_1-V_2
3 Negate	m_1, m_2, U_1-U_2, $-V_1+V_2$	m_1, m_2, U_1-U_2, $-V_1+V_2$	m_1, m_2, U_1-U_2, $-V_1+V_2$

Figure 9.8
Beginning of the momentum law discovery

second and third pairs by the DEPENDENT-PROPERTY-FOCUS heuristic, because V_1 and V_2 are dependent and U_1 and U_2 share the same property. None of the regularity spotters found any common patterns for the pairs in the three diagrams, so HUYGENS resorted to the DEFAULT-OPERATORS heuristic. The lines generated by the ADD and SUBTRACT operators are shown in middle two rows in figure 9.8, respectively. In the second cycle, the two new lines in each diagram were chosen by the SELECTION-BY-ATTRIBUTE heuristic. The NEGATIVE spotter was found to hold for the new lines generated by the SUBTRACT operator; the interest points of those lines in all three diagrams are on opposite sides of their shared origin. The SPOTTER-OPERATOR-MATCH then forced HUYGENS to generate a new set of diagrams by applying the NEGATE operator (row 3 of figure 9.8). In the third cycle, the EQUAL regularity was found to hold for the new pair of velocity lines, so HUYGENS was able to find the relation among the velocities given by equation 9.8.

However, in the fourth cycle, it became apparent that there were mass lines still to consider, so HUYGENS had not finished. The common distance of $U_1 - U_2$ and $V_2 - V_1$ was used as the basis for the application of the normalization operators and the construction points were taken as the new interest points. In the fourth cycle the five normalization operators are applied, as shown in figure 9.9 (the $U_1 - U_2$ and the $V_1 - V_2$ lines are shown at the top of each column, rather than repeating them next to each pair of mass lines). Each normalization operator was applied twice because either m_1 or m_2 may be associated with U_1. In the fifth and final cycle, HUYGENS found that the only regularity to hold was MEAN, for the groups produced by NORMALIZE-ADD-2, with m_2 associated with U_1. The distance from the interest point on the mass line to the ends of the lines for U_1 and $-V_1$ were equal. Thus, HUYGENS had found a relation between the velocities and masses:

$$m_2 / m_1 + m_2 (U_1 - U_2) = U_1 - V_1 / 2 . \tag{9.9}$$

With a little algebraic manipulation and given equation 9.8, previously found by HUYGENS, equation 9.9 can be easily shown to be equivalent to the momentum conservation law, equation 9.6.

HUYGENS has also been successfully run on data for a simplified version of Black's law on the temperatures of liquids.

Benefits and Limitations
Many systems already exist that successfully perform quantitative law induction (BACON, Langley et al. 1987; ABACUS, Falkenhainer and Michalski 1986). HUYGENS differs in that it searches the space of one-dimensional diagrams rather than the space of algebraic terms for regularities. This alternative representation motivates HUYGENS's use of a greater range of operators and regularity spotters than the other systems. Some of the operators and spotters consider triplets of lines on each cycle, whereas previous systems usually consider relations between pairs of variables at any one time. There is a corresponding reduction in the size of HUYGENS's search space because it can sometimes combine three lines into a single new line, when the other systems require two cycles to do the same. A manifestation of this can be seen in the need for the fifth version of BACON (Langley et al. 1987) to employ-high level search control heuristics, which assume symmetry and conservation in the data, to improve the efficiency with which more complex laws are found.

A deficit of HUYGENS is its inability to cope simply with laws with power terms. To deal with squares and square roots, Galileo and other early physicists employed the two-dimensional geometry of conic

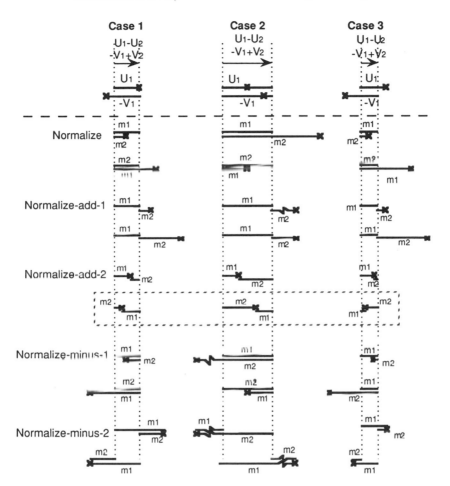

Figure 9.9
Momentum law discovery continued

224 Peter C.-H. Cheng and Herbert A. Simon

sections and circles (Cheng 1992b). A one-dimensional technique to find power laws is to take successive differences between the values of dependent variables until a linear series is obtained. However, this technique works only when the independent variable increases as an arithmetic progression and the index of the power law is a positive integer. Further, substantial amounts of drawing and redrawing are required.

Other abilities that HUYGENS will need are the means to recognize and define terms for intrinsic properties and to cope with noisy data, abilities that BACON possesses. Noisy data can be handled naturally under the diagrammatic approach by using error bars, similar to those used when plotting experimental errors on graphs. Briefly, the spotters would be allowed to match interest points so long as they fall within an interval, centered on the target position, whose length is some given percentage of the line of concern. Schemes for coping with noisy data can be devised using this technique.

Beyond One-Dimensional Diagrammatic Law Induction

Huygens's and Wren's diagrams encode the fairly complex momentum conservation laws in a deceptively simple manner, and in a way that makes it easy to reason qualitatively and quantitatively about different collisions (figures 9.6 and 9.7). The HUYGENS system has successfully modeled the diagrammatic discovery of the laws, thereby demonstrating how one-dimensional diagrammatic law induction can be performed in a manner consistent with the view that scientific discovery is problem solving characterized by heuristic search. In themselves, HUYGENS's operators, regularity spotters, and heuristics are quite straightforward, but in combination they provide an effective model of law induction. This is a further step toward understanding the processes of scientific discovery, which although seemingly mysterious can be rationally understood. In particular, HUYGENS provides further computational evidence for the view that switching back and forth between representations is an effective way to enhance creativity. From given numerical data, HUYGENS switches to a space of diagrams in its search for regularities by looking for patterns in the diagrams. When patterns have been found, the regularities are simply transformed back into equations. The change to diagrammatic representations permits different operators, regularity spotters, and heuristics to be employed that are more effective than those used in the direct search of a space of algebraic terms. The reasons for this are that diagrammatic representations often encode or index information in ways that help to reduce search (Larkin and Simon 1987) and that they enable perceptual inferences to be made in problem solving (Larkin 1989).

The wider implication of HUYGENS is that creative discovery with visual imagery, such as the episodes described by Shepard (1978, 1988), may be amenable to computational modeling in a similar fashion. One-dimensional diagrammatic law induction can be characterized as heuristic problem solving, but current research is exploring whether the same is true for diagrammatic discovery more generally, including one-dimensional deduction and two-dimensional induction and deduction. There are good reasons to think that the problem-solving view will cover other forms of diagrammatic discovery.

It seems possible to model two-dimensional diagrammatic discovery. Consider Koedinger and Anderson's (1990) diagram configuration model of expert problem solving. The central idea is that chunks of perceptual knowledge are stored as diagrammatic configuration schemas. Each schema holds various pieces of information, including a configuration, in the form of a diagram of the given situation; a whole-statement, which expresses the main theorem or idea of the schema; part-statements or part-properties, which indicate important features of the configuration; and sufficient conditions or ways-to-prove, which define sets of part-statements that are sufficient to prove the whole-statement. The way problem solving proceeds with the schemas involves mapping the configuration into a suitable part of the problem diagram and searching for part-statements that fulfill the sufficient conditions. If one set of the sufficient conditions is complete, then the whole-statement is applicable to the problem. Successive applications of different schema may fill in all the steps required for a complete problem solution.

Now it is possible to view the discoveries in Galileo's *Two New Sciences* as cases of problem solving under the Koedinger and Anderson model, treating each of the 38 propositions as a diagrammatic configuration schema. For example, how might Galileo have known that the sixth proposition (figure 9.2) was the right one to use for the problem of least time of descent? Quite simply, he could have found proposition 6 by searching through the space of all the diagrams encoding particular laws and theorems, which he had already discovered. Problem 6 can be reformulated as diagrammatic configuration schema. The configuration diagram is figure 9.2. The whole-statement says that the times of descent down all the inclined planes are equal. The part-statements would include facts, for example (1) each inclined plane runs from the circumference to the bottom of the circle, (2) each inclined plane runs from the top of the circle to the circumference, and (3) the circle is vertical. Sets of sufficient-conditions are 1 and 3 or

2 and 3. Hence, the schema for proposition 6 can be applied to the quickest descent time problem (figure 9.1) by adding a vertical circle to the problem diagram (figure 9.3), from which it is immediately seen that the first set of sufficient-conditions is satisfied.

New configuration schemas can be defined when a new proposition has been discovered using existing schemas. For example, a new configuration schema might be defined for Galileo's proposition 30. Its configuration diagram would be a triangle representing an inclined plane. The whole-statement would say that this inclined plane covering a fixed horizontal distance has the minimum descent time. The part-statement would indicate that the angle of the plane is 45 degrees or that the vertical height of the plane is equal to its horizontal length. A sufficient condition in this case would be either part-statement.

The propositions of the *Two New Sciences* can therefore be recast as diagrammatic configuration schemas, but it remains to be seen whether the discovery of all 38 of Galileo's propositions can be modeled under this approach. However, it seems that two-dimensional diagrammatic discovery is possible and that it does fall within the paradigm of problem solving as heuristic search.

Conclusions

Diagrams have an important role in scientific creativity because their representational properties make them effective for problem solving and discovery. This chapter has considered examples of the creative use of diagrams in the history of science and has described the HUYGENS discovery system, which uses one-dimensional diagrams to inductively discovery laws. The possibility of discovering laws with two-dimensional diagrams has also been considered. This research and other investigations have typically focused on the properties of diagrammatic representations in isolation or in comparison with other representations. However, scientific discovery probably does not usually rely on a single representation, diagrammatic or otherwise, but often involves the use of multiple representations in an integrated manner. Diagrams predominated in the Galilean examples, but they were not the only representational formalism he used. Galileo's knowledge of arithmetic and algebra was important in his discoveries, especially in the interpretation of the empirical data in his early work (Drake 1987), and they clearly interact in a complementary way with the diagrammatic representations in his discoveries. Future research must also consider discovery with multiple representations, how the best representations for a given problem can be chosen from those

available, and the ways in which different representations complement each other in problem solving and discovery.

Notes

P.C-H.C. was supported in part by a U.K. Science and Engineering Research Council
postdoctoral fellowship, which was held at Carnegie Mellon University, and by the
U.K. Economic and Social Research Council, which is funding the Centre for Research
on Development, Instruction and Training. H.A.S. was supported by the Defense
Advanced Research Projects Agency, Department of Defense, ARPA Order 3597, monitored by the Air Force Avionics Laboratory under contract F33615-81-K-1539. Reproduction in whole or in part is permitted for any purpose of the U.S. government.
Approved for public release; distribution unlimited.

References

Barbour, J. B. (1989). *Absolute or relative motion: The discovery of dynamics (vol. 1)*. Cambridge: Cambridge University Press.
Cheng, P. C.-H. (1991). Modelling experiments in scientific discovery. In *Proceeding of
the 12th International Joint Conference on Artificial Intelligence* (pp. 739–744). Mountain View, CA: Morgan Kaufmann.
Cheng, P. C.-H. (1992a). Approaches, models and issues in computational scientific
discovery. In M. T. Keane and K. Gilhooly (eds.), *Advances in the psychology of
thinking* (pp. 203–236). Hemel Hempstead, Hertfordshire: Harvester-Wheatsheaf.
Cheng, P. C.-H. (1992b). Diagrammatic reasoning in scientific discovery: Modelling
Galileo's kinematic diagrams. In H. Narayanan (ed.), *Working notes of the AAAI
Spring Symposium on Reasoning with diagrammatic representations* (pp. 33–38). Stan-
ford, CA: Stanford University.
Cheng, P. C.-H., and Simon, H. A. (1992). The right representation for discovery:
Finding the conservation of momentum. In D. Sleeman and P. Edwards (eds.),
Machine learning: Proceedings of the Ninth International Conference (ML92) (pp. 62–
71). San Mateo, CA: Morgan Kaufmann.
Drake, S. (1978). *Galileo at work*. Chicago: University of Chicago Press.
Falkenhainer, B. C., and Michalski, R. S. (1986). Integrating quantitative and qualitative
discovery: The ABACUS system. *Machine Learning, 1*(4), 367–401.
Galileo (1974). *Two new Sciences* (S. Drake, Trans.). Madison: University of Wisconsin
Press.
Gorman, M. E. (1992). Using experiments to determine the heuristic value of falsifica-
tion. In M. T. Keane and K. Gilhooly (eds.), *Advances in the psychology of thinking*
(pp. 147–176). Hemel Hempstead, Hertfordshire, UK: Harvester-Wheatsheaf.
Hutton, C. Shaw, G., and Pearson, R. (1804). *The philosophical transactions of the Royal
Society of London*. London: C&R Baldwin.
Klahr, D., and Dunbar, K. (1988). Dual space search during scientific reasoning. *Cognitive
Science, 12*, 1–48.
Koedinger, K. R., and Anderson, J. R. (1990). Abstract planning and perceptual chunks:
Elements of expertise in geometry. *Cognitive Science, 14*, 511–550.
Langley, P., Simon, H. A., Bradshaw, G. L., and Zytkow, J. M. (1987). *Scientific discovery:
Computational explorations of the creative process*. Cambridge, MA: MIT Press.
Larkin, J. H. (1989). Display-based problem solving. In D. Klahr and K. Kotovsky (eds.),
Complex information processing: The impact of Herbert A. Simon (pp. 319–341). Hills-
dale, NJ: Erlbaum.

Larkin, J. H., and Simon, H. A. (1987). Why a diagram is (sometimes) worth ten thousand words. *Cognitive Science, 11*, 65–99.

Narayanan, H. (Ed.) (1992). *AAAI Spring Symposium on Reasoning with Diagrammatic Representations:* Working notes. Stanford University, March 25–27, 1992.

Novak, G. S. (1977). Representations of knowledge in a program for solving physics problems. In *Proceedings of the Fifth International Joint Conference on Artificial Intelligence.* Mountain View, CA: Morgan Kaufmann.

Qin, Y. (1992). *From language to mental images to equations.* Unpublished doctoral dissertation, Carnegie Mellon University.

Qin, Y., and Simon, H. A. (1990). Laboratory replication of scientific discovery processes. *Cognitive Science, 14*, 281–312.

Schunn, C. D., and Klahr, D. (1992). Complexity management in a discovery task. In *Proceedings of the Fourteenth Annual Conference of the Cognitive Science Society* (pp. 177–182). Hillsdale, NJ: Erlbaum.

Shepard, R. N. (1978). Externalization of mental images and the act of creation. In B. S. Randhawa and W. E. Coffman (eds.), *Visual learning, thinking, and communication.* New York: Academic Press.

Shepard, R. N. (1988). The imagination of the scientist. In K. Egan and D. Nadaner (eds.), *Imagination and Education.* New York: Teachers College Press.

Shrager, J. (1990). Commonsense perception and the psychology of theory formation, In J. Shrager and P. Langley (eds.), *Computational models of scientific discovery and theory formation* (pp. 437–470). San Mateo, CA: Morgan Kaufmann.

Shrager, J., and Langley, P. (eds.). (1990). *Computational models of scientific discovery and theory formation.* San Mateo, CA: Morgan Kaufmann.

Tabachneck, H. (1992). *Computational difference in mental representations: The effects of mode of data presentation on reasoning and understanding.* Unpublished doctoral dissertation, Carnegie Mellon University.

Zytkow, J. (ed.). (1992). *Proceedings of the ML92 Workshop on Machine Discovery.* Aberdeen, Scotland.

Chapter 10

Making Machines Creative

Roger C. Schank and Chip Cleary

Why Study Creativity?

Our society views creativity as a rare and mystical gift. We put it on a pedestal, exalting artists, inventors, scientists and others we deem creative. At the same time, we believe that creativity is unattainable by the typical person. By so cherishing creativity in a few, our society inadvertently discourages it in most.

The workplace and the school are conspicuous arenas where creativity is discouraged. In most jobs, daydreaming (or creative thinking) is disparaged as a waste of time. Schoolchildren know that the teacher expects the "right answer" and will mark them incorrect unless they produce it on the test. They begin to think that a right answer always exists. The message is that it does not make sense to waste time trying to be creative. Instead, one should memorize the answers others have provided. Only the few who manage to climb up onto the pedestal of creativity need worry about generating new answers.

This message is false. The world is not full of standard problems amenable to standard solutions. Everybody needs to be somewhat creative simply to get through a typical day and deal with the innumerable shifts from the ordinary that arise. These small acts of creativity, though they differ in scope, are not different in kind from the brilliant leaps of an Einstein. Creativity is commonplace in cognition, not an esoteric gift bequeathed only to a few.

The social cost of this false message is immense. Because of it, many people do not take advantage of their potential for creativity. Living in an environment that exalts the creativity of a few while discouraging it in most, they internalize the belief that they lack the ability to be creative or they become fearful of taking the risk involved in being creative. The scientific cost is similarly large. For much of the history of artificial intelligence (AI) and cognitive science, creativity was viewed as an esoteric and perhaps somewhat magical process that was above and beyond normal processing. As a result, few researchers have risked tackling it.

Instead of being banished to the untouchable heights of cognition, creativity belongs squarely in its center. Far from being esoteric, creativity arises from relatively simple mental processes. Far from being magical, it depends on preexisting, though complex mental structures. The creative process is not above and beyond normal reasoning; but rather, it is central to it.

Besides being interesting in its own right, creativity is important to study for extrinsic reasons. In order to construct intelligent machines, we need to understand learning. And to build viable learning machines, we need to build machines that can be creative. Creativity is a critical component of the learning process.

What is creativity? It is the "intelligent misuse" of the knowledge structures underlying routine cognition. People depend on scripted knowledge in much of what they do. They can use pay telephones, for example, because they have dealt with them many times before. They have developed an internal script that tells them, among other things, to pick up the receiver before putting in money. But people are also able to function in situations in which they either have no scripts or want to look beyond them. When scripted knowledge does not directly apply, people find some knowledge that does not quite apply and then see how they can modify it. In other words, they intelligently misuse it.

We are not proposing that people simply loosen the constraints they use when searching for and applying knowledge. A system that worked in this way would not be creative but would instead progress from schizophrenia (as it leaped from one random idea to another) to catatonia (as it found itself buried under a combinatorial avalanche of attempts). Creativity may be hard work, but it is also knowledge based. A creative system must know which knowledge structures to retrieve and how to modify them. To paraphrase Thomas Edison, creativity is 99 percent perspiration and 1 percent inspiration.

What Do We Want to Know?

If I figure out for myself the tactic of bluffing in a game of poker, is that a creative act? It might be creative from my perspective, but it could hardly be considered creative from the perspective of society as a whole. When describing a creative act, it is important to spell out from which point of view the act should be considered creative. Boden follows this precept in her book *The Creative Mind*. She would label my personal invention of bluffing an example of "P-creativity" (psychological creativity) but not an act of "H-creativity" (historical creativity) (Boden 1990, p. 32).

In order to build a cognitive theory of creativity, we should not stop at the boundaries of the individual when asking what a creative act is creative *with respect to*. People use a variety of mental constructs in routine understanding and they intelligently misuse a similar variety in creative thinking. When we want to explain how some agent generated some creative act, we should ask ourselves; With respect to what knowledge structures inside the agent is the act creative? We should ask which types of knowledge structures were applied directly in the act and which types were intelligently misused.

By taking this stance, we can understand that instead of being an all-or-nothing affair, there are different types and levels of creativity. It is one type of creativity when someone responds to a new interruption in a standard routine with a type of repair he or she has used many times before. An office worker faced with a failure of the telephone network, for example, might decide to go to the corner store to make a call by applying the standard repair of finding a different source for an interrupted resource. It is another type of creativity when someone invents a type of repair that is new to the person. The same office worker might puzzle for a while and generate a new perspective, such as considering the situation to be a blessing in disguise, and use the lack of interruptions to get some work done. The worker did different processing in each case and engaged in different forms of creativity.[1] The fact that either of these plans seems like creative behavior is precisely the point. The creation of new plans—adapting them from old ones—is what creativity is all about.

Creativity does not flow from some elegant, unitary process. Rather, there is a different type of creativity for each type of knowledge structure that we are able to use for a purpose beyond that for which the structure was built. In other words, creativity is a set of processes, each creative with respect to some specific type of knowledge structure. Because people are able to use a number of different types of knowledge structures in a variety of ways, creativity can be achieved through a number of different processes. A theory of creativity should describe these processes and the knowledge structures each employs.

The Mechanics of Creativity

The Link between Creative and Routine Processing
Humans are remarkably effective at avoiding having to think very hard. When the world behaves just as we expect, we have little need to be creative. We can instead simply do routine processing, viewing our current situation in terms of situations we have experienced before

and behaving as we always do in those situations. This morning, for example, I went down to the garage, got in my car, and drove to work. No problem—and no creativity. I had a routine goal and I followed a routine plan.

It is only when routine knowledge structures fail that we need to be creative. If my car had died on a major street, if my planned route was clogged with construction, or if the driver in the car next to me began to make frantic hand signals that I could not interpret and these were problems I had not experienced many times before, so that I could handle them routinely, then I would need to be creative. People have knowledge structures that lay out plans for the goals they frequently encounter as well as typical paths for those plans to follow. If someone simply wants to make sense of the world and never encounters events out of the realm covered by his or her precoded knowledge structures, then this person need never be creative.

But what happens when something new or unexpected happens? What happens if I do not happen to know much about auto mechanics but am called on to restart a stalled car in the middle of traffic? I am faced with an anomaly, something that my top-down routine structures do not tell me how to handle. Such an anomaly indicates that I have a missing element in my knowledge or a flaw in my beliefs about the world. In order to make sense of the world, repair my beliefs, and expand my knowledge, I should try to *explain* the anomaly. The processes of anomaly detection and explanation are the link between routine and creative processing.

To perform such explanations, often we can apply routine explanations that we have used before for similar anomalies. For example, I might know that the explanation behind the occasional stalling fits my lawnmower suffers is that the wire leading to the mower's spark plug gets loose and needs to be jiggled. When my car stalls, I might react by jiggling the wires leading to its spark plugs. This action would be an example of using routine explanation to be creative with respect to routine processing. But routine explanation is not the only process people use to be creative. We cannot always find routine explanations, and even when we do find them, they do not always work. In the case of the stalled car, for example, what might I do if I have jiggled the wires and the car still does not start? Routine explanation has failed, and I have experienced another type of anomaly. I need a different type of creativity. I need to generate a new explanation. I need to be creative with respect to my explanation knowledge structures themselves.

In both of these types of creativity, anomaly detection provides the motivation to be creative, and explanation provides the mechanism.

We experience a problem in routine processing, we characterize the anomaly underlying the problem, we search for knowledge to explain the anomaly, and we see whether the explanation suits our needs.

An Unsatisfactory Theory: Bottom-up Inferencing
One way to try to understand creativity is to consider it bottom-up inferencing. Imagine a computer system that tries to understand a story using bottom-up inference. The program first analyzes the conceptualizations in the story and then chains through low level inference rules to tie those conceptualizations together. Such a system could construct some understandings that would strike us quite creative. It would also run *slowly*. Bottom-up inferencing would certainly be able to provide us with Edison's 99 percent perspiration.

In 1975 we built such a system, called MARGIE (Rieger 1975). We wanted not a creative understander but a routine understander, which we felt was a significant advance. MARGIE worked by performing bottom-up inference to try to relate sentences in an input text. Regardless of our intentions, MARGIE did not indeed produce creative explanations. Given a simple story such as "John hit Mary" and a long time to work, it would generate, among other understandings, the sadomasochistic hypothesis that "John wanted to be hit. He wanted Mary to be mad at him so she would hit him. So, he hit her."

As a theory of understanding, the program was quite a success, but MARGIE failed on psychological grounds. First, people can understand situations of much greater complexity than any system based on MARGIE's bottom-up inferencing would be able to. The MARGIE program suffered from combinatorial explosion, the number of inferences that the program could derive at each step was so large that the program quickly drowned relevant inferences in a swamp of irrelevant ones.[2] Second, it is clear that people understand familiar situations more easily than unfamiliar situations. MARGIE, with its exhaustive chaining, never got any better at understanding stories. It would read the same story 100 times, do the same processing each time, and never get bored.

As a theory of understanding, MARGIE ranks as a useful failure. As a theory of creativity, it fares somewhat better. Given enough resources, the program would generate every way of understanding an input that its inference rules licensed. In other words, MARGIE could hypothesize every interpretation, creative or not, that it could comprehend. Any program that exhaustively applies whatever inference rules it contains will be able to generate similarly "creative" outputs. In one sense, assuming no magical insights, no program could ever do better. No system will ever be able to generate outputs that do not come from some inference rule or knowledge structure the program contains. MARGIE's exhaustive inference provides a zeroeth-order theory of creativity. The question is, how can we do better? We managed to build a program based on 99 percent perspiration. Where is the 1 percent inspiration?

Starting at the Start: Routine Understanding
Our experience with MARGIE taught us that to understand creativity, we must first get a handle on how people perform routine cognition. We must determine what types of knowledge structures would allow an intelligent system to perform tasks such as routine understanding or routine planning. Only then may we determine what operations and, more important, what additional knowledge structures can enable an intelligent system to act creatively.

The primary problem in MARGIE was uncontrolled inference. Once the problem is described in this way, the solution is obvious: provide some method of controlling inference. Much of the work done at the Yale AI laboratory while Schank was director was aimed at determining the sorts of knowledge structures that could play this role. This work revolved around the fundamental idea that when people build useful inference chains, they generalize them and cache them away. When later faced with situations similar to those they have reasoned through before, they apply this cached knowledge without having to work through the detailed inferencing all over again.

Others have studies notions of "chunking" (Newell 1990). A concern with two questions sets the Yale work apart: What is the actual content of such structures? and What is the organization of a memory composed of them? We did a significant amount of work describing what people actually know about the situations and tasks they face every day and determining how an intelligent system might represent that knowledge in a way that would cause it to function efficiently. This work developed three types of knowledge structures: scripts, plans, and memory organization packets (MOPs)

Script-Based Understanding   We called the first of the knowledge structures we developed "scripts" (Schank and Abelson 1977; Cullingford 1978). Scripts packaged chains of atomic inferences that described typical sequences of events. We found that scripts could enable a computer to understand stories about topics ranging from auto accidents to state visits well enough to summarize and answer questions about them.

Unlike the bottom-up inference used in MARGIE, script-based processing was efficient. Systems using scripts could quickly infer that actions in stories occurred even if they had not been explicitly mentioned. To take an example, when told that Lucy went to a restaurant and had left a big tip, the SAM (script applier mechanism) program could readily infer that "Lucy had ordered," "Lucy had eaten," and "Lucy had enjoyed what she had eaten."

Script based systems could also quickly determine when something happened that was not expected. As an example, here's a small story:

The Mystery of Big-Tipping Lucy

Lucy went to a restaurant. She did not like her meal. But she left a big tip.

When processing this story, SAM was able to note that the big tip was not expected. But scripts did not indicate how to proceed from there. Once SAM had isolated this anomaly, it had no method of dealing with it. It ignored it and moved on.

Plan-Based Understanding People are clearly not limited to script-based understanding. They can readily hypothesize reasons why Lucy might have left a big tip. Perhaps she had just inherited a lot of money and wanted to share the wealth, or she liked the service but not the cooking, or she looked on the wrong row of her tipping chart. Such hypotheses share a curious characteristic: none of them seems script based.

To enable computer systems to generate such understandings, we develop additional knowledge structures that allowed them to explain stories by referring to the themes, goals, and plans of the actors in the story (Schank and Abelson 1977). The PAM (plan applier mechanism) program embodied these ideas (Wilensky 1981). When scripts fail, these knowledge structures provide an alternative method for an intelligent system to link actions in the world to mental constructs.

MOP-Based Understanding In *Dynamic Memory* (1982) Schank proposed how an organized memory might be built out of knowledge structures such as scripts and plans. In order to be integrated into a memory, the earlier structures needed to be altered. The major knowledge structure that resulted was MOP.

Like the earlier structures, the primary function of MOPs was to provide top-down expectations. But MOPs had additional advantages.

They provided a method for sharing knowledge between structures that was lacking in earlier theories and provided an organization that allowed us to understand how an intelligent system might learn new MOPs when old ones failed.

MOPs nevertheless retained a critical shortcoming of the earlier structures, a shortcoming that is endemic to top-down knowledge structures. What happens when the expectations provided by MOPs fail? While MOP-based programs such as CYRUS (Kolodner 1980) and IPP (Lebowitz 1980) could process stories of much greater complexity than MARGIE could, they could not duplicate MARGIE's flexibility. Because they were used for top-down processing, MOPs provided no bottom-up method to repair expectation failures.

Creative Understanding
We are now in a position to provide the missing 1 percent of inspiration and formulate an improved theory of creativity. The earlier theory we discarded was that creativity is the ability to use bottom-up inferencing. Our improved theory is that creativity is the ability to *target* bottom-up inferencing. Specifically, creativity is the ability of an intelligent system to access, adapt, and apply a top-down knowledge structure when that knowledge structure as it stands fails to address the system's current needs.

The way people understand and act in the world is strongly influenced by top-down structures. Someone who experiences something for the first time understands it in terms of similar experiences that person previously has had. The second time, the person understands it in terms of what happened the first time. This perspective on human reasoning, called case-based reasoning, has been a focus of work done in previous years at the Yale Artificial Intelligence Project and currently at Northwestern's Institute for the Learning Sciences (ILS) (Riesbeck and Schank 1989).

Work in case-based reasoning has shown that not everything can be understood directly in terms of previous experiences. Sometimes none of a person's prepackaged top-down structures immediately applies to the current situation. Other times, a person may have top-down structures that could apply yet not know to use them. Or a person might locate structures that seem to apply but propose an incorrect theory of the world and need to be corrected. In all of these situations, the person must find a way to make do with his or her top-down structures. Said differently, the person must find a way to use those top-down structures creatively.

Some form of bottom-up inferencing must be part of the answer. The tricky part about developing a theory of creativity is to target the use of bottom-up inference in a plausible way. A theory that suggests simply dropping into MARGIE-like exhaustive inference whenever an expectation failure is encountered is not plausible. It fails for the same reasons MARGIE failed: exhaustive inference is too expensive.

The 1 percent inspiration, the secret to developing a theory of creativity, lies in understanding what knowledge we use when faced with an expectation failure. For example, we use additional knowledge to characterize anomalies, determine which knowledge structure caused the anomaly, adapt the failed structure, and judge the appropriateness of repair. In order to understand creativity, we must understand what these additional knowledge structures look like and how they are used. They are what allow us to recover gracefully from processing failures without dropping into a computational catatonia.

We will examine two types of knowledge structures used in creative cognition. The first, called explanation patterns (XPs), are useful for adapting MOPs. The second group encompasses analogy molecules and restructuring rules. These are useful for adapting XPs.

Creativity with Respect to MOPs   What happens when the expectations that are generated by MOPs are violated? Among other things, such violations tend to pique our interest. As Schank and Kass (1986) point out, "the most interesting stories often contain anomalies—events that are not handled by active expectations. When we encounter anomalies, we feel the need to explain them. Explaining an anomaly means bringing knowledge to bear that will tie the anomalous action to something we understand, and thus render it non-anomalous" (p. 193).

Schank (1982) provides a model of how people respond to expectation failures. In brief, when an expectation fails, we try to *explain* the failure. Then we put the explained failure in a place in memory that will allow it to come to the fore if we encounter such a situation again. In particular, we attach it to the component of the MOP that generated the expectation, using the proposed explanation as an index. If we later encounter a failure involving the same component and the same type of explanation, we begin to believe that the combined failures reflect a problem with our understanding of how the world works.[3] To update our understanding, we create a new MOP that includes an expectation predicting what was previously the anomalous event. We use the explanations we generated for the anomalies to indicate when to use the new MOP instead of the old one.

Given this model, it becomes clear how closely related creativity is to learning. People depend on top-down structures to understand the world. Creativity is required to stretch those structures when they do not quite fit. When a structure is stretched in the same way a number of times, it is time to create a new top-down structure to compensate. Further, the explanations that stretch MOPs (they are creative with respect to MOPs) are also required to index memory so that recurrent failures can be efficiently matched. Without creativity, a person could neither stretch nor index.

How do people generate explanations? Quite easily. Think back to "The Mystery of Big-tipping Lucy," and try to generate a couple of explanations to explain Lucy's behavior. Doing so is not difficult, and so we tend to think that such hypothesis making is not creative. But unless these explanations followed some standard sequence of events cached in memory, they *are* creative with respect to your restaurant-meal MOP. They are stretching the MOP to cover a situation beyond those for which it was built.

How can people perform this stretching without falling into a MAR-GIE-like morass of bottom-up inferencing? As before, the answer is that we use additional knowledge to guide our work. Schank (1986) hypothesized that central to this process are XPs which provide "frozen explanations," prepackaged chains of inferences that can be used to explain a specified anomaly. Box 10.1 shows how XPs are used in routine explanation.

XPs have a different purpose from the previous knowledge structures we developed. The earlier structures provide an understanding system with places in memory to link in understandings-under-construction. XPs, however, do not provide another class of memory cubbyhole. Instead, they provide a more flexible way to fit understandings-under-construction into the previous set of cubbyholes. Systems that perform routine understanding require exact matches between input conceptualizations and cubbyholes. Systems that perform creative understanding can *build* exact matches by flexibly adapting their memory cubbyholes.

Creativity with Respect to XPs   When people encounter something new that does not fit in with the MOPs they have built from prior experience, they experience an anomaly. They then use XPs to try to tweak the MOPs of their previous experience and use them creatively. XPs allow for creativity with respect to MOPs but, are themselves just standard, routine explanations. And just as standard MOPs do not always allow us to understand the world, standard explanations do not always allow us to resolve the anomalies that result.

When an XP fails, we must generate a new explanation. We must achieve a higher level of creativity and be creative with respect to the XP. Imagine you are asked to explain Big-Tipping Lucy's behavior but

Box 10.1
The Explanation Process

---

1. Detect an anomaly
   1.1. Characterize the anomaly
   1.2 Develop a question that, when answered, will resolve the anomaly
2. Explain the anomaly
   2.1. Search for an XP that satisfies the question
   2.2. Apply the XP to generate an explanation
   2.3. Test the new explanation
3. Learn from the explanation
   3.1. Search for a similar expectation failure in memory
      3.1.1. If one exists, generate and index a new MOP based on the explanation
      3.1.2. If not, index the failed expectation using the explanation

Note: This process outlines only the basic method of explaining an anomaly: through accessing explanation patterns. An intelligent system must have a variety of more complex methods, such as coordinating anomalies or retrieving cases that contain similar failures. All of these methods, however, call on this basic method at some point. Essentially, the complex methods reduce the conceptual distance that the explanations produced by the basic method must cross. See Schank (1986) for a description of some of these other methods.

---

are told that none of the first five explanations you generate applies. You probably generated these first five directly from XPs. How would you go about generating a sixth? A tenth? At some point, you will run dry of standard explanations and will need to start creating new ones. Maybe Lucy enjoyed going to restaurants that served bad food because she could tell great stories later. Maybe she owned a competing restaurant and wanted to reward this restaurant for a bad performance, thereby training its owners to set their sights too low. What additional work does creating such new explanations entail?

Box 10.2 shows how the explanation process can be enhanced to allow explanations to be creative with respect to XPs. The italicized steps, processes that are creative from this new point of view. depend on two types of operations: (1) restructuring (taking an unsatisfactory explanation and modifying the relationships between its elements) and reformulating (seeing a thing of one type as a thing of another type). These two operations are the basis of creative explanation.

An example will explain restructuring. Consider a simple but unsatisfactory explanation for Big-Tipping Lucy's behavior: she was a customer and customers typically tip. The central relationship in the explanation is that Lucy is a customer of the restaurant. To restructure

Box 10.2
The *Creative* Explanation Process

1. Detect an anomaly
   1.1. Characterize the anomaly
   1.2. Develop a question that, when answered, will resolve the anomaly
2. Explain the anomaly
   2.1. Search for an XP that satisfies the goal
      2.1.1. *If none found, reformulate the situation as one for which an XP exists*
   2.2. Apply the XP to generate an explanation
   2.3. Test the new explanation
      2.3.1. *If the explanation does not work, restructure it*
3. Learn from the explanation
   3.1. Search for a similar expectation failure in memory
      3.1.1. If one exists, generate and index a new MOP based on the explanation
      3.1.2. If not, index the failed expectation using the explanation
   3.2. If the explanation comes from a tweaked XP, develop a new XP
      3.2.1. *Determine how to characterize (formulate) the elements of the explanation*
      3.2.2. Generate a candidate XP from the explanation
      3.2.3. Verify the candidate XP through reminding
      3.2.4. Index the verified candidate in memory

the explanation, we alter this relationship, assuming, for example, that Lucy is instead a *supplier*. This notion leads to the explanation that Lucy worked for a food supply company and that the company sold poor-quality food to the restaurant. This situation would explain both why Lucy did not like her meal and why she left a big tip. By restructuring the relationship between Lucy and the restaurant, we were led to a creative explanation.

When we are creative with respect to XPs, most of the interesting work is performed not by restructuring but by reformation. Restructuring is a simpler, weaker method. As such, it is often used only as a method of last choice, when other methods have failed. Restructuring is often accomplished by simply identifying the relationships in a faulty explanation, modifying one, and then testing out the new explanation, tweaking further as needed. In contrast, the process of reformulation depends on detailed knowledge about what sort of analogies are useful to build under what circumstances.

We coined the term *analogy molecules* to describe the class of knowledge structures used in reformulation.[4] The reason is that the process of reformulation is really the process of drawing a pointed analogy (one that serves a specific goal) between something that does not fit into an explanation as currently conceived and something that does. The purpose of the analogy is to enable the system to use the misfit explanation in the current situation. The role of analogy molecules is to provide a set of rules describing the conditions under which such a redescription is feasible. In the abstract, analogy molecules describe when some X may be seen as similar to some Y in order to correct some shortcoming Z in a current explanation.

Researchers at the Yale AI laboratory and at ILS have constructed two programs that are able to perform creative explanation using reformulation: SWALE and BRAINSTORMER. The SWALE program used creative explanation to hypothesize explanations for a mystery surrounding the racehorse Swale, a champion three year old who was found dead in his stall days after winning of one the biggest races of the year. (For details on the SWALE program, see Kass 1990; Leake 1990; Owens 1990; Schank 1986.) The BRAINSTORMER program used creative explanation in a planning task: generating proposals for how to react to terrorist attacks (Jones 1992).

Summary of the Processes of Creativity
Our basic theory is that creativity is the adaptation of top-down structures for situations to which they do not directly apply. This adaptation is performed by applying knowledge structures that allow for finer-grained inferences than those sanctioned by the misfit top-down structure. Sometimes these "corrective" knowledge structures themselves do not fit and must be tweaked.

This view provides a picture of a waterfall of corrective knowledge structures with each stage in the waterfall consisting of a type of knowledge structure. When that knowledge structure is applied to a situation that it does not immediately fit, it needs to be adapted. The structures at the next stage then supply suggestions for how to do the adaptation. Knowledge about how to use one stage creatively is contained in the next stage.

Our working hypothesis is that this waterfall is not very many levels deep. The waterfall bottoms out when an intelligent system is forced to use weak methods (like MARGIE's exhaustive search) in the attempt to use some knowledge structure creatively. The need to use weak methods indicates that no additional knowledge can be applied—in other words, that no lower-level knowledge structures used in the relatively simple process of restructuring XPs are bottom level. Because restructuring uses weak methods, it is one place where the waterfall terminates.

This is not to say that the products of creative thought must be as simple as the waterfall that produces them. One might think up a creative explanation for the story of Big-Tipping Lucy that would take pages to explain, but it would consist mostly of a linked set of sub-explanations. Our hypothesis about the depth of the waterfall does not have to do with any notion of how complex a network of explanations a person can construct as an output but rather with how many different sorts of knowledge structures might be involved in building any single component of that network.

Where the Tough Problems Are

What is the toughest challenge facing us as we construct theories of creativity? It is *not* elucidating the processes of creativity because they are not all that complex, as boxes 10.1 and 10.2 show. They outline two creative processes that are composed of standard AI methods like memory search and subgoaling and are far from complicated.

Creative power comes not from these simple processes but from the complex knowledge structures (or, better said, the complex of knowledge structures) on which these processes operate. To improve our understanding of creativity, we need to build content theories that describe what these knowledge structures contain and how they are organized in memory. We need to know what *types* of knowledge people have, but we need to know more what specific knowledge they have and how to represent that knowledge.

Accordingly, several projects at the ILS are concerned with representing knowledge in a way that allows an intelligent system to get reminded of that knowledge at appropriate times. The Dear Abby program, for example, is concerned with how to represent knowledge about social plans (Domeshek 1922). When told about a problem of the type for which one might write to Ann Landers (or her sister, Abigail Van Buren), the program uses this knowledge to retrieve relevant stories. The Creanimate program provides another example (Edelson 1993). It is concerned with how to represent relationships between form and function to support case-based design decisions in the realm of animal adaptation.

In doing such work, we have come to realize the importance of questions in triggering and channeling the need for explanations. As we have already seen with Big-Tipping Lucy, once we ask why Lucy left a big tip, hypotheses are not hard to construct. Once we ask what alternative relationships Lucy might have to the restaurant, we can readily build a whole new set of creative hypotheses. Because questions have buried within them the seeds of the answers they will permit, asking the right question sets the stage for a creative answer. But how do we generate a question?

One way is from the failure of expectations derived from scripts or MOPs. The SWALE program generated questions from the processing failures it experienced, as did the IVY program, which improved its performance on a diagnostic task over time by learning more about the task (Hunter 1989). It pursued questions generated by knowledge acquisition planning. The central question it posed itself was, What kinds of knowledge will help me avoid diagnostic failures I have previously experienced and are therefore worth looking for?

Pursuing processing failures is not the only way people generate questions: they have external goals that require them to understand things, they have open questions left over from before that they were never able to answer, or they simply become interested in some subject and delve in. To be more creative, computer systems will need to be able to question actively rather than simply react to expectation failures. They will need to seek out anomalies.

Two other programs actively generate questions, extending the range of questions computer systems can ask. The AQUA (asking questions and understanding answers) program developed a range of questions beyond those generated by script- or MOP-based understanders and illustrated how those questions can form the basis for a memory that extends itself over time (Ram 1989). The interview Coach program, under construction at ILS, takes a somewhat different approach to the task of constructing interesting questions. Aimed at helping a person perform a knowledge-acquisition interview, it suggests compelling questions for the interviewer to ask. The primary question it asks itself is Given what I know so far, what is it that I would like to know next? To answer, the program analyzes the structure of the knowledge in its memory, focusing on what it views as important holes in that structure. Essentially, it is an experiment in building a system with a primitive sense of curiosity.

Implications for a Theory of Creativity

The theory of creativity that we have described is quite different from that implicitly held by society. Society sees creativity as an exalted process, above the fray of normal processing. We posit that creativity is central to normal processing, required even in acts as small as reading novel misspelled wrods. Society sees creativity as a gift given to only a few. We posit that creativity is a skill everyone uses. Society sees creativity as a fixed quality: someone is either creative or is not.

Our theory is that anyone can practice and improve on his or her ability to be creative.

These differences raise an important question. What are the implications of this theory in the real world? One important area that this theory relates to is education. Since theories of creativity are so intimately bound up with learning, they allow us to move out of the academic realm of cognitive science and into the practical realm of one of society's most pressing problems, the troubled education system. Theories of creativity can be viewed not only as descriptions of how people learn, but as prescriptions for how we should structure the schools to help people learn. As Schank and Farrel (1987) said; "To teach students to be creative, we must teach them to become aware of just how strong everything is. They must notice when things around them don't work. They must seek out anomalies in the world around them, in people's behavior, in their own behavior. They must wonder why they do what they do every day. If they have been going through school thinking that everything is fine, this might be a shock to them."

Both creativity and learning start with questions. The work on routine understanding shows that people often cannot even understand an answer unless they themselves have first generated the underlying question. Why, then, do schools typically emphasize answers? To teach students to be creative, we must first teach them to ask good questions. Or, better yet, we must help them retain the natural talent all children have for generating questions. This talent, too often squelched in schools, needs rekindling.

Once students are able to generate questions that interest them, we should teach them how to answer those questions creatively. The creative process consists of a number of skills that are *learnable* and may be strengthened and improved. But like other skills, they cannot be taught directly. We cannot simply describe the laws of creativity to a student, have the student memorize them, and then expect the student to be creative. Rather, we must provide an environment in which students may practice and hone their creativity.

The tendency to squelch creative question asking that many learn in school carries through to adult life. Many people do not take advantage of their potential for creativity. Living in an environment that exalts the creativity of a select few while discouraging it in most, people become afraid of taking the risk of being creative, or they internalize the false message that they lack have the ability to be creative.

Everybody needs to be creative in response to anomalies. In this chapter, we have spoken about creativity mostly as a reaction to expectation failures. But what we have perhaps not made clear is that it is often useful to *create* understanding failures (Schank 1988). When we wish to understand something more deeply, develop a counter-argument to the opinions we hold, or simply create something new, it is often necessary to distance ourselves from our routine understandings. If I want to surprise my spouse on Valentine's Day, I know that I must disregard the first idea that comes into my mind for what to do. I will probably have to disregard the second as well. In order to be creative in routine situations, we must get beyond our cached standard knowledge structures and force ourselves to generate something new.

Such intentional creativity is not essentially different from the type of creativity that is forced on us by understanding failures. The differences lie in the way we choose questions to pursue creatively (the input to the system) and the way in which we evaluate the options we generate (the output of the system). The actual act of creativity itself is similar in both cases.

Intentional creativity is a skill all students should learn. To become intentionally creative, we must develop the ability to engage in a type of inner dialogue while working through the creative process. To help students become intentionally creative, we must provide environments in which they can engage in such inner dialogues and grow capable in them. We must give them the opportunity to propose new problems, fail in their attempted solutions, ask questions, explore anomalies, and create explanations.

Notes

1. It is difficult to judge from external behavior what type of creativity is involved in some act. In the example, we have assumed that the office worker already had a knowledge structure encoding the "find an alternate source" fix but would have had to generate one for the "make the curse into a blessing" fix. Another office worker with different experiences might habitually use "make the curse into a blessing" but need to be creative to generate "find an alternative source."
2. We implemented a "stopping rule," such as that later discussed by Raaijmakers and Shiffrin (1980), which allowed the program to give up and move on when faced with conceptualizations it was unable to link. But the stopping rule only allowed the program to quit trying. What it needed was a way to try better, a way to target the inferencing it performed more effectively.
3. Gick and McGarry (1992) provide experimental evidence supporting the position that people use an analysis of their processing failures to help store items in and retrieve items from memory.
4. Kass (1990) and Jones (1992) discuss two different sets of such structures. Kass proposes structures called component specifiers, component generalizers, and tweaks that contain the knowledge required to reformulate by specifying, generalizing, or substituting components. Jones proposes a knowledge structure called a

viewing schema to guide a system in inferring that one concept may be seen as an instance of another.

References

Boden, Margaret A. (1990) *The creative mind: Myths and mechanisms*. New York: Basic Books.

Cullingford, R. (1978). *Script application: Computer understanding of newspaper stories*. Unpublished doctoral dissertation, Yale University.

Domeshek, Eric A. (1992). *Do the right thing: A component theory for indexing stories as social advice*. Institute for the Learning Sciences Technical Report #26, Northwestern University.

Edelson, Daniel Choy (1993). *Learning from stories: Indexing and reminding in a case-based teaching system for elementary school biology*. Institute for the Learning Sciences Technical Report #43, Northwestern University.

Gick, Mary L., and McGarry, Susan J. (1992). Learning from mistakes: Inducing analogous solution failures to a source problem produces later successes in analogical transfer." *Journal of Experimental Psychology: Learning, Memory, and Cognition, 18* (3), 623– 629.

Hunter, Lawrence E. (1989). Knowledge acquisition planning: Gaining expertise through experience. Unpublished doctoral dissertation, Yale University.

Jones, Eric K. (1992). *The flexible use of abstract knowledge in planning*. Institute for the Learning Sciences Technical Report #28, Northwestern University.

Kass, Alex, M. (1990). *Developing creative hypotheses by adapting explanations*. Institute for the Learning Sciences Technical Report #6, Northwestern University.

Kolodner, J. L. (1980) *Retrieval and organizational strategies in conceptual memory: A computer model*. Unpublished doctoral dissertation, Yale University.

Leake, David Browder. (1990). *Evaluating explanations*. Unpublished doctoral dissertation, Yale University.

Lebowitz, M. (1980). *Generalization and memory in an integrated understanding system*. Unpublished doctoral dissertation, Yale University.

Newell, Allen. 1990. *Unified theories of cognition*. Cambridge, MA: Harvard University Press.

Owens, Christopher Charles (1990). *Indexing and retrieving abstract Planning knowledge*. Unpublished doctoral dissertation, Yale University.

Raaijmakers, J. G. W., and Shiffrin, R. M. (1980). SAM: A theory of probabilistic search of associative memory. *Psychology of Learning and Motivation, 14*, 207–262.

Ram, Ashwin. (1989). Question-driven understanding: An integrated theory of story understanding, memory, and learning. Unpublished doctoral dissertation, Yale University.

Rieger, Charles J. (1975). Conceptual memory and inference. R. C. Schank (ed.), In *Conceptual information processing* (pp. 157–288). Amsterdam: North-Holland.

Riesbeck, Christopher K., and Schank, Roger C. (1989). *Inside case-based reasoning*. Hillsdale, NJ: Erlbaum.

Schank, Roger C. (1982). *Dynamic memory: A theory of reminding and learning in computers and people*. Cambridge: Cambridge University Press, 1982.

Schank, Roger C. (1986). *Explanation patterns: Understanding mechanically and creatively*. Hillsdale, NJ: Erlbaum.

Schank, Roger C. and Abelson, Robert P. (1977). *Scripts, plans, goals, and understanding*. Hillsdale, NJ: Erlbaum.

Schank, Roger, with Childs, Peter (1988) *The Creative attitude*. New York: Macmillan.

Schank, Roger C., and Farrell, Robert (1987). *Creativity in Education: A standard for Computer-Based Teaching* New Haven: Computer Science Department, Yale University.

Schank, Roger, and Kass, Alex (1986). Knowledge representation in people and machines. *VS 44/45:* 181–200.

Wilensky, Robert. (1981). PAM. In R. Schank and C. K. Riesbeck (eds.), *Inside computer understanding* (pp. 136–179) Hillsdale, NJ: Erlbaum.

Chapter 11

Creativity and Connectionism

Colin Martindale

This chapter begins with an exploration of neural networks, examines what a theory of creativity needs to explain, and then describes a number of theories of creativity, in each case, pointing out how the theory could be translated into connectionist terms. Surprisingly, it turns out that behavioral, cognitive, and even psychoanalytic theories are essentially identical when expressed as a neural network theory. Even more surprisingly, this neural network theory is isomorphic to a set of existing connectionist models. These models, generally called Hopfield (1982) nets, have been applied to perception, learning, and problem solving. It is clear that they shed new light on the creative process as well.

A neural network theory tries to explain how mental processes could be explained by neuronlike components. To build a neural network, we need several components (Rumelhart, Hinton, and McClelland 1986):

1. A set of processing units or nodes. These are similar to neurons but not as complicated.
2. A state of activation. If some nodes are activated beyond a threshold, we are conscious of whatever they code. (Of course, some nodes, such as those controlling motor behavior, operate outside consciousness.) The one or two most activated nodes correspond to whatever is the focus of attention. Less activated nodes constitute the contents of short-term memory.
3. A pattern of connections among the nodes. The connections can be excitatory or inhibitory. They constitute long-term memory.
4. Input and output rules concerning how a node adds up its input and how outputs relate to current activation.
5. Learning rules. Current theorists use some variant of Hebb's (1949) idea that if two nodes are simultaneously activated, the connection between them is strengthened.

6. An environment for the network. I have argued that the network should be partitioned into modules devoted to specific tasks, such as reading, speech perception, and semantic memory (Martindale 1981, 1991). This is the way the brain is organized. I have also argued that each module is organized into several layers, with vertical connections being excitatory and lateral inhibition operating on each layer (cf. Grossberg 1980; Konorski 1967). Again, this is the way the brain seems to work.

According to neural-network theory, cognition is massively parallel; that is, all the nodes do whatever they do at the same time. This is quite unlike a conventional computer, which can do only one thing at a time. Another feature of neural networks is that they serve as content-addressable memories. A stimulus defines its place in memory. For example, seeing the word *cat* hypothetically corresponds to activating nodes coding angles, curves, and lines at various orientations. These nodes are connected to nodes standing for letters of the alphabet. In turn, these are connected to a node, or a pattern of nodes, representing the word. The latter are connected to a node or set of nodes in semantic memory representing the concept of cat. Finally, the latter are connected to nodes representing the features or attributes of the concept. This is unlike the way a computer works when a program needs to find something in memory.

Creative Ideas

A creative idea is one that is both novel and useful. Were someone to rediscover the theory of relativity, we would think the person to be quite clever but not creative because the idea has already been discovered. Creative ideas also have to be useful in the broad sense of the term. By *useful* I do not mean capable of turning a profit. Recall Michael Faraday's remark that he could not see any practical utility at all in his research on electricity, but he imagined that some day politicians would be putting a tax on the stuff. Rather, I mean appropriate for the domain in which the idea occurs. The utility criterion is meant to rule out ideas that are novel but wrong or silly. When analyzed, creative ideas are always new combinations of old ideas. A poet does not generally make up new words. Rather, old words are put together in a new way. Consider Einstein's equation, $E = mc^2$. Einstein did not invent the concepts of energy, mass, or speed of light. Rather, he combined these old ideas in a novel and useful way.

The Creative Process

Based on self-reports of eminently creative people, it is usually argued that the creative process can be segmented into four successive stages. Wallas (1926), drawing on the observations of Helmholtz (1896), labeled these stages preparation, incubation, illumination, and verification. Helmholtz said that when he was first confronted with a problem, he would often work very intensively on it but arrive at no solution. This is the preparation stage, in which ideas presumed relevant to the problem are learned and manipulated in an intellectual fashion. When no progress was forthcoming, Helmholtz set the problem aside. This is the incubation stage. After some time, usually with no clear cause, the solution simply occurred to him. Usually it was not the ideas manipulated during the preparation stage that provided the insight but ideas not previously thought to be relevant. The verification or elaboration stage involves intellectual scrutiny of the idea, putting it into its final form, and so on.

This sequence of stages seems to be very general. After reviewing a large number of autobiographical reports, Ghiselin (1952) came to the strong conclusion that "production by a process of purely conscious calculation seems never to occur" (p. 5). A number of others who have studied creative inspiration argue that it seems to be an effortless and nonintellectual process (Harding 1965; Weber 1969). The self-reports are quite striking, so a few are worth quoting. Blake (1803) said of one of his poems, "I have written this poem from immediate dictation, twelve or sometimes twenty or thirty lines at a time without premeditation, and even against my will" (p. 115). Scientists and mathematicians give similar testimony. Everyone knows the story of Kekulé's discovering the structure of benzene while having a reverie about a snake that happened to circle around and bite its tail. Here is how Poincaré (1913) discovered a set of mathematical functions: "One evening contrary to my custom, I drank black coffee and could not sleep. Ideas rose in crowds; I felt them collide until pairs interlocked, so to speak, making a stable combination. By the next morning I had established the existence of a class of Fuchsian functions, those which come from the hypergeometric series; I had only to write out the results, which took but a few hours" (p. 387).

Theories of Creativity

Common Sense and Some Facts
If a creative idea is a new combination of previously existing ideas, it would seem that the more mental elements one had, the more likely

one would be to have a creative idea. This is reasonable, but a moment's thought reveals that the crucial factor is what sorts of ideas one has. If one considers the mental furniture of the average person—who is going to win the Superbowl this year, what did little Johnny do in school today, what kind of tulips should be planted and where—no creative combinations are possible. A person who does not know anything about chemistry, say, cannot possibly make any discoveries in that domain, creative or uncreative. Even though I know the algorithm, I could not rediscover the structure of benzene for the simple reason that I have forgotten—if I ever knew—which atoms compose benzene molecules.

Common sense would suggest that the more one knew about a given domain, the more creative one would be, yet creative ideas in a domain often come from people who would not be characterized as experts. The longer one has been in a field, the more of an expert he or she is going to be and the older he or she is also going to be. Yet creativity shows an inverted-U relationship with age (Simonton 1984). A person cannot have creative ideas before he or she has learned at least some of the crucial facts, theories, and problems in a domain. In mathematics and the physical sciences, the ages of peak creativity are twenty-five to thirty-five. People at these ages would be amateurs turning into experts. An expert can solve problems because he or she knows what is relevant and—the disastrous part—what is irrelevant. A creative solution is one involving ideas that were previously thought to be irrelevant.

Creative ideas often involve taking ideas from one discipline and applying them to another. Hopfield (1982) took a set of ideas and equations from solid-state physics and, with minor modifications, came up with a neural network theory. Specifically, spin glasses are magnetic substances in which the atoms have a spin (up or down) and interact in either a positive or negative way with each other. The brain is composed of neurons that are either on or off and either excite or inhibit one another. Physicists know a lot about spin glass. Why not apply the equations to the brain? This is what Hopfield did, and the results are interesting indeed.

Hopfield is a physicist. Had he been a narrow specialist on spin glass, the analogy to the brain would never have occurred. Had he been a narrow expert on cognitive psychology, he would not have known anything about spin glass. It would seem that to maximize creativity, one's best bet is to have knowledge about a wide variety of things. A number of studies have shown that creative people have a very wide range of interests (Martindale 1989).

The more intelligent one is, the more one can learn. There should, then, be a correlation between intelligence and creativity, and there is—but only up to an IQ around 120 or so, and then the correlation essentially vanishes (Simonton 1984). One finds extremely intelligent people who are not in the slightest bit creative and extremely creative people who are not wildly intelligent. William Shockley, the inventor of the transistor, was not quite intelligent enough to get into Terman's (1925) longitudinal study of highly intelligent children (Eysenck in press). The children who were included have been relatively success-ful but not notably creative (Terman and Oden 1959). It must be that creativity has to do not with the amount of knowledge one has but with how this knowledge is accessed.

Blind Variation and Selective Retention
D. T. Campbell (1960) argued that there may be nothing special about creativity at all. We all think about 16 hours per day. Campbell argues that these thoughts are not random but quasi-random. If our thoughts are of no interest, we do not remember them. Just by chance, one may think of something creative. Consider someone confronted with a scientific problem. As the person goes about his or her daily business, almost everything that occurs will be random with respect to this particular problem. Purely by chance, some random event could sug-gest a solution to the problem. In this case, the thought will be retained or remembered. Campbell makes an analogy with biological evolution: random variants that are fit are retained; those that are unfit are not retained.

Campbell's theory can easily enough be put into neural-network terms. Thinking consists of the activation of nodes. If these nodes are already strongly connected, thinking is routine and unsurprising. At the moment, I am simply reading out the contents of my long-term memory concerning Campbell's theory, and other nodes are being activated as well. I notice the arrangement of my desktop, for example. It is just as it always is. There is no connection between the theory and the desk; the nodes coding the two are unconnected. By chance, there might have been an analogy, as with Kekulé's snakes and atoms. This would have been surprising, and I would have remembered it.

The connections between nodes that are simultaneously activated are strengthened. If the connections are already at maximal strength (e.g., those concerning my desktop), nothing happens. If there are no connections (e.g., between my desktop and Campbell's theory), noth-ing happens. If there is a weak or undirect connection (e.g., Kekulé's atoms and snakes), then we get a quick sequence of events: the arousal system bombards the cortex with nonspecific activation; the latter multiplies with the activation of already activated nodes (Grossberg 1980; Hull 1943; Martindale 1981); as a consequence, the activated nodes become extremely activated, and the connection strength between them is quickly increased. This provides a mechanism for Campbell's selective retention.

The process just described could be called creative insight or could just as well be called conditioning. As Rescorla (1988) has pointed out, "Organisms adjust their Pavlovian associations only when they are 'surprised.'" He goes on to remark that rather than saying that Pavlov's dogs were conditioned, one could say that they developed a "theory" about the relationship between laboratory assistants and meat powder. By the same token, rather than saying that Pavlov developed a theory, we could say that he was conditioned (Martindale 1991). Pavlov noticed that his dogs started to drool prematurely when a laboratory assistant entered the room. Another way of putting this is that the strength of the association between the laboratory assistant nodes and the drooling dog nodes was strengthened. Thus, he was conditioned.

Pavlov was studying the chemical composition of saliva rather than learning. He happened to notice what had been known since the dawn of time: one's mouth waters when expecting food. His discovery of conditioning could be taken as an example of Campbell's theory of random variation and selective retention. The discovery also poses a problem for Campbell's theory. If the theory were correct, we would expect on average that any given person should have at most one creative idea. Yet Pavlov had a number of creative ideas, and the same is true of most other creators. Most people never have an important creative idea, whereas some have a lot of them. The theory cannot explain why, as Pasteur put it, "chance favors the prepared mind."

Although apparently developed without knowledge of Campbell's theory, genetic algorithms (Koza 1992) implement his analogy with evolution almost exactly. Genetic algorithms are most frequently used in optimization problems—that is, finding the maximum or minimum of a complex function. The values of the function are typically represented by a string of 0's and 1's called a chromosome. A population of chromosomes is generated at random. Each chromosome is a binary number. If one is looking for the minimum of a function, the smaller the number is, the more fit the chromosome is. The more fit, the more chances it gets to breed (exchange genes) with other fit chromosomes to produce the next generation of chromosomes. Mutation—random flipping of bits—is also included. Thus, genetic algorithms are modeled explicitly on natural selection. Surprisingly, they can solve some quite difficult problems.

Holland (1975) pointed out that genetic algorithms can be thought of as representing connection strengths in a neural network, and Goldberg (1989) pointed out that they could in principle be used to mimic creative insight. Both Campbell (1960) and Dawkins (1986) note that a monkey hitting typewriter keys at random would eventually type out all of *Hamlet*. This is true, but we would need a monkey with a lifespan of trillions of years. Dawkins considers just one phrase, Hamlet's "Methinks it is like a weasel." There are 28 characters and spaces in this sentence. The probability of the monkey's typing it correctly is $1/28^{27}$, a very small number indeed. Dawkins wrote a computer program that produced a population of random letter strings (blind variation). The one closest to the target was retained (selective retention), and a new population was produced by randomly replacing incorrect letters. The "fittest" string in the new population was selected, and the procedure was reiterated. The target string was correctly produced in from 10 to 50 generations. In contrast, it would generally take trillions of trials if a purely random procedure had been used.

Defocused Attention
Campbell's theory gives us a possible way of explaining how creative ideas arise, but it does not shed much light on the psychological processes involved. To have a creative idea, one obviously has to be conscious of it. That is, the elements to be combined have to be in the focus of attention. Mendelsohn (1976) proposed that differences in attentional capacity can explain individual differences in creativity. As he put it, "The greater the attentional capacity, the more likely the combinational leap which is generally described as the hallmark of creativity." Consider someone who can attend to two ideas—A and B—at the same time. At any instant, the person has a chance of thinking of a creative combination AB. A person who could attend to three ideas—A, B, and C—simultaneously has three potentially creative combinations: AB, AC, and BC. Someone who could attend to four ideas simultaneously has six possible creative combinations, and so on. Such a person should be six times more likely to think of a creative ideas than the person with narrowly focused attention. Several lines of experimental evidence support Mendelsohn's contention that creative people tend to have less focused attention than uncreative people (Dykes and McGhie 1976; Mendelsohn and Griswold 1966).

In neural network terms, we can divide consciousness into attention (the most activated nodes) and short-term memory (nodes that are activated but less so than those in the focus of attention). Where the division between attention and short-term memory should be drawn is rather arbitrary. I have suggested that Mendelsohn's theory should be revised to refer to the total number of elements in consciousness (Martindale 1981, 1989). Perhaps more nodes can be simultaneously activated in creative people than in uncreative people, regardless of whether these nodes are in focal attention or only in short-term memory.

During the preparation stage of the creative process, attention must be too focused. That is, a few nodes are highly activated and dominate consciousness. These nodes encode ideas thought to be relevant to the problem at hand. Of course, the creative solution lies in ideas thought to be irrelevant. During incubation, the nodes coding the problem remain primed or partially activated in the creative mind. In the uncreative person, the nodes coding the problem are deactivated. Rather than remaining in the back of the mind, the problem is forgotten. As the creator goes about his or her business, many nodes will be activated. If one of these happens to be related to the nodes coding the problem, the latter became fully activated and leap into attention. This is inspiration, the discovery of the creative analogy. It would not have happened if the nodes representing the problem had not been partially activated, because the path connecting the two sets of nodes is presumably long and circuitous. During the verification stage, attention is focused, and the new idea is scrutinized for flaws.

Associative Hierarchies and Creativity
In a network with recurrent lateral inhibition, total activation in any layer of nodes is normalized or kept relatively constant (Grossberg 1980). When attention is focused, a few nodes are highly activated. They exert strong lateral inhibition on other nodes and prevent them from becoming activated. As attention is defocused, activation is more equitably spread out among a larger number of nodes. Since no nodes are extremely activated, there is less lateral inhibition. Thus, nodes receiving small amounts of input become activated rather than being inhibited by strongly activated nodes. In a state of defocused attention, nodes in short-term memory are more activated—relative to units in the focus of attention—than in a state of focused attention. Consider a word association task. The examiner says a word, activating the node coding the word. In turn, this node activates nodes with which it is connected. The subject responds with whichever of these nodes is most activated. The set of activated nodes corresponds to the associative hierarchy or habit-family hierarchy (Hull 1943) elicited by the word. When attention is focused, the word will strongly activate only a few other nodes. Thus, the associative hierarchy will be steep (figure 11.1a). When attention is less focused, more nodes will be activated

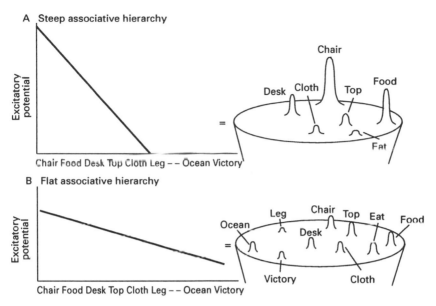

Figure 11.1
Steep (*A*) and flat (*B*) associative hierchies

but to a lesser degree. Thus, the associative hierarchy will be relatively flat (figure 11.1b).

A person with steep associative gradients responds in a stereotyped manner. The dominant response to a stimulus will always be given. A person with flat associative hierarchies responds in a more variable fashion. On a word association task, such a person is more likely to make remote associations. The person with steep associative gradients should thus be uncreative, and the person with flatter gradients should be creative. This is, in fact, Mednick's (1962) theory of creativity. Defocused attention versus flat associative hierarchy are cognitive and behavioristic ways of describing exactly the same phenomenon (Martindale 1981; Mendelsohn and Griswold 1966).

Mednick's idea is that the relative ordering of associative hierarchies is the same in creative and uncreative people. What differs is the steepness of the hierarchies. Thus, on a continuous word association task, the most likely sequence of responses to the stimulus *table*—for both creative and uncreative people—would be *chair, food, desk, top, cloth, eat,* or something similar. Uncreative people should produce this series quickly—because the nodes coding these words are highly activated—and then stop responding—because no other nodes are activated. On the other hand, creative people should respond at a slower rate—because the nodes are not as activated—and should continue responding with remote associations—because more nodes have been activated. This is exactly what was found (Mednick 1962).

Primary Process Thinking and Creativity
The psychoanalytic theorist Ernst Kris (1952) proposed that creative people are more able to alternate between primary process and secondary process cognition than are uncreative people. The primary process–secondary process continuum may be thought of as the main dimension along which consciousness varies. It is isomorphic with Wundt's (1896) associative versus intellectual and Werner's (1948) dedifferentiated versus differentiated thinking. Primary process thinking is analogical, autistic, and free associative. Secondary process thinking is abstract, logical, goal oriented, and reality oriented. According to Kris, creative inspiration involves a movement toward a primary process state of mind. Because primary process thinking is associative, it makes the discovery of new combinations more likely. Creative elaboration or verification involves a movement toward secondary process thinking.

Throughout this chapter, I use the terms *primary process* and *secondary process* as purely descriptive labels rather than as psychoanalytic constructs. I could just as well have used Wundt's or Werner's terms. Kris's theory should be taken as purely descriptive. In this light, all he said is that a person is more likely to have a creative idea in a reverie than when his or her thinking is extremely intellectual. The theory should also be modified so as to state that there is a curvilinear relationship between creativity and primary process thinking. A moderate amount of primary process thinking, as in fantasy or reverie, may facilitate discovery of creative ideas, but extreme primary process thinking—such as dreaming—does not produce creative ideas (Martindale 1990a).

The most extreme form of secondary process thinking is deductive logic. A creative insight is not possible with this sort of thinking because the conclusion is implicit in the premises. We could think of secondary process thinking as crystalline. It is nicely structured, but the probability of two remote atoms' bumping into each other is zero. We could compare movement toward primary process thinking as analogous to heating the crystal. When heated enough, it turns into a fluid. In the fluid state, the probability of two remote atoms' colliding and combining is tremendously increased. If we had a flawed or imperfect crystal (compare imperfect understanding of some phenomenon), this is, in fact, just what we would do: heat it so that it turned into a fluid (move toward primary process thinking) and then gradually lower the temperature (move back toward secondary process thinking). The result would be a flawless crystal (compare a creative scientific hypothesis).

Kris also argued that creative people can use primary process thinking to deal with abstract or neutral material, whereas uncreative people use it only to deal with affect-laden, personally relevant ideas. Thus, a creative person may have fantasies or reveries about, say, prime numbers. The reveries of the uncreative person, according to Kris, are restricted to his or her drives and emotions.

Kris's theory nicely accounts for the self-reports of creative inspiration. There are also other lines of evidence supportive of the theory. For example, creative people report more fantasy activity (Lynn and Rhue 1986), remember their dreams better (Hudson 1975) and are more easily hypnotized (Aston and McDonald 1985) than uncreative people. Suler (1980) gave a review of such studies.

Shallice (1978) argued that primary process thinking corresponds to a state in which large numbers of nodes are weakly and about equally activated. In such a state, there would be relatively little lateral inhibition. As a consequence, concepts would be dedifferentiated or holophrastic. This allows us to explain primary process mechanisms such as condensation, displacement, symbolism, and part-for-whole thinking—albeit in a very different way than Freud (1900) explained them. The crucial point is that such a state of a large number of weakly and equally activated nodes corresponds exactly to what Mednick call flat associative hierarchies. Secondary process thinking is best modeled as a state of focused attention, where a few nodes are strongly activated (Martindale 1981). Thus, it would seem that Kris, Mednick, and Mendelsohn all had the same theory but stated it in quite different terms.

Creativity and Arousal
Creative people can get themselves into primary process states of defocused attention. I have modeled these as states in which a large number of nodes are almost equally activated. A possible—but wrong—explanation would be that the nodes in a creative network are weakly but densely interconnected. This is wrong because a creative person can obviously shift to a secondary process state of focused attention, which I have suggested is a situation in which only a few nodes are very active.

I have suggested a neural network model in which each node receives "informational" input from other nodes and nonspecific input from the arousal system (Martindale 1981, 1991). Activation of a node is computed by adding up excitatory input, subtracting inhibitory input, and multiplying the result by input from the arousal system. In other words, the network follows Hull's (1943) behavioral law: increases in arousal make behavior more stereotyped. Whereas decreases in arousal make behavior more variable. In Hull's terms, the excitatory potential or probability of a behavior (compare activation of a node) is equal to its habit strength (compare informational inputs) multiplied by drive—what we now call general arousal.

If we assume that the total amount of activation in a layer of nodes is kept relatively constant (Grossberg 1980), one node would have all the activation at a very high level of arousal. As arousal was lowered, more nodes would be activated. What I called associative gradients would become flatter and flatter. Another way of saying this is that attention would become less and less focused. There is evidence that focus of attention is related to arousal (Callaway 1959; Easterbrook 1959). Simple introspection shows that as we decrease arousal (e.g., dozing off after solving calculus problems), thinking moves from secondary process to primary process in nature.

We need evidence that creativity is related to arousal. Virtually anything that increases arousal causes decreases on tests of creativity (see Martindale 1989, 1990b). Creative people actually show higher levels of cortical arousal than do uncreative people under resting or baseline conditions, but the difference is slight (Martindale 1990b). However, we do find differences in arousal just where we would expect them. Martindale and Hines (1975) monitored electroencepalogram activity while subjects took an intelligence test and a creativity test. Cortical arousal increased about equally while creative and uncreative subjects took the intelligence test. For uncreative subjects, arousal while taking the creativity test was the same as while taking the intelligence test. For creative subjects, arousal while taking the creativity test was actually below resting or baseline levels. This is surprising because virtually any mental task generally induces an increase in cortical arousal. Martindale and Hasenfus (1978) measured cortical arousal while people thought up a fantasy story (inspiration) and while they wrote it out (as close as we could come to operationalizing elaboration). Uncreative subjects showed the same high level of arousal during both stages, whereas creative subjects exhibited low arousal during inspiration and high arousal during elaboration. It is unlikely that these differences are due to differences in self-control, as creative people are notoriously bad at self-control (Martindale 1989) and worse than uncreative people at biofeedback tasks (Martindale and Hines 1975).

It is likely that creative people are in general more variable in their level of arousal, but there is not yet much quantitative evidence for this (Eysenck 1993; Martindale 1989, 1993). The idea that creative people should show more extreme spontaneous fluctuations in level of arousal comes directly from Kris's (1952) hypothesis that they show more variation along the secondary process–primary process continuum. It can also be derived from the correlation between creativity and the personality trait of psychoticism, which is associated with fluctuations in arousal (Eysenck in press).

Some Conclusions

To build a neural network capable of creative insights, first we need to fill the nodes with a wide diversity of knowledge. Second, we need to present the network with a problem that it cannot solve. If the problem can be solved at first glance, the solution will most likely be algorithmic or uncreative (Amabile 1985). Next, we want the nodes representing the problem to remain partially activated so they can "filter" other nodes corresponding to perception and thoughts. If these other nodes give a hint at the solution, connections will be strengthened, and the solution will pop into mind.

To fix ideas, let us say that the problem concerns a relationship between $node_1$ and $node_2$. Why the two are related is unclear. More or less by chance, $node_3$ is activated. It happens to be weakly connected to both $node_1$ and $node_2$. Since the latter are partially activated, all the connections are strengthed. If they are strengthened sufficiently, one has the "insight" as to why $node_1$ and $node_2$ are related. All that is necessary is to get all of the crucial nodes activated at the same time. To do that, it would be best to settle into a state of low arousal, with the relevant nodes at least partially activated. As arousal decreased, more and more nodes would become activated. Purely by chance, the crucial ones could become activated enough so that an insight occurred. As Eysenck (1993) has pointed out, using different terminology, if we let nodes come on and off totally at random, the "search space" for problem solving of other than a trivial nature is so large that a solution could never be found. We must cut down what he calls the "associative horizon" to a reasonable level. If we trim it too far, though, only "relevant" nodes will be activated, and they do not contain the crucial hint. We want a network that will at least periodically go to a low-arousal state in order to "search" for a solution and return to a higher arousal state to see if the solution is a good one.

Simulated Annealing and Creativity

Neural networks have an analogy with spin glass models in solid-state physics. This analogy is quite direct in the type of network first discussed by Hopfield (1982). Related models have been described by Geman and Geman (1984), Hinton and Sejnowski (1986), and Smolensky (1986). Consider a network composed of n nodes with each of the nodes connected to each of the other nodes. Hopfield (1982) proposed such a network in which connection strengths are symmetrical. That is, the strength of the connection from node i to node j is the same as the strength of the connection from j to i. The nodes can take values of 1 or -1 and are updated one at a time by a function such as

$$\text{Probability (activation} = 1) = \frac{1}{1 + e^{-I/T}} ,$$

where e is the base of the natural logarithms, I is the net input to the node, and T is temperature if we are thinking of a physical system. The equation produces sigmoid functions such as those shown in figure 11.2. When temperature is low, we have something close to a step function, with the node being on if input is above 0 and off if input is below 0. At higher temperature, nodes behave more randomly. A node may take a value of -1 even if input is positive or a value of $+1$ even if input is negative.

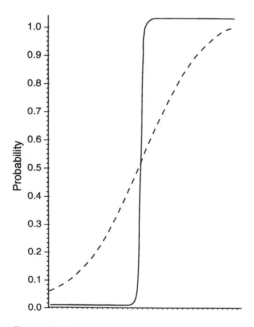

Figure 11.2
Probability that a node will be on or off as a function of amount of input and of temperature. $T = .5$: ——— ; $T = 10$: - - - -

If we consider all possible combinations of nodes being on or off, the network can be in any of 2^n states, where n is the number of nodes in the network. This is the phase space or energy space of the network. Each possible state can be thought of as the corner of an n-dimensional hypercube. Hopfield showed that such a network will evolve so as to minimize what he called energy. That is, states of minimal energy are fixed-point attractors for the network. (A fixed-point attractor is the state toward which a system will move. For example, when we are very hungry, eating is a fixed-point attractor.) The reason to say this is that all physical systems evolve so as to minimize free energy, and Hopfield's hypothesis—a creative one—is that neural networks do the same. Energy is minimized for any given node when the constraints placed on it by other nodes are satisfied. Thus, if two nodes are positively connected, energy is minimal if both are on. If two nodes are negatively connected, one should be on and the other off. This would be easy enough to accomplish in one step if the network had only two nodes; however, with a large number of nodes, the network will have to try various combinations before finding the global energy minimum. That is, we must iteratively update activation of the nodes until global energy has reached a minimum.

Let us say that such a network has been taught to recognize letters of the alphabet. The task Hopfield (1982) originally set for his network was to recognize patterns even when they were degraded or only partially presented. Energy minimization means making the correct response (e.g., responding A when an A is presented). Such a network responds A even if the input pattern is considerably degraded. It would be quite nice to have a network that behaved as Hopfield did: input some information about the brain, and the network outputs "spin glass." There are enough similarities between brains and spin glass that energy is minimized by using the same equations for both. This is certainly not a global minimum, but it is a better solution than treating the two as totally unrelated. For the moment, it is the best energy minimum that has been found.

A Hopfield net has a number of constraints, such as symmetric connections and complete interconnectedness, that do not apply to the brain. Campbell, Sherrington, and Wong (1989) reviewed studies of what happens when these constraints are loosened. Reducing connectivity has rather small effects on performance. Making the weights asymmetric, as they are in the brain, does not affect performance, but it does introduce cyclic and chaotic attractors into the phase space. This is actually good. A Hopfield net will "recognize" any input by settling onto the nearest attractor. It does not know when to switch from recognition to learning. In an asymmetric net, an input too dissimilar to stored patterns would almost certainly get the network into a cyclic or chaotic state. That is, there is no stable energy minimum, and activation of nodes in the system will oscillate either periodically or chaotically. This sustained activity could serve as a signal to stop trying to recognize and start learning. Hopfield (1984) himself has shown that better results are obtained if nodes can take on a continuum of values—as in the networks discussed earlier in this chapter—rather than just values of $+1$ and -1.

A problem with Hopfield's (1982) network was that it tended to get caught in a local minima. Consider figure 11.3 as representing an energy surface. If we drop a marble from the left side, it will end up at the global minimum on the left. If we drop it from the right side, it will get caught in the local minimum on the right. Recall Fermat's Last Theorem: There are no integer solutions to the equation, $a^n = b^n + c^n$, for n greater than 2. The phase space for this theorem is full of local minima. The global minimum is the general proof, which has apparently finally been found after a 300-year search. There is a local minimum for even numbers. That is, the proof for even numbers does not generalize to odd numbers. There is a local minimum around every

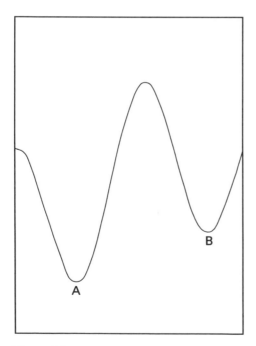

Figure 11.3
Illustration of a global (A) and a local (B) minimum

prime number. One can prove the theorem for any prime number he or she chooses, but the proof does not generalize to other prime numbers. For any scientific problem, we are trying to find a global minimum: an explanation that satisfies all the constraints imposed by the data and by the rules of scientific method.

Hopfield's (1982) perception of a similarity between atoms and neurons allows us to bring to bear on neural networks much of the powerful mathematics of statistical mechanics. It also inspires us to look around and see what else we can purloin from physics. Flaws in a crystal occur when the atoms are misaligned. This happens because the crystal formed too quickly. A flawed crystal has gotten caught in a local minimum. To fix the crystal, one uses annealing—heating the crystal until it is in a fluid state and then gradually cooling it to allow the atoms to "communicate" information about their orientation throughout the whole system. If annealing is done correctly, a global energy minimum—a perfect crystal—is reached.

Kirkpatrick, Gelatt, and Vecchi (1983) suggested that what they called simulated annealing could be used to avoid the problem of getting trapped in local minima. Hinton and Sejnowski (1986) use the analogy of shaking a system such as the one shown in figure 11.3 to give an intuitive understanding of annealing. To get the marble into the global minimum, we first shake the system violently and gradually shake less and less violently. The marble should end up at the global minimum.

To do simulated annealing on a Hopfield net, we start out with the temperature very hight. With high temperature, the nodes are going on and off in a quasi-random fashion. So long as a node gets enough positive or negative input, it will be on or off; however, nodes receiving moderate inputs do not yet have to commit themselves to being on or off and thus are not trapped in the system as a whole in a local minimum. Gradually temperature is lowered. At high temperatures, nodes can increase as well as decrease their contribution to total energy. This allows the system to crawl out of local minima. Thus, by the time the system freezes, it is likely to be at the global minimum.

If we imagine a network that anneals periodically—that is, oscillates between high and low temperature—this sounds exactly like the creative network I have described. When temperature is high, the network could be said to be operating in a primary process fashion. When temperature is low, it is operating in a secondary process fashion. The analogy between simulated annealing and the explanation of creativity given in previous sections suggests that the biological analogue of temperature is the inverse of cortical arousal. That is, high temperature corresponds to low arousal.

Something like annealing must occur in all thinking, creative or not. Arousal fluctuates on several time scales. The cortical scanning hypothesis of the EEG alpha rhythm is that it represents slight variations in arousal caused when the arousal system sends arousal to the cortex not continuously but about 10 times per second (Harter 1967). When we work on a problem, we tend to alternate between intense concentration (higher arousal) and pondering or taking a break (lower arousal). There is also an ultradian 90-minute cycle in cortical arousal (Kripke and Sonnenschien 1978) as well as a diurnal cycle (Dermer and Berscheid 1972). A possible function of these cycles would be to provide periodic annealing, allowing us to escape from local minima—false starts or dead ends in our thinking. If there is any truth at all to this speculation, it would seem that creative thought and normal problem solving are not fundamentally different. Both must involve annealing. However, the annealing is more extreme in creative insight than in day-to-day problem solving.

Conclusions

When the major theories of creativity are translated into neural-network theories, we see that they are identical. Even more surprising, they seem to be identical with connectionist theories involving simulated annealing. If they are identical, then the analogue of temperature in simulated annealing must be the inverse of general cortical arousal. If nothing else, equating the theories allows us at least to guess the meaning of the previously undefined temperature of a neural network. Furthermore, the equation allows us to look at creative problem solving in terms of energy minimization, thus bringing to bear the powerful mathematical machinery of statistical mechanics and thermodynamics.

My conclusions could be tested in several ways. On the physiological level, we would predict that more creative people should show more fluctuations in arousal, on a variety of time scales, than less creative people. This should be the case especially during creative problem solving. On the level of computer simulation, consider a connectionist poetry writing program. Run at very low temperatures, we would expect it to produce prosaic statements (e.g., "I climbed the stairs sadly"). Run at very high temperatures, it should produce nonsense (e.g., "I shoveled the stairs with ice"). With simulated annealing, we would predict something creative. Victor Hugo's, "I climbed the bitter stairs," would be a bit much to hope for, but we would expect outputs more creative than those produced by the program run at a single temperature.

References

Amabile, T. M. (1985). Motivation and creativity: Effects of motivational orientation on creative writers. *Journal of Personality and Social Psychology, 48,* 393–339.

Aston, M. A., and McDonald, R. D. (1985). Effects of hypnosis on verbal and nonverbal creativity. *International Journal of Clinical and Experimental Hypnosis, 33,* 15–26.

Blake, W. (1803). Letter to Thomas Butts. In *The letters of William Blake,* edited by A. G. B. Russell. London: Methuen.

Callaway, E. (1959). The effect of amobarbital (amylobarbiton) and methamphetamine on the focus of attention. *Journal of Mental Science, 105,* 382–392.

Campbell, C., Sherrington, D., and Wong, K. Y. M. (1989). Statistical mechanics and neural networks. In *Neural computing architectures,* edited by I. Aleksander. Cambridge, MA: MIT Press.

Campbell, D. T. (1960). Blind variation and selective retention in creative thought as in other knowledge processes. *Psychological Review, 67,* 380–400.

Dawkins, R. (1986). *The blind watchmaker.* New York: Norton.

Dermer, M., and Berscheid, E. (1972). Self-report of arousal as an indicant of activation level. *Behavioral Sciences, 17,* 420–429.

Dykes, M., and McGhie, A. (1976). A comparative study of attentional strategies of sow of human experience. New York: Plenum.

Helmholtz, H. von (1896). *Vorträge and Reden.* Brunswick: Friedrich Viewig und Sohn.

Hinton, G. E., and Sejnowski, T. J. (1986). Learning and relearning in Boltzmann machines. In D. E. Rumelhart and J. H. McClelland (eds.), *Parallel distributed processing: Explorations in the microstructure of cognition* (Vol. 1). Cambridge, MIT Press.

Holland, J. H. (1975). *Adaptation in natural and artificial systems.* Ann Arbor: University of Michigan Press.

Hopfield, J. J. (1902). Neural networks and physical systems with emergent collective computational abilities. *Proceedings of the National Academy of Sciences, USA, 79,* 2554–2558.

Hopfield, J. J. (1984). Neurons with graded response have collective computational properties like those of two-state neurons. *Proceedings of the National Academy of Sciences, USA, 81,* 3008–3092.

Hudson, L. (1975). *Human beings: The psychology of human experience.* New York: Anchor Press.

Hull, C. L. (1943). *Principles of behavior.* New York: Appleton-Century-Crofts.

Kirkpatrick, S., Gelatt, C. D., Jr., and Vecchi, M. P. (1983). Optimization by simulated annealing. *Science, 220,* 671–680.

Konorski, J. (1967). *Integrative activity of the brain.* Chicago: University of Chicago Press.

Koza, J. R. (1992). *Genetic programming: On the programming of computers by means of natural selection.* Cambridge, MA: MIT Press.

Kripke, D. F., and Sonnenschein, D. (1978). A biologic rhythm in waking fantasy. In *The stream of consciousness: scientific investigations into the flow of human experience.* New York: Plenum.

Kris, E. (1952). *Psychoanalytic explorations in art.* New York: International Universities Press.

Lynn, S. J., and Rhue, J. W. (1986). The fantasy-prone person: Hypnosis, imagination, and creativity. *Journal of Personality and Social Psychology, 51,* 404–408.

Martindale, C. (1981). *Cognition and consciousness.* Homewood, IL: Dorsey.

Martindale, C. (1989). Personality, situation, and creativity. In J. A. Glover, R. R. Ronning, and C. R. Reynolds (eds.), *Handbook of creativity.* New York: Plenum.

Martindale, C. (1990a). *The clockwork muse: The predictability of artistic change.* New York: Basic Books.

Martindale, C. (1990b). Creative imagination and neural activity. In R. Kunzendorf and A. Sheikh (eds.), *Psychophysiology of mental imagery: Theory, research, and application.* Amityville, NY: Baywood.

Martindale, C. (1991). *Cognitive psychology: A neural-network approach.* Pacific Grove, CA: Brooks/Cole.

Martindale, C. (1993). Psychoticism, degeneration, and and creativity. *Psychological Inquiry, 4,* 209–211.

Martindale, C., and Hasenfus, N. (1978). EEG difference as a function of creativity, stage of the creative process, and effort to be original. *Biological Psychology, 6,* 157–167.

Martindale, C., and Hines, D. (1975). Creativity and cortical activation during creative, intellectual, and EEG feedback tasks. *Biological Psychology, 3,* 71–80.

Mednick, S. A. (1962). The associative basis of the creative process. *Psychological Review, 69,* 220–232.

Mendelsohn, G. A. (1976). Associative and attentional processes in creative performance. *Journal of Personality, 44,* 341–369.

Mendelsohn, G. A., and Griswold, B. B. (1966). Assessed creative potential, vocabulary level, and sex as predictors of the use of incidental cues in verbal problem solving. *Journal of Personality and Social Psychology, 4,* 423–431.

Poincaré, H. (1913). *The foundations of science.* Lancaster, PA: Science Press.

Rescorla, R. A. (1988). Pavlovian conditioning: It's not what you think it is. *American Psychologist, 43,* 151–160.

Rumelhart, D. E., Hinton, G. E., and McClelland, J. L. (1986). A general framework for parallel distributed processing. In D. E. Rumelhart and J. L. McClelland (eds.), *Parallel Distributed Processing: Explorations in the Microstructure of Cognition* (Vol. 1). Cambridge, MA: MIT Press.

Shallice, T. (1978). The dominant action system: An information-processing approach to consciousness. In K. S. Pope and J. L. Singer (eds.), *The stream of consciousness: Scientific investigations into the flow of human experience.* New York: Plenum.

Simonton, D. K. (1984). *Genius, creativity, and leadership: Historiometric inquiries.* Cambridge, MA: Harvard University Press.

Smolensky, P. (1986). Information processing in dynamical systems: Foundations of harmony theory. In D. E. Rumelhart and J. L. McClelland (eds.), *Parallel distributed processing: Explorations in the microstructure of cognition* (Vol. 1). Cambridge, MA: MIT Press.

Suler, J. (1980). Primary process thinking and creativity. *Psychological Bulletin, 88,* 155–165.

Terman, L. M. (1925). *Mental and physical traits of a class of gifted children.* Stanford: Stanford University Press.

Terman, L. M., and Oden, M. (1959). *The gifted child at midlife.* Stanford: Stanford University Press.

Wallas, G. (1926). *The art of thought.* New York: Harcourt, Brace & World.

Weber, J. P. 91969). *The psychology of art.* New York: Delacorte.

Werner, H. (1948). *Comparative psychology of mental development.* New York: International Universities Press.

Wundt, W. (1896). *Lectures on human and animal psychology.* New York: Macmillan.

Part III

General Issues in Creative Cognition

Chapter 12

An Investment Approach to Creativity: Theory and Data

Todd I. Lubart and Robert J. Sternberg

What enables a person to be creative? Why do some people generate novel ideas and pursue them, while others join the crowd with humdrum contributions? We suggest that specific aspects of six resources—intellectual processes, knowledge, intellectual styles, personality, motivation, and environmental context—contribute to creativity (Sternberg and Lubart 1991, 1992). The cognitive resources work together with the conative and environmental ones to form an individual's "investment" in creative enterprise.

In any number of domains, a person may apply the six resources to initiate a project and bring it to fruition. For creative work, we propose that the choice of domains, projects, and ideas for those projects will involve a basic investment strategy of "buying low and selling high." Buying low means pursuing ideas that are unknown or at least slightly out of favor but with growth potential. A person can buy low in terms of both the primary idea for a project and the secondary ideas needed to develop it. Buying low inherently links risk taking to creative performance. Selling high involves presenting one's work and moving on to new projects when an idea or product becomes valued and yields a significant return. Analogous to stock market investment success, sometimes creativity fails to occur because a person puts forth ("sells") an idea prematurely or holds an idea so long that it becomes common or obsolete. We suggest that selling high is important for creative success on an individual project and for a career of creative work.

In addition to the buy low–sell high theme, the investment metaphor highlights aspects of the definition and judgment of creativity. First, the evaluation of both financial worth and creativity involves social consensus. A stock is valuable, in part, because investors collectively desire to possess it. A product is labeled creative at a point when appropriate judges collectively agree on this evaluation (Amabile 1982). Previous theoretical and empirical accounts of people's conceptions of creativity suggest that novelty or statistical rarity, appropriateness, and high quality are the main criteria for judging creative performance (Amabile 1982; Jackson and Messick 1965; MacKinnon 1962; Sternberg 1985b, 1988a). Second, the investment metaphor points out the importance of concentrating the evaluation of creativity on *observable products*. In the evaluation of financial investments, the measurement of performance is tangible—monetary gain. A potential stock investor who has good ideas but does not participate in the stock market is not a successful investor in stocks. In our view of creativity, a similar distinction exists between latent creative potential and creative performance. Our investigation of the investment approach focuses on creative performance—creativity that is manifested in some kind of overt form (Albert 1983). Third, the investment approach highlights that there is a continuum of creative performance, as there is a continuum of risk and profit in the financial realm.

As with any other metaphor between disparate subjects, there are points of correspondence and points of noncorrespondence, which also bring insights. One example is the differences between the investment and creative realms is the starting point for each endeavor. Financial investors generally buy into existing stocks or other instruments. For creative work, people may join an existing field or genre but must also generate the specific project or starting ideas. Another example involves the source of the "value added" after buying into a stock or idea, respectively. The financial investor usually monitors a stock, which may gain in value because the business or economy as a whole succeeds; the investor does not actually go to work for the company. For creativity, however, the individual must roll up his or her sleeves, apply the cognitive, conative, and environmental resources to the problem, push the project toward a final product, and sometimes promote the product to win acceptance. Thus, for creative work, an individual's resources are actively applied throughout a project, whereas, in the financial realm, an investor uses his or her resources primarily to make just the buy and sell decisions.

To conclude our sketch of the investment approach, we turn to a brief description of the cognitive, conative, and environmental resources that a person can invest in a project and the manner in which these resources combine (see Sternberg and Lubart 1991 for details). We propose that the six resources we have identified can lead a person to buy low, develop an innovative project, and sell high.

Six Resources for Creativity and Their Confluence

Problem definition (or redefinition) and insightful thinking are vital to creative performance (Davidson and Sternberg 1984; Getzels and

Csikszentmihalyi 1976; Sternberg 1985a). Getzels and Csikszentmihalyi's (1976) seminal research on problem finding showed that art students who produced highly original still-life drawings spent longer periods of time formulating their compositions than less creative peers. Creative work often involves taking an existing problem and redefining it by approaching the problem from a new angle. The insight processes of selective encoding, comparison, and combination are hypothesized to facilitate problem redefinition and problem solution. Selective encoding occurs when a person notices the relevance of information to a task. When Fleming noticed the bactericidal properties of the penicillium mold that had ruined an experiment, he had a selective-encoding insight. Selective comparison involves the judicious use of analogies and metaphors to conceptualize and complete a task. Kekulé, for example, allegedly used a dream of a snake's biting its tail to aid him in discovering the ringlike structure of the benzene molecule. Selective combination is the meaningful synthesis of disparate information. Darwin synthesized into a unified whole disparate facts that served as a basis for his theory of natural selection. Analogously, the successful investor must selectively encode information others do not see as relevant, compare the current case to other investment situations, and synthesize the implications of this information to make the best investment decisions.

Knowledge, the second resource, is necessary to make an informed creative contribution in any domain. Knowledge provides a large part of the raw material on which intellectual processes operate. Knowledge of the "state of the market" in a domain helps a person to avoid reinventing ideas or products that society has already experienced. Knowledge also allows a person to be contrarian—to move away from the popular trends, as successful investors often do in financial markets (Dreman 1982). With further benefits to creative performance, knowledge helps a person to produce high-quality work, notice and use beneficial chance occurrences, and devote greater cognitive resources to the processing of new ideas. Given these benefits of knowledge, it is important to note, however, that experts operating on knowledge-rich tasks may become entrenched in a standard or "correct" way of approaching a problem (Frensch and Sternberg 1989; Langer 1989). For creativity, therefore, very high levels of knowledge can be detrimental (Simonton 1984, Sternberg and Lubart 1991).

Intellectual styles, the third resource, refer to preferences in using one's intellectual skills. Certain intellectual styles facilitate the application of intellectual processes and knowledge by directing an individual toward problem approaches conducive to novelty. Based on a model of mind as mental self-government, three of the style clusters are called legislative-executive, conservative-liberal, and global-local (Sternberg 1988b). People with a legislative style prefer work that allows them to make new rules and structures, whereas those with an executive style prefer to apply their thinking skills to the execution of tasks by following rules. A preference for sequential completion of tasks one at a time, the monarchic style, often co-occurs with the executive style. The conservative-liberal styles contrast those with a proclivity for tasks that involve old approaches with those preferring new approaches. Finally, the global style refers to people who prefer to focus on the broader, general aspects of a task, whereas the local style describes those who prefer detail-oriented work. An individual can be characterized by a combination of styles reflecting person-situation interactions (Cantor and Mischel 1979), but one style may dominate over others for a given individual. The legislative, liberal, and global styles are hypothesized to make positive contributions to creative performance. The executive, conservative, monarchic, and local styles are predicted to affect creativity negatively.

In terms of the creative personality, we identify five attributes as essential. Each of these attributes helps the cognitive resources to be used effectively. The first, tolerance of ambiguity (Barron and Harrington 1981; Golann 1963), is necessary during these periods of creative endeavor in which things are not quite fitting together but in which premature closure would prevent the intellectual processes from having a sufficient opportunity to get a handle on the problem. The second attribute, perseverance (Golann 1963; Roe 1952), is essential in any kind of contrarian efforts when one is going against entrenched ideas and against those who have a stake in the existing order. Intellectual processes and knowledge often need to be applied repeatedly to solve a problem. Without perseverance, the problem solver may very well become tired and stop the cognitive work early. Third, a willingness to grow becomes important as one attempts to go beyond one's past knowledge and previously successful uses of intellectual skills to make new ones that are genuinely novel. Fourth, a willingness to take risks (Glover 1977; McClelland 1956) is emphasized in our investment approach. During creative work, there is a potential for gain (internal and external rewards) or loss (e.g., time, energy, criticism), and the outcome is uncertain. A general principle of investment is that, on average, greater return involves greater risk. The link between risk taking, cognitive resources, and creative performance is developed in detail later in the chapter. Finally, the fifth attribute is individuality and a supporting courage of one's convictions (Amabile 1983; Barron and Harrington 1981; Dellas and Gaier 1970; Golann 1963; MacKinnon 1962, 1965). One needs to value one's novel cognitions and the differences between these cognitions and other people's ideas. To achieve creativity, a person needs to believe in novel ideas even if they go against the crowd's opinion. These aspects of personality are viewed as necessary for the maintenance of high levels of creative performance over long periods of time.

Closely related to personality characteristics is the motivation to use intellectual processes, knowledge, or intellectual styles for creative purposes. In the financial realm, "money makes the world go around." For creative work, intrinsic rewards such as realizing one's potential and satisfying one's curiosity have often been viewed as important driving forces for creativity (Amabile 1983; Crutchfield 1962; Golann 1962; Rogers 1954). These motivators share a common feature: all tend to focus attention on the task, which concentrates the effect of whatever cognitive resources are available. Goal-focusing motivators, in contrast, lead people to see a task as a means to an end. If the goal, which may be money, recognition, or an intangible reward, remains salient during task completion, then creative performance suffers because attention is drawn away from the task itself. Thus, we emphasize the way in which motivation focuses attention (task versus goal) rather than the specific motivator. We suggest that, at moderate levels, motivators (both intrinsic and extrinsic) will be most effective for creativity because people will have a desire to work and be able to maintain a focus on their work. Thus, in accord with the Yerkes-Dodson principle, motivation is hypothesized to bear an inverted U relationship to creativity.

The final resource for creativity is the environmental context. Environments can provide physical or social stimulation, either of which helps new ideas to form by "jump-starting" a person's thinking processes. Environments also differ in the extent to which creativity is fostered (Amabile 1983; Lubart 1990; Rubenson and Runco 1992; Simonton 1984). The earliest inklings of new ideas, which Finke, Ward, and Smith (1992) call "preinventive forms," need an atmosphere that permits and encourages further idea growth and developments. When conformity is valued, new ideas may be squelched as soon as they are conceived. In investment terms, these conditions would constitute a "bear market" for creative work. In a third role, social environments provide a subjective evaluation of a product's creativity or an individual's creative performance. For example, the work of a young poet could be considered very creative by her peers but not by literary critics, who might regard the poetry as too offbeat. Thus, the environment sets standards for creative products that individuals may come to internalize as part of their cognitive processes.

A confluence of resources is also necessary. The combined contributions of the individual resources plus interactions among the resources lead to a proclivity for "buying low" and achieving creative performance (see Sternberg and Lubart 19910. The nature of the resource confluence may vary with the specific domain and task that is involved.

Taken together, we believe that these ideas on the conceptualization of the resources and their confluence themselves represent an integrative approach to creativity. We have attempted to combine the strongest elements of specialized and alternative theories using a new investment metaphor and confluence hypotheses. In particular, the investment approach draws on Amabile's (1983) componential model of creativity, Csikszentmihalyi's (1988) system approach, Getzels and Csikszentmihalyi's (1976) research on problem finding, and Walberg's (1988) ideas on creativity and "human capital."

The investment approach also connects with Finke, Ward, and Smith's (1992) work on creative cognition. The creative cognition approach focuses on the information processes and structures that lead to creativity. Similar to the investment view, creativity is seen as the result of several mental processes that are used to generate and develop new ideas. Also, Finke, Ward, and Smith mention the importance of motivation, overcoming a fear of failure, and personal involvement on a task, which leads to perseverance and a conviction in one's ideas. Unlike the investment approach, however, creative cognition work (as the label indicates) concentrates on the cognitive side of creativity. We balance our attention between cognitive and noncognitive (personality, motivation, environment) resources. Thus, one could view the work on creative cognition as an extended and specialized treatment of the cognitive portion of creativity, compatible with our more general multivariate approach.

We will expand on the potential links between creative cognition and the investment approach after considering two preliminary empirical studies conducted within the investment approach. The first study focuses on the cognitive and conative resources for creative work. The second study provides an in-depth look at cognitive risk taking and the concept of buying low and selling high.

Study 1: Testing the Investment Resources for Creativity

Although some recent work has begun to acknowledge that different aspects of creativity are best studied together (Csikszentmihalyi 1988; Gruber 1981; Hill 1990; Rossman and Horn 1972), previous empirical work has often treated the antecedents of creativity in relative isolation from each other. For example, a large literature explores the connection between creativity and intelligence. However, this work has remained separate from other studies on personality and creativity (Barron and Harrington 1981). Our research simultaneously studies multiple resources of the investment approach. We seek to describe the contribution to creativity of each resource alone *and* in the context of the other resources. For example, we explore how aspects of intelligence relate to creative performance and then whether the variability in creative performance that intelligence "explains" is different from the variability that the other resources "explain." We hypothesize that each resource will uniquely contribute to creative performance. The resources will also contribute in ways that overlap statistically with other resources and cannot be isolated at this time. The relative contribution of each resource to creative performance depends on three variables: (1) the general importance of the resource for creativity (e.g., intellectual processes may be more important than knowledge), (2) the specific requirements of the creativity task (e.g., short-term tasks may decrease the importance of cognitive style or personality), and (3) the extent to which each resource is operationalized and measured well. With these points in mind, the findings we report should be considered suggestive rather than definitive.

The research, with its multivariate design, also allows us to examine potential interactions between the resources for creativity. We hypothesize that high levels on two or more resources (such as intellectual processes and knowledge) may boost creativity more than does the simple additive effect of the individual resources.

The focus of the current study is on the person-centered resources for creativity (intellectual processes, knowledge, intellectual styles, personality, and motivation); thus, it does not directly address the environmental resource. Also, the study uses a sample of laypeople to test the investment approach (see also Finke, Ward, and Smith 1992). Others, such as Gruber (1981), have examined the lives of extremely creative people (e.g., Charles Darwin). The investment approach should apply to all levels of creative achievement. There are large- and small-scale investors in both the financial and creative realms. However, the use of a sample of laypeople focuses the test on more typical, everyday levels of the creative-performance continuum.

Method
The subjects for the primary phase of the study consisted of 48 people from the New Haven, Connecticut, area (24 males, 24 females). The mean age of the sample was 33.40 years ($SD = 13.79$), with a range of 18 to 65 years. Fifteen additional New Haven subjects (8 males, 7

females) judged the creativity of the work produced in the first phase. These raters had a mean age of 41.07 years ($SD = 13.02$) and ranged in age between 21 and 70.

The study employed multiple measures of creative performance and of the resources, which were chosen to reflect both the investment approach and alternative perspectives. The materials consisted of creativity tasks, cognitive tests designed to measure the intellectual processes relevant to creativity, and self-report measures pertaining to the knowledge, intellectual styles, personality, and motivation resources of the investment framework.

Drawing, writing, advertising, and scientific tasks were composed to allow a broad assessment of creative performance. These tasks involve the production of substantive products that can exhibit a range of creativity. The tasks have a parallel form across the four domains and include topic selection as an integral part of the creative process. Amabile (1983) and others have used similar types of tasks (e.g., collage making and poem writing) to measure creative performance.

The materials for each task consisted of a list of topics and an array of supplies (e.g., pens, paper, pastels). Some drawing topics were "hope," "rage," and "earth from an insect's point of view." Examples of topics used for the other domains were "Beyond the Edge" and "The Octopus's Sneakers" as titles to be expanded into stories; "Bowties," "brussels sprouts," and "the IRS" as topics for television commercials; and "How could we detect aliens among us?" as an open-ended scientific problem. Three to ten topics were provided for each domain.[1]

Four tests of intellectual ability were used as convergent measures of the investment approach's intellectual processes resource: (1) the Stroop color-word interference task, individual form (Golden 1975), to measure selective encoding; (2) the Letter Series Test (Thurstone 1962) to measure induction, (3) the Culture-Fair Test of g, Scale 3, Form A (Cattell and Cattell 1963) to measure fluid intelligence; and (4) a Coping with Novelty test designed for this study to measure selective encoding, combination, and comparison skills. The Coping with Novelty test consisted of 7 insight problems, 17 verbal, and 13 figural problems that involved unusual and counterfactual reasoning and 10 verbal learning from context problems (inter-item reliability = .89). These items were drawn from previous research on the triarchic theory of human intelligence (Sternberg 1980, 1985a, 1986)

Knowledge was assessed with a biographical questionnaire concerning educational history, knowledge level, and activities in the domains studied. For knowledge level, subjects were asked to compare their knowledge in a domain with an average person's knowledge. For relevant activities, subjects were asked how often they engaged in drawing, painting, writing short stories, writing poetry, looking at advertisements, selling products, conducting science experiments, electronics, working on social problems, plus other activities.

Two instruments, the Intellectual Styles Questionnaire, an operationalization of Sternberg's (1988b) theory of mental self-government, and the Myers-Briggs Type Indicator (MBTI), Form G (Myers and McCaulley 1985), were used to assess intellectual styles. The Intellectual Styles Questionnaire (ISQ) has 130 items measuring 13 thinking styles, including the legislative, executive, monarchic, conservative, liberal, global, and local styles specified in the investment approach. A sample item measuring the global style is: "When working on a project, I care more about its general impact than about the details of it." Previous research on the ISQ has also shown adequate scale reliability and construct validity (Martin 1988). The MBTI provides convergent validity with its intuitive-sensing style dimension, which is related to the investment framework's conception of styles.

A wide range of personality characteristics was measured by the Adjective Check List (ACL) (Gough and Heilbrun 1983) and the Personality Research Form (PRF), Form E (Jackson 1984). The ACL provides a list of adjectives that the subject may check as self-descriptors. The PRF uses brief statements of behaviors that the subject may find indicative. These instruments provide converging measures for the personality resource.

Motivation was assessed by a motivational questionnaire composed for this study and the Creative Motivation Scale (Torrance in press). The 50-item motivational questionnaire was constructed on the basis of previous experimental work (see Amabile 1985); subjects used a 7-point scale to rate how well domain-specific statements like "I would write a short story to challenge myself" described them. The "intrinsic" motivations of relaxation, self-expression, gaining insights, enjoying order in a product, personal challenge, and enjoying a sense of accomplishment and "extrinsic" motivations of money, impressing others, fulfilling external expectations, and obtaining a future job were assessed across artistic, literary, advertising, scientific, and general life domains. Items were standardized and used to form intrinsic (6 items), extrinsic (4 items), and comprehensive motivation scales (10 items) for each of the domains (15 scales in total). The scales showed high inter-item reliability with a median alpha of .80. The Creative Motivation Scale (Torrance in press) contains 28 true-false behavioral statements regarding intrinsic motivation and other creativity-relevant motivations. The Creative Motivation Scale is included for comparative purposes.

Subjects completed the creativity tasks and resource measures during the course of three 2⅓-hour sessions. The sessions occurred, on average, two days apart. The first session began with the drawing, writing, advertising, and scientific tasks, which were presented in counterbalanced orders across subjects. Each task involved the selection of a topic from a list of possible topics and the creation of a product. Subjects worked individually and were encouraged to "be imaginative" and to "have fun." They worked on the drawing and writing tasks for 20 minutes each and the advertising and scientific tasks for 10 minutes each. After completion of these four tasks, the Intellectual Styles Questionnaire, ACL, and Stroop color-word interference test were administered. In the second session, each subject received the drawing, writing, advertising, and scientific tasks in a new sequence. This time, however, subjects chose a new topic from each task list and then proceeded. Following these tasks, subjects completed the knowledge questionnaire, Torrance's Creative Motivation Scale, the motivational questionnaire, the Myers-Briggs Type Indicator, the letter series test, and the Culture Fair Test of g. The third session consisted of the Coping with Novelty test and the Personality Research Form. In all sessions, subjects occasionally shared the experimental testing room.

Our creativity rating procedure was modeled on Amabile's (1983) consensual assessment technique, with the exception that peer judges were used. Peers, rather than experts, were chosen to be raters because peers are the most likely audience for laypersons' work, and peers typically evaluate each others' work. Our peer raters worked individually and were asked to use their own definition of creativity. They judged each product on a scale of 1 (low creativity) to 7 (high creativity). The need for raters to judge products that varied on topic choice made the rating task more difficult than if all products were on the same topic. However, the presence of multiple topics in a set of products to be judged is characteristic of many, if not most, real-world judgment situations, and interjudge reliabilities were high. Raters reported that they judged the products against each other and used some external standards as well. Following the creativity ratings, a single random selection of 24 pieces from each product set was presented for further rating. The subject of products from each domain was rated for novelty, aptness to the topic chose, aesthetic value, integration of disparate elements, technical skill, and perceived effort employed by the creator.

Results and Discussion

Aspects of Creative Performance

Descriptive statistics. The creativity score for each product was the mean creativity rating given by 15 raters. The mean creativity ratings for the eight products generated by each subject (two drawings, two writings, two advertisements, two scientific solutions) were all close to the 4.0 midpoint of the rating scale (X = 3.68–4.22), demonstrating that neither a ceiling nor a floor effect occurred. Standard deviations were slightly less than one point on the rating scale (SD = .78–.91). For each subject, a composite creativity score was generated for each domain by averaging the two products from the domain.[2] These scores are referred to simply as the "drawing," "writing," "advertising," and "scientific" creativity scores. The mean creativity score across all four domains is termed the 'overall" creativity score.

The interjudge reliabilities (alpha coefficients) of the ratings for the various domains ranged from .81 to .89, demonstrating high interjudge consistency (Amabile 1982). For the overall creativity score, the mean interjudge correlation was .43, and the reliability was .92. We examined raters' implicit criteria for creativity by gathering additional ratings on a subset of 24 products from each task domain. Each product was characterized by a creativity rating and ratings on the dimensions of novelty, aptness, aesthetic value, integration of disparate elements, technical goodness, and effort exhibited. In general, the specialized ratings correlated significantly with creative performance ratings and with each other. Of primary interest, creativity ratings correlated .65 ($p<.001$) with novelty ratings, .49 ($p<.001$) with aptness ratings, and .57 ($p<.001$) with technical goodness ratings. Novelty ratings were relatively independent (r = .09, n.s.) of aptness ratings and correlated .37 ($p<.001$) with technical goodness.

Based on theoretical definitions and previous research (Amabile 1982), a hierarchical forward regression was performed on the raters' data. Novelty and aptness ratings were entered first as predictors of creativity ratings. With novelty (β = .62, $p<.001$) and aptness (β = .43, $p<.001$) in the model, 61 percent of the variance in creativity ratings was explained ($F(2,93)$ = 73.21, MSe = .25, $p<.001$). Integration ratings then entered as a third significant predictor variable. This final model explained 70 percent of the variance using novelty (β = .40, $p<.001$), aptness (β = .15, $p<.05$), and integration (β = .47, $p<.001$) ($F(3.92)$ = 71.67, MSe = .19, $p<.001$). Separate regressions by domain supported the generalizability of the overall analysis to writing, advertising, and scientific products. In the drawing-product analysis, aesthetic value rather than integration entered as a third significant predictor of creativity ratings.

Performance across time. How stable was creative performance? A repeated-measures analysis of variance across time and domain showed no significant mean differences for the creativity of work produced during sessions 1 and 2. Correlations across time suggest moderate stability. The correlations between the products within each domain were .37 ($p<.05$) for drawing 1 with drawing 2, .63 ($p<.001$) for writings, .65 ($p<.001$) for advertisements, .52 ($p<.001$) for science, and .67 ($p<.001$) for overall creative performance between sessions. While all of these correlations across time are significant, some fluctuations in creative performance obviously occur. We believe that these fluctuations are inherent to creativity and derive from day-to-day changes in the resources that lead to creative performance. The drawing, writing, advertising, and science creativity scores used throughout this study provide a more stable estimate of creative performance than individual products because the domain scores represent the mean performance on two occasions.

Performance across domains. There was a significant difference in rated creativity across the four domains ($F(3,138) = 5.51$, $MSe = .69$, $p <.01$). The mean creativity ratings for the drawings were 4.13, for the writings 4.14, for the advertisements 3.91, and for the scientific products 3.71. A contrast showed that the science domain was significantly lower than the drawing and writing domains. These mean differences may reflect subjects' differential familiarity with the domains.

Addressing the issue of domain specificity of creative performance, table 12.1 presents the correlations across the domains. These ranged

Table 12.1
Correlations across Creative Performance Domains ($N = 48$)

| | Creative Performance Domain | | | |
	Drawing	Writing	Advertising	Science
Drawing	.85	.32*	.31*	.23
Writing		.89	.41**	.62***
Advertising			.81	.44**
Science				.87

Note: The diagonal elements give the alpha coefficient interrater reliabilities.
* $p < .05$.
** $p < .01$.
***$p < .001$.

from .23 (n.s.) to .62 ($p<.001$), with a median correlation of .37 ($p<.01$). The results suggest that creativity is moderately domain specific; however, there is more overlap between domains than would be expected just by chance. Others, such as Runco (1987) who studied children's self-reported creative achievements across several domains, also find that creativity is somewhat but not completely domain specific. This balance makes sense within our investment approach because some resources, such as intellectual processes, may apply widely across domains (leading to generalized creativity), but other resources, such as the personality trait of risk taking, may be more domain specific, especially for advanced levels of creative work (Sternberg and Lubart 1993).

Person-Centered Resources and Creative Performance

Intellectual processes. The Culture Fair Test of g (IQ), series completion test, and Coping with Novelty test all correlated strongly with creative performance ($r = .41$ to $r = .68$, $p<.001$). These tests require selective encoding, comparison, and combination processes; the results therefore provide convergent evidence for the importance of the insight skills specified in the intellectual processes resource. The Stroop color-word test involved selective encoding alone and showed somewhat lower correlations with creative performance ($r = .22$, n.s. to $r = .35$, $p<.05$). For subsequent confluence analysis, an overall intellectual-process measure was created by linearly combining standardized scores for all the individual tests. The correlations of this combined measure with creative performance ranged from .50 ($p<.001$) to .61 ($p<.001$) across domains (table 12.2).

In a separate study, a second sample of 44 New Haven subjects also completed the drawing and writing creativity tasks, the Culture Fair Test of g, the Extended Range Vocabulary Test, and other measures. The Culture Fair Test of g again correlated significantly with creative performance in drawing ($r = .35$, $p<.05$) and writing ($r = .36$, $p<.05$). These correlations were slightly lower but not significantly different ($z < 1$) from those observed in this study. Demonstrating discriminant validity, the Extended Range Vocabulary test, a measure of crystallized intelligence, showed nonsignificant correlations with creative performance ($r = -.08$, n.s. for drawing; $r = .13$, n.s. for writing). Perhaps the low correlations ($-.05$ to $+.31$) previously observed between intelligence and creativity (Barron and Harrington 1981) were due to the use of intelligence measures that emphasized crystallized intelligence and did not fully tap relevant processing abilities (see Horn 1976 for an alternate view). Historically, there have also been speculations that

Table 12.2
Correlations of Resources with Rated Creative Performance ($N = 48$)

Resource	Creative Performance Domain				
	Drawing	Writing	Advertising	Science	Overall
Intellectual processes	.51***	.59***	.50***	.61***	.75***
Knowledge	.35*	.37**	.33*	.41**	.49***
Intellectual styles	−.08	−.28	−.51***	−.28	−.39**
Personality	.25	.25	.26	.32*	.36*
Motivation[a]	.28	.34*	.61***	.34*	.53***
Combined resources[b]	.61**	.63***	.73***	.66***	.83***

a. Expressed as a combined score containing negative linear and negative quadratic (inverted-U) trends.
b. The regression-based multiple correlation of the five resources with creative performance.
* $p < .05$.
** $p < .01$.
***$p < .001$.

increases in intellectual ability to a certain level (IQ < 120) benefit creative performance, whereas increases in intellectual skill beyond the threshold show no consistent effect on creative performance (Golann 1963; Meer and Stein 1955; Schubert 1973). Our data did not show any significant threshold or asymptotic effects for the intellectual measures employed with either of our samples (see Cohen and Cohen 1983 for statistical methods used).

Taken together, we believe that the current results support a conceptualization of the intellectual resource for creativity that centers on insight abilities. However, insight processes do not necessarily form the complete set of intellectual skills for creativity. Indeed, an ability to alternate strategically between divergent and convergent modes of thinking during a project and the judicious use of evaluation to monitor one's progress on a task may be relevant high-level skills (Sternberg and Lubart 1993). In their recent work on creative cognition, Finke, Ward, and Smith (1992) have proposed other sets of cognitive skills that are involved in the generation of preinventive forms and then the exploration of these ideas. Generative processes include association of items in memory, synthesis and transformation of ideas, and analogical transfer. Exploratory processes include searching for useful attributes, shifting contexts when interpreting preinventive forms, and searching for limitations. Some of these processes, such as synthesis, analogical transfer, and searching for limitations, overlap with those that we highlight in the investment approach. The diverse set of intellectual processes mentioned in the creative cognition approach, the investment approach, and other approaches will need to be tested more completely in future work.

Knowledge. Subjects reported three types of information: (1) educational level achieved; (2) perceived knowledge about drawing, writing, advertising design, and scientific problem solving; and (3) the frequency of domain-related activities. The frequency data provided a measure of familiarity for each of the task domains.

Subjects' years of education showed positive correlations of approximately .30 ($p < .05$) for the domains of writing, advertising, and science. Self-reported knowledge level in a domain was unrelated to creative performance, with the exception of advertising knowledge, which correlated .35 ($p < .05$) with creative performance on the advertising task. In contrast to self-reported knowledge level, the frequency-familiarity measures showed some strong positive relationships to creative performance. Frequency of writing, for example, correlated .45 ($p < .01$) with writing performance. Writing frequency also correlated with advertising performance ($r = .33$, $p < .05$). This domain generality was expected because knowledge is often relevant to more than one specific task. In the scientific domain, social problem-solving frequency ($r = .51$, $p < .001$) was more important than formal scientific activity levels ($r = .08$, n.s.). Given that the scientific problems used in this study involved social rather than laboratory settings, the stronger correlation with social problem solving was reasonable.

An overall knowledge score was formed from a composite of education, knowledge level, and frequency reports. This overall score showed moderate correlations to creative performance (table 12.2) and is used in the analysis for a confluence of resources. Four domain-specific knowledge scores were also analyzed. The pattern of results for each domain when using domain-specific versus overall scores was very similar. We view the overall knowledge score as more useful, however, because there is relevance and value of knowledge from outside domains (e.g., writing and drawing) to a target domain (e.g., advertising).

Intellectual styles. For overall creative performance, a higher level of creativity was associated with lower levels on the executive ($r = -.35$, $p < .05$) conservative ($r = -.40$, $p < .01$), and monarchic styles ($r = -.28$, $p < .10$). This correlational pattern was consistent across task domains and is theoretically meaningful; a preference for conservative, rule-following behavior is antithetical to creativity. The correlations for the liberal and local styles with creative performance were in the predicted direction but did not reach significance. The legislative

($r = -.02$, n.s.) and global styles ($r = -.35$, $p < .05$) did not relate to creative performance as predicted. For purposes of testing the role of the intellectual-styles resource in the confluence analyses, a combined score was created using executive, conservative, and monarchic styles. As expected, this combined score for the intellectual-styles resource shows negative correlations with creative performance and negative correlations with the other resources (tables 12.2 and 12.3).

For the Myers-Briggs questionnaire, the only significant correlation involved the sensing-intuition style. Sensing types tend to be reality oriented, to prefer rules, and to emphasize facts and precision. Intuitive types are the opposite. They concentrate on inferences, meanings, and hidden patterns. A preference for an intuitive style as opposed to the sensing style was significantly correlated with creative performance in the writing ($r = .33$, $p < .05$), advertising ($r = .34$, $p < .05$), and overall domains ($r = .39$, $p < .05$). This result corresponds to previous studies on the relationship of the Myers-Briggs inventory to creative performance (Myers and McCaulley 1985). Furthermore, the negative role of the sensing type offers convergent evidence for the negative roles that Sternberg's executive and conservative styles displayed.

In summary, the original conceptualization of the intellectual-style resource was partially supported. Perhaps the executive, conservative, and monarchic styles are detrimental to creativity in general, while the global and legislative styles are beneficial to creativity only when the problem-finding phase of creative work is emphasized.

Personality. The five personality dimensions hypothesized as relevant to creativity are tolerance of ambiguity, perseverance, desire to grow,

Table 12.3
Intercorrelations of Resources ($N = 48$)

	IP	K	IS	P	M
Intellectual processes (IP)	—	.25	−.44**	.22	.57***
Knowledge (K)		—	−.32*	.68***	.09
Intellectual styles (IS)			—	−.51**	−.32*
Personality (P)				—	.18
Motivation (M)[a]					—

a. Expressed as a combined score containing negative linear and negative quadratic (inverted-U) trends.
* $p < .05$.
** $p < .01$.
*** $p < .001$.

willingness to take risk, and individuality with a supporting courage of one's convictions. Based on the content of the ACL and PRF scales, relevant scores from the Personality Research Form and the Adjective Check List were standardized and then combined to form five new, reliable theory-based scales.[3] An overall personality resource measure was also formed by linear combination of the five theoretically based scales.

The correlations between personality dimensions and creative performance were relatively consistent across task domains. Tolerance of ambiguity correlated .19 (n.s.) with overall creative performance, willingness to take risk correlated .25 ($p<.10$), individuality correlated .26 ($p<.10$), and desire to grow correlated .39 ($p<.01$). Due, perhaps to the short-term nature of our study, perseverance was unrelated to creativity on our tasks. In general, the influence of personality on a project probably accrues over time, leading correlations of the personality resource with creative performance during a brief task to underestimate the influence of the resource (Abelson 1985). The combined personality resource measure correlated .25 ($p<.10$) with drawing creativity, .25 ($p<.10$) with writing creativity, .26 ($p<.10$) with advertising creativity, .32 ($p<.05$) with scientific creativity, and .36 ($p<.05$) with overall creative performance.

Motivation. The self-report motivational questionnaire assessed a variety of intrinsic and extrinsic motivators in the drawing, writing, advertising, scientific, and general-life domains. The mean response on the 7-point scale for the strength of each motivator was approximately 4.0, with a standard deviation of approximately 2 points. Intrinsic, extrinsic, and comprehensive motivation scales for the drawing, writing, advertising, and science domains showed a pattern of significant positive correlations with the general-life scales. For the sample, self-reported motivation in the specific domains studied does not appear to be highly differentiated from self-reported motivation for activities in general. Furthermore, the domain-specific scores did not provide independent contributions beyond the general-life motivation scores in any of the analyses to be reported. Results involving intrinsic, extrinsic, and comprehensive general-life motivation scales, therefore, are our focus.

The intrinsic, extrinsic, or comprehensive motivation scales did not show any significant linear relation to creative performance. However, as predicted, meaningful inverted-U relationships did occur; there was an optimal level for general motivation (comprehensive scale) beyond which additional motivation was negatively related to creative performance. Curvilinear trends were assessed by statistical tests following

Cohen and Cohen's (1983) procedures. Hierarchical regressions showed a significant negative quadratic (inverted-U) trend for the writing, advertising, science, and overall creative performance analyses.[4] In the drawing domain, the quadratic trend was negative but nonsignificant. The incremental variance (ΔR^2) explained by the quadratic motivation trend in each domain was .04 (n.s.) for drawing, .15 ($p<.01$) for writing, .40 ($p<.001$) for advertising, .11 ($p<.05$) for science, and .28 ($p<.001$) for the overall analysis.

Further supporting the investment framework's conception of the motivational resource, both intrinsic (relaxation, self-expression, gaining insights, enjoying order in a product, personal challenge, and enjoying a sense of accomplishment) and extrinsic motivation scales (earn money, desire to impress others, fulfill external expectations, and obtain a future job) showed significant inverted-U relationships to overall creativity. This result suggests that different types of motivators (intrinsic, extrinsic) are not themselves inherently good or bad for creative work. Rather, there appears to be an optimal level of motivation, beyond which a person might become too goal focused to concentrate on the creative work itself.

In terms of the confluence analyses, a combined score containing negative linear and negative quadratic (inverted-U) trends was used to represent the motivational resource (table 12.2); the linear and quadratic terms from the comprehensive, general-life motivation scale were standardized first and then given equal weight in the new combination score. On this new motivation-resource score, subjects with intermediate levels of motivation receive high scores and subjects with very low or very high levels of motivation receive low scores. Thus, scores on the new motivation-resource variable are expected to correlate in a positive, *linear* fashion with creative performance; the motivational resource exhibited these correlations with creative performance (table 12.2).

The Creative Motivation Scale (Torrance in press), another measure of intrinsic motivation used in this study, correlated .38 ($p <.01$) with the intrinsic motivation score in the general-life domain, $-.06$ (n.s.) with the extrinsic motivation score, and .23 (n.s.) with the comprehensive motivation score. These results offer some validation for the intrinsic items on the motivation questionnaire constructed for this study. The Creative Motivation Scale, however, showed no significant linear or quadratic relationships with creative performance. Examination of the Creative Motivation Scale suggests that several items measure personality characteristics, such as perseverance, curiosity, and willingness to grow. The heterogeneity of the item content probably affected the scale's correlations with creative performance and our own motivation measure. In general, regarding the motivation results, our findings contrast with Amabile's (1983) findings, which suggest a positive, linear relationship between intrinsic motivation and creativity. The issue of task-focused and goal-focused motivation for creativity needs to be studied further, and the current findings need to be replicated.

A developmental trend. An influence of the social environment may have occurred through the raters: the evaluative component of the environment. In the advertising domain, age was positively related to creative performance through 30 years, at which point the relationship turned negative. A hierarchical regression for the advertising domain showed that there was a nonsignificant linear trend ($F<1$), and a significant quadratic trend ($F(2,45) = 3.30$, $MSe = .48$, $p<.05$, $R^2 = .13$). These trends might have been the result of generational differences in creativity standards; as the producer moves away in age from the rater, the two may differ increasingly on their standards for novelty and creativity. For example, a 65-year-old subject might have produced an advertisement that she considered creative; a 30-year-old rater might have regarded this product as outdated. In fact, the work judged as most creative was produced by subjects who were approximately ten years younger than the average age of the raters.

The generational-differences explanation for the negative age trends in the advertising domain fits with the notion that within certain fields, the type of work that is considered creative changes rapidly. For example, the characteristics of creative work in the literary domain may shift more slowly than the views of creative work in advertising. An alternative explanation of the inverted-U age effects through age decrements in intellectual processes ($r = -.17$, n.s.), a more conservative and executive style ($r = .14$, n.s.), less tolerance of ambiguity ($r = -.46$, $p<.001$), or less willingness to take risks ($r = -.47$, $p <.001$) seems less plausible because of the domain specificity of the age results. We are investigating these age effects further.

Testing the Confluence of Resources   The investment approach predicts that high levels of creativity emerge from an interactive combination of the resources. The composite scores created for each resource were used as predictors for creative performance. Zero-order correlations of each predictor with the creativity criterion variables are presented in table 12.2. In general, intellectual processes and then knowledge and motivation show the highest correlations. Intellectual styles and personality show some significant relationships to creative performance, but there is more variability across domains.

The intercorrelations of the resource variables ranged in absolute value from .09 (n.s.) to .68 ($p<.001$) (table 12.3). All the correlations between resources were positive except for correlations with the intellectual-styles resource, which were negative. The intercorrelations support the idea of a "creativity syndrome"; the determinants of creativity seem to co-occur to a moderate extent (Mumford and Gustafson 1988).

Multiple regressions of creative performance on the five measured resources provide evidence that the resources, although related, make some independent (unique) contributions to creative performance. Forward selection, backward selection, and full regression procedures all lead to virtually identical results; the results for the full regression procedure are discussed.

In the drawing domain model, only the intellectual processes resource accounted for a significant portion of unique variability ($\beta = .55, p<.01$) ($F(5,42) = 4.96, MSe = .36, p<.01, R^2 = .37$). For the writing domain, intellectual processes again bore a strong relationship to performance ($\beta = .53, p<.01$). Knowledge showed a weight of .36 ($p<.05$). We also found a significant linear interaction of intellectual processes and knowledge for the writing domain ($\beta = .29, p<.05$). This interaction showed that a high level of both resources was especially beneficial. Inclusion of the interaction term increased the writing variance explained from .40 for the 5-resource equation to .48 ($F (6,41) = 6.33$, $MSe = .39, p<.001$).

The results for the advertising domain suggest that the resources may receive domain-specific emphases. The resources with significant weights in the advertising model were motivation ($\beta = .49, p<.001$), intellectual styles ($\beta = -.35, p<.05$), and knowledge ($\beta = .32, p<.05$) ($F (5, 42) = 9.72, MSe = .27, p<.001, R^2 = .53$). The negative beta weight for intellectual styles indicates that as the proclivity toward executive, conservative, and monarchic styles increased, creative performance decreased.

The science domain results and overall (multiple domain) performance analyses return us to the relevance of the intellectual processes resource in terms of unique predictors. For science, the intellectual resource had a significant regression weight ($\beta = .56, p<.001$), and the knowledge resource parameter ($\beta = .24$) was marginal ($F (5,42) = 6.69, MSe = .33, p<.001, R^2 = .44$). For overall performance, intellectual processes ($\beta = .57, p<.001$) and knowledge ($\beta = .36, p<.001$) were significant, and motivation showed a marginally significant parameter ($\beta = .19, p<.10$) ($F (5,42) = 18.41, MSe = .11, p<.001, R^2 = .69$). In closing this section on the confluence results, we note that all of the regression results should be viewed as tentative and remain to be replicated.

Study 2: Cognitive Risk Taking and Creative Performance

We conducted a second study to focus on the notion of buying low and taking risks for creative performance. The financial market illustrates the rules of risk taking in a monetary domain. Investment in a long-standing company with a record of slow growth involves less risk than investment in a new company that promises fast growth. The new company is unproved, and although the opportunity for larger profits exists, there is also increased uncertainty that the profit will materialize. Investors may choose to "buy low" and risk their money on the unproved company, hoping for the big payoff, or to "buy high," choose an established firm, and be relatively sure of small profits.

Analogous to the financial world, most endeavors offer more and less risky alternatives; in any domain, buying low involves taking risks. For creative work, the risks tend to be intellectual ones (which carry social and monetary ramifications). An artist, for example, may choose between several projects. Within each project, there may be further options for topics, topic development, materials, and style. Typically, the choices at each step fall into two risk-payoff options. One option can be labeled low risk–low payoff because a high probability of success is usually associated with following a well-worn problem-solving path. The other option, high risk–high payoff, offers a chance of great success, but the path is treacherous and less traveled.

Willingness to take risk, a personality trait, guides the problem-solving route that a person will pursue. Risk taking influences whether cognitive abilities, such as insight processes, will be applicable during problem solving or unnecessary because a routine path is being pursued. Thus risk taking can be viewed as one of the keys to creative performance because it opens opportunities for creativity-relevant cognitive resources to be utilized.

In a variety of contexts (general decision making, business, and school), studies show that people tend to avoid risks, preferring the low risk–low payoff option (Clifford 1988; Dreman 1977; Kahneman and Tversky 1982; MacCrimmon and Wehrung 1985), or, put another way, a bird in hand is worth two in the bush. The investment approach suggests that this general aversion to risk partially accounts for the infrequency of creative performance. Although buying low and taking risk does not guarantee that creative performance will occur, buying high basically guarantees that it will not.

Two studies offer preliminary support of the risk taking–creative performance link. Eisenman (1987) presented 200 adult subjects with a contest situation and found that selection of the high risk–high payoff option was related to high performance on both a measure of creative attitudes and a divergent thinking test ($r = .34$ to $r = .37$, $p<.01$). Glover (1977) induced risk taking in college students through group discussions of risky decision-making situations. Compared with control subjects, the risk-induced subjects showed higher originality and flexibility scores on the Torrance Tests of Creative Thinking ($p<.01$). Our study builds on this work and uses multiple assessments or risk-payoff preferences and multiple domains of creative performance.

Method
Forty-four subjects from the New Haven area (22 males, 22 females) with an average age of 32.37 years ($SD = 13.13$, range, 18–67) completed four kinds of tasks: (1) creativity tasks, (2) cognitive tests of intellectual ability, (3) risk-taking contests, and (4) self-report measures of risk taking, personality, and biographical information.

For creativity measures, drawing and writing tasks from our first study were used. The cognitive tests consisted of the Cattell Culture Fair Test of g, Scale 3, Form A (Cattell and Cattell 1963), for fluid intelligence and the Extended Range Vocabulary Test, Scale V-3 (French, Ekstrom, and Price 1963) for crystallized intelligence.

Two contests provided behavioral measures of risk taking. Subjects were given the opportunity to enter their drawing in one contest and their short story in another contest. Each contest established two pools of work from which the best entries would be selected. One pool was described as high risk and high payoff. In this pool, there was one winner of $25. The other pool involved lower risk and lower payoff, with five winners of $10 each. The instructions allowed subjects to enter one pool for the drawing contest and a different pool for the writing contest if they desired. Based on our judges' ratings, prizes were awarded at the conclusion of the study.

The self-report questionnaires measured propensity toward risk taking in a very different way. Three choice-dilemma questionnaires assessed risk taking in the drawing, writing, and general-life domains. The general-life questionnaire was an updated version of Kogan and Wallach's (1964) original instrument; gender-specific language and some factual details were revised. The drawing and writing questionnaires were constructed for this study as domain-specific forms of Kogan and Wallach's questionnaire.

Each questionnaire contained 12 hypothetical situations that subjects were asked to imagine themselves in. Each scenario presented a choice between two courses of action: a high risk, potentially high-payoff alternative, and a low risk, low-payoff alternative. Subjects selected the minimum odds of success that they would require before pursuing the high-risk option. A sample scenario from the drawing-domain questionnaire follows:

> You are a potter, making a large vase to be displayed at a pottery craft show. You hope to receive recognition in the pottery guild's magazine that will be doing a feature story on the show. You have two ideas for a vase. Idea A would us a potter's wheel to form a vase with smooth contours that are pleasing to look at. You know that several other potters at the show use the same method but you feel confident that you will receive a little recognition for technical skill in your vase. Idea B would use a hand coil method in which you roll clay into strips and piece the strips together. This method yields an unusual primitive vase. The magazine editors may feature your coil vase because of its uniqueness or they may not even mention it because it could be seen as too far out of the mainstream. Listed below are several probabilities or odds that the coil vase (idea B) will turn out successfully. Please check the lowest probability that you would consider acceptable to make it worthwhile to pursue the coil vase.

The possible odds for success were 1 in 10, 3 in 10, 5 in 10, 7 in 10, or 9 in 10. A subject could also refuse the risk alternative "no matter what the probabilities" and then would receive a score of 10 out of 10 for that scenario. The questionnaire reliabilities were adequate (.74–.78). The scores are reflected (multiplied by −1) to maintain consistency with other risk measures. High (reflected) scores on these choice-dilemma questionnaires therefore indicate risk taking.

Risk taking was further assessed with items on the biographical questionnaire. Subjects used a 7-point scale to describe their risk tendencies in drawing and writing for the overall task, topic selection, topic development, and materials and style used. Subjects were also asked if they would describe themselves as a high or low risk taker in the drawing and writing domains.

Another portion of the biographical questionnaire provided a brief assessment of educational history, knowledge level, activities and interests in the domains studied, and personality-motivational tendencies. The Adjective Check List (Gough and Heilbrun 1983) also measured personality characteristics. On the final portion of the biographical questionnaire, subjects judged the creativity of their own products using 7-point response scales.

Subjects were tested individually during a 3-hour session. The drawing and writing tasks were administered first, followed by the choice-dilemma questionnaires, the Adjective Check List, biographical questionnaire, Cattell Culture Fair Test of g, and Extended Range Vocabulary Test. Subjects chose a contest group in which to enter their work either at the start of the session before they worked on the creativity tasks or at the very end, after finishing the creativity tasks. We therefore manipulated the timing of the contest decision.

A separate group of 15 New Haven subjects (8 males, 7 females; X age $= 31,73$, $SD = 6.83$, range, 22–45) judged the creativity of the drawing and writing work, with good interrater reliability.

Results and Discussion

Aspects of Cognitive Risk Taking   In accord with previous research, people were relatively risk avoidant. In the drawing contest, 32 of the subjects chose the low risk–low payoff option, in contrast to 12 who chose the high risk–high payoff alternative. In the writing contest, 29 subjects selected the low risk and 15 selected the high risk. In both cases, the bias toward lower risk was significant ($p < .05$). On the hypothetical scenario measures, subjects were slightly risk averse. For each questionnaire where low scores (-120) indicate risk aversion, the means scores were -64.14 ($SD = 19.85$) for drawing scenarios, -60.61 ($SD = 19.14$) for writing scenarios, and -71.77 ($SD = 19.19$) for general-life scenarios. Subjects also described themselves as somewhat risk averse on the self-report items. On a 7-point scale with low scores indicating risk aversion, the mean response was 3.06 ($SD = 1.77$) for the drawing domain and 3.64 ($SD = 1.78$) for the writing domain.

The tests of intelligence as well as years of education were essentially unrelated to risk taking. However, self-reported levels of knowledge for drawing and writing correlated with self-reported risk taking in the respective domains (drawing: $r = .48$, $p < .01$; writing: $r = .33$, $p < .05$). Similarly, the frequency with which a subject engaged in drawing or writing activities and liked these activities correlated moderately with domain-specific risk taking on contest, hypothetical scenario, and self-report measures (median $r = .31$, $p < .05$). Scores on the self-confidence, desire for change, and the creative personality scales from the Adjective Check List were moderately related to risk taking on the hypothetical scenario measures.

We varied whether subjects had to choose their contest option (high or low risk) before beginning their drawings and short stories or after finishing them. The manipulation had no measurable effect on the level of risk taking or the relationship between risk taking and creative performance. This null finding suggests that risk taking does not depend especially on the producer's looking at the final product and judging whether it is good enough to enter into a high-risk contest. We suggest that risk taking is a personality trait that develops and is influenced by prior experiences in a domain. Early, successful experiences increase self-confidence and the tendency for risk taking. The results that link creative performance with risk taking in hypothetical scenarios (different from our creative performance tasks) further support the idea that risk taking is not simply a pragmatic choice once a product has been completed but rather a pervasive tendency that can influence each step of problem solving.

Risk Taking and Creative Performance   The main question of interest is whether higher levels of risk taking are associated with higher levels of creative performance. For the drawing contest, subjects choosing the high risk–high payoff option showed a mean creativity score of 4.21 ($SD = .99$), whereas subjects choosing the low risk–low payoff option shoed a mean score of 3.90 ($SD = .75$). Although this result did not reach significance, a follow-up analysis using creativity ratings from three graduate student judges with artistic background showed stronger results. The high risk group received a mean creativity score of 4.36 ($SD = 1.98$), and the low-risk group's mean score was 2.86 ($SD = 1.57$), $t(42) = 2.62$, $p<.05$). The "artistic" judges also showed high reliability (alpha $= .83$).

The scenario-based measures of risk taking supported a connection between risk taking and creativity. Risk taking on the drawing scenarios correlated significantly with drawing creativity ($r = .39$, $p<.01$). A multiple regression of the drawing, writing, and general-life scenario scores on creative performance in the drawing task tested for domain specificity between risk taking and creativity ($F(3,40) = 3.91$, $MSe = .56$, $p<.05$, $R^2 = .23$). The drawing scenario measure was the best predictor ($\beta = .54$, $p<.05$). The general-life scenario measure acted as a suppressor effect, enhancing the domain-specific nature of the drawing risk measure ($\beta = -.38$, $p<.06$). Further supporting domain specificity, the writing scenario measure showed a nonsignificant weight in the equation.

In contrast to the situational scenario and behavioral contest measures of risk, self-report items showed little relationship to creative performance. Only one item that assessed overall risk taking on drawings related to creative performance ($r = .34$, $p<.05$).

In summary, we found some support for the hypothesized link between risk taking and creative performance in the drawing domain. The drawing scenario measure of risk taking showed this relationship most clearly. In the writing domain, no significant results were obtained. However, examination of the writings produced by subjects who scored in the top 20 percent and bottom 20 percent on the writing risk scenario measure suggested an interesting trend: we believed the stories of the high risk takers to be more unconventional than those of the low risk takers. We had three additional peer judges rate unconventionality and found a significant difference in the ratings for high-risk takers ($X = 4.00$, $SD = .75$) versus low-risk takers ($X = 3.11$, $SD = .85$), $t(16) = 2.36$, $p<.05$).

An investigation of the stories suggests that the unconventional stories did not receive high creativity ratings, on average, because of the controversial issues with which the stories dealt. For example, one high-risk-taking subject chose "It's Moving Backward" as a title and offered a negative view of American politics. In this case, as well as others, the risk did not pay off with respect to the judges. Perhaps our judges had a narrower view of what constitutes a creative short story compared to a creative drawing, so the range of risk taking that could lead to an acceptable product was limited.

Conclusions

The current results provide initial support for the investment approach but also suggest revisions and areas for further research. The basic conceptualization of the intellectual processes, knowledge, and personality resource was supported by the results; these results also support and extend earlier theoretical and empirical work (Amabile 1983; MacKinnon 1962, 1965; McClelland 1956). The intellectual styles resource did not operate completely as expected. Executive, conservative, and monarchic styles were negatively related to creative performance, but the legislative and global styles did not promote creative work. These findings may be due to the semistructured nature of our creativity assessments. In any case, the intellectual styles resource requires further study and possible revision. Finally, the motivational resource showed an inverted-U relationship to creative performance, which is consistent with our task-focused versus goal-focused distinction.

In terms of the relative importance and confluence of resources, several promising results were also obtained. First, creative performance was most related to the intellectual processes resource. This result is sensible because the creative performance measures involved short-term, timed tasks. We noted earlier that certain resources such as personality may show their importance in long-term projects rather than short-term tasks. Second, regression analyses showed significant involvements for multiple resources. For example, the analysis of overall creative performance showed that intellectual processes, knowledge, and motivation accounted for unique portions of variance. Third, the creative performance measures and the confluence analyses addressed the issue of domain specificity. For example, the motivation and intellectual styles resources received emphasis in the advertising domain. And an interaction between intellectual processes and knowledge was observed as specific to the writing domain. Together, these results demonstrate the utility of a multivariate approach to creative performance.

At a general level, the results are congruent with many recent proposals that suggest the need for a convergence of cognitive and conative elements for creativity (Amabile 1983; Arieti 1976; Barron 1988; Csikszentmihalyi 1988; Feldman 1988; Gardner 1988; Gruber 1981; Mumford and Gustafson 1988; Simonton 1988). For example, Amabile (1983) describes creativity as a result of domain-relevant skills (knowledge and abilities), creativity-relevant skills (styles, personality traits, and idea-generation heuristics), and motivation (primarily intrinsic motivation). High levels of these components must co-occur in an appropriate environment to yield high levels of creative performance. Portions of the results noted in this chapter can be seen as supportive of both Amabile's model and the investment approach.

At this time a rigorous test between various confluence theories of creativity is not possible for two reasons. First, confluence theories need to become more specific. We acknowledge that the investment approach must move toward greater specificity. The results reported here suggest that domain and task variables are important for determining the nature of a resource confluence for creativity. Second, studies need to test both competing theories' concepts of the resources for creativity and these theories' concepts of the confluence of resources. It is possible that empirical support for a specific resource confluence will depend on the specification of the resources involved.

Next, we can consider the investment concept of buying low and selling high. The results of the study on cognitive risk taking provide some support for the benefits of buying low, but we want to note that the test of the investment metaphor was limited. In general, the investment approach is part of an emerging economic perspective on creativity. Contributing to this perspective, Rubenson and Runco (1992) propose an account of societal levels of creativity using the concepts of supply and demand. They apply cost-benefit analysis to people's decisions to seek creativity training. Also, Walberg (1988) has emphasized society's need to develop "human capital," the "knowledge, skills, and talents" necessary for creative work.

The investment approach and the new economic perspective on creativity offer many avenues for research. The investment approach still remains to be tested over longer periods of time using significant work produced prior to the investigation, using more eminent samples, and using samples with broader distributions on the resources to test the confluence hypotheses better. Also, the measurement of the resources needs to be improved, the direct effects of the environment need to be assessed, and the relationship between risk taking and creative performance needs to be studied more completely.

Finally, the investment approach and the creative cognition approach can benefit by drawing connections between each other. For example, creative cognition research has attempted to analyze problem tasks and specify the particular generative processes, preinventive structures, and exploratory processes that are employed in each task. the investment approach needs to move toward this type of specific modeling. Also, the investment approach needs to be linked to a process model of creative problem solving. This process model may be a general one that covers problem solving in a wide range of domains, such as the generation-exploration model of Finke, Ward, and Smith (1992). Alternatively, domain-specific process models may be necessary. Within each task's process model, we would want to specify the points at which various intellectual processes are most active, when and how knowledge is utilized, and whether intellectual styles, personality, motivation, or environmental resources influence specific portions of the process or act in general ways. For example, insight processes and tolerance of ambiguity may be especially important during the initial conception of a project, whereas solution monitoring and perseverance may be most important in the later stages of a project.

Our work with the investment approach also suggests new directions for creative cognition research. First, work on creative cognition may consider how a general strategy, such as attempting to buy low and sell high, could pervade creative work and influence actions at each problem-solving step. Second, creative cognition research may consider the impact of noncognitive (personality, motivational, and environmental) variables on the effectiveness and use of cognitive processes. Third, creative cognition research may investigate whether beneficial interactions occur when certain generative processes are used together with particular exploratory processes or preinventive structures.

In conclusion, the results provide initial support for many aspects of the investment approach's person-centered resources for creativity: intellectual processes, knowledge, intellectual styles, personality, and motivation. The results also demonstrate the relative importance of cognitive resources, show beneficial effects from a partial confluence of the person-centered resources, and show a partial link between buying low and creative performance. We suggest that the investment approach offers a framework within which previous work can be integrated and the current results can be understood. The investment approach also offers a base from which future links can be developed to other multivariate approaches, other economic-based approaches, and work in the creative cognition approach.

Notes

This chapter was written while the first author was supported by a Jacob K. Javits Fellowship and a Yale University Graduate Fellowship. Research was further supported by the Javits Act Program (grant R206R00001) as administered by the Office of Educational Research and Improvement, U.S. Department of Education. Grantees undertaking such projects are encouraged to express freely their professional judgment. This chapter therefore does not necessarily represent positions or policies of the government, and no official endorsement should be inferred. We thank members of Robert Sternberg's research seminar, Mahzarin Banaji, Robert G. Crowder, J. Steven Reznick, and anonymous reviewers for helpful comments. We also thank Michael Sanders for his assistance.

1. The topics for each domain were: *Drawing*: a dream, a quark, hope, rage, pleasure, earth from an insect's point of view, contrast, tension, motion, beginning of time; *Writing*: Beyond the Edge, A Fifth Chance, Saved, Under the Table, Between the Lines, Not Enough Time, The Keyhole, The Octopus's Sneakers, 2983, It's Moving Backward; *Advertising*: double-pane windows, brussels sprouts, Internal Revenue Service (portray positive image), brook, iron, cufflinks, bowties, doorknobs, sugar substitute; *Science*: detecting whether aliens are living among us, determining if someone has been on the moon in the past month, devising a way for the SDI Star Wars system to destroy real missiles but avoid empty decoy missiles sent to overload the defense system.

2. One subject was missing a science product for time 2. This subject's scientific creativity score equaled the score for the first science project.

3. The theory-based personality scores were formed from standardized scores as follows: Tolerance of ambiguity = -1(PRF cognitive structure + PRF order + ACL order), reliability = .91; Perseverance = (PRF endurance + ACL endurance), reliability = .85; Desire to grow = (PRF change + PRF achievement + PRF sentience + PRF understanding + ACL change + ACL achievement), reliability = .82; Willingness to take risk = -1 (PRF harmavoidance + ACL self-control), reliability = .86; Individuality = (PRF autonomy + PRF dominance + ACL autonomy + ACL dominance + ACL self-confidence), reliability = .89. Reliability of the theory-based scales was computed following Nunnally (1967) and used established inter-item reliabilities for each of the ACL and PRF scales.

4. Full regressions containing linear and quadratic terms were used to follow up the hierarchical regression results (Cohen and Cohen 1983). Across domains, the linear and quadratic components had significant negative beta weights with approximately the same magnitude. The resultant equation ($y = -x - x^2$) produces an inverted-U

function with creative performance scores (y) increasing until a moderate level of motivation (x) is reached. After this point, higher levels of motivation lead to a rapid decline in creative performance.

References

Abelson, R. P. (1985). A variance explanation paradox: When a little is a lot. *Psychological Bulletin, 97*(1), 129–133.
Albert, R. S. (1983). Toward a behavioral definition of genius. In R. S. Albert (ed.), *Genius and eminence: The social psychology of creativity and exceptional achievement* (pp. 57–72). New York: Pergamon Press.
Amabile, T. M. (1982). Social psychology of creativity: A consensual assessment technique. *Journal of Personality and Social Psychology, 43*(5), 997–1013.
Amabile, T. M. (1983). *The social psychology of creativity.* New York: Springer-Verlag.
Amabile, T. M. (1985). Motivation and creativity: Effects of motivational orientation on creative writers. *Journal of Personality and Social Psychology, 48*(2), 393–399.
Arieti, S. (1976). *Creativity, the magic synthesis.* New York: Basic Books.
Barron, F. (1988). Putting creativity to work. In R. J. Sternberg (ed.), *The nature of creativity* (pp. 76–98). New York: Cambridge University Press.
Barron, F., and Harrington, D. M. (1981). Creativity, intelligence, and personality. *Annual Review of Psychology, 32*, 439–476.
Cantor, N., and Mischel, W. (1979). Prototypes in person perception. In L. Berkowitz (ed.), *Advances in experimental social psychology* (Vol. 12). New York: Academic Press.
Cattell, R. B., and Cattell, A. K. (1963). *Test of g: Culture fair, Scale 3.* Champaign, IL: Institute for Personality and Ability Testing.
Clifford, M. M. (1988). Failure tolerance and academic risk taking in ten- to twelve-year-old students. *British Journal of Educational Psychology, 58*(1), 15–27.
Cohen, J., and Cohen, P. (1983). *Applied multiple regression/correlation analysis for the behavioral sciences* (2d ed.). Hillsdale, NJ: Erlbaum.
Crutchfield, R. (1962). Conformity and creative thinking. In H. Gruber, G. Terrell, and M. Wertheimer (eds.), *Contemporary approaches to creative thinking* (pp. 120–140). New York: Atherton Press.
Csikszentmihalyi, M. (1988). Society, culture, and person: A systems view of creativity. In R. J. Sternberg (ed.), *The nature of creativity* (pp. 325–339). New York: Cambridge University Press.
Davidson, J. E., and Sternberg, R. J. (1984). The role of insight in intellectual giftedness. *Gifted Child Quarterly, 28*, 58–64.
Dellas, M., and Gaier, E. L. (1970). Identification of creativity: The individual. *Psychological Bulletin, 73*, 55–73.
Dreman, D. (1977). *Psychology and the stock market.* New York: AMACOM.
Dreman, D. (1982). *The new contrarian investment strategy.* New York: Random House.
Eisenman, R. 1987. Creativity, birth order, and risk taking. *Bulletin of the Psychonomic Society, 25*, 87–88.
Feldman, D. H. (1988). Creativity: Dreams, insights, and transformations. In R. J. Sternberg (ed.), *The nature of creativity* (pp. 271–297). New York: Cambridge University Press.
Finke, R. A., Ward, T. B., and Smith, S. M. (1992). *Creative cognition: Theory, research, and applications.* Cambridge, MA: MIT Press.
French, J. W., Ekstrom, R. B., and Price, I. A. (1963). *Kit of reference tests for cognitive factors.* Princeton, NJ: Educational Testing Service.

Frensch, P. A., and Sternberg, R. J. (1989). Expertise and intelligent thinking: When is it worse to know better? In R. J. Sternberg (ed.), *Advances in the psychology of human intelligence* (Vol. 5, pp. 157–188). Hillsdale, NJ: Erlbaum.

Gardner, H. (1988). Creative lives and creative works: A synthetic scientific approach. In R. J. Sternberg (ed.), *The nature of creativity* (pp. 298–321). New York: Cambridge University Press.

Getzels, J., and Csikszentmihalyi, M. (1976). *The creative vision: A longitudinal study of problem-finding in art.* New York: Wiley-Interscience.

Glover, J. A. (1977). Risky shift and creativity. *Social Behavior and Personality, 5*(2), 317–320.

Golann, S. E. (1962). The creativity motive. *Journal of Personality, 30,* 588–600.

Golann, S. E. (1963). Psychological study of creativity. *Psychological Bulletin, 60,* 548–565.

Golden, C. J. 1975. A group version of the Stroop color and word test. *Journal of Personality Assessment, 39*(4), 386–388.

Gough, H. G., and Heilbrun, A. B. (1983). *The Adjective Check List Manual.* Palo Alto, CA: Consulting Psychologists Press.

Gray, C. E. (1966). A measurement of creativity in Western civilization. *American Anthropologist, 68,* 1384–1417.

Gruber, H. E. (1981). *Darwin on man: A psychological study of scientific creativity* (2d ed.). Chicago: University of Chicago Press.

Hill, K. (1990). *An ecological approach to creativity and motivation: Trait and environment influences in the college classroom.* Unpublished doctoral dissertation, Brandeis University.

Horn, J. L. (1976). Human abilities: A review of research and theory in the early 1970s. *Annual Review of Psychology, 27,* 437–485.

Jackson, D. N. (1984). *Personality research form manual* (3d ed.). Port Huron, MI: Research Psychologists Press.

Jackson, P., and Messick, S. (1965). The person, the product and the response: Conceptual problems in the assessment of creativity. *Journal of Personality, 33,* 309–329.

Kahneman, D., and Tversky, A. (1982). The psychology of preferences. *Scientific American, 246*(1), 160–173.

Kogan, N., and Wallach, M. A. (1964). *Risk taking: A study in cognition and personality.* New York: Holt, Rinehart, and Winston.

Langer, E. J. (1989). *Mindfulness.* Reading, MA: Addison-Wesley.

Lubart, T. I. (1990). Creativity and cross-cultural variation. *International Journal of Psychology, 25,* 39–59.

McClelland, D. C. (1956). The calculated risk: An aspect of scientific performance. In C. W. Taylor (ed.), *The 1955 University of Utah research conference on the identification of creative scientific talent* (pp. 96–110). Salt Lake City, UT: University of Utah Press.

MacCrimmon, K. R., and Wehrung, D. A. (1985). A portfolio of risk measures. *Theory and Decision, 19*(1), 1–29.

MacKinnon, D. W. (1962). The nature and nurture of creative talent. *American Psychologist, 17,* 484–495.

MacKinnon, D. W. (1965). Personality and the realization of creative potential. *American Psychologist, 20,* 273–281.

Martin, M. C. (1988). *Mind as mental self-government: Construct validation of a theory of intellectual styles.* Unpublished master's thesis, Yale University.

Meer, B., and Stein, M. I. (1955). Measures of intelligence and creativity. *Journal of Psychology, 39,* 117–126.

Mumford, M. D., and Gustafson, S. B. (1988). Creativity syndrome: Integration, application, and innovation. *Psychological Bulletin, 103*(1), 27–43.

Myers, I. B., and McCaulley, M. H. (1985). *Manual: A guide to the development and use of the Myers-Briggs Type Indicator.* Palo Alto, CA: Consulting Psychologists Press.

Nunnally, J. (1967). *Psychometric theory.* New York: McGraw-Hill.

Roe, A. (1952). *The making of a scientist.* New York: Dodd, Mead.

Rogers, C. R. (1954). Toward a theory of creativity. *Etc, 11,* 249–260.

Rossman, B. B., and Horn, J. L. (1972). Cognitive, motivational and temperamental indicants of creativity and intelligence. *Journal of Educational Measurement, 9*(4), 265–286.

Rubenson, D. L., and Runco, M. A. (1992). The psychoeconomic approach to creativity. *New Ideas in Psychology, 10*(2), 131–147.

Runco, M. A. (1987). The generality of creative performance in gifted and nongifted children. *Gifted Child Quarterly, 31,* 121–125.

Schubert, D. S. P. (1973). Intelligence as necessary but not sufficient for creativity. *Journal of Genetic Psychology, 122,* 45–47.

Simonton, D. K. (1984). *Genius, creativity, and leadership.* Cambridge, MA: Harvard University Press.

Simonton, D. K. (1988). Creativity, leadership, and chance. In R. J. Sternberg (ed.), *The nature of creativity* (pp. 386–426). New York: Cambridge University Press.

Sternberg, R. J. (1980). *Stalking the elusive humunculus: Isolating the metacomponents of intelligence.* Unpublished manuscript.

Sternberg, R. J. (1985a). *Beyond IQ: A triarchic theory of human intelligence.* New York: Cambridge University Press.

Sternberg, R. J. (1985b). Implicit theories of intelligence, creativity, and wisdom. *Journal of Personality and Social Psychology, 49,* 607–627.

Sternberg, R. J. (1986). *Intelligence applied: Understanding and increasing your intellectual skills.* Orlando, FL: Harcourt Brace Jovanovich.

Sternberg, R. J. (ed.). (1988a). *The nature of creativity.* New York: Cambridge University Press.

Sternberg, R. J. (1988b). Mental self-government: A theory of intellectual styles and their development. *Human Development, 31,* 197–224.

Sternberg, R. J., and Lubart, T. I. (1991). An investment theory of creativity and its development. *Human Development, 34,* 1–31.

Sternberg, R. J., and Lubart, T. I. (1992). Buy low and sell high: An investment approach to creativity. *Current Directions in Psychological Science 1,* 1–5.

Sternberg, R. J., and Lubart, T. I. (1993). Creative giftedness: A multivariate investment approach. *Gifted Child Quarterly, 37*(1), 7–15.

Thurstone, T. G. (1962). *Primary mental abilities.* Chicago: Science Research Associates.

Torrance, E. P. (in press). *Creative motivation scale: Norms technical manual.* Bensenville, IL: Scholastic Testing Service.

Walberg, H. J. (1988). Creativity and talent as learning. In R. J. Sternberg (ed.), *The nature of creativity* (pp. 340–361). New York: Cambridge University Press.

Chapter 13

Creative Realism

Ronald A. Finke

The previous chapters have considered many different aspects of creative cognition, the goal of which is to use the methods of cognitive science to understand how creative ideas are generated, to explore the mental processes and structures that underlie creative thinking, and to identify the various properties of those structures that promote creative exploration and discovery. This chapter considers an important next step in the creative cognition approach.

Creative realism refers to the study of creative ideas that make contact with realistic issues and problems or, equivalently, of realistic ideas that have creative potential. Creativity should consist of more than just new ideas or wild imagination; it should also have realistic, enduring consequences. Thus, creative cognition needs to distinguish between creativity that goes nowhere and creativity that really counts.

The popular view of creativity is that it is unrealistic—the opposite of thinking that is sensible or practical. Yet creativity in and of itself serves no end. There needs to be a realistic focus to make creativity work. By the same token, ideas that address realistic issues and concerns but offer little in the way of creative inspiration or enlightenment are equally unsatisfying. In creative realism, one tries to have the best of both worlds: to develop ideas that are not only original and inspiring but are also likely to have a genuine impact on real-world problems, needs, and values.

Interest in creative realism is not new. In *Cognition and Reality*, Neisser (1976) called for an ecological approach to cognitive psychology that makes contact with structures that naturally exist in the real world rather than simply focusing on the creative, constructive qualities of the human mind. Others have called attention to the importance of "problem finding" in creative thinking, which often leads to successful innovations (Getzels and Csikszentmihalyi 1976; Perkins 1981). With recent advances in creative cognition, it is now possible to specify more precisely how creative realism can be assessed and achieved.

The usual procedure for achieving creative realism has been to generate lots of new ideas and then simply weed out the ones that are nonsensical or unrealistic (Findlay and Lumsden 1988; Perkins 1988). In the present approach, the goal is to discover how to generate realistic, creative ideas from the very outset and to determine whether the ideas are likely to have an impact on realistic issues and problems. Creative realism is thus relevant to all forms of creativity and can occur at many levels, ranging from major scientific theories and artistic creations down to the simplest, everyday activities.

In addition to providing a brief introduction to the basic concepts and issues in creative realism, this chapter will consider some practical suggestions for how to enhance creative realism when generating new ideas. Most of the recommendations will consist of general principles and guidelines rather than explicit rules or prescriptions.

One major theme is that to achieve creative realism, there needs to be some degree of continuity between old and new ideas. This property is termed *structural connectedness* (see also Weisberg, chap. 3). In order to be realistic, creative ideas need to be structured, and that structure needs to have evolved from previously established ideas and principles. For example, successful analogies in creative problem solving often preserve higher-order structural relations from solutions that have worked for other types of problems, as in the planetary model of the atom (Gentner 1989; Cheng and Simon, chap. 9). As another example, it is often easier to generate new ideas for inventions by taking existing designs and varying them in creative ways while maintaining their essential structure (Finke, Ward, and Smith 1992). Even when a new idea consists of extensive transformations of previous ideas, one should still be able to discover a connective path that links the structures (Shepard and Cooper 1992).

Structure alone does not guarantee creative realism. There can be unrealistic ideas that are marvelously structured but unconnected in any sensible way to prior, realistic concepts. The structure needs to have evolved from those ideas that have exhibited creative realism in the past. Also, it is important to distinguish between structured creativity and planned creativity. Creative ideas can be structured without being predetermined; in fact, having some degree of ambiguity in the structure allows new, unanticipated insights to emerge. Thus, structural connectedness does not mean that the ideas will be entirely predictable or devoid of opportunities for creative discovery.

A second theme is that ideas in creative realism must also exhibit inspirational qualities that excite the imagination and lead to meaningful explorations. This is referred to as *imaginative divergence*. It distinguishes genuinely exciting and innovative ideas from those that appear sensible and realistic but lead nowhere. Imaginative divergence promotes what has been called *divergent thinking*, in which one explores unconventional possibilities, associations, and interpretations (Guilford 1968).

Studies on creative cognition have shown that certain properties of mental structures encourage imaginative divergence, such as novelty and ambiguity (Finke 1990; Finke, Ward, and Smith 1992). However, novelty alone does not ensure that an idea will have these inspirational qualities or will lead to creative realism. Not every novel idea excites the imagination. And even if a novel idea does lead to imaginative divergence, structural connectedness is still required. The structural and inspirational aspects of creative realism are both important and will be considered throughout this chapter.

After describing the major dimensions and characteristics of creative realism, I will propose various criteria, based on structural connectedness, imaginative divergence, and other properties, that can be used to assess the likelihood that a new idea will result in creative realism. Some consequences of failing to satisfy these criteria will then be considered.

Dimensions of Creative Realism

The dimensions creative-conservative and realistic-idealistic define four general categories into which every new idea can, in principle, be classified (figure 13.1).

Conservative Realism

The upper right-hand quadrant of figure 13.1 represents conservative realism, which describes most ideas that are generated in traditional, highly structured fields such as engineering, medicine, government, and law. These ideas focus on realistic issues and problems but are generally conservative, often excessively. They exhibit a high degree of structural connectedness, in that they tie in closely with previous, established ideas, but they are usually low in imaginative divergence, for they seldom lead to enlightened explorations. There is a tendency to resort to conservative realism whenever one wishes to avoid ambiguity or uncertainty.

Creative Idealism

Creative idealism, represented in the lower left-hand quadrant of figure 13.1, describes most crackpot ideas—those that are often quite original but excessively fanciful. For instance, many New Age concepts would fall into this category, such as the claim that razor blades

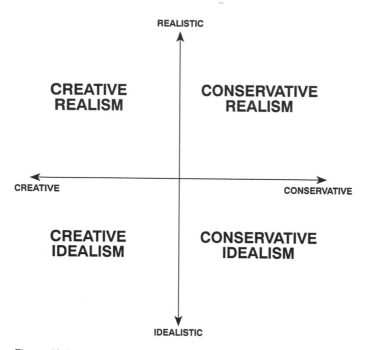

Figure 13.1
Four general, conceptual domains into which new ideas can be classified, according to
whether the ideas are creative, conservative, realistic, or idealistic

will stay sharper when placed inside miniature pyramids. The novelty
and imaginative possibilities of an idea are considered its primary
virtues, regardless of whether the idea is sensible or realistic. Ideas
exhibiting creative idealism are thus high in imaginative divergence
but generally low in structural connectedness.

When someone attempts to relate such ideas to familiar concepts or
principles, the connections usually end up vague or inappropriate.
For example, attempts to explain alleged paranormal phenomena using principles of quantum mechanics are likely based on an illusory
connectedness to modern physics (Gardner 1981). The same can be
said of overextended metaphors, which often imply structural connections that do not truly exist.

Throughout this chapter, the term *idealism* will be used in the sense
of "fanciful." Of course, some notions that are idealistic now may turn
out to be realistic at some later time, as with science fiction that one
day comes true. Creative idealism refers to ideas that are novel but
unlikely to make contact with realistic needs and issues in the fore-
seeable future. Thus, science fiction concepts that are highly improb-

able, such as the notion of beaming people through space, or truly wild forms of artistic expression would be considered examples of creative idealism. As a rule, one resorts to creative idealism when one is more concerned with escaping from reality than with enhancing or expanding it.

Conservative Idealism
Probably the least interesting category is conservative idealism, represented in the lower right-hand quadrant of figure 13.1. This consists of simple extensions of common ideas that were unrealistic to begin with, such as conventional misconceptions and irrational prejudices— for example, the belief, once quite common, that women are inherently inferior to men. Ideas exhibiting conservative idealism are low in both structural connectedness and imaginative divergence, since they tend to be arbitrary, have no basis in fact or scientific support, and display little imagination. One might engage in conservative idealism to avoid innovative thinking at all costs and thus embrace traditional ideas that make little sense.

Creative Realism
The category of primary interest, creative realism, is represented in the upper left-hand quadrant of figure 13.1. Ideas in this category show imaginative divergence and yet are structurally connected to realistic issues and concepts. They are meaningful and inspirational without being excessively fanciful or detached from established principles. They are the direct opposite of ideas that exhibit conservative idealism.

Distinguishing creative and conservative ideas has been the main focus of creative cognition, whereas distinguishing realistic and idealistic ideas has been the main focus of studies of crackpot science and human gullibility (Gardner 1957; Randi 1982). In creative realism, both considerations are important; one wants to identify those ideas that are creative as well as realistic. This is not always easy, however, because ideas can vary along a continuum in the extent to which they are creative or realistic and can thus exhibit creative realism to varying degrees.

Examples of Creative Realism

Invention and Design
Most of the major inventions that have helped to shape modern technology, such as radio, television, and the computer, are prime exam-

ples of creative realism. In nearly every case, these inventions displayed both structural connectedness and imaginative divergence. Consider Edison's phonograph, which incorporated many of the same principles and structural features in an earlier device he had successfully designed for recording telegraph messages (Burke 1978). In addition to having structural connectedness, the phonograph had a remarkable power to excite the imagination; one could envision preserving the voices of famous people, recreating great musical performances, and revolutionizing home entertainment. In this regard, the phonograph could be distinguished from the many inconsequential, gimmicky inventions that existed at the same time, which exhibited structural connectedness but not imaginative divergence.

As another example of creative realism, consider car designs. Certain cars become classics because they combine structural connectedness and imaginative divergence. They inspire one's imagination but without departing too radically from previous, successful designs. Cars that are too conventional usually fail to excite the public (conservative realism), whereas cars that are too imaginative often end up having unrealistic features (creative idealism). A good example of the latter is the Edsel, which became an epic violation of creative realism.

Some recent studies from my laboratory have explored a person's ability to generate ideas for new inventions that are both creative and practical and are thus more likely to result in creative realism (Finke 1990). Subjects in these experiments imagined combining three simple object parts or geometric shapes to form *preinventive forms,* which they were then to try to interpret as representing practical devices belonging to various object categories, such as "appliances" and "scientific instruments." The resulting inventions were scored according to their originality and practicality. Most of the subjects were able to come up with at least one invention concept that scored highly on both of these measures.

Figure 13.2 presents examples of inventions in these studies that correspond to each of the four categories in figure 13.1. Part A presents a contact lens remover, representing creative realism. The user places the rubber cone against the lens, covers the air hole in back with a finger, and then lifts off the lens by moving the device away from the eye. This device displays structural connectedness to previous designs for suction cups yet is highly imaginative. Part B displays a practical but conventional design for a heavy-duty pair of scissors, representing conservative realism. The scissors are made out of a thicker metal so they will not break as easily. This shows structural connectedness without imaginative divergence.

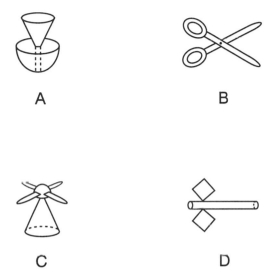

Figure 13.2
Examples of invention concepts in experiments on imagining preinventive forms, which represent each of the four categories shown in figure 13.1: (A) A contact lens remover, a practical and original design that represents creative realism. One places the rubber cone against the lens, covers the air hole in back with a finger, and then lifts off the lens by moving the device away from the eye. (B) A practical but conventional design for a heavy-duty pair of scissors, representing conservative realism. The scissors are made out of a thicker metal so they will not break as easily. (C) A universal energy transporter, representing creative idealism. The omnidirectional sensor at the top of the device allows any form of energy to be detected and then transferred from one location to another. (D) An unoriginal and impractical design for an airplane, representing conservative idealism. The side panels flap up and down, presumably allowing the airplane to fly like a bird. (From Finke 1990).

Part C presents a universal energy transporter, representing creative idealism. The omnidirectional sensor at the top of the device allows any form of energy to be detected and then transferred from one location to another. It is highly imaginative but not very realistic; it lacks structural connectedness to established principles for transporting energy. Part D displays an unoriginal and impractical design for an airplane, representing conservative idealism. The side panels flap up and down, presumably allowing the airplane to fly like a bird. The design is based on traditional misconceptions and exhibits little imagination or connectedness to established principles of flight.

Scientific Theories
There are many instances of creative realism in scientific thinking. Some classic examples are the theory of relativity, the theory of evo-

lution, and the quantum theory. All exhibited a high degree of structural connectedness, for they were based on established findings and principles of their time, and imaginative divergence, for they raised many new, exciting possibilities and implications. These theories also helped to resolve apparent contradictions that defied explanation by conventional theories.

At the opposite extreme, there have been many cases of misguided science, in which a person continued to pursue an inspiring idea in spite of growing evidence that it was almost certainly wrong. These range from instances of outright lunacy, as in serious, determined efforts to show that the earth is really flat and is surrounded by an enormous shell, to saner misconceptions, such as the belief that gravity can be neutralized (Gardner 1957). In such cases, conservative or creative idealism replaces creative realism.

Art, Music, and Film
Creative realism also exists in art. Here one can make a distinction between works that are structurally connected to previous styles and forms and naturally inspire the imagination—for example, the great works of impressionism, cubism, and surrealism—and those that are structurally dissociated from previous forms and are novel merely for novelty's sake. Examples of the latter would be performance art, in which the artist tries to be outrageous for the mere effect of shocking the observer, or art that has to be "defined" as meaningful by virtue of the concepts that it supposedly represents (Wolfe 1976).

In musical composition, a similar distinction can be made between new works that exhibit structural connectedness to previous forms and excite the imagination, and uninspired imitations of previous works or experimental music that results from arbitrary combinations of notes and sounds. Some would argue, perhaps, that the latter are no less valid as legitimate forms of music than the great classical works of Mozart or Beethoven. This may be, but they fall into the category of creative idealism, not creative realism.

There is also creative realism in filmmaking. A classic film often presents a novel theme in such a way that the audience can both relate to it and become inspired by it. Such films are timeless, in part because their content is not only fresh but also highly meaningful. Films that fail to achieve creative realism usually fall into one of two categories: *high-concept* films, which are very creative but may be difficult for an audience to relate to, and tend to result in creative idealism, and *formula* films, which are relatively uncreative but easy for audiences to relate to, and tend to result in conservative realism.

Everyday Thinking

Creative realism is not restricted to major inventions, grand theories, or great works of art; it can also occur in everyday life. For example, one might discover a creative way of doing an ordinary task, such as buying food at the grocery store, that results in a considerable savings in time and effort. Or one might explore new ways of driving to work each day in an attempt to make the task more imaginative. Even something like inventing a joke can exhibit creative realism. Consider the contrast between jokes and witticisms that bear on current problems and hypocrisies in wonderfully creative and clever ways, versus those that are original but are seemingly pointless or that are very much to the point but are dull, crude, and unimaginative.

The Need for Creative Realism

Future work in creative cognition should be concerned with creative realism for several reasons. First, it is important to direct creative thinking toward the development of ideas that are most likely to succeed or endure. Creativity abounds in modern society, but much of it is transient and fatuous —as in the case of highly creative parade floats that appear and then vanish every holiday. Even now, people continue to waste time and energy trying to build perpetual motion machines and other fanciful devices. Similarly, we find many cases in everyday life where a creative impulse leads to the capricious abandonment of realistic considerations, as when a person suddenly quits a steady job to pursue some idealistic fantasy. We can no longer afford to encourage creativity for its own sake.

Second, there has always been a conflict between the unbridled enthusiasm for new ideas, in which one becomes intrigued by their many fresh and exciting implications, and critical evaluation, which attempts to impose realistic constraints and perspectives. People tend to either accept creative ideas without critically examining them or reject those ideas prematurely, in the name of skepticism. This relates back to the classic problem of trying to reconcile belief and analysis. In creative realism, one allows creative exploration and critical assessment to coexist. Some thoughts on how this might best be achieved are provided at the end of the chapter.

Third, even highly intelligent and informed people often confuse creative realism and creative idealism. For example, there have been many cases in which reputable scientists have been taken in by highly creative ideas that seemed appealing at first but then turned out to be preposterous, as in the case of the notorious "N-Ray" affair at the turn of the century, where many prominent scientists imagined that they were seeing interference patterns from a nonexistent form of radiation (Klotz 1980). One can also point to cases in which supposed photographic experts "certified" that fairies had actually been captured on film (Randi 1982), incidents that now seem almost beyond belief. Although often necessary for creative realism, expertise is no assurance of it.

Fourth, people sometimes reject a genuinely creative idea because it seems too closely connected to familiar things. Some artists have deliberately destroyed works they considered inferior because the structure or form struck them as too conventional. Yet some contact with prior structure is important in creative realism; art and science usually fail when previous structures are abandoned completely (Weisberg, 1986). On the other hand, there is the opposite problem: a person begins to think that every new idea is important and must be expressed, irrespective of its true novelty or merit. Both of these problems can be avoided in creative realism.

Fifth, it is important to try to establish general criteria for assessing creative realism. It would be fairly uninteresting if creative realism depended solely on consensual approval or varied capriciously from one domain to another. The next section will consider objective and subjective criteria that can be used to assess creative realism in general, as well as psychological criteria that bear on conceptual impediments to achieving creative realism.

Finally, creative realism can help one to gauge when an original idea is likely to succeed. This is more efficient than using a strictly Darwinian approach, in which one generates lots of creative ideas and then selects out those that survive a lengthy process of testing and evaluation. Although one usually cannot predict the final form that successful, creative ideas will take, one can learn to recognize, in advance, various properties of those ideas that increase the probability that creative realism will be achieved.

Assessing Creative Realism

There are three types of criteria for assessing the likelihood of creative realism: objective, subjective, and psychological.

Objective Criteria

Objective criteria are based on the general, structural properties of an idea and on whether the idea meets certain standards for acceptance.

1. *Does the idea display structural connectedness, or is it dissociated from established ideas?* Structural connectedness is one of the major features of creative realism; an idea needs to be connected in meaningful ways

to established principles and concepts. Structure alone does not necessarily result in creative realism, however, because highly fanciful ideas often display intricate structures that are disconnected from realistic considerations. An example is zone therapy, which proposes that certain areas of the feet are connected through a complex, neural network to each of the major organs of the body. In failing to meet this criterion, a person might try to claim that the idea represents a totally unique concept, subject to entirely different laws and principles. This, however, severs structural connectedness and leads to creative idealism.

Structural connectedness does not exclude the global restructuring of existing concepts, as long as the emerging structures are still related to conventional structures in meaningful ways. The theory of relativity, for example, resulted in a revolutionary restructuring of physics, yet it remained connected to the classical concepts of space and time, which remained valid within certain limits. However, if the restructuring process removes this connectedness altogether, one is likely to lose creative realism and end up with creative idealism. An example is Alfred Lawson's self-proclaimed transformation of physics, in which he proposed that every law of nature could be understood according to the principle of "zig, zag, and swirl"(Gardner 1957).

Although structural connectedness does not exclude the emergence of novel structures during the creative process, the emergent structures must be connected in at least some respects to earlier structures in order to exhibit creative realism (Finke, Ward, and Smith 1992; Koestler 1964). For example, most successful inventions are structurally connected to previous inventions, despite their uniqueness and emergent properties.

How might structural connectedness be measured? First, one could examine the degree of direct, one-to-one correspondence, or isomorphism, between the old and new structures, which can be determined using a variety of empirical methods (Shepard and Chipman 1970). Second, one could explore whether the new idea represents a transformation of some previous, established idea. For example, a mental image representing a new invention might have been derived from various transformations on a previous design (Shepard and Cooper 1982). These transformations, however, must retain some meaningful relations between the structures; structural connectedness is lost if the transformations become so extensive or unconstrained that only arbitrary connections remain.

One could also examine whether the new idea retains many of the same features of the old idea (Ward in press, this volume). Here one would need to take into account not just the total number of shared features but also their configural properties and the types of features. Some features might be important to retain, whereas others would be irrelevant or even detrimental. For example, in generating a new design for the interior of a car, certain traditional features, such as a steering wheel, might be essential, whereas other features, such as a gas pedal, might not be.

2. *Does the idea fulfill its intended purpose, or does one need to invent reasons to justify it?* In creative realism, an idea needs to be successful in some legitimate sense. A new design for a car engine, for example, should perform according to established guidelines or specifications. A new painting or composition should satisfy the general expectations that define a successful work. There is, of course, always the possibility that a new design or concept can turn out to be successful in unexpected ways, and this possibility must also be taken into consideration. However, creative realism is usually not achieved by searching after the fact for arbitrary justifications for an idea, as when one's theory is refuted but the person continues to claim that the theory has succeeded in other respects. This merely encourages creative or conservative realism.

3. *Is the idea internally consistent, or does it contradict itself?* New ideas, especially those that express complex concepts or theories, can turn out to be inconsistent. This happens not only in scientific thinking but also in everyday thinking and planning. For example, one might come up with a highly creative idea for rearranging one's work schedule but which leads to impossible situations and conflicts.

There is a general tendency for people to overlook the inconsistencies in their ideas, regarding them as much more complete or coherent than they actually are (Wason and Johnson-Laird 1972). Consistency is therefore an important criterion for assessing creative realism. Although creative insights can sometimes arise from apparent contradictions, as when old ideas are combined in novel ways (Koestler 1972), in creative realism an idea cannot be truly self-contradictory.

4. *Is the validity of the idea easily tested, or does it become elusive and hard to pin down?* Some creative ideas start out sounding important and significant but are actually so ambiguous that they cannot be evaluated critically (Popper 1968). This tends to be more of a problem in fields in which they key concepts are not yet quantified or precisely defined, and promotes creative idealism. In failing to meet this criterion, a person might offer the excuse that the idea really is testable but is simply being misunderstood or misinterpreted.

5. *Is the idea based on simple assumptions, or does it require making multiple assumptions?* Increasing the number of assumptions in justifying a new idea generally increases the risk of failing to achieve creative realism.

In science, this occurs when one makes too many qualifying assumptions in proposing a theory and strays too far from established concepts (Gardner 1981). In art, this can happen when the artist begins to paint or compose according to increasingly abstract principles, requiring the observer or listener to make increasing assumptions in order to appreciate the work (Wolfe 1976). These increasing assumptions reduce structural connectedness.

Subjective Criteria

The next set of criteria are more subjective; they are based on the effect an idea has on one's imagination and sense of enlightenment.

1. *Does the idea promote imaginative divergence, or does it tend to stagnate the imagination?* In other words, does the idea encourage new explorations and discoveries, or does it seem to be headed toward a dead end? In creative realism, ideas should have an enlightening, dynamic quality; they should encourage one's imagination to spread out, make new connections, and raise new possibilities.

Virtually every scientific field has its share of makeshift theories that appear to account for much of the data but then lead nowhere. Similarly, there are numerous inventions that combine features in novel ways but are seemingly pointless. To achieve creative realism, an idea must engage the imagination sufficiently to result in meaningful insights, in addition to having realistic implications. Otherwise, the idea usually leads to conservative realism.

Imaginative divergence means more than simply having an imaginative idea. The idea needs to engage the imagination to the extent that one becomes intrigued by it and begins to explore where it might lead. One's imagination should "flow" from the idea, leading to new insights and feelings of enlightenment, a process I have previously called intuitive spreading (Finke 1989). The inherent, dynamic qualities that many mental representations possess can often be useful in stimulating imaginative divergence (Freyd 1987; Freyd and Pantzer, chap. 8).

2. *Does the idea provide deeper understandings, or does it merely offer some other point of view?* People often claim that because an event *could* have happened in some other way, the alternative deserves equal attention. Yet the mere possibility that some other interpretation might be correct does not excuse one from being discriminating. For example, JFK conspiracy theories have offered various alternative accounts of the assassination, some of which are highly creative, and they have even received some small degree of support, but they do not provide major new insights or understandings about the assassination. Similarly, creationist theories about the origin of species can be quite inventive,

and some support for them can be found, but they do not provide any real insight into the evolutionary process. Great scientists, artists, and inventors are normally selective about what interests them and what they consider to be worthy of their attention. They recognize the difference between creative realism and creative idealism.

3. *Is the idea truly innovative, or does it simply imitate previous ideas?* In assessing creative realism, one needs to distinguish between ideas that show genuine originality and insight and those that merely consist of simple variations of familiar concepts and themes. Although this assessment is highly subjective, it constitutes an important criterion. Cheap imitations of things that have been successful in the past, such as bad sequels to good movies, dreary songs that spring from familiar melodies, and uninspired books that are based on well-worn plots, are all clearly lacking in creative realism.

4. *Can the idea be shared, or does its creator attempt to conceal or protect it?* New ideas that make contact with many important issues and result in enlightened insights and discoveries will usually seem so exciting and obvious that the person will naturally want to share them. Trying to protect a creative idea is often a sign that it is unrealistic or unexciting, as when a person says, "This new theory of mine is so advanced that you will probably not be able to understand it, so I won't even try to explain it to you." Most creative ideas that really matter are fundamentally shareable (Freyd 1983).

5. *Does the idea reflect the relevant works of others, or does it seem to exist as an isolated creation?* A new idea is more likely to achieve creative realism when it displays a sensitivity to the successful contributions that others have made. When one prefers to work entirely within one's own private world, it becomes all too convenient to reject off-handedly the relevant ideas of others (Gardner 1957). This promotes creative idealism, often to an astonishing degree.

Psychological Criteria
The various psychological criteria for assessing creative realism refer mainly to the avoidance of certain conceptual illusions that can cause one to misjudge the true significance of an idea. The reason these criteria are also needed is that the previous criteria do not always enable one to make an accurate assessment of creative realism, especially if one is highly motivated to believe in an idea and is naive to the psychological mechanisms underlying various forms of self-deception.

1. *The illusion of magical validity.* Just because a creative idea seems meaningful and inspirational does not mean that it must therefore have external validity. Yet one can become so absorbed in the imagi-

native divergence of an idea as to become convinced that the idea is indisputably correct (Hilgard 1977). It is like becoming so enthralled by a magic act that one becomes convinced that the magic must be real. This promotes creative idealism, as opposed to creative realism. The scientist or inventor who claims, "This new idea seems so incredible that it can't possibly be wrong," has fallen victim to the illusion of magical validity.

One consequence of this illusion is that a person may become so convinced that an idea is correct that he or she easily finds confirming evidence for it even though none actually exists. This has been referred to as *confirmation bias* (Wason and Johnson-Laird 1972). In the case of the N-Ray affair, some scientists believed so strongly in the reality of N-Rays that they began finding evidence for them practically everywhere they looked—even on photographs—when in fact no such evidence existed (Klotz 1980).

The illusion of validity may also be related to the general tendency for people to believe in their ideas at the time they initially generate them (Gilbert 1991). For instance, a person might come up with an idea for a new invention that is clearly idealistic but tacitly assume that the idea is valid until proved otherwise. Thus, people may suspend disbelief whenever they entertain a new concept. This tendency is likely to be even stronger when the ideas engage the imagination.

2. *The illusion of synchronicity.* Remarkable coincidences occur in all aspects of daily life. These can be so striking that they can lead to the conclusion that the events must be connected in deeper, fundamental ways, as was suggested by Koestler (1972) and Jung (1960). In most cases, however, this apparent connectedness, or "synchronicity," is simply an illusion (Gardner 1981). Superficial similarities have often resulted in exaggerated claims about causal relations, as in recent claims that apparent faces on the surface of Mars are causally linked to the face of the Sphinx.

One reason this illusion occurs is that people tend to remember striking coincidences and forget less meaningful ones, which leads them to overestimate the frequency with which the striking coincidences occur (Tversky and Kahneman 1973). In addition, sometimes the current zeitgeist leads people who are not in direct contact to arrive at similar ideas and concepts. To attribute special meaning or significance to such coincidences encourages creative idealism and inhibits creative realism.

3. *The illusion of linearity.* A common belief, especially among scientists, engineers, and business executives, is that the only valid extensions of existing ideas are those that occur in a direct, linear, predictable manner. This illusion promotes conservative realism. In

actuality, many important innovations come about not as simple extensions of existing ideas but as broad reconceptualizations or transformations of those ideas (Kuhn 1962). The illusion of linearity often encourages one to extend an idea beyond its natural boundaries, as in failed attempts to apply the principles of behaviorism to language learning and conceptual development (Chomsky 1972; Fodor 1968).

4. *The illusion of explanatory power.* Sometimes a new theory gains widespread appeal because it appears to explain a great many things. This can make the theory seem more powerful than it actually is, especially if it is sufficiently complicated and flexible. Such theories could conceivably explain virtually any outcome whatsoever—even opposite results. A good example is Freud's psychoanalysis; it fulfills most of the objective criteria for creative realism, and it certainly led to many new insights and understandings, but it has fallen into disfavor because much of its explanatory power was illusory.

5. *The illusion of destiny.* Another common belief is that people are often destined to have certain insights or to make certain discoveries, given the issues or problems at hand. Once these insights or discoveries occur, it seems as if no others would have been as appropriate or meaningful. In creative realism, imaginative divergence can follow many paths, resulting in a diversity of valid insights and discoveries.

Recent experiments from my own research have shown how powerful the illusion of destiny can be. A preinventive form, once it is interpreted as a specific invention, often gives the impression that it was designed for that explicit purpose, when in fact the form preceded the discovery and could just as easily have resulted in many different types of inventions (Finke 1990).

Failures to Achieve Creative Realism

There are important consequences of failing to achieve creative realism, particularly in scientific thinking. These failures can take several forms, which are related to the various illusions just described.

Overextensions of Imaginative Divergence
Certain ideas can engage the imagination to such an extent that one can lose the distinction between creative possibility and reality. A person can become so involved in a good science fiction movie, for instance, as to come to believe in the reality of humanoid aliens, futuristic weapons, and fanciful methods of interstellar travel. These experiences represent overextensions of imaginative divergence. One becomes so involved in the engaging qualities of the experience that creative idealism is confused with creative realism.

This often happens, unfortunately, in many scientific fields, particularly those on the fringes of legitimacy. For example, many concepts in parapsychology have fallen prey to the illusions of magical validity and synchronicity. These concepts are highly creative, are intensely meaningful to many people, and clearly excite the imagination—but they have failed to achieve creative realism. For example, the notion that one can levitate objects merely by concentrating on them raises all kinds of intriguing possibilities—indeed, one can easily imagine oneself doing it—but this does not mean that such abilities are therefore any more likely to exist.

Even an entire scientific field can make a wrong turn, moving further away from creative realism. When this happens, one has to back up and try a more promising path. For instance, Gestalt psychology led to many significant insights at first, but then researchers began looking for imaginary neural fields that would supposedly represent extensions of the Gestalt principles (Kohler 1947). These searches failed, and this was one of the reasons that Gestalt psychology eventually faded.

These overextensions occur, in part, because of a failure to distinguish the usefulness of an idea as a metaphor or catalyst for creative exploration and the external validity of the idea. Highly fanciful concepts could still be valuable in the role of metaphors, without having to be externalized. For instance, the notion that people can pick up the thoughts of others through paranormal means, though unrealistic, could conceivably function as a useful metaphor in arriving at new insights about novel forms of communication that would be sensible and realistic (Gordon 1961).

Absence of Imaginative Divergence
At the opposite extreme, there are many cases in which new ideas are completely lacking in imaginative divergence. Theories based on computer simulations, for example, are often devoid of these inspirational qualities and function mainly to account for the results of an experiment in as complete a manner as possible (Dreyfus 1972). Such theories are particularly susceptible to the illusions of linearity and explanatory power; they represent straightforward extensions of previous ideas and appear to explain many things. Yet many of these theories are quickly forgotten, having done little to inspire the imagination.

In much of science, there is a tendency to constrain the direction of future explorations, in the spirit of conservative realism, and to minimize imaginative divergence, which is seen as promoting carelessness and lack of discipline. Yet imaginative divergence is an essential part of creative realism; it distinguishes ideas that are truly enlightening and innovating from those that are realistic but inconsequential. To exclude or suppress imaginative divergence is to sterilize a scientific field or conceptual domain.

Overstructuring the Creative Process

Another way in which there could be a failure to achieve creative realism is by overstructuring the creative process, regarding it as somehow predetermined or inevitable. This bears on the illusion of destiny, in which one has the impression, in retrospect, that the creative process has unfolded in a uniquely rewarding direction. In fact, many potential discoveries can result from the very same initial conditions; there is no single correct or optimal path for creative exploration.

Creative thinking is sufficiently structured on its own that it need not be deliberately structured or prescribed in advance (Ward in press). To attempt to do so is to encourage conservative realism. Often, structural connectedness is not even recognized until after an insight has been achieved (Schooler and Melcher, chap. 5.) Moreover that connectedness is not necessarily unique; the same insight can be structurally connected in different ways to different ideas. For these reasons, structural connectedness should not be artificially imposed on the creative process.

A related problem is that one is often drawn to the structural complexity of a new idea without thinking about its true meaningfulness or appropriateness. For instance, a complex, structural theory in philosophy or psychology might be appealing because the structure itself is impressive, irrespective of whether it provides any real enlightenment or understanding. Or a highly technical theory that has been successful in one domain might be extended to another domain and considered a creative achievement, though it is not actually relevant to that domain. A good example is the attempt to use some of the formal principles of quantum mechanics to explain paranormal events.

Enhancing Creative Realism

The following are some practical suggestions for increasing the likelihood of generating new ideas that result in creative realism and how to recognize when creative realism is likely to be missing.

Generating New Ideas with Creative Realism in Mind

As discussed, structural connectedness is an important characteristic of creative realism. How does one encourage structural connectedness when coming up with creative ideas, without artificially imposing it, or overstructuring the creative process?

One recommendation is to take existing designs or concepts and to vary them in playful, interesting ways, without departing too radically from the original structure—at least at first. One can then explore the creative implications of these simple variations, which are likely to retain structural connectedness. Also, one could generate completely novel structures, such as preinventive forms, and then explore how the structures might make contact with existing concepts or designs. Often these connections turn out to be both unexpected and meaningful. Another recommendation is to return to earlier, established ideas and look for new ways in which those ideas could be extended. For instance, if new developments in art seem to be headed in pointless or meaningless directions, one might try returning to earlier artforms and extending them along different paths. This recommendation can help when structural connectedness appears to have been lost.

Imaginative divergence, the other major characteristic of creative realism, can be increased by generating structures that seem inherently interesting, or are sufficiently novel or ambiguous, and then exploring their possibilities. This should be done without initial concern for critical evaluation. It often helps to visualize potential consequences of the ideas and to involve oneself completely in these explorations, in much the same way that one might become totally absorbed in a movie or novel. One can also think of other issues and concepts that might be associated with the ideas while exploring their creative implications.

In addition, one could make an explicit point to try to avoid the various psychological illusions that were considered in this chapter. For example, one could simply consider whether any of these illusions might apply to a creative idea that one has just generated, especially if it is unusually appealing. This should probably be done, however, only after developing or exploring the idea sufficiently. One does not want to dismiss the idea prematurely, before having a chance to adequately assess its creative potential.

There are also certain attitudes and traits that seem to foster creative realism. These include aesthetic sensitivity, concern for quality, lack of interest in competition, concern for long-range as opposed to short-term benefits, interest in sharing ideas and discoveries, tolerance for novelty and imperfection, and a willingness to explore imaginative possibilities without taking them too seriously.

Recognizing Failures of Creative Realism
In most cases, likely failures of creative realism can be recognized by applying the general criteria considered previously. In addition, there

are various other symptoms of impending failures of creative realism: the tendency to try to pressure others to accept one's ideas instead of simply allowing them the opportunity to share those ideas, the need to satisfy professional ambitions instead of wanting to contribute to the general spirit of the field, the lack of concern for aesthetics or craftsmanship, and the inability to distinguish ideas from opinions. Although these refer to attitudes and character traits rather than to properties of the ideas themselves, they are nonetheless helpful in determining whether creative realism is likely to result.

Implications of Creative Realism

Creative Cognition and the Geneplore Model
The Geneplore model of creative cognition (Finke, Ward, and Smith, 1992) distinguishes between generative and exploratory processes in developing creative ideas (figure 13.3). Generative processes, such as retrieval, association, mental synthesis, mental transformation, and analogical transfer, give rise to preinventive structures. These may consist of mental images, verbal combinations, category exemplars, or mental models. The structures are then explored to assess their creative possibilities. These exploratory processes include attribute

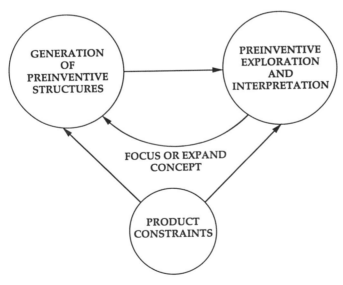

Figure 13.3
The Geneplore model of creative cognition. (From Finke, Ward, and Smith 1992).

finding, conceptual interpretation, functional inference, hypothesis testing, and searching for limitations. For instance, a person might use mental synthesis to combine parts of objects to create a novel form and then explore how the form might be useful as a metaphor representing a new concept.

Once these exploratory processes are completed, the preinventive structure can be refined or regenerated, depending on what one discovers during the exploratory phase. The cycle can then be repeated until the structure has been developed to a desired extent. At any point in the Geneplore cycle, constraints can be imposed onto the generative and exploratory phase, restricting the nature of the final product. These include constraints on the type of product, the general category to which it belongs, the features it possesses, and the functions it can have. For instance, one might impose the constraint that the new concept must provide some insights into how to solve a certain type of problem. Experimental studies can determine the optimal time for imposing these constraints.

Creative realism can provide some additional constraints on the Geneplore model. For example, one might want to identify and emphasize generative processes that maximize structural connectedness but without sacrificing imaginative divergence. For instance, mentally blending two familiar designs or structures might result in an optimal balance between structural connectedness and the emergence of unexpected features. These features could then be explored to determine their imaginative possibilities. It might also be possible to identify which properties of the preinventive structures are most relevant to promoting imaginative divergence, such as novelty, ambiguity, incongruity, and meaningfulness.

Applications of Creative Realism
Creative realism can have widespread applications. In product development, it could facilitate the discovery of new, creative designs that must meet required specifications, help designers to overcome design fixation (Jansson and Smith 1991), and enhance both structural connectedness and imaginative divergence in the design process. This would result in more efficient ways of developing innovative products.

In science, creative realism could reduce the number of theories that are excessively idealistic or conservative. It could improve ways of engaging in imaginative thought experiments, in which one explores new theoretical possibilities and their implications. In addition, one could avoid the common problem that an entire scientific theory is thrown out based on a single flaw or shortcoming, in an effort to be overly critical and conservative, where it still might have been possible to use or expand on the promising and enlightening aspects of the theory, and thus encourage imaginative divergence.

In business, creative realism could help one to avoid entering into ventures that seem imaginative and exciting but are unrealistic, to explore investments that are both sensible and innovative, and to develop marketing strategies that are both effective and creative. It could also help one to avoid making career choices that are appealing but excessively idealistic.

There are also implications of creative realism for improving education. One reason there has been resistance to creativity training within traditional educational systems is that it is often regarded as silly and impractical. Creative realism could help to change this attitude by showing how creative thinking can be focused in realistic and practical directions.

Creative Talent

A further proposal concerns the relation between creative realism and talent. People who possess genuine talent can usually judge whether a new concept in art, a new style of musical composition, or a new scientific theory are promising. In contrast, people who seem to lack talent are more susceptible to being impressed by superficial novelty or excessive conservatism. They are always inventing reasons for why a new idea is important when it really is not. In short, the lack of talent encourages conservative realism and idealism, whereas creative realism will generally follow one's talents, in the sense that those talents will naturally lead the person in realistic and enlightening directions.

Concluding Comments

Creative realism represents the next step in the creative cognition approach. Once one understands how to generate creative ideas, using the methods of creative cognition, one can then focus on developing creative ideas that are likely to have realistic implications, and thus avoid many of the common impediments to creative achievement. People have always been interested in trying to make their dreams come true; in creative realism, they learn how to select the dreams that are most worth pursuing.

Creative realism can also promote the critical examination of new and unusual claims without minimizing the creative aspects of those claims. Critics of novel ideas, especially in the sciences, are often accused of being captious, closed-minded, and "anticreative." By applying the principles of creative realism, one can examine the realistic prospects of new ideas while taking into account their imaginative and inspirational qualities.

Although the ideas presented in this chapter provide useful guidelines for future developments in creative cognition, they are not intended as a complete theory of creative realism. The exact nature of structural connectedness and imaginative divergence, and how they interact to produce creative realism, still need to be established. It also needs to be shown that the various proposed criteria for creative realism have predictive value.

Are there absolute standards for creative realism? Probably not, since context and cultural values will always play some role in evaluating a new idea (Simonton 1984; Sternberg and Lubart 1991; Lubart and Sternberg, chap. 12). Also, as with Galileo's ridicule of the notion that the moon can influence the tides, there will always be cases whereby a seemingly preposterous idea later turns out to be correct. Nevertheless, in most cases, the proposed criteria can help to distinguish between ideas that are likely to result in creative realism and those that almost certainly will not.

References

Burke, J. (1978). *Connections.* Boston: Little, Brown.

Chomsky, N. (1972). *Language and mind.* New York: Harcourt Brace Jovanovich.

Dreyfus, H. (1972). *What computers can't do: A critique of artificial reason.* New York: Harper & Row.

Findlay, C. S., and Lumsden, C. J. (1988). The creative mind: Toward an evolutionary theory of discovery and invention. *Journal of Social and Biological Structures, 11,* 3–55.

Finke, R. A. (1989). *Principles of mental imagery.* Cambridge, MA: MIT Press.

Finke, R. A. (1990). *Creative imagery: Discoveries and inventions in visualization.* Hillsdale, NJ: Erlbaum.

Finke, R. A., Ward, T. B., and Smith, S. M. (1992). *Creative cognition: Theory, research, and applications.* Cambridge, MA: MIT Press.

Fodor, J. A. (1968). *Psychological explanation: An introduction to the philosophy of psychology.* New York: Random House.

Freyd, J. J. (1983). Shareability: The social psychology of epistemology. *Cognitive Science, 7,* 191–210.

Freyd, J. J. (1987). Dynamic mental representations. *Psychological Review, 94,* 427–438.

Gardner, M. (1957). *Fads and fallacies in the name of science.* New York: Dover.

Gardner, M. (1981). *Science: Good, bad, and bogus.* Buffalo, NY: Prometheus.

Gentner, D. (1989). The mechanisms of analogical learning. In S. Vosniadou and A. Ortony (eds.), *Similarity and analogical reasoning.* Cambridge: Cambridge University Press.

Getzels, J. W., and Csikszentmihalyi, M. (1976). *The creative vision: A longitudinal study of problem finding in art.* New York: Wiley.

Gilbert, D. T. (1991). How mental systems believe. *American Psychologist, 46,* 107–119.

Gordon, W. (1961). *Synectics: The development of creative capacity.* New York: Dutton.

Guilford, J. P. (1968). *Intelligence, creativity, and their educational implications.* San Diego: Knapp.

Hilgard, E. R. (1977). *Divided consciousness: Multiple controls in human thought and action.* New York: Wiley-Interscience.

Jansson, D. G., and Smith, S. M. (1991). Design fixation. *Design Studies, 12,* 3–11.

Jung, C. G. (1960). *Collected works.* New York: Pantheon.

Klotz, I. M. (1980). The N-Ray affair. *Scientific American, 242,* 168–175.

Koestler, A. (1964). *The act of creation.* New York: Macmillan.

Koestler, A. (1972). *The roots of coincidence.* New York: Random House.

Kohler, W. (1947). *Gestalt psychology.* New York: Liveright.

Kuhn, T. S. (1962). *The structure of scientific revolutions.* Chicago: University of Chicago Press.

Neisser, U. (1976). *Cognition and reality.* San Francisco: W. H. Freeman.

Perkins, D. N. (1981). *The mind's best work.* Cambridge, MA: Harvard University Press.

Perkins, D. N. (1988). The possibility of invention. In R. J. Sternberg (ed.), *The nature of creativity: Contemporary psychological perspectives* (pp. 362–385). Cambridge: Cambridge University Press.

Popper, K. R. (1968). *The logic of scientific discovery.* New York: Harper & Row.

Randi, J. (1982). *Flim-flam! Psychics, ESP, unicorns, and other delusions.* Buffalo, NY: Prometheus.

Shepard, R. N., and Chipman, S. (1970). Second-order isomorphism of internal representations: Shapes of states. *Cognitive Psychology, 1,* 1–17.

Shepard, R. N., and Cooper, L. A. (1982). *Mental images and their transformations.* Cambridge, MA: MIT Press.

Simonton, D. K. (1984). *Genius, creativity, and leadership.* Cambridge, MA: Harvard University Press.

Sternberg, R. J., and Lubart, T. I. (1991). An investment theory of creativity and its development. *Human Development, 34,* 1–31.

Tversky, A., and Kahneman, D. (1973). Availability: A heuristic for judging frequency and probability. *Cognitive Psychology, 5,* 207–232.

Ward, T. B. (in press). Structured imagination: The role of category structure in exemplar generation. *Cognitive Psychology.*

Wason, P. C., and Johnson-Laird, P. N. (1972). *Psychology of reasoning: Structure and content.* Cambridge, MA: Harvard University Press.

Weisberg, R. W. (1986). *Creativity, genius, and other myths.* New York: Freeman.

Wolfe, T. (1976). *The painted word.* New York: Bantam.

Conclusion

Paradoxes, Principles, and Prospects for the Future of Creative Cognition

Steven M. Smith, Thomas B. Ward, and Ronald A. Finke

Paradoxes and Principles

The contributing authors to this book have addressed, and in many cases clarified or resolved, some of the major issues and controversies that have surrounded the subject of creativity. In doing so, they demonstrate the value of the creative cognition approach (Finke, Ward, and Smith 1992), showing that creativity can be better understood if it is studied in the context of contemporary cognitive science. The chapters show how creativity can be effectively studied scientifically, using experiments, case studies, and computational modeling. In this concluding chapter we will review and integrate the major themes in these chapters, attempt to resolve some of creativity's paradoxes, suggest ways in which creative thinking might be improved, and conclude by considering future prospects for the creative cognition approach.

One paradox the authors addressed is that creative thinking appears to involve special processes and abilities, such as insight, incubation, or divergent thinking, yet creativity is also considered to be part of our regular collection of cognitive skills, underlying such everyday activities as recalling events, forming images, using language, and dreaming. Does creative thinking involve special abilities, or normal everyday processes?

Many of the authors clearly endorse the claim that creative thinking consists of the same mental processes involved in noncreative thinking (Bowers, Farvolden, and Mermigis; Freyd and Pantzer; Mandler; Schank and Cleary; Smith; Ward; Weisberg). Mandler, for example, states that the ability to produce novelty is necessary even in common everyday thinking, suggesting that the mechanisms that underlie creative thinking are normal ones. Weisberg and Ward emphasize the importance of prior knowledge in creative endeavors—Weisberg from the standpoint of knowledge retrieval and Ward in terms of antecedent cognitive structures that underlie idea generation and exploration. Incubation, a seemingly mysterious phenomenon in creative problem solving, has also been attributed to normal cognitive mechanisms, such as spreading activation (Bowers, Farvolden, and Mermigis) or contextual fluctuation (Smith). Dynamic qualities of creative thinking are linked by Freyd and Pantzer to dynamic mental representations that typically give rise to memory distortions. Schank and Cleary show that only slight variations of computational models of comprehension are needed to account for creative thinking. These cognitive mechanisms—knowledge retrieval, spreading activation, contextual fluctuation, memory distortion, and comprehension—are the same as those currently studied in noncreative contexts.

On the other hand, other chapters indicate that special creative processes do exist. Dominowski emphasizes the importance of insight and productive thinking in creative problem solving, distinguishing them from reproductive uses of prior experience. Schooler and Melcher indicate that the processes that underlie insight in problem solving are not verbalizable; in fact, these authors find that verbalization inhibits success on insight problems, suggesting that insight processes differ from analytical problem-solving operations. Martindale also characterizes the special nature of creative processes, describing how the simultaneous activation of disparate elements during creative cognition differs from noncreative cognition.

How can creative thinking be both special and ordinary? Although this paradox may not be completely resolved, it can at least be clarified. First, it should be obvious that not all creative thinking follows exactly the same pattern. Whereas some classic discoveries appear to have resulted from flashes of insight (e.g., Archimedes' displacement principle, Kekulé's benzene ring), others seem to have resulted from incremental applications of prior knowledge (e.g., Watson and Crick's discovery of the structure of DNA). Just as different memory tasks may require different types of cognitive processes, so, too might different creative endeavors. One task may be done by restructuring, another by reproductive knowledge retrieval, and yet another by a combination of the two operations.

Also helping to resolve this special-vs.-ordinary paradox is evidence that special processes such as insight, incubation, and activation of disparate elements can also be seen in noncreative tasks. Verbalization, which interferes with insight problem solving (e.g., Schooler and Melcher, chap. 5), also interferes with face recognition (e.g., Schooler and Engstler-Schooler 1990). Incubation has been found not only in problem-solving situations but in memory tasks as well (e.g., Smith and Vela 1991). Likewise, dreaming, a daily activity, often involves juxtapositions of disparate elements. Whether or not a particular cognitive process is deemed special, it is clear that none are uniquely encountered in creative thinking.

Another paradox addressed by the chapter authors is that, whereas creativity involves the use of old knowledge, it also requires that we do things in new ways. Are we therefore to use or reject prior knowledge in creative thinking? How are we to decide when we are told not to fall into ruts in our thinking and yet to have the sense not to repeat the mistakes of history?

The predominant view expressed in these chapters is that prior knowledge is usually needed for creative cognition. For example, both Mandler and Bowers, Farvolden, and Mermigis note the importance of Pasteur's idea that a prepared mind is essential for creative thinking. Weisberg's thesis is that major creative leaps can arise from the reproductive use of prior knowledge. Smith's description of the use of plans in constructive searches also underscores the importance of prior knowledge in creative thinking. The use of established concepts that guide the generation and exploration of new ideas is also a basic theme of Ward's chapter.

But is the prepared mind sufficient for producing creative ideas? Perhaps some would agree, but most of the contributing authors do not. Schank and Cleary, who support the idea that knowledge is necessary for creative thinking, define creative thinking as an "intelligent misuse" of knowledge. That is, knowledge that one has acquired must be playfully manipulated to achieve creative ends. Similarly, Mandler describes how the nondeliberate use of memory structures in dreaming can produce novelty. Having knowledge is not enough; one must use that knowledge in unconventional ways to produce creative thoughts. Finke describes an excessive adherence to prior knowledge as "conservative realism," which consists of uninteresting extensions of what is already known, whereas "creative realism" requires an imaginative use of known cognitive structures.

Acknowledging the importance of prior knowledge in creative cognition helps to resolve another paradox: are creative methods and abilities domain specific, or are there general principles that describe and explain creative thinking in all domains? Although there have been notable exceptions, most people who have made significant creative contributions have done so in only a single domain, such as sports, science, or the arts, rather than shining in many unrelated domains. Paradoxically, the creative cognition approach posits that the basic cognitive processes that underlie creativity are essentially the same in all domains. If one's creative abilities can function across domains, why does that tend not to occur?

Because domain-specific knowledge is necessary for most creative contributions, as noted in many of these chapters, it follows that most individuals can make creative advances only in the domains in which they have cutting-edge expertise. Therefore, the playful or "intelligent misuse" of expertise, which can yield creative ideas in any domain, tends to be seen only in an individual's area of specialization.

The idea that creativity involves a playful or unusual use of expert knowledge helps to resolve another paradox: that imagination and practicality are the two primary criteria used to assess creativity. We typically think of these as the opposite ends of a continuum rather than as qualities that are found together. Imagination so often seems impractical, and practicality seems so unimaginative. How can imaginative ideas by practical or realistic? Ideas can be practical if they are based on expert knowledge that is well integrated, and they can be imaginative if the underlying knowledge is used in novel ways. Finke's emphasis on structural connectedness in creative realism and Ward's assertion that knowledge structures are used to guide creative thought show how creative ideas can also be practical.

The rarity of important creative discoveries makes real-world creativity difficult to study in a scientific way. The idea of "everyday" creativity, however, is endorsed by many of these chapters as psychologically similar to that which underlies great discoveries. As Mandler notes, the important question to the psychologist is how someone gets an idea rather than the personal or cultural importance of the idea. Therefore, researchers have turned to relatively simple laboratory tasks that require no expertise beyond that of an average college-aged adult. These laboratory tasks, which include insight problems (e.g., Bowers, Farvolden, and Mermigis; Dominowski; Schooler and Melcher), Remote Associates Test (RAT) problems (e.g., Bowers, Farvolden, and Mermigis; Smith), and mental synthesis problems (Finke 1990) are used as microcosms for creative problem-solving activities. From studies of these problems, one can learn to overcome mental blocks, reformulate problems, restructure knowledge, and acquire new insights.

Another approach to studying creative thinking that does not require special expertise has been to use activities that are normatively familiar to subjects. For example, Smith, Ward, and Schumacher (1993) asked subjects to generate novel ideas for toys or imaginary creatures. Subjects may not have extraordinary expertise in the domains of these tasks, but they nonetheless have enough knowledge about toys and animals to display a good deal of creativity about them.

Although the apparent conflict between the use of knowledge versus the suspension of it in creativity has been somewhat clarified, it has not been completely resolved. Dominowski cites obstacles to solving insight problems: functional fixedness, inappropriate organization of the problem, inadequate monitoring of the efficacy of one's solution, and fixation. Smith notes that memory processes, such as priming of inappropriate information, can negatively affect problem solving and creative idea generation, even among professional design engineers (Jansson and Smith 1991). Weisberg, on the other hand, notes the importance of using, rather than rejecting, prior knowledge in real-world examples of creative discovery. Distinguishing between situations in which prior knowledge must be used and those in which it should be rejected continues to be important issue.

Another paradox in creative cognition is that creative ideas might not occur when one deliberately attempts to work on a problem but rather when one's attention is turned away, at least momentarily, from the problem at hand. This "catch-22—" that you can do something creative only when you are not trying— resembles other phenomena that can be attributed to implicit processes, such as the performance of certain motor skills or the forgetting of unwanted information. Finke's research with preinventive forms, for example, has shown that more creative inventions are discovered if subjects do not have a specific purpose in mind at the time they generate their forms, which then inspire their subsequent creative thinking. Lubart and Sternberg note that creative performance in their studies was negatively affected by having too high a level of motivation, also suggesting that too much goal focus may detract from creative thinking.

Several explanations of the role of nontask processing in creative cognition are offered in these chapters. Bowers, Farvolden, and Mermigis suggest that unconscious semantic activation may support the generation of solutions to problems, a notion that has been used to explain incubation effects (Yaniv and Meyer 1987). Mandler states that novel concatenations of existing knowledge, such as those generated during dreams, arise from problem-initiated activation that spreads throughout one's knowledge without the typical constraints of reality. He cites a number of cognitive mechanisms that may explain why deliberate work on ideas is sometimes fruitless. If deliberate processing encourages verbalization, then Schooler and Melcher's research shows that insights may be prevented by trying to verbalize one's thoughts. Smith theorizes that rather than allowing unconscious processes to construct solutions, nontask processing changes one's cognitive context, leading to a new problem representation that avoids the mental blocks encountered on previous attempts. Finally, Martindale's emphasis on the importance of combining disparate elements in discovering creative ideas suggests that nontask processing increases the accessibility of material that is not obviously related to the problem. Any or all of these explanations of nontask processing may occur in creative cognition, and all are empirically testable.

The chapters also show different ways in which creative cognition can be computationally modeled. Schank and Cleary consider how creative ideas could be generated by a computer program, tracing the development of artificial intelligence programs designed to understand and explain discrepancies in text and natural language. Cheng and Simon model a different aspect of creative cognition, looking at the way one- and two-dimensional diagrams can be used to guide the induction of scientific principles. Their HUYGENS program spots systematic regularities in diagrams and uses heuristics and logical operators to simulate scientific discoveries. Martindale's connectionist approach considers the type of knowledge that is activated during creative work on a problem. This model uses simulated annealing to characterize a search for ideas; when the search becomes bogged down in a local minimum (analogous to blocking or fixation), an increase in "temperature" (analogous to lowering arousal) helps extricate the search from the block and improve the chances of finding a global minimum (analogous to a creative idea or solution).

Finally, the chapters indicate various ways in which people can improve their creative thinking. The principles noted above suggest some general strategies for improving creative performance. One principle is that both prior knowledge and a playful or imaginative use of that knowledge are important in creative thinking. The classic educational question—whether to focus on skills and knowledge in the classroom, or allow students to think freely so that their creativity will not be stifled—is thus resolved: knowledge is necessary but not sufficient for creativity.

Another principle is that one should try to recognize mental blocks and implicit assumptions that may prevent insight. When a design engineer, architect, artist, scientist, or writer is at an impasse, working harder with traditional methods might not bring success. An awareness of what is blocking success may be the first step toward a solution and might be achieved by sticking with the task and developing a more abstract representation that makes underlying assumptions explicit. An alternative strategy for dealing with implicit blocks is to put the task aside momentarily. Nontask processing may therefore be helpful, particularly when impasses are reached, because it can destabilize the use of inappropriate approaches, encourage restructuring, and make remotely associated knowledge more accessible.

Another principle—that nonverbal processing, including visualization, often enhances creative insight—also suggests useful applications. One is that protocol analyses of interviews with experts may be limited because the verbalization required by the procedure may inhibit creative thinking. It also indicates that both people and computer programs can make use of visual representations to recognize systematic or meaningful relationships.

Other principles for enhancing creativity can also be found in these chapters. Lubart and Sternberg note the importance of knowing when to invest one's efforts in creative endeavors, recommending that one should take risks and work hardest on a creative idea while it is still popularly unknown and withdraw efforts once the idea becomes a bandwagon if one is to achieve success with creativity. To encourage creative realism, Finke suggests taking advantage of structural connectedness without overstructuring the creative process by blindly adhering to a plan. Dominowski states that practice on insight problems, as well as reformulation training, in which solutions and false assumptions in practice problems are pointed out, can improve performance on unfamiliar insight problems. Cheng and Simon note the usefulness of diagrams as representations for data when searching for higher-order rules that explain one's observations. The usefulness of these principles is underscored by the fact that they are based not only on logic and the internal consistency of the ideas but also on empirical findings.

The Future of the Creative Cognition Approach

The research and ideas in these chapters represent important advances in our understanding of creative cognition, but they by no means answer or even address all of the important and relevant issues. Researchers must continue to investigate creative cognition in such areas as knowledge retrieval, conceptual structure, problem solving, visual representation, comprehension, and computational modeling. In addition, inquiry in other areas of cognition is also essential. Those issues, which have only been touched on in this book, include analogy, metaphor, mental models, conscious and unconscious processes, metacognition, and language.

The creative cognition approach also suggests new strategies for studying conventional issues in human cognition. For example, memory retrieval can be considered as a constructive search with open-ended outcomes rather than as a task with a single correct answer. Representations of categories in studies of concept formation, for instance, must be flexible enough to account for the wide range of novel variations that subjects can create in exemplar generation tasks. A model of comprehension that relies too heavily on bottom-up inferencing in the course of explaining propositions may be thorough in terms of discovering every possible interpretation of an ambiguous text, but it would be too slow to understand complex texts that people can easily comprehend, and it would fail to take advantage of prior experiences with similar texts. Future research in cognitive science could thus benefit by examining phenomena of interest in flexible, open-ended, creative situations.

The development of computational models of creativity described here and elsewhere suggests that computer programs may eventually be constructed that will generate creative ideas and products. On the other hand, Lubart and Sternberg point out the importance of motivational variables in creativity, and Mandler notes that affect is also an important consequence of novel thought. Machines, outside of science fiction, do not appear to have motivational or affective qualities and may therefore fail to be truly creative (however, see Boden 1991 for a consideration of some philosophical aspects of this issue). It is possible that cognitive scientists will eventually find ways to combine human and computer systems, with both humans and machines enhancing creativity by contributing to different components of the creative process.

Developing theoretically motivated and empirically tested methods for training and improving creative expertise should be another goal of future research in creative cognition. In personality approaches to creativity, one assumes that traits are enduring characteristics of individuals; consequently, this approach is concerned more with the creative individual than the creative process. The creative cognition approach, on the other hand, focuses on the process and therefore should be more directly relevant to teaching people how to be more creative. The chapters consider training to some extent, but there is much more to be learned about how to improve creativity.

Will there eventually be a single overarching theory of creativity that can explain all aspects of creative functioning across situations? The chapters in this book make it very clear that such a theory is not likely. Creative cognition, like noncreative cognition, is by its very nature diverse and affected by many processes. To understand creativity, we must begin to assess those processes in creative contexts. An overarching theory of creativity is no more likely to be found than a unified theory that could explain all cognitive phenomena. Instead, it might be better to pursue more focused theories that can inform us about the role of specific processes in creative functioning.

Finally, the impact and potential of the creative cognition approach, as shown by the contributions to this book, marks the fall of yet another barrier previously assumed to be insurmountable: the idea that creativity cannot be studied scientifically. Historically, sober-minded scientists have avoided, spurned, or denied important cognitive phenomena that were supposedly intractable to scientific research, such as higher-level mental processes. These phenomena are now studied routinely with increasingly sophisticated methods of manipulation, observation, and analysis. With barriers to the scientific study of creative cognition removed, we can expect important strides in this area in the coming years.

References

Boden, M. (1991). *The creative mind: myths and mechanisms.* New York: Basic Books.

Finke, R. A. (1990). *Creative imagery: Discoveries and inventions in visualization.* Hillsdale, NJ: Erlbaum.

Finke, R. A., Ward, T. B., and Smith, S. M. (1992). *Creative cognition: Theory, research, and applications.* Cambridge, MA: MIT Press.

Jansson, D. G., and Smith, S. M. (1991). Design fixation. *Design Studies, 12* (1), 3–11.

Schooler, J. W., and Engstler-Schooler, T. Y. (1990). Verbal overshadowing of visual memories: Some things are better left unsaid. *Cognitive Psychology, 22,* 36–71.

Smith, S. M., and Vela, E. (1991). Incubated reminiscence effects. *Memory and Cognition, 19,* 168–176.

Smith, S. M., Ward, T. B., and Schumacher, J. S. (1993). Constraining effects of examples in a creative generation task. *Memory and Cognition, 21,* 837–845

Yaniv, I, and Meyer, D. E. (1987). Activation and metacognition of inaccessible stored information: Potential bases for incubation effects in problem solving. *Journal of Experimental Psychology: Learning, Memory, and Cognition, 13,* 187–205.

Name Index

Subject Index

ABACUS, 222
Abilities, individual, 1
Abstraction, 172–174, 176, 258, 259
Activation, 105, 249
Accumulated Clues Task (ACT), 36, 37, 38, 39, 43–46
Adjective Check List (ACL), 279–280, 287, 293–294, 299
Advertising, 281–282, 284–285, 287–290
Aesthetic, 21, 33, 106, 198–199
Affect, 3, 23
AIDS, 99
Algorithm, 261
  genetic, 254–255
Ambiguity, 274
Analogy, 59–60, 71, 102, 128, 240–241, 252–253, 256, 258, 261, 265, 271, 273, 304, 333. *See also* Mental model; Metaphor
  local, 62
  molecules, 240–241
  regional, 63
  remote, 63 (*see also* Transfer, remote analogical)
  transfer of, 62, 284 (*see also* Transfer, analogical)
Annealing, 261, 265–266
Anomaly, 232–233, 237–240, 243–245
Appropriateness, 77, 167–168, 174, 250, 272, 320
Arousal, 4, 20, 253, 259–261, 332
  cortical, 260, 266
Art, 21, 28, 57, 64, 67–68, 69, 77, 273, 291, 295, 304, 310, 312, 315, 329, 332. *See also* Painting; Sculpture
  primitive, 64, 67

Associationism, 1
Assumption
  false, 104
  implicit, 141–142, 152–153, 167, 174, 332 (*see also* Implicit assumption)
  unwarranted, 99, 101
Asymmetry, 185, 188. *See also* Symmetry
Attention, 74, 81, 85, 256, 275, 331
  defocused, 255–256, 259
  focus of, 255, 275
Attractor, fixed-point, 263
Attribute. *See also* Feature; Property
  central, 167, 176
  correlated, 165
  finding, 322
  listing, 167, 176
Authoritarian, 21
Autism, 258
Awareness, 16, 18, 100, 105, 142, 144, 153–154, 332. *See also* Consciousness
  of relations, 74
  and remembering, 144, 152
  restriction of, 19

Backing up, 142
BACON, 213, 222, 224
Behavioral, 249, 318
Biographical, 278, 292–293
Blind variation, 253
Block, 1, 20, 81, 143–144, 148, 151, 331–332. *See also* Fixation
  implicit, 332
  of memory, 153
  recovery from, 152 (*see also* Recovery)
  and retrieval, 144, 149, 172
BRAINSTORMER, 241